Rick Steves®

BELGIUM:
BRUGES, BRUSSELS, ANTWERP & GHENT

Rick Steves & Gene Openshaw

CONTENTS

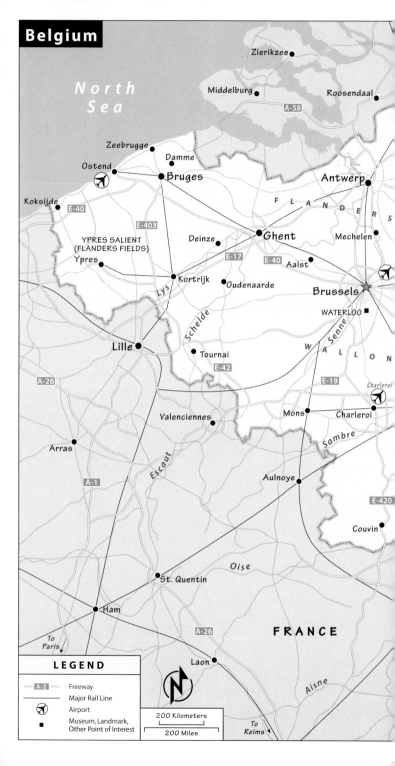

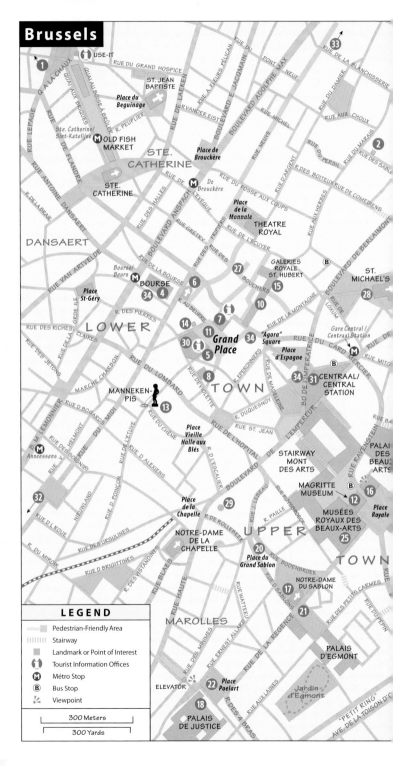

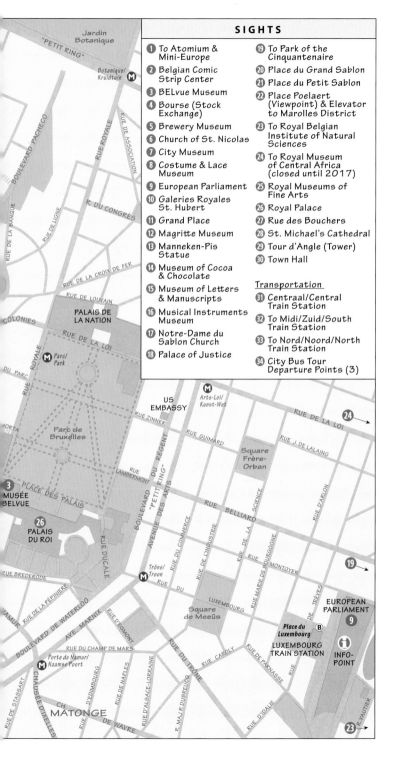

SIGHTS

1 To Atomium & Mini-Europe
2 Belgian Comic Strip Center
3 BELvue Museum
4 Bourse (Stock Exchange)
5 Brewery Museum
6 Church of St. Nicolas
7 City Museum
8 Costume & Lace Museum
9 European Parliament
10 Galeries Royales St. Hubert
11 Grand Place
12 Magritte Museum
13 Manneken-Pis Statue
14 Museum of Cocoa & Chocolate
15 Museum of Letters & Manuscripts
16 Musical Instruments Museum
17 Notre-Dame du Sablon Church
18 Palace of Justice

19 To Park of the Cinquantenaire
20 Place du Grand Sablon
21 Place du Petit Sablon
22 Place Poelaert (Viewpoint) & Elevator to Marolles District
23 To Royal Belgian Institute of Natural Sciences
24 To Royal Museum of Central Africa (closed until 2017)
25 Royal Museums of Fine Arts
26 Royal Palace
27 Rue des Bouchers
28 St. Michael's Cathedral
29 Tour d'Angle (Tower)
30 Town Hall

Transportation

31 Centraal/Central Train Station
32 To Midi/Zuid/South Train Station
33 To Nord/Noord/North Train Station
34 City Bus Tour Departure Points (3)

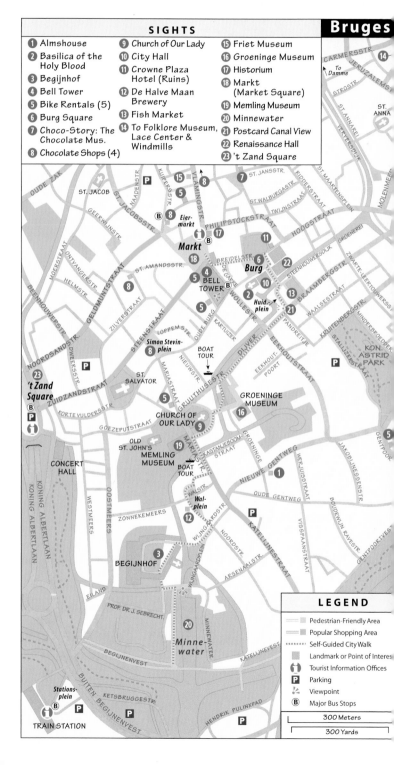

Bruges

SIGHTS

1. Almshouse
2. Basilica of the Holy Blood
3. Begijnhof
4. Bell Tower
5. Bike Rentals (5)
6. Burg Square
7. Choco-Story: The Chocolate Mus.
8. Chocolate Shops (4)
9. Church of Our Lady
10. City Hall
11. Crowne Plaza Hotel (Ruins)
12. De Halve Maan Brewery
13. Fish Market
14. To Folklore Museum, Lace Center & Windmills
15. Friet Museum
16. Groeninge Museum
17. Historium
18. Markt (Market Square)
19. Memling Museum
20. Minnewater
21. Postcard Canal View
22. Renaissance Hall
23. 't Zand Square

LEGEND

- Pedestrian-Friendly Area
- Popular Shopping Area
- Self-Guided City Walk
- Landmark or Point of Interest
- Tourist Information Offices
- **P** Parking
- Viewpoint
- **B** Major Bus Stops

300 Meters
300 Yards

Rick Steves®

BELGIUM:
BRUGES, BRUSSELS, ANTWERP & GHENT

INTRODUCTION

Digging into a dish of mussels while seated on a sunny square beneath the outline of a lacy medieval spire...you're in Belgium.

This book presents the best of Belgium—its great cities, fine food, rich history, and sensuous art, as well as the modern scene that makes Belgium the face of Europe today. You'll see the predictable biggies and experience a healthy dose of Back Door intimacy. Bruges—once mighty, now mighty cute—comes with fancy beers in fancy glasses, lilting carillons, and filigreed Gothic souvenirs of a long-gone greatness. Brussels—the de facto capital of Europe, with a low-rise Parisian ambience—exudes joie de vivre, from its tasty cuisine to its love of chocolate and comic strips. Design-forward Antwerp thrills with window displays of ladies in high-fashion couture, as well as ladies in bras and panties in its racy red light district. In Ghent, you'll find a richly detailed Renaissance altarpiece amid a vibrant urban landscape. Belgium offers all this and more. (Did I mention chocolate?)

Along with sightseeing, this book gives you tips on how to save money, plan your time, and ride Belgium's excellent rail system, as well as recommendations on hotels, restaurants, shopping, and entertainment.

This book is selective, including only the top sights. The best is, of course, only my opinion. But after spending more than half of my adult life exploring and researching Europe, I've developed a sixth sense for what travelers enjoy.

Belgium is ready for you. Like sampling a flavorful praline in a chocolate shop, that first enticing taste just leaves you wanting more. Go ahead, it's OK...buy a whole box of Belgium.

INTRODUCTION

Map Legend

↙	View Point	✈	Airport	⬚	Park
↟	Entrance	Ⓣ	Taxi Stand	▬▬▬	Pedestrian Zone
❶	Tourist Info	Ⓜ	Metro Stop	------	Railway
WC	Restroom	Ⓣ	Tram Stop	....	Ferry/Boat Route
🏠	Church	Ⓑ	Bus Stop	⊢—⊢	Tram
▪	Statue/Point of Interest	Ⓟ	Parking	ⅢⅢⅢⅢ	Stairs
◎	Fountain	⚓	Boat/Cruise Line	• • • • •	Walk/Tour Route

Use this legend to help you navigate the maps in this book.

ABOUT THIS BOOK

Rick Steves Belgium is a personal tour guide in your pocket. Better yet, it's actually two tour guides in your pocket: The co-author of this book is Gene Openshaw. Since our first "Europe through the gutter" trip together as high-school buddies in the 1970s, Gene and I have been exploring the wonders of the Old World. An inquisitive historian and lover of European culture, Gene wrote most of this book's self-guided museum tours and neighborhood walks. Together, Gene and I keep this book up-to-date and accurate (though for simplicity, from this point "we" will shed our respective egos and become "I").

This book is organized by destination. Each is a mini-vacation on its own, filled with exciting sights, strollable neighborhoods, affordable places to stay, and memorable places to eat.

Here's what you'll find in the following chapters:

Orientation includes specifics on public transportation, helpful hints, local tour options, easy-to-read maps, and tourist information. The "Planning Your Time" section suggests how to best use your limited time.

Sights describes the top attractions and includes their cost and hours.

Self-Guided Walks take you through interesting neighborhoods, pointing out sights and fun stops. **Self-Guided Tours** lead you through Belgium's most fascinating museums and sights. In Bruges choose from a city walk and tours of the Groeninge and Memling museums; in Brussels, take a Grand Place walk, an Upper Town walk, and a tour of the Royal Museums of Fine Arts; in Antwerp, stroll through the city center and tour the Rubens House; and in Ghent, walk the core of the old town and visit the Cathedral of St. Bavo, home of the renowned Ghent Altarpiece.

Sleeping, Eating & More is a one-stop compendium describing my favorite hotels (from good-value deals to cushy splurges),

Key to This Book

Updates

This book is updated regularly—but things change. For the latest, visit www.ricksteves.com/update.

Abbreviations and Times

I use the following symbols and abbreviations in this book:

Sights are rated:

▲▲▲	Don't miss
▲▲	Try hard to see
▲	Worthwhile if you can make it
No rating	Worth knowing about

Tourist information offices are abbreviated as **TI,** and bathrooms are **WC**s. To categorize accommodations, I use a **Sleep Code** (described on page 329).

Like Europe, this book uses the **24-hour clock.** It's the same through 12:00 noon, then keeps going: 13:00, 14:00, and so on. For anything over 12, subtract 12 and add p.m. (14:00 is 2:00 p.m.).

When giving **opening times,** I include both peak season and off-season hours if they differ. So, if a museum is listed as "May-Oct daily 9:00-16:00," it should be open from 9 a.m. until 4 p.m. from the first day of May until the last day of October (but expect exceptions).

If you see a ✪ symbol near a sight listing, it means that sight is described in far greater detail elsewhere—either with its own self-guided tour, or as part of a self-guided walk.

For **transit** or **tour departures,** I first list the frequency, then the duration. So a train connection listed as "2/hour, 1.5 hours" departs twice each hour and the journey lasts an hour and a half.

eating options (from inexpensive cafés to fancy restaurants), shopping neighborhoods and tips, and fun things to do after dark. The "Connections" section outlines your travel options by train, bus, plane, and cruise ship (with detailed information on major airports).

The **Belgian History** chapter gives you a quick overview of the country's past and a timeline of major events.

Practicalities is a traveler's tool kit, with my best advice about money, sightseeing, sleeping, eating, staying connected, and transportation (trains, buses, car rentals, driving, and flights). There's also a list of recommended books and films.

The **appendix** is a nuts-and-bolts guide with useful phone numbers and websites, a festival list, a climate chart, a handy packing checklist, and Dutch and French survival phrases.

Browse through this book, choose your favorite destinations, and link them up. Then have a *prachtig* trip! Traveling like a temporary local, you'll get the absolute most out of every mile, minute, and dollar. As you visit places I know and love, I'm happy that you'll be meeting some of my favorite Belgian people.

Planning

This section will help you get started planning your trip—with advice on trip costs, when to go, and what you should know before you take off.

TRAVEL SMART

Your trip to Belgium is like a complex play—easier to follow and really appreciate on a second viewing. While no one does the same trip twice to gain that advantage, reading this book in its entirety before your trip accomplishes much the same thing.

Design an itinerary that enables you to visit sights at the best possible times. Note festivals, holidays, specifics on sights, and days when sights are closed or most crowded (all covered in this book). For example, many museums in Bruges are closed on Mondays. To get between destinations smoothly, read the tips in Practicalities on taking trains and buses, or renting a car and driving. A smart trip is a puzzle—a fun, doable, and worthwhile challenge.

When you're plotting your itinerary, strive for a mix of intense and relaxed stretches. To maximize rootedness, minimize one-night stands. It's worth taking a long drive after dinner (or a train ride with a dinner picnic) to get settled into a town for two nights. Every trip—and every traveler—needs slack time (laundry, picnics, people-watching, and so on). Pace yourself. Assume you will return.

Reread this book as you travel, and visit local tourist information offices (abbreviated as TI in this book). Upon arrival in a new town, lay the groundwork for a smooth departure; get the schedule for the train or bus that you'll take when you depart. Drivers can figure out the best route to their next destination.

Update your plans as you travel. Use your phone, tablet, or laptop to find out tourist information, learn the latest on sights (special events, tour schedule, etc.), book tickets and tours, make reservations, reconfirm hotels, research transportation connections, and keep in touch with your loved ones. If you don't want to bring a mobile device, use guest computers and phones at hotels instead.

Enjoy the friendliness of the Belgian people. Connect with the culture. Set up your own quest to find the best local beer, lace doily, or handmade praline. Slow down and be open to unexpected experiences. Ask questions—most locals are eager to point you in their idea of the right direction. Keep a notepad in your pocket for noting directions, organizing your thoughts, and confirming prices. Wear your money belt, learn the currency, and figure out how to estimate prices in dollars. Those who expect to travel smart, do.

TRIP COSTS

Five components make up your trip costs: airfare, surface transportation, room and board, sightseeing and entertainment, and shopping and miscellany.

Airfare: A basic round-trip flight from the US to Brussels can cost, on average, about $1,000-2,000 total, depending on where you fly from and when (cheaper in winter). Consider saving time in Europe by flying into one city and out of another; for instance, into Brussels and out of Amsterdam. If you're sticking to Belgium, you're never more than about two hours from Brussels' international airport. Overall, Kayak.com is the best place to start searching for flights on a combination of mainstream and budget carriers.

Surface Transportation: For getting around, you're best off enjoying tiny Belgium's excellent and affordable train system. Trains travel several times hourly between its major cities. It costs about $15 for a ticket from Ghent to Brussels. If you'll be renting a car, allow $200 per week, not including tolls, gas, and supplemental insurance. If you'll be keeping the car for three weeks or more, look into leasing, which can save you money on insurance and taxes for trips of this length. Car rentals and leases are cheapest if arranged from the US. Train passes normally must be purchased outside Europe but aren't necessarily your best option—you may save money by simply buying tickets as you go. If you'll be traveling elsewhere in Europe, consider flying, as budget airlines can be cheaper than taking the train (check www.skyscanner.com for intra-European flights). For more on public transportation and car rental, see "Transportation" in the Practicalities chapter.

Room and Board: You can thrive in Belgium on $125 a day per person for room and board. This allows $20 for lunch, $30 for dinner, and $70 for lodging (based on two people splitting the cost of a $140 double room that includes breakfast). That leaves you $5 for *frieten*, beer, or chocolate. To live and sleep more elegantly, I'd propose a budget of $145 per day per person ($20 for lunch, $40 for dinner, $5 for snacks, and $80 each for a $160 hotel double with breakfast). Students and tightwads can enjoy Belgium for as little as $60 a day ($30 for a bed, $30 for meals and snacks).

Sightseeing and Entertainment: In big cities, figure about $12-15 per major sight (Royal Museums, Rubens House, Ghent Altarpiece); $6-10 for minor ones (climbing church towers or windmills); $10-18 for guided walks, boat tours, and bike rentals; and $30-60 for splurge experiences such as concerts, special art exhibits, and big-bus tours. An overall average of $25 a day works for most people. Don't skimp here. After all, this category is the driving force behind your trip—you came to sightsee, enjoy, and experience Belgium.

Shopping and Miscellany: Figure $1-2 per postcard, tea, or ice-cream cone. Shopping can vary in cost from nearly nothing to a small fortune. Good budget travelers find that this category has little to do with assembling a trip full of lifelong and wonderful memories.

SIGHTSEEING PRIORITIES

So much to see, so little time. How to choose? With affordable flights from the US, minimal culture shock, almost no language barrier, and a well-organized tourist trade, Belgium is a good place to start a European trip. Depending on the length of your trip, and taking geographic proximity into account, here are my recommended priorities for a great week in Belgium:

2 days:	Bruges
4 days, add:	Brussels and Ghent
6 days, add:	Antwerp
7 days, add:	Flanders Field (near Bruges) plus time to just slow down

WHEN TO GO

For tourist hotspots like Bruges, peak season is summer, especially June and early July. Business towns like Brussels, Antwerp, and Ghent tend to be more crowded in spring and fall. With long days, lively festivals, and sunny weather, summer is a great time to visit despite the crowds in places like Bruges. It's rarely too hot for comfort. Plus, Brussels' fancy business-class hotels are deeply discounted in the summer.

Late spring and fall are also pleasant, with generally mild weather and lighter tourist crowds (except during holiday weekends—see page 365).

Travel from late October through mid-March is cold and wet, as coastal winds whip through the low, flat country. It's fine for city visits, but smaller towns and countryside sights feel dreary. Some sights and TIs keep shorter hours, and many outdoor activities vanish altogether.

KNOW BEFORE YOU GO

Your trip is more likely to go smoothly if you plan ahead. Check this list of things to arrange while you're still at home.

You need a **passport**—but no visa or shots—to travel in Belgium. You may be denied entry into certain European countries if your passport is due to expire within three months of your ticketed date of return. Get it renewed if you'll be cutting it close. It can take up to six weeks to get or renew a passport (for more on passports, see www.travel.state.gov). Pack a photocopy of your passport in your luggage in case the original is lost or stolen.

Book rooms well in advance if you'll be traveling during busy months or any major holidays (see page 365).

Call your **debit- and credit-card companies** to let them know the countries you'll be visiting, to ask about fees, request your PIN code (it will be mailed to you), and more. See page 321 for details.

Do your homework if you want to buy **travel insurance.** Compare the cost of the insurance to the likelihood of your using it and your potential loss if something goes wrong. Also, check whether your existing insurance (health, homeowners, or renters) covers you and your possessions overseas. For more tips, see www.ricksteves.com/insurance.

If you plan to hire a **local guide,** reserve ahead by email. Popular guides can get booked up.

If you're bringing a **mobile device,** download any apps you might want to use on the road, such as translators, maps, and transit schedules. Check out **Rick Steves Audio Europe,** featuring hours of travel interviews and other audio content about Belgium (via the Rick Steves Audio Europe free app, www.ricksteves.com/audioeurope, iTunes, or Google Play; for details, see page 361).

Check the **Rick Steves guidebook updates** page for any recent changes to this book (www.ricksteves.com/update).

Because **airline carry-on restrictions** are always changing, visit the Transportation Security Administration's website (www.tsa.gov) for a list of what you can bring on the plane and for the latest security measures (including screening of electronic devices, which you may be asked to power up).

Traveling as a Temporary Local

We travel all the way to Belgium to enjoy differences—to become temporary locals. You'll experience frustrations. Certain truths that we find "God-given" or "self-evident," such as cold beer, ice in drinks, bottomless cups of coffee, and bigger being better, are suddenly not so true. One of the benefits of travel is the eye-opening

realization that there are logical, civil, and even better alternatives. A willingness to go local ensures that you'll enjoy a full dose of Belgian hospitality.

Europeans generally like Americans. But if there is a negative aspect to the Belgian image of Americans, it's that we

How Was Your Trip?

Were your travels fun, smooth, and meaningful? If you'd like to share your tips, concerns, and discoveries, please fill out the survey at www.ricksteves.com/feedback. To check out readers' hotel and restaurant reviews—or leave one yourself—visit my travel forum at www.ricksteves.com/travel-forum. I value your feedback. Thanks in advance—it helps a lot.

are loud, wasteful, ethnocentric, too informal (which can seem disrespectful), and a bit naive.

My Belgian friends place a high value on speaking quietly in restaurants and on trains. Listen while on the bus or in a restaurant—the place can be packed, but the decibel level is low. Try to adjust your volume accordingly to show respect for their culture.

While Belgians look bemusedly at some of our Yankee excesses—and worriedly at others—they nearly always afford individual travelers all the warmth we deserve.

Judging from all the happy feedback I receive from travelers who have used this book, it's safe to assume you'll enjoy a great, affordable vacation—with the finesse of an independent, experienced traveler.

Thanks, and have a *goede vakantie* and a *bon voyage!*

Rick Steves

Back Door Travel Philosophy

From *Rick Steves Europe Through the Back Door*

Travel is intensified living—maximum thrills per minute and one of the last great sources of legal adventure. Travel is freedom. It's recess, and we need it.

Experiencing the real Europe requires catching it by surprise, going casual..."through the Back Door."

Affording travel is a matter of priorities. (Make do with the old car.) You can eat and sleep—simply, safely, and enjoyably—anywhere in Europe for $125 a day plus transportation costs. In many ways, spending more money only builds a thicker wall between you and what you traveled so far to see. Europe is a cultural carnival, and time after time, you'll find that its best acts are free and the best seats are the cheap ones.

A tight budget forces you to travel close to the ground, meeting and communicating with the people. Never sacrifice sleep, nutrition, safety, or cleanliness to save money. Simply enjoy the local-style alternatives to expensive hotels and restaurants.

Connecting with people carbonates your experience. Extroverts have more fun. If your trip is low on magic moments, kick yourself and make things happen. If you don't enjoy a place, maybe you don't know enough about it. Seek the truth. Recognize tourist traps. Give a culture the benefit of your open mind. See things as different, but not better or worse. Any culture has plenty to share.

Of course, travel, like the world, is a series of hills and valleys. Be fanatically positive and militantly optimistic. If something's not to your liking, change your liking.

Travel can make you a happier American, as well as a citizen of the world. Our Earth is home to seven billion equally precious people. It's humbling to travel and find that other people don't have the "American Dream"—they have their own dreams. Europeans like us, but with all due respect, they wouldn't trade passports.

Thoughtful travel engages us with the world. In tough economic times, it reminds us what is truly important. By broadening perspectives, travel teaches new ways to measure quality of life.

Globetrotting destroys ethnocentricity, helping us understand and appreciate other cultures. Rather than fear the diversity on this planet, celebrate it. Among your most prized souvenirs will be the strands of different cultures you choose to knit into your own character. The world is a cultural yarn shop, and Back Door travelers are weaving the ultimate tapestry. Join in!

BELGIUM

Belgium falls through the cracks. Wedged between Germany, France, and the Netherlands, and famous for waffles, Smurfs, and a statue of a little boy peeing, it's no wonder it can get lost in the mix.

But Belgium rewards with richer sights than you might expect—and fewer tourist crowds. You'll encounter some of Europe's finest cuisine, including the best beer, creamiest chocolates, and tastiest French fries. Belgium's town squares bristle with soaring spires and warm-brick gables. Its museums house lush paintings celebrating the glories of everyday life. From funky urban neighborhoods to tranquil convents, from old-fashioned lace to high-powered European politics—little Belgium delights.

With nearly 900 people per square mile, Belgium is the second most densely populated country in Europe (after the Netherlands). When viewed from space, Belgium shines at night as a single patch of light—a phenomenon NASA astronauts call the "Belgian Window."

Despite its small size, Belgium is diverse. It's divided—linguistically, culturally, and politically—between French-speaking Wallonia in the south and Dutch-speaking Flanders in the north, with bilingual Brussels in between. ("Flemish," the Dutch spoken in Belgium, is even more guttural than textbook Dutch—insert your own "phlegmish" pun here.) And, because of its international business and political connections, more than 25 percent of its residents are foreigners who speak English as their common language.

Belgium is at the crossroads of Western Europe, where Romance languages meet the German world, and where the Protestant north meets the Catholic south. It was born as a merchant entity in medieval times (c. 1300-1500), when energetic traders made it one of Europe's richest, most cosmopolitan, and sophisticated lands. On the other hand—located as it is in the cross fire

Belgium

North Sea

NETHERLANDS

GERMANY

Zeebrugge
Ostend · Damme
Bruges
YPRES
SALIENT
(FLANDERS FIELDS) **Ghent**
·**Antwerp**
FLANDERS
·Ypres
Brussels
Hasselt ·Maastricht
Waterloo · Leuven
Aachen
Lille
BELGIUM
Liège
·Spa
Charleroi Namur Meuse
WALLONIA
Bastogne
N
FRANCE
ARDENNES
LUXEM-
BOURG ·Trier
50 Kilometers
Luxembourg
City
50 Miles

BELGIUM

between larger powers—it's also been Europe's battlefield. From Charlemagne to Napoleon, from the Austrian Habsburgs to Germany in two world wars, this country has paid a heavy price.

But tiny Belgium has survived by producing savvy businesspeople and excellent linguists, and by welcoming new trends. I recently asked a local, "What is a Belgian?" He said, "We are a melting pot. We're a mix culturally: one-third English for our sense of humor, one-third French for our love of culture and good living, and one-third German for our work ethic."

Belgians have a directness that some find refreshing (and others term brusque). They revel in their wry, sardonic sense of humor—it can be hard sometimes to tell whether they're putting you on. The art of the comic strip is deeply respected—the Smurfs and Tintin were created by Belgians. If you ask a twentysomething Belgian what career they're pursuing, and he says "comic books," nobody snickers.

Belgians are said to be born with a "brick in their stomach"— meaning they feel a deep-seated need to own a house, decorate it just so (hence the abundance of furniture shops), and invite their friends for dinner. Belgians are social, meeting up at sidewalk cafés or cozy pubs after work. On a beautiful spring day, it might seem like nobody here has a job—they're all outside drinking beer.

This book showcases several destinations in this surprisingly

The Battle for Belgium: Flanders vs. Wallonia

Although little, peace-loving Belgium seems like a warm and cozy place, its society is split right down the middle by a surprisingly contentious linguistic divide: the Dutch-speaking people of Flanders (in the north) versus the French speakers of Wallonia (in the south). To travelers, it almost seems as if Flanders and Wallonia are different countries. Each region has its own "national" tourist office, which effectively ignores the other half of the country.

From its earliest days, "Belgium" was less a country than a patchwork of dukedoms joined awkwardly together not by language, but by foreign rulers. For centuries, the two language groups co-existed side-by-side as they were successively dominated by Burgundian, Habsburg, Spanish, French, and Dutch overlords.

That changed in 1830, when the modern nation-state of Belgium was born, forcing the two regions together. It was Belgium's French-speaking aristocracy and industrialists that had led the drive for independence from the Netherlands. They said, "Belgium will be French, or it will not be." And so it was: Linguistic and cultural oppression ruled the day, as the Dutch language spoken in Flanders was suppressed. Education at prestigious universities, for example, was only in French. These days, the tables have turned—Flanders today has the healthier, wealthier economy and more inhabitants than Wallonia.

Language issues still dominate Belgium's politics. Some Flemish feel they'd have been better off had Belgium remained part of the Netherlands, which would have respected their native tongue. That's why most Flemish people are not particularly nationalistic about their language—rather than being blinded by Flemish pride, they readily acknowledge that what they speak is a dialect of Dutch.

Whereas a generation ago, virtually every Belgian spoke both Dutch and French, nowadays when Flemish students choose a "second" language to study, many choose English. Meanwhile, in a strange role reversal, Francophones are choosing to learn Dutch, which they realize will open up employment options. On my last visit to Brussels, I saw a sign in a shop window saying, "Bilingual staff wanted."

The Belgian government has taken steps to involve everyone. In 1970, Belgium began decentralizing itself, over time becoming a federal state with three semi-autonomous regions: Flanders, Wallonia, and the bilingual city-state of Brussels. Each group is now free to pursue its own agenda.

diverse country. **Bruges** is the Belgium of the past—a wonderfully preserved medieval gem that once was one of the largest cities in the world. The thriving towns of **Ghent** and **Antwerp**—also former medieval powerhouses—demonstrate how the country has rebounded to again be a global trendsetter. The Flemish countryside shows off Belgium's peasant foundation, and a visit to **Flanders Fields** gives a powerful glimpse into Belgium's traumatic experience in World War I.

And finally, there's **Brussels:** the unofficial capital of the European Union and one of Europe's great cities. With the finest town square in the country (if not the Continent), a chocolate shop on every corner, a French taste for class and cuisine, and a smattering of intriguing museums, it's equally ideal for a quick stopover as it is for a multiday visit. Wherever you go, find time to leave the quaint-but-touristy central square to wander the back streets. You'll find a Belgium that's lived-in, a bit funky, and authentic.

Belgium flies the flag of Europe more vigorously than any other place on the Continent. There's a feeling of being at the center of global events. Under a new king (and his young family), the country is on the rise, and it's kick-started gentrification throughout the country. With a thousand years of history behind it, Belgium seems poised to write a new chapter in its long and illustrious tale.

BELGIUM

Belgium Almanac

Official Name: Royaume de Belgique/Koninkrijk België, or simply Belgique in French and België in Dutch.

Population: About 10.5 million Belgians are packed into their little country—58 percent are Flemish, 31 percent are Walloon, and 11 percent are "mixed or other." About three-quarters are Catholic, and the rest are Protestant or other.

Latitude and Longitude: 50°N and 4°E. The latitude is similar to Calgary, Canada.

Area: With only 12,000 square miles, it's slightly smaller than the state of Maryland, and one of the smallest countries in Europe.

Geography: Belgium's flat coastal plains in the northwest and central rolling hills make it easy to invade (just ask Napoleon or Hitler). There are some rugged hills and ridges in the southeast Ardennes Forest. The climate is temperate.

Biggest Cities: Antwerp has a half-million inhabitants, Ghent has 250,000, and little Bruges has 120,000. Brussels has about 170,000 people in the city proper, but about 1.2 million in the capital region.

Economy: With few natural resources, Belgium imports most of its raw materials and exports a large volume of manufactured goods, making its economy unusually dependent on world markets. It can be a sweet business—Belgium is the world's number-one exporter of chocolate. It's prosperous, with a Gross Domestic Product of nearly $510 billion and a GDP per capita of about $45,000. As the "crossroads" of Europe, Brussels is the headquarters of NATO and the de facto capital of the European Union.

Government: Belgium is a parliamentary democracy, and its official head of state is King Philippe. He's the father of four cute kids (two princes and two princesses) and married to the popular Queen Mathilde. Belgium has adopted a federal state model since 1994, giving each linguistic community (Dutch and French) autonomy in education, culture, and regional economic policy. The division has made it increasingly difficult for the Belgian Senate to form ruling coalitions. One prime minister recently said that Belgians are united only by the king, a love of beer, and the national soccer team. Voting is compulsory. More than 90 percent of registered voters participated in the last general election (compared with approximately 62 percent in the US).

Flag: Belgium's flag is composed of three vertical bands of black, yellow, and red.

The Average Belgian: The average Belgian is 42 years old and will live to be 79. He or she is also likely to be divorced—Belgium has the highest divorce rate in Europe, with 60 for every 100 marriages. Beer is the national beverage: On average, Belgians drink 26 gallons a year, just behind the Austrians and just ahead of the Brits.

BRUGES

ORIENTATION TO BRUGES

Brugge • Bruges

With pointy gilded architecture, stay-a-while cafés, vivid time-tunnel art, and dreamy canals dotted with swans, Bruges is a heavyweight sightseeing destination, as well as a joy. Where else can you ride a bike along a canal, munch mussels and wash them down with the world's best beer, savor heavenly chocolate, and see Flemish Primitives and a Michelangelo, all within 300 yards of a bell tower that jingles every 15 minutes? And do it all without worrying about a language barrier?

The town is Brugge (BROO-ghah) in Dutch, and Bruges (broozh) in French and English. Its name comes from the Viking word for wharf. Right from the start, Bruges was a trading center. In the 11th century, the city grew wealthy on the cloth trade.

By the 14th century, Bruges' population was 35,000, as large as London's. As the middleman in the sea trade between northern and southern Europe, it was one of the biggest cities in the world and an economic powerhouse. In addition, Bruges had become the most important cloth market in northern Europe.

In the 15th century, while England and France were slugging it out in the Hundred Years' War, Bruges was the favored residence of the powerful Dukes of Burgundy—and at peace. Commerce and the arts boomed. The artists Jan van Eyck and Hans Memling had studios here.

But by the 16th century, the harbor had silted up and the economy had collapsed. The Burgundian court left, Belgium became a minor Habsburg possession, and Bruges' Golden Age abruptly ended. For generations, Bruges was known as a mysterious and dead city. In the 19th century, a new port, Zeebrugge, brought renewed vitality to the area. And in the 20th century, tourists discovered the town. These days, Bruges seems to be a particularly hot destination among British people—for whom it's an easy weekend getaway (and the popularity of the 2008 film *In Bruges* didn't hurt, either).

Today, Bruges prospers because of tourism: It's a uniquely well-preserved Gothic city and a handy gateway to Europe. It's no secret, but even with the crowds, it's the kind of place where you don't mind being a tourist.

PLANNING YOUR TIME

Bruges needs at least two nights and a full, well-organized day. Even non-shoppers enjoy browsing here, and the Belgian love of life makes a hectic itinerary seem a little senseless. With one day—other than a Monday, when the Groeninge and Memling museums are closed—a speedy visitor could try this ambitious Bruges blitz (also included in my Bruges City Walk):

9:30	Climb the bell tower on the Markt (Market Square).
10:00	Tour the sights on Burg Square.
11:30	Tour the Groeninge Museum.
13:00	Eat lunch and buy chocolates.
14:00	Take a short canal cruise.
14:30	Visit the Church of Our Lady and see Michelangelo's *Madonna and Child*.
15:00	Tour the Memling Museum at St. John's Hospital.
16:00	Catch the De Halve Maan Brewery tour (note that on winter weekdays, their last tour runs at 15:00).
17:00	Relax in the Begijnhof courtyard.
18:00	Ride a bike around the quiet back streets of town or take a horse-and-buggy tour.
20:00	Enjoy the low light of magic hour on the Markt, then lose the tourists and find dinner elsewhere. Finish the evening with a unique Belgian beer in a local pub.

If this schedule seems insane, skip the bell tower and the brewery—or stay another day.

Bruges Overview

The tourist's Bruges is less than one square mile, contained within a canal (the former moat). Nearly everything of interest and importance is within a convenient cobbled swath between the train station and the Markt (Market Square; a 20-minute walk). Most tourists are concentrated in the triangle formed by the Markt, Burg Square, and the Church of Our Lady; outside of that tight zone, the townscape is sleepy and relatively uncrowded. Many of my charming recommended accommodations lie just beyond this zone.

BRUGES ORIENTATION

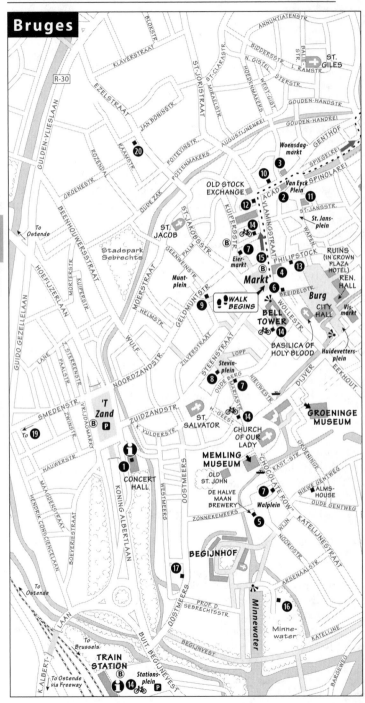

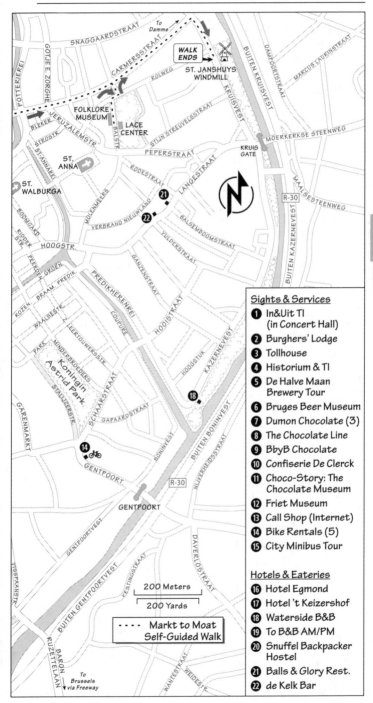

Sights & Services

1. In&Uit TI (in Concert Hall)
2. Burghers' Lodge
3. Tollhouse
4. Historium & TI
5. De Halve Maan Brewery Tour
6. Bruges Beer Museum
7. Dumon Chocolate (3)
8. The Chocolate Line
9. BbyB Chocolate
10. Confiserie De Clerck
11. Choco-Story: The Chocolate Museum
12. Friet Museum
13. Call Shop (Internet)
14. Bike Rentals (5)
15. City Minibus Tour

Hotels & Eateries

16. Hotel Egmond
17. Hotel 't Keizershof
18. Waterside B&B
19. To B&B AM/PM
20. Snuffel Backpacker Hostel
21. Balls & Glory Rest.
22. de Kelk Bar

TOURIST INFORMATION

The main TI, called **In&Uit** ("In and Out"), is in the big, red concert hall on the square called 't Zand (daily 10:00-18:00, take a number from the touch-screen machines and wait, 't Zand 34, tel. 050-444-646, www.brugge.be, toerisme@brugge.be). They have three terminals with free Internet access and printers. Don't bother with the Sound Factory interactive music museum that's also inside the concert hall (hefty price, sparse exhibits, partially obstructed views).

Other TI branches include one at the **train station** (Mon-Fri 10:00-17:00, Sat-Sun 10:00-14:00) and one on the **Markt,** sharing a building with the Historium museum (daily 10:00-17:00, Markt 1).

TIs sell the €2.50 *Love Bruges Visitors' Guide,* which comes with a map (costs €0.50 if bought separately), a few well-described self-guided walking tours, bike maps, and listings of all the sights and services (free with Brugge City Card—see sidebar). You can also pick up a free monthly English-language program called *events@brugge* and information on train schedules and tours. Many hotels give out free maps with more detail than the map the TIs sell. The TIs also have a free "Use-It" map available for young-at-heart travelers—filled with tips for backpackers and well worth asking for.

ARRIVAL IN BRUGES

By Train: Bruges' train station is what all stations under construction aspire to: in a clean, park-like setting, where travelers step out the door and are greeted by a taxi stand and a roundabout with center-bound buses circulating through every couple of minutes. Coming in by train, you'll see the bell tower that marks the main square (Markt, the center of town). Upon arrival, stop by the train station TI to pick up the *Love Bruges Visitors' Guide* (with map). The station has ATMs and lockers (€3-4).

The best way to get to the town center is by **bus.** Buses #1, #3, #4, #6, #11, #13, #14, and #16 go to the Markt (all marked *Centrum*). Simply hop on, pay €2 (€1.20 if you buy in advance at Lijnwinkel shop just outside the train station), and you're there in four minutes (get off at third stop—either Markt or Wollestraat). Buses #4 and #14 continue to the northeast part of town (to the windmills and recommended accommodations on and near Carmersstraat, stop: Gouden  Handstraat). If you arrive after 20:30, catch the (less-frequent) "evening line" buses to the Markt: buses marked *Avondlijn Cen-*

Bruges Museum Tips

Admission prices are steep, but they often include great audioguides—so plan on spending some time and really getting into it. For information on all the art and historical museums, call 050-448-711 or visit www.brugge.be/musea.

Museum Passes: The 't Zand TI and city museums sell a "Museumpas" **combo-ticket** for €20 (valid for 3 days at 16 locations). Because the Groeninge and Memling museums cost €8 each, you'll save money with this pass if you plan to see at least one other covered sight.

The **Brugge City Card** is a more extensive pass covering entry to 27 museums, including all the major sights (€43/48 hours, €48/72 hours, sold at TIs and many hotels). If you'll be doing some serious sightseeing, this card can save you money. It also includes, among other things, a free canal boat ride (March-Nov), a visitors' guide, and discounts on bike rental, parking, and some performances.

Blue Monday: If you're in Bruges on a Monday, when several museums are closed, consider the following activities or attractions: bell-tower climb on the Markt, Begijnhof, De Halve Maan Brewery tour, Basilica of the Holy Blood, City Hall's Gothic Room, Bruges Beer Museum, Historium, chocolate shops and museum, and Church of Our Lady. You can also join a boat, bus, or walking tour, or rent a bike and pedal into the countryside.

trum, *Avondlijn Noord*—#91, *Avondlijn Oost*—#92, and *Avondlijn Zuid*—#93. If traveling from the Markt to the train station, catch bus #2 or #12 (from in front of the Historium).

The **taxi** fare from the train station to most hotels is about €8.

It's a 20-minute **walk** from the station to the center—no fun with your luggage. If you want to walk to the Markt, cross the busy street and canal in front of the station, head up Oostmeers, and turn right on Zwidzandstraat. You can rent a **bike** at the station for the duration of your stay, but other bike-rental shops are closer to the center (see "Helpful Hints," next page).

By Car: Park in front of the train station in the handy two-story garage for just €3.50 for 24 hours. The parking fee includes a round-trip bus ticket into town and back for everyone in your car. There are pricier underground parking garages at the square called 't Zand and around town (€9/day, all of them well-marked). Paid parking on the street in Bruges is limited to four hours. Driving in town is very complicated because of the one-way system. The best plan for drivers: Park at the train station, visit the TI at the station, and rent a bike or catch a bus into town.

HELPFUL HINTS

Market Days: Bruges hosts markets on Wednesday morning (on the Markt) and Saturday morning ('t Zand). On good-weather Saturdays, Sundays, and public holidays, a flea market hops along Dijver in front of the Groeninge Museum. The Fish Market sells souvenirs daily and seafood Wednesday through Saturday mornings until 13:00.

Internet Access: There are free computer terminals at the **TI** on 't Zand. **Call Shop,** just a block off the Markt, is the most central of the city's many "telephone shops" offering Internet access (€1.50/30 minutes, €2.50/hour, daily 9:00-20:00, Philipstockstraat 4).

Post Office: It's on the Markt near the bell tower (Mon-Fri 9:00-18:00, Sat 9:30-15:00, closed Sun, tel. 050-331-411).

Bookstore: A good travel bookstore (which carries my guidebooks) is at #12 on the Markt.

Laundry: Bruges has three self-service launderettes, each a five-minute walk from the center; ask your hotelier for the nearest one.

Bike Rental: Bruges Bike Rental is central and cheap, with friendly service and long hours (€3.50/hour, €5/2 hours, €7/4 hours, €10/day, show this book to get student rate—€8/day, no deposit required—just ID, daily 10:00-22:00, free city maps and child seats, behind the far-out iron facade at Niklaas Desparsstraat 17, tel. 050-616-108, Bilal). **Fietsen Popelier Bike Rental** is also good (€4/hour, €8/4 hours, €12/day, 24-hour day is OK if your hotel has a safe place to store bike, no deposit required, daily 10:00-19:00, sometimes open later in summer, free Damme map, Mariastraat 26, tel. 050-343-262). **Koffieboontje Bike Rental** is just under the bell tower on the Markt (€4/hour, €9/day, €20/day for tandem, these prices for Rick Steves readers, daily 9:00-22:00, free city maps and child seats, Hallestraat 4, tel. 050-338-027). **De Ketting** is less central, but cheap (€6/day, Mon-Fri 9:00-12:15 & 13:30-18:30 except Mon opens at 10:00, Sat 9:30-12:15, closed Sun, Gentpoortstraat 23, tel. 050-344-196, www.deketting.be). **Fietspunt Brugge** is a huge outfit at the train station (7-speed bikes, €12/24-hours, €7/4 hours, free maps, Mon-Fri 7:00-19:30, Sat-Sun 9:00-21:30, just outside the station and to the right as you exit, tel. 050-396-826).

Best Town View: The bell tower overlooking the Markt rewards those who climb it with the ultimate Bruges view.

Updates to This Book: For updates to this book, check ricksteves. com/update.

GETTING AROUND BRUGES

Most of the city is easily walkable, but you may want to take the bus or taxi between the train station and the city center at the Markt (especially if you have heavy luggage).

By Bus: A bus ticket is good for an hour (€1.20 if you buy in advance at Lijnwinkel shop just outside the train station, or €2 on the bus). Though various day passes are available, there's really no need to buy one for your visit. Nearly all city buses go directly from the train station to the Markt and fan out from there; they then return to the Markt and go back to the train station. Note that buses returning to the train station from the Markt also leave from the library bus stop, a block off the square on nearby Kuiperstraat (every 5 minutes). Your key: Use buses that say either *Station* or *Centrum*.

By Taxi: You'll find taxi stands at the station and on the Markt (€8/first 2 kilometers; to get a cab in the center, call 050-334-444 or 050-333-881).

Tours in Bruges

Boat Tours

The most relaxing and scenic (though not informative) way to see this city of canals is by boat, with the captain narrating. The city carefully controls this standard tourist activity, so the many companies all offer essentially the same thing: a 30-minute route (roughly 4/hour, daily 10:00-17:00), a price of €7.60 (cash only), and narration in three or four languages. Qualitative differences are because of individual guides, not companies. Always let them know you speak English to ensure you'll understand the spiel. Two companies give the group-rate discount to individuals with this book: **Boten Stael** (just over the canal from Memling

Museum at Katelijnestraat 4, tel. 050-332-771) and **Gruuthuse** (Nieuwstraat 11, opposite Groeninge Museum, tel. 050-333-393).

Bike Tour

QuasiMundo Bike Tours leads daily five-mile English-language bike tours around the city (€25, €3 discount with this book, 2.5 hours, departs March-Oct at 10:00, in Nov only with good weather, no tours Dec-Feb). For more details and contact info, see their listing under "Near Bruges," later.

City Minibus Tour

City Tour Bruges gives a rolling overview of the town in an 18-seat, two-skylight minibus with dial-a-language headsets and video support (€16, 50 minutes, pay driver). The tour leaves hourly from the Markt (10:00-19:00, until 18:00 in fall, less in winter, tel. 050-355-024, www.citytour.be). The narration, though clear, is slow-moving and a bit boring. But the tour is a lazy way to cruise past virtually every sight in Bruges.

Walking Tours

Your Bruges is enthusiastically run by Andy. His entertaining two-hour walks focus on Bruges' back streets, less-discovered sights, and a few silly legends and stories. This is more affordable than hiring your own guide, since Andy charges per person—with no minimum—and may collect several of my readers into a small group (€10/person, cheaper for groups of more than 10, typically available afternoons and weekends, arrange in advance, tel. 0468-174-700, yourbruges@gmail.com).

The **TI** also arranges walks through the core of town (€9, 2 hours, daily July-Aug, Sat-Sun only mid-April-June and Sept-Oct, depart from TI on 't Zand Square at 14:30—just drop in a few minutes early and buy tickets at the TI desk). Though earnest, the tours are heavy on history and given in two languages, so they may be less than peppy. Still, to propel you beyond the pretty gables and canal swans of Bruges, they're good medicine. In the off-season, "winter walks" leave from the same TI four evenings a week (€9, Nov-Feb Sat-Mon and Wed at 17:00).

Local Guides

Daniëlle Janssens gives two-hour walks for €80, three-hour walks for €120, and full-day tours of Bruges and Brussels for €210 (mobile 0476-493-203, www.tourmanagementbelgium.be, tmb@skynet.be). You can also hire a guide through the **TI** (typically €70/2-hour tour, reserve at least one week in advance, for contact information see "Tourist Information," earlier).

Horse-and-Buggy Tour

The buggies around town can take you on a clip-clop tour (€36, 35 minutes; price is per carriage, not per person; buggies gather in Minnewater, near entrance to Begijnhof, and on the Markt). When divided among four or five people, this can be a good value.

Other Tours

Several tours are available to those with special interests, including **photography tours** (www.phototourbrugge.com), guided **jogging**

tours (www.touristrunbrugge.be), a **beer tour bus** that connects countryside pubs around Belgium (www.thebelgianbeertourbus. be), and more. See details online, or pick up brochures at the TI.

NEAR BRUGES

Popular tour destinations from Bruges are Flanders Fields (famous WWI sites about 40 miles to the southwest; see that chapter for more information) and the picturesque town of Damme (four easy-to-bike miles to the northeast).

Quasimodo Countryside Tours

This company offers those with extra time two entertaining, all-day, English-only bus tours through the rarely visited Flemish countryside. The "Flanders Fields" tour concentrates on WWI battlefields, trenches, memorials, and poppy-splattered fields (Tue-Sun at 9:15, no tours Mon or in Jan, 8 hours, visit to In Flanders Fields Museum not included). The other tour, "Triple Treat," focuses on Flanders' medieval past and rich culture, with tastes of chocolate, waffles, and beer (departs Mon, Wed, and Fri at 9:15, 8 hours, no tours Dec-mid-Feb). Be ready for lots of walking.

Tours cost €65, or €55 if you're under 26 (cash preferred, €10 discount on second tour if you've taken the other, includes sandwich lunch, 9- or 30-seat bus depending on demand, non-smoking, reservations required—call 050-370-470, www.quasimodo.be). After making a few big-hotel pickups, the buses leave town from the Park Hotel on 't Zand Square (arrange for pickup when you reserve).

Bike Tours

QuasiMundo Bike Tours (listed earlier) also offers a daily "Border by Bike" tour through the nearby countryside to Damme (€25, €3 discount with this book, March-Oct, departs at 13:00, 15 miles, 4 hours, tel. 050-330-775, www.quasimundo.com). Both their city and border tours include bike rental, a light raincoat (if necessary), water, and a drink in a local café. Meet at the metal "car wash" fountain on Burg Square 10 minutes before departure. If you already have a bike, you're welcome to join either tour for €15. Jos, who leads most departures, is a high-energy and entertaining guide.

Charming Mieke of **Pink Bear Bike Tours** takes small groups on an easy and delightful 3.5-hour guided pedal along a canal to the historic town of Damme and back, finishing with a brief tour of Bruges. English tours go daily through peak season and nearly daily the rest of the year (€23, €2 discount with this book, €16 if you already have a bike, meet at 10:25 under bell tower on the Markt, tel. 050-616-686, mobile 0476-744-525, www. pinkbear.freeservers.com).

For do-it-yourself bike tours, see my "Self-Guided Bike Ride to Damme" (page 43). My "Self-Guided Walk from the Markt to the Moat" is also good fun on a bike (page 32). For bike rental shops in Bruges, see "Helpful Hints," earlier.

SIGHTS & EXPERIENCES IN BRUGES

While Bruges has several worthwhile museums and churches, the ultimate sight here is the town itself. After seeing the essential sights, I enjoy slowing down and savoring the city, whether it's getting lost on the back streets, away from the lace shops and waffle stands, taking a bike ride along a quiet canal, learning about beer from passionate locals, or sampling chocolate at one of Bruges' fine chocolatiers. This chapter covers both the top sights and best experiences Bruges has to offer.

Sights in Bruges

These sights are listed by neighborhood, covering the area around the Markt (Market Square) and Burg Square, the cluster of sights south of the Markt, as well as the less touristy area northeast of the core.

ON OR NEAR THE MARKT

All of these sights (except the Historium) are described in greater detail in the ✪ Bruges City Walk chapter.

▲Markt (Market Square)

The crossroads of Bruges is one of the most enjoyable town squares in Belgium—and in this country, that's really saying something. In Bruges' heyday as a trading center, a canal came right up to this square. And today it's still the heart of the modern city. The square is ringed by the frilly post office, enticing restaurant terraces, great old gabled buildings, and the iconic bell tower. Under the bell tower are two great Belgian-style french-fry stands. The streets spoking off this square are lined with tempting eateries and

BRUGES SIGHTS & EXPERIENCES

Bruges at a Glance

▲▲**Bell Tower** Overlooking the Markt, with 366 steps to a worthwhile view and a carillon close-up. **Hours:** Daily 9:30-17:00. See page 28.

▲▲**Burg Square** Historic square with sights and impressive architecture. **Hours:** Always open. See page 30.

▲▲**Groeninge Museum** Top-notch collection of mainly Flemish art. **Hours:** Tue-Sun 9:30-17:00, closed Mon. See page 31.

▲▲**Church of Our Lady** Tombs and church art, including Michelangelo's *Madonna and Child*. **Hours:** Mon-Sat 9:30-17:00, Sun 13:30-17:00. See page 31.

▲▲**Memling Museum at St. John's Hospital** Art by the greatest of the Flemish Primitives. **Hours:** Tue-Sun 9:30-17:00, closed Mon. See page 32.

▲▲**Begijnhof** Peaceful medieval courtyard and Beguine's House museum. **Hours:** Courtyard open daily 6:30-18:30; museum open Mon-Sat 10:00-17:00, Sun 14:00-17:00, shorter hours off-season. See page 32.

▲▲**De Halve Maan Brewery Tour** Fun tour that includes beer. **Hours:** April-Oct Mon-Fri tours approximately on the hour between 10:00-17:00, Sat-Sun until 18:00; Nov-March Mon-Fri 10:00 and 15:00 only, Sat 10:00-17:00, Sun 11:00-16:00. See page 38.

shops. Most city buses run from near here to the train station—use the library bus stop, a block down Kuiperstraat from the Markt.

▲▲Bell Tower (Belfort)

Most of this bell tower has presided over the Markt since 1300, serenading passersby with cheery carillon music. The octagonal lantern was added in 1486, making it 290 feet high—that's 366 steps. The view is worth the climb...and probably even the pricey admission. Some mornings and summer evenings, you can sit in the courtyard or out on the square to enjoy a carillon concert (for details, see page 96).

Cost and Hours: €8, daily 9:30-17:00, 16:15 last-entry time strictly enforced—best to show up before 16:00, pay WC in courtyard.

▲Historium

I despise the Disneyfication of Europe, but this glitzy sight right on the Markt is actually entertaining—and it takes a genuine interest

▲**Markt** Main square that is the modern heart of the city, with carillon bell tower. **Hours:** Always open. See page 27.

▲**Historium** Glitzy multimedia exhibit that re-creates the sights, sounds, and even smells of 1430s Bruges. **Hours:** Daily 10:00-18:00. See page 28.

▲**Basilica of the Holy Blood** Romanesque and Gothic church housing a relic of the blood of Christ. **Hours:** Daily 9:30-12:00 & 14:00-17:00; Nov-March closed on Wed afternoon. See page 30.

▲**City Hall** Beautifully restored Gothic Room from 1400, plus the Renaissance Hall. **Hours:** Daily 9:30-17:00, Renaissance Hall closed 12:30-13:30. See page 30.

▲**Folklore Museum** Well-presented exhibits of life in Bruges' industrious Golden Age. **Hours:** Tue-Sun 9:30-17:00, closed Mon. See page 35.

▲**Bruges Beer Museum** History of Belgian beer and the brewing process, with tastings. **Hours:** Daily 10:00-17:00. See page 38.

▲**Choco-Story: The Chocolate Museum** The delicious story of Belgium's favorite treat. **Hours:** Daily 10:00-17:00. See page 40.

in history. It's pricey and cheesy—sort of "Pirates of the Belgianean" (or maybe "Hysterium")—but it immerses you in the story of Bruges in a way a textbook cannot.

Cost and Hours: €11, includes audioguide, daily 10:00-18:00, last entrance one hour before closing, may be too creepy for kids, Markt 1, tel. 050-270-311, www.historium.be.

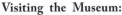

Visiting the Museum: The 35-minute audioguide tour leads you from room to room as it tells the story of an apprentice to the painter Jan van Eyck helping the master prepare to create his famous altarpiece (described on page 65). Using giant video screens, animatronic mannequins, fake fog, and even smell-o-vision, the rooms re-create life in Bruges during its heyday in the 1430s, bringing to life the gritty harbor, the sensuous (R-rated) bath houses, and Van Eyck's studio. The story is engaging and—most important—rooted in real history, providing beautifully rendered glimpses of a medieval age when Bruges was a bustling and important metropolis.

You emerge into a small museum that's as good an introduction to the city's history as you'll find in Bruges. Don't miss the panoramic terrace overlooking the Markt. One floor down, the Duvelorium, a self-described "grand beer café" (see details on page 93), lets you enjoy a pricey beer on the terrace with that same great view.

▲▲Burg Square

This opulent, prickly-spired square is Bruges' civic center, the historic birthplace of Bruges, and the site of the ninth-century castle of the first count of Flanders. It's home to the Basilica of the Holy Blood and City Hall (described next). Today, it's an atmospheric place to take in an outdoor concert while surrounded by six centuries of architecture.

▲Basilica of the Holy Blood

Originally the Chapel of Saint Basil, this church is famous for its relic of the blood of Christ, which, according to tradition, was

brought to Bruges in 1150 after the Second Crusade. The lower chapel is dark and solid—a fine example of Romanesque style. The upper chapel (separate entrance, climb the stairs) is decorated Gothic. An interesting treasury museum is next to the upper chapel.

Cost and Hours: Church-free, treasury-€2, daily 9:30-12:00 & 14:00-17:00; Nov-March closed on Wed afternoon; Burg Square, tel. 050-336-792, www.holyblood.com.

▲City Hall (Stadhuis)

This complex houses several interesting sights, including a room full of old town maps and paintings, and the highlight—the grand, beautifully restored **Gothic Room** from 1400, starring a painted and carved wooden ceiling adorned with hanging arches. Your ticket also covers the less impressive **Renaissance Hall** (Brugse Vrije), next door and basically just one ornate room with a Renaissance chimney (separate entrance—in corner of square at Burg 11a).

Cost and Hours: €4, includes audioguide; daily 9:30-17:00, Renaissance Hall closed 12:30-13:30, last entry 30 minutes before closing; tel. 050-448-711, www.brugge.be.

SOUTH OF THE MARKT

All of the following sights are covered in more detail either in a separate self-guided tour or walk chapter. Also in this area is the De Halve Maan Brewery, with an excellent beer tour (described later, under "Experiences in Bruges").

▲▲Groeninge Museum

This museum houses a world-class collection of mostly Flemish art, from Memling to Magritte. While there's plenty of worthwhile modern art, the highlights are the vivid and pristine Flemish Primitives. (In Flanders, "Primitive" simply means "before the Renaissance.") Flemish art is shaped by its love of detail, its merchant patrons' egos, and the power of the Church. Lose yourself in the halls of Groeninge: Gaze across 15th-century canals, into the eyes of reassuring Marys, and through town squares littered with leotards, lace, and lopped-off heads.

Cost and Hours: €8, more for special exhibits, ticket also covers nearby Arentshuis Museum (described on page 63); Tue-Sun 9:30-17:00, closed Mon; Dijver 12, tel. 050-448-743, www.brugge.be/musea.

✪ See the Groeninge Museum Tour chapter.

▲▲Church of Our Lady (Onze-Lieve-Vrouwekerk)

The church stands as a memorial to the power and wealth of Bruges in its heyday. The delicate *Madonna and Child* is said to be the only Michelangelo statue to leave Italy in his lifetime (thanks to the wealth generated by Bruges' cloth trade). If you like tombs and church art, pay to wander through the apse, but note that the church is undergoing a major, years-long renovation, during which different parts of the interior will be closed to visitors.

Cost and Hours: The rear of the church is free to the public. To get into the main section costs €6; Mon-Sat 9:30-17:00, Sun 13:30-17:00, Mariastraat, tel. 050-448-711, www.brugge.be/musea.

✪ See page 58 of the Bruges City Walk chapter.

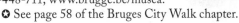

▲▲Memling Museum at St. John's Hospital (Sint Janshospitaal)

The former monastery/hospital complex has a fine collection in what was once the monks' church. It contains several much-loved paintings by the greatest of the Flemish Primitives, Hans Memling. His *St. John Altarpiece* triptych is a highlight, as is the miniature, gilded-oak shrine to St. Ursula.

Cost and Hours: €8, Tue-Sun 9:30-17:00, closed Mon, last entry 30 minutes before closing, includes good audioguide, across the street from the Church of Our Lady, Mariastraat 38, tel. 050-448-713, www.brugge.be/musea.

○ See the Memling Museum Tour chapter.

▲▲Begijnhof

Inhabited by Benedictine nuns, the Begijnhof courtyard almost makes you want to don a habit and fold your hands as you walk under its wispy trees and whisper past its frugal little homes. For a good slice of Begijnhof life, walk through the simple Beguine's House museum.

Cost and Hours: Courtyard-free, daily 6:30-18:30; museum-€2, Mon-Sat 10:00-17:00, Sun 14:00-17:00, shorter hours off-season, English explanations, museum is left of entry gate; tel. 050-330-011.

Nearby: Just south of the Begijnhof is the waterway called **Minnewater**, an idyllic world of flower boxes, canals, and swans.

○ For more on the Begijnhof and Minnewater, see page 61 of the Bruges City Walk chapter.

LESS TOURISTY SIGHTS NORTHEAST OF THE MARKT

The streets north and east of the Markt don't suffer from the intense crowd congestion of the main Markt-Burg-Church of Our Lady thoroughfare and are worth a wander.

▲Self-Guided Walk from the Markt to the Moat

This tranquil stroll takes you along postcard canals and through sleepy residential areas to the moat, where you can climb up inside a working windmill (for the route, see the map on page 18). The walk takes about 20 minutes (longer if you enter the sights). It also works great on a bike and can be extended with a longer ride to Damme (described on page 43).

• *From the Markt, head up Vlamingstraat (with the bell tower at your back, exit straight ahead up the top-right corner of the square).*

Vlamingstraat: Two short blocks up this street, on the left, you'll spot the stately, Neo-Renaissance-style **City Theater** (Stadsschouwburg). Notice how atypically broad this street is for claustrophobic Bruges. That's because several old buildings were torn down to build this theater in 1869. This was a time of Flemish cultural revival—when Dutch-speaking people began to take pride in what differentiated them from the dominant French-speaking Belgians—and Dutch-language theater was an important symbol of Flemish pride. Notice the large plaza in front of the main entrance, dating from a time when regal horse carriages would drop off well-heeled theatergoers. French speakers wish actors a hearty "break a leg!" with the expression, *Je te dis merde!* ("I say crap to you!"). Back then, more *merde* meant more horse carriages...and a bigger audience.

• *A few steps past the theater, on the left, notice the **Friet Museum**, dedicated to the esteemed fry (for details, see page 42). Then, just a bit farther up and also on the left, look for the angled building set slightly back from the street, with yellow bricks and narrow windows. This marks a small square known as...*

Oude Beursplein: While Amsterdam likes to lay claim to inventing the stock market, Bruges' actually predates it. (See the old sign reading *Huis Ter Beurze*—House of the Stock Market.) In the mid-13th century, the Van der Beurse family built an inn here and offered discounted beers to passing merchants on their way between the tollhouse (which we'll see soon) and the Markt. Gradually these hangouts began to host more formalized trading of goods and services. Much of this business took place out in this square; traders would scurry under awnings in case of bad weather. To kick off these meetings amid this chaos, they'd ring a bell, which is still used today to start and end stock trading sessions. And to this day, in most European languages, some variation of the word "Beurse" (*Börse, borsa*, etc.) means "stock market." (Conveniently, the family name also means "purse.")

Just after the old stock market, turn right up Academiestraat. The big building near the end of the street on your right is the **Burghers' Lodge** (Poortersloge)—a meeting place of the local businessmen, similar to today's Rotary clubs. Pause at the building's ornate doorway, just before the square. Just above, notice the Latin message in golden letters with a few seemingly random capitalized letters; if you add them up, they represent the year of the building's reconstruction after a devastating fire (VIXXCIVVIVMD-VIVI—1655).

• *You'll pop out into a square called...*

Jan Van Eyckplein: A large **statue** honors the painter in the middle of this charming waterfront square. In this bilingual city, he's carefully identified twice: the Dutch *Jan van Eyck* on the side facing you, and the French *Jean van Eyck* on the side facing the canal.

On the left side of the square, you can't miss the building with the big, fire-engine-red doors. Sure enough, this was once the firehouse. But before that, it was the **tollhouse** *(tolhuis)*. Although this canal once went all the way to the Markt (and water still runs under this square to the far side), entering vessels had to pause here to pay duties. Today it's the library and archive for the province of West Flanders.

The extremely skinny facade just left of the tollhouse (with the four carved figures over the red door) is the **Dockworkers' House**

(Pijndershuisje). Above the door, notice the detailed carvings showing hardworking stevedores hunched beneath heavy loads. It's no wonder the Dutch word for this thankless occupation was *pijnder*—"one who feels pain."

As the entry point for trade into the city, this neighborhood was an eclectic zone of sailors from around the world. Many international dockworkers lived in little enclaves near here. Looking at a map of this neighborhood, you'll see street names that echo this past: Spanjaardstraat ("Spaniard Street"), Biskajerplein ("Basque Square"), and Engelsestraat ("English Street").

Facing the canal, find the brick house on the left corner. On the upper story, a **statue of Mary** stands in a niche, next to an old lamp. In the 18th century, when Bruges was in decline and in need of beautification, local authorities made landowners a deal: If they added a statue of Mary to their house, the city would install a gas light to illuminate it (the homeowner would benefit from more light and security). Many burghers took them up on the offer, and more than 350 statues of Mary continue to decorate the city (many still with a lamp nearby). Once you start looking for them, you'll see them everywhere.

• *From here, enjoy a stroll through a...*

Residential Canal Zone: From the square, head straight along the canal (left side), simply enjoying the serene scenery. When you hit the wide cross-canal, jog left, cross the bridge, and continue straight up Carmersstraat. At the fifth street on the right—tiny

Korte Speelmansstraat—you're a short block from the **Folklore Museum** and the **Lace Center** (both described later). Once finished there, backtrack to Carmersstraat and carry on straight until you pop out at the dike that separates Bruges from the old moat that surrounds it.

• *Sitting on top of the dike is the...*

St. Janshuys Windmill: In its heyday, bustling Bruges had 29 windmills, mostly used to grind grains. Built in 1770, this one was

funded by several local bakers. Notice how its narrow base allows it to swivel to catch the prevailing wind. Windmill keepers had to be as skilled at riggings as sailors—ready to cover the blades with canvas when the conditions were right. If it's open and you're curious how this remarkable old technology operated, you can climb up the steep, narrow, ladder-like stairs to enter the windmill (€3, May-Aug Tue-Sun 9:30-12:30 & 13:30-17:00, closed Mon, closed Sept-April, last entry 30 minutes before closing, tel. 0499-690-987). In the top section, you'll see the mighty gears and appreciate how wind power not only spun the giant millstones, but also harnessed pulleys to hoist heavy sacks of grain up from the ground below. The grain was steadily trickled into the ever-spinning millstones, which ground it and poured it down the spout, in the lower area of the windmill. There it could be bagged and hoisted back down to send off to the awaiting baker.

• *If you're on foot, you can keep strolling and explore the moat and other nearby windmills, including the tourable **Koelewei Windmill** (covered by St. Janshuys ticket, different style and an interesting complement to St. Janshuys but open only in July and Aug). When you're ready to head back, retrace your steps—and consider detouring to the Folklore Museum and Lace Center, if you haven't yet visited these.*

If you're on a bike, you can turn left and head up along the moat—past three more windmills—before you angle off to the right and head for Damme (see directions on page 43).

OLD-TIMEY ATTRACTIONS ON BALSTRAAT

Balstraat, a tranquil cobbled lane between the Markt and the moat, has two humble but engaging museums. To reach them, follow my self-guided walk, earlier.

▲Folklore Museum (Volkskundemuseum)

While "folklore" usually indicates farming lifestyles and colorful costumes, urbane Bruges dedicates its Folklore Museum to the

Lace

Lace originated as a poor person's profession—because it begins with very cheap raw materials, it was a way to be paid for one's painstaking labor.

In the 1500s, lace collars, sleeves, headdresses, and veils were fashionable among rich men and women. For the next 200 years, the fashion raged (peaking in about 1700). All this lace had to be made by hand, and many women earned extra income from the demand. But the French Revolution of 1789 suddenly made lace for men undemocratic and unmanly. Then, in about 1800, machines replaced human hands, and except for ornamental pieces, the fashion died out among women, too.

These days, handmade lace is usually also homemade—not produced in factories, but at home by dedicated, sharp-eyed hobbyists who love their work. Unlike knitting, it requires total concentration as the lacemaker follows intricate patterns. Lacemakers create their own patterns or trace tried-and-true designs. A piece of lace takes days, not hours, to make—which is why a handmade tablecloth can easily sell for €250.

There are two basic kinds of lace: bobbin lace (which originated in Bruges) and needle lace. To make bobbin lace, the lacemaker juggles many different strands tied to bobbins, "weaving" a design by overlapping the threads. Because of the difficulties, the resulting pattern is usually rather rough and simple compared with other techniques.

Needle lace is more like sewing—stitching premade bits onto a pattern. For example, the "Renaissance" design is made by sewing a premade ribbon onto a pattern in a fancy design. This is then attached as a fringe to a piece of linen—to make a fancy tablecloth, for instance.

In the "Princess" design, premade pieces are stitched onto a cotton net. This method is often used to make all sorts of pieces, from small doilies to full wedding veils.

"Rose point"—no longer practiced—used authentic bits of handmade antique lace as an ornament in a frame or to fill a pendant. Antique pieces can be very expensive.

occupations that kept the city humming through its industrious Golden Age. It's a well-presented little slice of Bruggian life, with modern exhibits filling a row of eight charming, interconnected, 17th-century almshouses.

As you enter, borrow the English descriptions, which bring each room to life. You'll see a schoolhouse, cobbler, clogmaker's shop (where they'd carve a shoe out of a chunk of wood), grocery, and cooper (barrelmaker), as well as exhibits featuring devotional objects and pipes. After spilling out into the tranquil garden courtyard, head back up to the main entrance building to see the rest of the collection: the late 19th-century inn/pub (In de Zarte Kat—look for the resident black cat, Aristide), a typical living room, fragrant candy shop, pharmacy, hatmaker, tailor, costume collection, and more.

Cost and Hours: €4, Tue-Sun 9:30-17:00, closed Mon, last entry 30 minutes before closing, Balstraat 43, tel. 050-448-764, www.brugge.be/musea. To find it, ask for the Jerusalem Church.

Lace Center (Kant Centrum)

Across the street from the Folklore Museum, this lace museum and school lets you learn about lace-making and then see lace actually

being made. Observe as ladies toss bobbins madly while their eyes go bad.

Cost and Hours: €5, Mon-Sat 10:00-17:00, closed Sun, demonstrations usually 14:00-17:00, Balstraat 16, www.kantcentrum.eu.

Nearby: Nearly across the street from the Lace Center is a lace shop with a good reputation, **'t Apostelientje** (Tue 13:00-17:00, Wed-Sat 9:30-12:15 & 13:15-17:00, Sun 10:00-13:00, closed Mon, Balstraat 11, tel. 050-337-860, mobile 0495-562-420).

Experiences in Bruges

While Bruges has some top-notch museums, many of its charms are more experiential. This section covers beer, chocolate, and a delightful bike ride.

BEER

Much as wine flows through all aspects of French or Italian cuisine, Belgians prize beer above all else. Bruges offers a wide variety of places to sample brews, one of the most accessible and enjoyable brewery tours in Belgium, and an interesting museum on beer. For more on Belgian beers, see page 338. For recommendations on shops where you can buy bottles, see page 94.

Pubs and Beer Halls

Hoisting a glass of beer is a quintessential ▲▲▲ Bruges experience. Here, pubs are not just pubs, they're destinations, and places in the old center—which you'd think would be overrun by tourists—are the proud domain of locals, who are happy to educate you on the (sometimes) hundreds of choices. I've listed some of my favorite spots to sample Bruges beer starting on page 90.

▲▲De Halve Maan Brewery Tour

Belgians are Europe's beer connoisseurs, and this handy tour is a great way to pay your respects. The brewery makes the only beers brewed in Bruges: Brugse Zot ("Fool from Bruges") and Straffe Hendrik ("Strong Henry"). The happy gang at this working-family brewery gives entertaining and informative 45-minute tours in two languages (lots of steep steps but a great rooftop panorama). Avoid crowds by visiting at 11:00.

During your tour, you'll learn that "the components of the beer are vitally necessary and contribute to a well-balanced life pattern. Nerves, muscles, visual sentience, and healthy skin are stimulated by these in a positive manner. For longevity and lifelong equilibrium, drink Brugse Zot in moderation!"

Their bistro, where you'll drink your included beer, serves quick, hearty lunch plates. You can eat indoors with the smell of hops, or outdoors with the smell of hops. This is a good place to wait for your tour or to linger afterward.

Cost and Hours: €7.50 tour includes a beer; tours run April-Oct Mon-Fri approximately on the hour 10:00-17:00, Sat-Sun until 18:00; Nov-March Mon-Fri 10:00 and 15:00 only, Sat 10:00-17:00, Sun 11:00-16:00; check the chalkboard for the schedule when you arrive; tours can fill up; Walplein 26, tel. 050-444-223, www.halvemaan.be.

▲Bruges Beer Museum

With a red-carpet entrance just off the Markt, this ode to beer's frothy history overlooks the square from the top of the post office. Head up three flights of stairs to the museum's entrance, where you'll get an iPad and headphones to tour the exhibit and learn about the history of beermaking. The most interesting section is on the top floor, where you can run your hands through raw hops, yeast, and barley while getting a step-by-step guide to modern brewing.

When you've had your historical fill, saunter down to the bar and trade the iPad for three tokens good for your choice of tasting-size beers from a rotating list of 15 local drafts. The bar offers Markt views and is also open to the public (ticket not required).

Cost and Hours: €11 ticket includes three tastings, daily 10:00-17:00, Breidelstraat 3, tel. 0479-359-567, www.brugesbeermuseum.com.

BRUGES SIGHTS & EXPERIENCES

CHOCOLATE

Bruggians are connoisseurs of fine chocolate. You'll be tempted by chocolate-filled display windows all over town. While Godiva is the best big-factory/high-price/high-quality brand, there are plenty of smaller family-run places in Bruges that offer exquisite handmade chocolates. All of the following chocolatiers are proud of their creative varieties and welcome you to assemble a 100-gram assortment of five or six chocolates.

A rule of thumb when buying chocolate: Bruges' informal "chocolate mafia" keeps the price for midrange pralines quite standard, at about €24 per kilogram (or €2.40 for 100 grams). Swankier and "gastronomical" places (like The Chocolate Line or BbyB) charge significantly more, but only aficionados may be able to tell the difference. On the other hand, if a place is priced well *below* this range, be suspicious: Quality may suffer.

By the way, if you're looking for value, don't forget to check the supermarket shelves. Since the country is the largest producer of raw chocolate, Belgium's stores always have a wall of quality chocolate. Try Côte d'Or Noir de Noir for a simple bar of pure dark chocolate that won't flatten in your luggage.

▲Chocolate Shops

Katelijnestraat, which runs south from the Church of Our Lady, is "Chocolate Row," with a half-dozen shops within a few steps. Locals rarely buy chocolate along here (as the prices are marked up for tourists), but this is a convenient place to shop. For locations, see the map on page 18.

Dumon: Perhaps Bruges' smoothest, creamiest chocolates are at Dumon, just off the Markt (a selection of 5 or 6 chocolates are

a deal at €2.30/100 grams). Nathalie Dumon runs the store with Madame Dumon still dropping by to help make their top-notch chocolate daily and sell it fresh. The Dumons don't provide English labels because they believe it's best to describe their chocolates in person— and they do it with an evangelical fervor. Try a small mix-and-match box to sample a few out-of-this-world flavors, and come back for more of your favorites. The original location is just north of the Markt at Eiermarkt 6 (Wed-Mon 10:00-18:00, closed Tue, old chocolate molds on display in basement, tel. 050-346-282). A bigger, glitzier Dumon branch is at Simon Stevinplein 11 (near The Chocolate Line, described next). While technically the Dumon flagship store, this lacks the family-run charm of the original. But they produce similar chocolates, offer additional types of pralines (including sugar-free varieties), and have a full coffee and hot chocolate bar (daily 10:00-18:30, tel. 050-333-360). A third, less-interesting branch is farther south, at Walstraat 6.

The Chocolate Line: Locals and tourists alike flock to The Chocolate Line (pricey at €5.60/100 grams) to taste the *gastronomique* varieties concocted by Dominique Person—the mad scientist of chocolate. His unique creations mix chocolate with various, mostly savory, flavors. Even those that sound gross can be surprisingly good (be adventurous). Options include Havana cigar (marinated in rum, cognac, and Cuban tobacco leaves—so, therefore, technically illegal in the US), lemongrass, lavender, ginger (shaped like a Buddha), saffron curry, spicy chili, Moroccan mint, Pop Rocks/cola chocolate, wine vinegar, fried onions, bay leaf, sake, lime/vodka/passion fruit, wasabi, and tomatoes/olives/basil. The kitchen—busy whipping up 80 varieties—is on display in the back. Enjoy the window display, refreshed monthly (daily 9:30-18:00 except Sun-Mon opens at 10:30, between Church of Our Lady and the Markt at Simon Stevinplein 19, tel. 050-341-090).

BbyB: This chichi, top-end chocolate gallery (whose name stands for "Babelutte by Bartholomeus," for the Michelin-starred restaurateur who owns it) lines up its pralines in a minimalist display case like priceless jewels, each type identified by number. If you don't mind—or actually enjoy—the pretense, the chocolates are top-notch (about €4 for a 5-flavor sleeve, €9 for a sleek 10-flavor sampler box; Tue-Fri 10:00-12:00 & 13:00-18:00, Sat 10:00-18:00, closed Sun-Mon; Sint-Amandsstraat 39, tel. 050-705-760, www.bbyb.be).

Confiserie De Clerck: Third-generation chocolatier Jan sells his handmade chocolates for just €1.20/100 grams, making this one of the best deals in town. Some locals claim his chocolate's just as good as at pricier places, while others insist that any chocolate this cheap must be subpar—taste it and decide for yourself. The time-warp candy shop itself is so delightfully old-school, you'll want to visit one way or the other (Mon-Wed and Fri-Sat 10:00-19:00, closed Thu and Sun, Academiestraat 19, tel. 050-345-338).

▲Choco-Story: The Chocolate Museum
With lots of artifacts well-described in English, this kid-friendly museum fills you in on the production of truffles, bonbons, hollow figures, and solid bars of chocolate. Head up the stairs by the gigantic chocolate egg to fol-

A Brief History of Chocolate

While Belgium's chocolatiers rake in the euros today, their customers are just the latest in a long line of chocoholics.

Ancient Central American indigenous groups—from the Aztecs to the Mayans to the Olmecs—indulged in cocoa products for centuries; the earliest evidence of cocoa consumption dates to around 2000 B.C. Cocoa was so prized that some societies used it as a currency.

In 1519, the Aztec emperor Montezuma served Spanish conquistador Hernán Cortés a cup of hot cocoa (xocoatl) made from cocoa beans, which were native to the New World. It ignited a food fad in Europe—by 1700, elegant "chocolate houses" in Europe's capitals served hot chocolate (with milk and sugar added) to wealthy aristocrats. By the 1850s, the process of making chocolate candies was developed, and Belgium, with a long tradition of quality handmade luxuries, was at the forefront.

Cocoa comes from a big orange fruit that grows—like coffee—primarily in the tropical climates of Central and South America. The fruit's gooey pulp and beans are scooped out and left to ferment, then sun-dried for two weeks. Then the beans are roasted, creating "nibs"—the essence of cocoa. Chocolate straight from the bean is very bitter, so nibs are processed to create cocoa paste or cocoa butter, and the byproduct is ground again to make cocoa powder. Cocoa butter and cocoa paste are mixed together and sweetened with sugar to make chocolates. (Dark chocolate has a higher concentration of cocoa paste, while milk chocolate has more cocoa butter as well as milk powder.)

Europeans created the first chocolate bar in 1847. In 1876, a Swiss man named Henry Nestlé added concentrated milk, creating milk chocolate. And in 1912, Swiss confectioner Jean Neuhaus invented the Belgian praline in Brussels. Later innovators perfected the process, among them the Greek-American chocolatier Leonidas Kestekides, who started his internationally renowned company in Belgium.

Belgians divide their confections into two categories: **Truffles** have soft, crumbly chocolate shells filled with buttercream, while **pralines** are made of a hard chocolate shell with a wide range of fillings—totally different from the sugar-and-nuts French praline.

Belgians take chocolate seriously, and rightly so: It's an essential—and delicious—part of the economy.

low the chronological exhibit, tracing 4,000 years of chocolate history. You'll learn why, in the ancient Mexican world of the Maya and Aztec, chocolate was considered the drink of the gods, and cocoa beans were used as a means of payment. Higher up, you'll learn how chocolates are made and how Belgian pioneers perfected the process. And on the top floor, you'll view a delicious little video (8 minutes long, runs continuously, English subtitles) and learn more about the big-name Belgian chocolatiers (including some less-than-subtle product placement for Belcolade, which owns this museum). The finale is downstairs in the "demonstration room," where—after a 10-minute cooking demo—you get a taste.

Cost and Hours: €8, ticket includes chocolate bar; various combo-tickets also include the adjacent Lamp Museum, Friet Museum, and the Diamond Museum across town—consider your options before buying a ticket; daily 10:00-17:00, last entry 45 minutes before closing; where Wijnzakstraat meets Sint Jansstraat at Sint Jansplein, 3-minute walk from the Markt; tel. 050-612-237, www.choco-story-brugge.be.

Related Sights: The owners of the Chocolate Museum operate two other, similarly hokey but endearing museums that are open the same hours. Neither one is worth its €7 individual admission, but both are cheap add-ons with one of the Chocolate Museum's combo-tickets, mentioned above.

The museum owner's wife got tired of his ancient lamp collection...so he opened a **Lamp Museum** next door. While obscure, it's an impressive and well-described collection showing lamps through the ages.

The same folks also run the **Friet Museum,** a few blocks away (at Vlamingstraat 33, www.frietmuseum.be). While this fun-loving and kid-friendly place tries hard to elevate the story of the potato, this is—for most—one museum too many. Still, it's the only place in the world that enthusiastically tells the story of french fries, which, of course, aren't even French—they're Belgian.

BIKING

The Dutch word for bike is *fiets* (pronounced "feets"). And though Bruges' sights are close enough for easy walking, the town is a treat for bikers. A bike quickly gets you into dreamy back lanes without a hint of tourism. Take a peaceful evening ride through the town's nooks and crannies and around the outer canal. Consider keeping a bike for the duration of your stay—it's the way the locals get around. You can try one of the following rides, or ask at the rental shop for maps and ideas (see "Bike Rental" on page 22 for more info).

▲Biking from the Markt to the Moat

My self-guided walk from the Markt to the Moat (described on page 32) is equally as fun on a bike. As this area is less touristy, it's less congested and easy to navigate on a bike. When you reach the end of the described route, you can circle the moat in either direction on the fine bike paths or continue riding, following the route described next.

▲Self-Guided Bike Ride to Damme

For the best short bike trip out of Bruges, pedal four miles each way to the nearby town of Damme. You'll enjoy a whiff of the country-

side and see a working windmill while riding along a canal to a charming (if well-discovered) small market town. While Damme is cute, it's sleepy, with little to see—take this ride mostly as an excuse to pedal through the country-side, between canals and farm fields. Allow about two hours for the leisurely round-trip bike ride and a brief stop in Damme. The Bel-gium/Netherlands border is a 40-minute pedal (along the same canal) beyond Damme.

• *Head east from Bruges' Markt through Burg Square and out to the canal. (Or, for a more enter-taining route, follow my self-guided tour through Jan Van Eyckplein, described on page 32.) At the canal, circle to the left, riding along the former town wall and passing four windmills (includ-ing the St. Janshuys Windmill, described on page 35). After the last windmill, at Dampoort, turn right across the second of two bridges (at the locks), then continue straight along the north/left bank of the Damme Canal (via Noorweegse Kaai/Damse Vaart-West).*

The Damme Canal (Damse Vaart): From Dampoort you'll pedal straight and level along the canal directly to Damme. There's

no opportunity to cross the canal until you reach the town. The farmland to your left is a *polder*—a salt marsh that flooded each spring, until it was reclaimed by industrious local farmers. The Damme Canal, also called the Na-poleon Canal, was built in

1811 by Napoleon (actually by his Spanish prisoners) in a failed at-tempt to reinvigorate the city as a port. Today locals fish this canal for eels and wait for the next winter freeze. Old-timers have fond

memories of skating to Holland on this canal—but nowadays it's a rare event (ask locals about the winter of 2008-2009).

Schelle Windmill (Schellemolen): Just before arriving in Damme, you'll come upon a working windmill that dates from 1867. More clever than the windmills in Bru-ges, this one is designed so just the wood cap turns to face the wind—rather than the entire building. If it's open, climb up through the creaking, spinning, wind-powered gears to the top floor (free, April-Sept Sat-Sun 9:30-12:30 & 13:00-18:00, closed Mon-Fri and Oct-March).

In its day (13th-15th century), Bruges was one of the top five European ports...and little Damme was important as well. Today all you see is land—the once-bustling former harbors silted up, causing the sea to retreat. Pause atop the bridge just beyond the windmill, with the windmill on your right and the spire of Bruges' Church of Our Lady poking up in the distance. It's easy to imagine how, at Napoleon's instructions, the canal was designed to mimic a grand Parisian boulevard—leading to the towering church back in Bruges.

• *From here, the canal continues straight to Holland. (If tempted...you're a third of the way to the border.) Instead, cross the bridge and follow Kerkstraat, which cuts through the center of town, to Damme's main square and City Hall.*

Damme: Once a thriving medieval port, and then a moated garrison town, Damme is now a tourist center—a tiny version

of Bruges. It has a smaller-but-similar City Hall, a St. John's Hospital, and a big brick Church of Our Lady. You can tell by its 15th-century City Hall that, 500 years ago, Damme was rolling in herring money. Rather than being built with Belgian bricks (like other buildings around here), the City Hall was made of French limestone. Originally the ground floor was a market and fish warehouse, with government offices upstairs.

• *Continue on Kerkstraat as it leads two blocks farther to the Church of Our Lady. Along the way, you could side-trip to the left, down Pottenbakkersstraat, which takes you to a quaint little square called Haringmarkt (named for the Herring Market that made Damme rich in the 15th century). The trees you see from here mark the lines of the town's long-gone 17th-century ramparts.*

Returning to Kerkstraat, continue on to the big church.

The Church of Our Lady: This church, which rose and fell with the fortunes of Damme, dates from the 13th century. Inside

are two Virgin Marys: To the right of the altar is a 1630 wooden statue of Mary, and to the left is Our Lady of the Fishermen (c. 1650, in a glass case). Over the nave stands Belgium's oldest wooden statue, St. Andrew, with his X-shaped cross.

Outside, behind the 13th-century church tower, is a three-faced, modern fiberglass sculpture by the Belgian artist Charles Delporte. Called *View of Light*, it evokes three lights: morning (grace), midday (kindness), and evening (gentleness). If you like his work, there's more at his nearby gallery.

• *To return to Bruges, continue past the church on Kerkstraat. Just before crossing the next bridge, follow a scenic dirt lane to the right that leads you back to the Damme Canal (and Damse Vaart-Zuid). Take this road back to Bruges. If you want a change of pace from the canal, about halfway back turn off to the left (at the white bridge and brick house), then immediately turn right on Polderstraat and follow the smaller canal back to the outskirts of Bruges.*

BRUGES CITY WALK

Bruges is made for walking. In just a couple of hours, you can get the lay of the land, pop in to a few sights, and mentally bookmark others to come back to later. On this walk, we'll get a sampling of what makes Bruges Bruges. We'll start on the vast square with a towering bell tower that shows off the Golden Age of the 1400s, when Bruges was one of the richest cities on earth. We'll see art by Memling and Michelangelo, oak pilings from Bruges' foundations, the pious home of cloistered women, and maybe even a few drops of Christ's blood. Along the way you can sample local beer, watch swans glide beneath willow trees, and enjoy postcard views of a tranquil city reflected in a quiet canal.

Orientation

Length of This Walk: Allow two hours for the walk, plus more time for touring sight interiors.

Sightseeing Tip: If you're planning to visit all the sights listed on this walk, save money by buying one of the city's sightseeing passes (explained on page 21).

Bell Tower: €8, daily 9:30-17:00, 16:15 last entry strictly enforced—best to show up before 16:00.

Basilica of the Holy Blood: Church-free, treasury-€2, daily 9:30-12:00 & 14:00-17:00, Nov-March closed on Wed afternoon.

City Hall and Renaissance Hall: €4 ticket includes City Hall's Gothic Room and Renaissance Hall; daily 9:30-17:00, Renaissance Hall closed 12:30-13:30, last entry 30 minutes before closing; includes audioguide.

Church of Our Lady: Free to glance down the nave, €6 to see art-filled apse and choir; Mon-Sat 9:30-17:00, Sun 13:30-17:00.

Memling Museum at St. John's Hospital: €8, Tue-Sun 9:30-

17:00, closed Mon, last entry 30 minutes before closing, includes good audioguide.

De Halve Maan Brewery Tour: €7.50, tours run April-Oct Mon-Fri approximately on the hour 10:00-17:00, Sat-Sun until 18:00 (11:00 is least crowded); Nov-March Mon-Fri 10:00 and 15:00 only, Sat 10:00-17:00, Sun 11:00-16:00.

Begijnhof: Courtyard-free, daily 6:30-18:30; museum-€2, Mon-Sat 10:00-17:00, Sun 14:00-17:00, shorter hours off-season.

The Walk Begins

❶ Markt (Market Square)

Ringed by the frilly-spired post office, lots of restaurant terraces, great old gabled buildings, and the bell tower, this is the modern

heart of the city. And, in Bruges' heyday as a trading city, this was also the center. The "typical" old buildings here were rebuilt in the 19th century in an exaggerated Neo-Gothic style (Bruges is often called "more Gothic than Gothic"). This pre-Martin Luther style was a political statement for this Catholic town.

In the 1300s, a canal came right up to this square. Imagine boats moored where the post office stands today. Cranes (powered by humans in hamster wheels) loaded and unloaded the boats. Along that whole side of the square once stretched the spacious Waterhalle, a covered warehouse where businessmen from all nations stored and traded goods. On the opposite side of the square, locate the house with the modern gold ball on top—this is Bruges' oldest house (15th century). In former times, farmers shipped their cotton, wool, flax, and hemp to the port at Bruges. The industrious locals would spin, weave, and dye it into a finished product, then load it onto boats to ship throughout the known world.

By 1400, they were trading more refined goods, such as trendy clothes, tapestry, chairs, jewelry, and paper—a new invention (replacing parchment) made in Flanders with cotton that was shredded, soaked, and pressed. One of the Continent's first bookmakers worked here in Bruges.

The square is adorned with **flags,** including the red-white-and-blue lion flag of Bruges, the yellow-with-black-lion flag of Flanders, the black-yellow-and-red flag of Belgium, and the blue-with-circle-of-yellow-stars flag of the European Union.

The **statue** depicts two friends, Jan Breidel and Pieter de Coninc, clutching sword and shield and looking toward France as

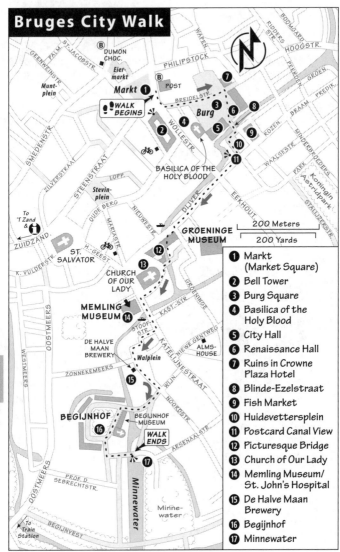

Bruges City Walk

1. Markt (Market Square)
2. Bell Tower
3. Burg Square
4. Basilica of the Holy Blood
5. City Hall
6. Renaissance Hall
7. Ruins in Crowne Plaza Hotel
8. Blinde-Ezelstraat
9. Fish Market
10. Huidevettersplein
11. Postcard Canal View
12. Picturesque Bridge
13. Church of Our Lady
14. Memling Museum/ St. John's Hospital
15. De Halve Maan Brewery
16. Begijnhof
17. Minnewater

they lead a popular uprising against the French king in 1302. The rebels identified potential French spies by demanding they repeat two words—*schild en vriend* (shield and friend)—that only Flemish locals (or foreigners with phlegm) could pronounce. They won Flanders its freedom. Cleverly using hooks to pull knights from their horses, they scored the medieval world's first victory of foot soldiers over cavalry, and of common people over nobility. The French knights, thinking that fighting these Flemish peasants would be a cakewalk, had worn their dress uniforms. The peasants had a field day afterward scavenging all the golden spurs from the fallen soldiers after the Battle of the Golden Spurs (1302).

Geldmuntstraat, a block west of the square, has fun shops and eateries. Steenstraat, the people-packed main shopping street, stretches from in front of the belfry to the big 't Zand Square, and eventually all the way to the train station. More than ever, in peak season, the crowds here include cruise groups following the numbered ping-pong paddles of their guides. Want a coffee? Stop by the Café-Brasserie Craenenburg on the Markt. Originally the house where Maximilian of Austria was imprisoned in 1488, it's been a café since 1905 (daily 7:30-23:00, Markt 16).

❷ Bell Tower (Belfort)

Most of this bell tower has stood over the Markt since 1300. The octagonal lantern was added in 1486, making it 290 feet high.

The tower combines medieval crenellations, pointed Gothic arches, round Roman arches, flamboyant spires, and even a few small flying buttresses (two-thirds of the way up).

Try some Belgian-style fries from either stand at the bottom of the tower. While the fries come with an array of exotic sauces, traditionally Belgians dip in mayonnaise—while kids and Americans enjoy ketchup.

Enter the courtyard. The public sits on benches here to enjoy free carillon concerts (normally Wed, Sat, and Sun at 11:00, plus mid-June-mid-Sept Mon and Wed at 21:00—see the posted schedule). A pay WC is in the courtyard.

Climb the tower (the price is steeper than its 366 steps). Just before you reach the top, peek into the carillon room. The 47 bells

can be played mechanically with the giant barrel and movable tabs (as they are on each quarter hour), or with a manual keyboard (as they are during concerts). The carillonneur uses his fists and feet, rather than fingers. Be there on the quarter hour, when things ring. The bell experience is best at the top of the hour.

Atop the tower, survey Bruges. On the horizon, you can see the towns along the North Sea coast.

• *Leaving the bell tower, turn right (east) onto Breidelstraat, and thread yourself through the lace and waffles to...*

❸ Burg Square

This opulent square is Bruges' historical birthplace, political center, and religious heart. Today it's the scene of outdoor concerts and local festivals.

Pan the square counter-clockwise to see six centuries of architecture. You'll go from Romanesque (the interior of the fancy, gray-and-gold **Basilica of the Holy Blood** in the corner), to the pointed Gothic arches and prickly steeples of the white sandstone **City Hall,** to the well-proportioned windows of the **Renaissance Hall** (next door, under the gilded statues). Continue spinning, past the park, until you reach the elaborate 17th-century Baroque of the **Provost's House** (at the head of Breidelstraat). The park is where Bruges' first cathedral once stood. It was demolished during the French Revolutionary period. Today, the foundation is open to the public in the **Crowne Plaza Hotel** basement (we'll visit it in a few minutes).

• *Approach the small, fancy, gray-and-gold building in the corner of Burg Square.*

❹ Basilica of the Holy Blood

The gleaming gold knights and ladies on the church's gray facade remind us that this double-decker church was built (c. 1150) by a brave Crusader to house the drops of Christ's blood he'd brought back from Jerusalem.

Visiting the Basilica: Enter the **lower chapel** through the door labeled *Basiliek.* The stark and dim decor reeks of the medieval piety that drove crusading Christian Europeans to persecute Muslims. With heavy columns and round arches, the style is pure Romanesque. The annex along the right aisle displays somber statues of Christ being tortured and entombed, plus a 12th-century relief panel over a doorway showing St. Basil (a

fourth-century scholarly monk) being baptized by a double-jointed priest, and a man-size dove of the Holy Spirit.

Go back outside and up the stair-case to reach the **upper chapel.** After being gutted by secular-humanist French revolutionaries in 1799, the

The Legend of the Holy Blood

Several drops of Christ's blood, washed from his lifeless body by Joseph of Arimathea, were preserved in a rock-crystal vial in Jerusalem. In 1150, the patriarch of Jerusalem gave the blood to a Flemish soldier, Derrick of Alsace, as thanks for rescuing his city from the Muslims during the Second Crusade. Derrick (also called Dedric or Thierry) returned home and donated it to the city. The old, dried blood suddenly turned to liquid, a miracle repeated every Friday for the next two centuries, and verified by thousands of pilgrims from around Europe who flocked here to adore it. The blood dried up for good in 1325.

Every year on Ascension Day (May 14 in 2015, May 5 in 2016), Bruges' bankers, housewives, and waffle vendors put on old-time costumes for the parading of the vial through the city. The slow-mo parade involves 1,700 locals and 50 floats: Crusader knights re-enact the bringing of the relic, Joseph of Arimathea washes Christ's body, and ladies in medieval costume with hair tied up in horn-like hairnets come out to wave flags. If you stand at one point, it takes 1.5 hours to watch the entire processional trudge past from beginning to end. Most of the remaining Bruges citizens just take the day off.

upper chapel's original Romanesque decor was redone by 19th-century Romantics in a Neo-Gothic style. The nave is colorful, with a curved wooden ceiling, painted walls, a round pulpit carved from a single massive oak, and stained-glass windows of the dukes who ruled Flanders, along with their duchesses.

The painting at the main altar tells the story of how the Holy Blood got here. Derrick of Alsace, having helped defend Jerusalem *(Hierosolyma)* and Bethlehem *(Bethlema)* from Muslim incursions in the Second Crusade, kneels (left) before the grateful Christian patriarch of Jerusalem, who rewards him with the relic. Derrick returns home (right) and kneels before Bruges' bishop to give him the vial of blood.

The relic itself—some red stuff preserved inside a clear, six-inch tube of rock crystal—is kept in the adjoining room (through the three arches). It's in the tall, silver tabernacle on the altar. (Each Friday—and many other days as well—the tabernacle's doors will be open, so you can actually see the vial of blood.) On holy days, the relic is shifted across the room and displayed on the throne under the canopy.

Next to the upper chapel, the **treasury** contains the impressive gold-and-silver, gem-studded, hexagonal reliquary (c. 1600, left wall) that the vial of blood is paraded around in on feast days. The vial is placed in the "casket" at the bottom of the three-foot-tall structure. Flanking the shrine are paintings of kneeling residents who, for centuries, have tended the shrine and organized the pageantry as part of the 31-member Brotherhood of the Holy Blood. Elsewhere in the room are the Brothers' ceremonial objects: necklaces, chalices, a hunting horn, and so on. A video shows the Brotherhood in action today, parading the relic across Burg Square.

Find the small lead box holding a broken glass tube. This is a replica of the precious rock-crystal vial that holds the blood of Christ. The lead box once protected the vial of blood from Protestant extremists (1578) and French Revolutionaries (1799) bent on destroying what, to them, was a glaring symbol of Catholic mumbo jumbo.

• *Go back out into the square.*

❺ City Hall (Stadhuis)

Built in about 1400, when Bruges was a thriving bastion of capitalism with a population of 35,000, this building served as a model for

town halls elsewhere, including Brussels. The white sandstone facade is studded with statues of knights, nobles, and saints with prickly Gothic steeples over their heads. A colorful double band of cities' coats of arms includes those of Bruges (Brugghe) and Dunkirk (Dunquerke). Back then, Bruges' jurisdiction included many towns in present-day France. The building is still the City Hall; on Fridays and Saturdays, it's not unusual to see couples arriving here to get married.

Visiting City Hall: The ground-level lobby leads you to a **picture gallery** (free, closed Mon) with scenes from Belgium's history, from the Spanish king to the arrival of Napoleon, shown meeting the mayor here at the City Hall in 1803.

• *You can pay to climb the stairs for a look at the...*

Gothic Room: Some of modern democracy's roots lie in this ornate room, where, for centuries, the city council has met to discuss the town's affairs. In 1464, one of Europe's first parliaments, the Estates General of the Low Countries, convened here. The fireplace at the far end bears a proclamation from 1305, which says, "All the artisans, laborers... and citizens of Bruges are free—all of them."

The elaborately carved and painted wooden ceiling (a Neo-Gothic reconstruction from the 19th century) features tracery in gold, red, and black. Five dangling arches ("pendentives") hang down the center, now adorned with modern floodlights.

The late 19th-century Romantic **wall murals** depict episodes in the city's history. Start with the largest painting along the left wall, and work clockwise.

In the **big painting on the left wall,** everyone cheers, flags wave, trumpets blare, and dogs bark, as Bruges' knights, dressed

in gold with black Flemish lions, return triumphant after driving out French oppressors and winning Flanders' independence. The Battle of the Golden Spurs (1302) is remembered every July 11.

Next, the **painting on the fireplace wall** shows cardinals in red flocking to this elaborate ceremony. In what may have been Bruges' high-water mark, Philip the Good of Burgundy (seated, in black) assembled his court here in Bruges and solemnly founded the knightly Order of the Golden Fleece (1429).

Next, the Crusader knight, Derrick of Alsace, returns from the Holy Land and kneels at the entrance of St. Basil's Chapel to present the relic of Christ's Holy Blood (c. 1150).

On the **right wall,** a nun carries a basket of bread in this scene from St. John's Hospital.

A town leader stands at the podium and hands a sealed document to a German businessman, renewing the Hanseatic League's business license. Membership in this club of trading cities was a key to Bruges' prosperity.

As peasants cheer, a messenger of the local duke proclaims the town's right to self-government (1190).

The mayor visits a Bruges painting studio to shake the hand of Jan van Eyck, the great Flemish Primitive painter (1433). Jan's wife, Margareta, is there, too. In the 1400s, Bruges rivaled Florence and Venice as Europe's cultural capital. See the town in the distance, out Van Eyck's window.

Bruges' book printer—the first on the Continent—sells his modern books in 1446.

City fathers grab a ceremonial trowel from a pillow to lay the fancy cornerstone of the City Hall (1376). Bruges' familiar towers (before the lantern was added to the bell tower) stand in the background.

The city's best-known medieval poet gazes out the window for inspiration.

On the **back wall,** it's a typical market day at the Halls (the courtyard behind the bell tower). Arabs mingle with Germans in fur-lined coats and beards in a market where they sell everything from armor to lemons.

And finally, a bishop blesses a new canal (1404) as ships sail right by the city. This was Bruges in its heyday, before the silting of the harbor. At the far right, the two bearded men with moustaches are the brothers who painted these murals.

In the **adjoining room,** old paintings and maps show how little the city has changed through the centuries. Find one well-

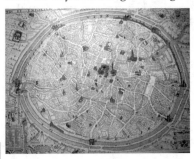

known **map** (in pale white-aqua-gold colors, on the left wall). It shows in exquisite detail the city as it looked in 1562. Find the bell tower, the Church of Our Lady, and Burg Square, which back then was bounded on the north by a cathedral. Notice the canal (on the west) leading

from the North Sea right to the Markt. A moat encircled the city with its gates, unfinished wall, and 28 windmills (four of which survive today). The mills pumped water to the town's fountains, made paper, ground grain, and functioned as the motor of the Middle Ages. Most locals own a copy of this map that shows how their neighborhood looked 400 years ago.

• *Back on the square, leaving the City Hall, turn right and go to the corner to enter...*

❻ Renaissance Hall (Brugse Vrije)

This elaborately adorned mansion has served Bruges as a governing palace, a courthouse, and (today) as the city archives. The white-gold-red facade dates from the 1720s. Notice the crowned heads, each with their unique personality.

Visiting the Hall: Go inside to find the elaborately decorated Renaissance Hall, with its grand fireplace mantelpiece carved from oak by Bruges' Renaissance Man, Lancelot Blondeel, in 1531. If you're into heraldry, it's fascinating. If not, you'll wonder where the rest of the museum is.

The centerpiece of the incredible carving is the most powerful man in Europe—Holy Roman Emperor Charles V. The home-

town duke, on the far left, is related to Charles V. By making the connection to the Holy Roman Emperor clear, this carved family tree of Bruges' nobility helped substantiate their power. The double-eagle emblem is Charles' Habsburg family symbol. The other coats of arms are the many European nobles under Charles' powerful reign. Notice the well-guarded family jewels (i.e., Charles' bulging codpiece). And check out the expressive little cherubs.

Notice the painting that stands nearby. It depicts this same hall: There's the fireplace, the same paneled walls, and the raised green table where justices sat in judgment. The painting shows the room in action in 1659, as a repentant man stands before the lace-collared justices to hear his punishment. One of the judges is about to pull that long chain to ring a bell and decide his fate.

• *Leaving the building, walk straight ahead and hook around the cream-colored building to your right.*

❼ Ruins in the Crowne Plaza Hotel

One of the old town's newest buildings (1992) sits atop the ruins of the town's oldest structures. In about A.D. 900, when Viking ships regularly docked here to rape and pillage, Baldwin Iron Arm built a fort *(castrum)* to protect his Flemish people. In 950, the fort was converted into St. Donatian's Church, which became one of the city's largest.

Visiting the Ruins: Ask politely at the hotel's reception desk to see the archaeological site—ruins of the fort and the church. If there's no conference in progress, they'll let you walk down the stairs and have a peek. (They were only allowed to build here on condition they allow visitors to see the antiquities upon which the building sits.)

In the basement, the modern conference rooms are lined

with old stone walls and display cases of objects found in the ruins of earlier structures. Trace the history.

See thousand-year-old oak pilings, carved to a point, once driven into this former peat bog to support the original fort and shore up its moat. Next, see paintings that show the church that replaced it. The curved stone walls you walk among are from the foundations of the ambulatory around the church altar.

A document (*Vente de Materiaux,* posted back where you entered) announces the "sale of material" when Napoleon destroyed the church in the early 1800s and auctioned off the bricks. A local builder bought them, and now the pieces of the old cathedral are embedded in other buildings throughout Bruges.

Display cases around the room show what modern archaeologists found around here—the refuse of a thousand years of habitation: pottery, animal skulls, rosary beads, dice, coins, keys, thimbles, pipes, spoons, and Delftware. There's also a 14th-century sarcophagus painted with the crucifixion on the west end and a Virgin and Child on the east.

• *Back on Burg Square, head down the passageway by Renaissance Hall. This alley is called...*

❽ Blinde-Ezelstraat

Midway down on the left side (thigh level), see an original iron hinge from the city's south gate, back when the city was ringed by a moat and closed nightly at 22:00. On the right wall, at eye level, a square black patch shows you just how grimy the city had become before a 1960s cleaning. Despite the cleaning and a few fanciful reconstructions, the city today looks much as it did in centuries past.

The name "Blinde-Ezelstraat" means "Blind Donkey Street." Perhaps in medieval times, the donkeys, carrying fish from the North Sea on their backs, were stopped here so that their owners could put blinders on them. Otherwise, the donkeys wouldn't cross the water between the old city and the fish market.

From the end of the alleyway, look back and up for a nice photo-op of the Goldfinger family standing atop the alley's sky bridge.

• *Cross the bridge over what was the 13th-century city moat. On your left are the arcades of the...*

❾ Fish Market (Vismarkt)

The North Sea is just 12 miles away, and the fresh catch is sold here (Wed-Sat 6:00-13:00, closed Sun-Tue). Locals love the shrimp—cooked on the boat and sold fresh here. Once a

BRUGES CITY WALK

thriving market, today it's mostly crafts and souvenirs...and the big catch is the tourists.

• *Take an immediate right (west), entering a courtyard called...*

⑩ Huidevettersplein

This tiny, picturesque, restaurant-filled square was originally the headquarters of the town's skinners and tanners. The lions on the

column hold the tanners' logo. On the facade of the Hotel Duc de Bourgogne, four old relief panels above the windows show scenes from the leather trade—once a leading Bruges industry. First, tan the hide in a bath of acid; then, with tongs, pull it out to dry; then beat it to make it soft; and, finally, scrape and clean it to make it ready for sale.

• *Continue a few steps to Rozenhoedkaai street, where you can look back to your right and get a great...*

⑪ Postcard Canal View

The bell tower reflected in a quiet canal lined with old houses—this view is the essence of Bruges. Seeing buildings rising straight

from the water makes you understand why this was the Venice of the North. Can you see the bell tower's tilt? It leans about four feet. The tilt has been carefully monitored since 1740, but no change has been detected.

As you face the view, to your left (west) down the Dijver canal (past a flea market on weekends) looms the huge spire of the Church of Our Lady,

the tallest brick spire in the Low Countries. Between you and the church are the Europa College (a post-graduate institution for training future "Eurocrats" about the laws, economics, and politics of the European Union) and a fine museum.

• *Continue walking with the canal and the bell tower on your right. About 100 yards ahead, on the left, is the copper-colored sign that points the way to the* **Groeninge Museum.** *This sumptuous collection of paintings takes you from the 15th to the 20th century. The highlights are its Flemish Primitives, with all their glorious detail (✪ see the Groeninge Museum Tour chapter).*

Continue another half-block past the Groeninge Museum. At Dijver 16, turn left into a quiet courtyard. You'll pass by the entrance to the

BRUGES CITY WALK

Arentshuis Museum (see page 71). Continue through the courtyard to the far right corner, where you'll find a...

⑫ Picturesque Bridge

Standing atop this tiny stone bridge over a little canal, take in the scene and savor its beauty. Start with the back end of the church,  admiring Our Lady's big buttresses and round apse. Panning clockwise, find a teeny-tiny window at the corner of a building—a toll-keeper's lookout. Below that, at canal level, you could snap a photo of your travel partner at the iron bars. Continue panning until you find the old relief panel of a boat (directly behind you). Next comes the old wooden house along the canal. Finally, in the garden, there's a bust of Juan Luis Vives (1492-1540), the Spanish-born resident of Bruges whose writings on the connection between the body and the soul made him the "father of psychology."

• *Cross the bridge, veer left along the hedge-lined path, and find the church entry on the right.*

⑬ Church of Our Lady (Onze-Lieve-Vrouwekerk)

This towering brick church stands as a memorial to the power and wealth of Bruges in its heyday. Step inside. While you can stand in the back and marvel at its interior in general, to get a close-up look at the Michelangelo and historic tombs and art, you'll need to pay for a ticket. As the church is undergoing a major renovation, some parts of the interior may be closed to visitors.

Visiting the Church: Enter and stand in the back to admire the Church of Our Lady. Its 14th- and 15th-century stained glass was destroyed by iconoclasts, so the church is lit more brightly today than originally. Like most of Belgium, it is Catholic. The medieval-style screen divided the clergy from the commoners who gathered here in the nave. Worshippers are still attended by 12 Gothic-era statues of apostles, each with his symbol and a grandiose Baroque wooden pulpit, with a roof that seems to float in midair. It was from this fancy perch that the priest would interpret the word of God.

Madonna and Child **by Michelangelo:** Pay and pass through

the turnstile, entering first a chapel featuring a small marble Michelangelo statue. The delicate statue is somewhat overwhelmed by the ornate Baroque niche it sits in. It's said to be the only Michelangelo statue to leave Italy in his lifetime, bought in Tuscany by a wealthy Bruges businessman, who's buried in the same chapel (to the right).

As Michelangelo chipped away at the masterpiece of his youth, *David*, he took breaks by carving this one in 1504. Mary, slightly smaller than life-size, sits while young Jesus stands in front of her. Their expressions are mirror images—serene, but a bit melancholy, with downcast eyes, as though pondering the young child's dangerous future. Though they're lost in thought, their hands instinctively link, tenderly. The white Carrara marble is highly polished, something Michelangelo only did when he was certain he'd gotten it right.

Tombs at the High Altar: The reclining statues mark the tombs of the last local rulers of Bruges: Mary of Burgundy, and her father, Charles the Bold. The dog and lion at their feet are symbols of fidelity and courage. Underneath the tombs are the actual excavated gravesites with mirrors to help you enjoy the well-lit, centuries-old tomb paintings.

Bruges residents would stand before these tombs and ponder the great decline of their city. In 1482, when 25-year-old Mary of Burgundy tumbled from a horse and died, she left behind a toddler son and a husband who was heir to the Holy Roman Empire. Beside her lies her father, Charles the Bold, who also died prematurely, in war. Their twin deaths meant Bruges belonged to Austria, and would soon be swallowed up by the empire and ruled from Vienna by Habsburgs—who didn't understand or care about its problems. Trade routes shifted, and goods soon flowed through Antwerp, then Amsterdam, as Bruges' North Sea port silted up. After these developments, Bruges began four centuries of economic decline. The city was eventually mothballed. The sleeping beauty of Flemish towns was later discovered by modern-day tourists to be remarkably well-pickled, which explains its current affluence. The first tourists were Americans and Canadians who came to visit the graves of loved ones in nearby WWI cemeteries after that war.

The Rest of the Church: The wooden balcony to the left of the painted altarpiece is part of the Gruuthuse mansion next door, providing the noble family with prime seats for Mass. Along the outside of the choir, to the left as you face the balcony, notice the row of dramatic wooden statues. (Contrast these with the meek figures in the apse's stained glass.)

BRUGES CITY WALK

In a side chapel in the apse you'll see excavations that turned up fascinating grave paintings on the tombs below and near the altar. Dating from the 14th and 15th centuries, these show Mary represented as Queen of Heaven (on a throne, carrying a crown and scepter) and Mother of God (with the baby Jesus on her lap). Since Mary is in charge of advocating with Jesus for your salvation, she's a good person to have painted on the wall of your tomb. Tombs also show lots of angels—generally patron saints of the dead person—swinging incense burners.

• *Just across Mariastraat from the church entrance and about 20 yards farther south on Mariastraat and to the left is the entrance to perhaps the city's most visit-worthy museum, the...*

⓮ Memling Museum at St. John's Hospital (Sint Janshospitaal)

Located in the former wards and church of St. John's Hospital, the Memling Museum offers a glimpse into medieval medicine, displaying surgical instruments, documents, and visual aids as you work your way to the museum's climax: several of Hans Memling's glowing masterpieces.

Hans Memling's art was the culmination of Bruges' Flemish Primitive style. His serene, soft-focus, motionless scenes capture a medieval piety that was quickly fading. The popular style made Memling (c. 1430-1494) one of Bruges' wealthiest citizens, and his work was gobbled up by visiting Italian merchants, who took it home with them, cross-pollinating European art. (◎ See the Memling Museum Tour chapter.)

• *Leaving the museum, turn right and go about 30 paces to enjoy a fine canal view. Before you is one of many canal tour boat companies. (As they share city waterways, they all have the same price and standards.) The canal here was part of the city moat. Standing here in the 15th century, you would have just left town through the Maria Gate. Continue on down Katelijnestraat. After about 50 yards, turn right and go down a tiny lane, Stoofstraat. This was "Stove Street"—where the neighborhood's public bathhouse stood—which in times past served (like ancient Roman baths) as a place to bathe, work out, and socialize. Stoofstraat leads you into the pleasant square called Walplein, where you'll find the...*

⓯ De Halve Maan Brewery

If you like beer, take a tour here. On busy days, tours can fill up, so you may want to reserve a spot on a later tour (see page 38).

• *Leaving the brewery, head right, then turn right on Wijngaartstraat. You'll reach a horse-head fountain, where the*

horse-and-buggy horses stop to drink. From the fountain, turn right and pause in the center of a picturesque pedestrian bridge. Before you, above the gate, a sign reads Sauve Garde—*you are entering the protection of the sisters and leaving the jurisdiction of the city. The relief above shows St. Elizabeth taking care of the handicapped. Walk through the gate and, as the lacy charm of Bruges crescendos, enter the...*

⓰ Begijnhof

Begijnhofs (pronounced gutturally: buh-*H*INE-hof) were built to house women of the lay order, called Beguines. Though obedient to

a mother superior, they did not have to take the vows of a nun. They spent their days deep in prayer, spinning wool, making lace, teaching, and caring for the sick. The Beguines' ranks swelled during the Golden Age, when so many women were widowed or unwed due to the hazards of war and overseas trade. The order of Beguines offered such women a dignified place to live and work. When the order died out, many begijnhofs were taken over by towns for subsidized housing. Today, single religious women live in the small homes. Benedictine nuns live in a building on the far side.

There are several sights here. You can tour the simple **museum** to get a sense of Beguine life. It's a typical Beguine's residence—kitchen, dining room, bedroom—with period furniture (spinning wheel, foot warmer). Don't miss the bedroom out back across the tiny cloister. The "Liturgical Center" is little more than a gift shop.

In the **church,** enjoy the peaceful interior, with its carved pulpit and tombstones on the floor. The altar has corkscrew columns and a painting of the Beguines' patron, St. Elizabeth. On the right wall is an 800-year-old golden statue of Mary. The rope that dangles from the ceiling is yanked by a nun to announce a sung vespers service. The Benedictine nuns gather at 11:55, proceed through the garden, and sing and chant a capella in the choir of the church. The public is welcome for this service.

• *Exiting the church, turn left, and leave the Begijnhof courtyard. Take your first left, through the gate, to a view of the lake known as...*

⓱ Minnewater

Just south of the Begijnhof is Minnewater ("Water of Love"), a peaceful, lake-filled park with canals, weeping willows, and swans. This was once far from quaint—it was a busy harbor where small boats shuttled cargo from the big, ocean-going ships into town. From this point, the cargo was transferred again to flat-bottomed boats that went through the town's canals to their respective warehouses and to the Markt.

When locals see these swans, they recall the 15th-century mayor—famous for his long neck—who collaborated with the Austrians. The townsfolk beheaded him as a traitor. The Austrians warned them that similarly long-necked swans would inhabit the place to forever remind them of this murder. And they do. With this sweet little murder story, we end our tour of perhaps the cutest town in Europe.

• *You're a five-minute walk from the train station (where you can catch a bus to the Markt) or a 15-minute walk from the Markt. If you walk back to the town center, consider a detour along Nieuwe Gentweg to visit one of about 20 **almshouses** in the city. At #8, go through the door marked Godshuis de Meulenaere 1613 into the peaceful courtyard (free). This was a medieval form of housing for the poor. The rich would pay for someone's tiny room here in return for lots of prayers.*

GROENINGE MUSEUM TOUR

Groeningemuseum

In the 1400s, Bruges was northern Europe's richest, most cosmopolitan, and most cultured city. New ideas, fads, and painting techniques were imported and exported with each shipload. Beautiful paintings were soon an affordable luxury, like fancy clothes or furniture. Internationally known artists set up studios in Bruges, producing portraits and altarpieces for wealthy merchants from all over Europe.

Understandably, the Groeninge Museum has one of the world's best collections of the art produced in the city and surrounding area. Early Flemish art is less appreciated and understood today than the Italian Renaissance art produced a century later. This chapter highlights several masterpieces to give you an introduction to this subtle, technically advanced, and beautiful style. Hey, if you can master the museum's name (*H*ROON-ih-guh), you can certainly handle the art.

As you wander, notice that many artists, having lived and worked in Bruges, included scenes of the picturesque city in their pieces, proving that it looks today much as it did way back when. Enjoy the many painted scenes of old Bruges as a slice-of-life peek into the city and its people back in its glory days.

Orientation

Cost: €8, more for special exhibits, ticket also includes entry to nearby Arentshuis Museum (described at the end of this chapter).

Hours: Tue-Sun 9:30-17:00, closed Mon.

Getting There: The museum is well-signed at Dijver 12, near the Church of Our Lady.

Information: Tel. 050-448-743, www.brugge.be/musea.

Length of This Tour: Allow one hour.

Starring: The meticulous details and limpid atmosphere of Flemish Primitive art; Jan van Eyck's *Canon Joris* and *Portrait of Margareta van Eyck;* and Rogier van der Weyden's *Duke Philip the Good.*

The Tour Begins

The collection fills 10 rooms on one easy floor, arranged chronologically from the 15th to the 20th century. As the collection is far bigger than the actual gallery, some of the paintings featured here may be rotated out or moved.

GOLDEN AGE MASTERS
• *Starting in Room 1, look for...*

Gerard David—*Judgment of Cambyses* (1498)
That's gotta hurt.

A man is stretched across a table and skinned alive in a very businesslike manner. The crowd hardly notices, and a dog just scratches himself. According to legend, the man was a judge arrested for corruption (left panel) and flayed (right panel), then his skin was draped (right panel background) over the new judge's throne.

Gerard David (c. 1455-1523), Memling's successor as the city's leading artist, painted this for the City Hall. City councilors could ponder what might happen to them if they abused their offices.

By David's time, Bruges was in serious decline, with a failing economy and struggles against the powerful Austrian Habsburg family. The Primitive style also was fading. Italian art was popular, so David tried to spice up his retro-Primitive work with pseudo-Renaissance knickknacks—*putti* (baby angels, over the judgment throne), Roman-style medallions, and garlands. But he couldn't quite master the Italian specialty of 3-D perspective. We view the flayed man at an angle from slightly above, but the table he lies on is shown more from the side.

GROENINGE MUSEUM

Attributed to Hieronymus Bosch—
Last Judgment (late 15th century)

It's the end of the world, and Christ descends in a bubble to pass judgment on puny humans. Little naked people dance and cavort in a theme park of medieval symbolism, desperately trying

to squeeze in their last bit of fun. Meanwhile, some wicked souls are being punished, victims either of their own stupidity or of genetically engineered demons. The good are sent to the left panel to frolic in the innocence of paradise, while the rest are damned to hell (right panel) to be tortured under a burning sky. Bosch paints the scenes with a high horizon line, making it seem that the chaos extends forever.

The bizarre work of Bosch (c. 1450-1516)—who, by the way, was not from Bruges—is open to many interpretations, but some see it as a warning for the turbulent times. He painted during the dawn of a new age. Secular ideas and materialism were encroaching, and the pious, serene medieval world was shattering into chaos.

• *Head to Rooms 2-4 for the following paintings—the core of the collection.*

Jan van Eyck—*Virgin and Child with*
Canon Joris van der Paele (1436)

Jan van Eyck (c. 1390-1441) was the world's first and greatest oil painter, and this is his masterpiece—three debatable but defensible assertions.

Mary, in a magnificent red gown, sits playing with her little baby, Jesus. Jesus glances up as St. George, the dragon-slaying knight, enters the room, tips his cap, and says, "I'd like to introduce my namesake, George (Joris)." Mary glances down at the kneeling Joris, a church official dressed in white. Joris takes off his glasses and looks up from his prayer book to see a bishop in blue, St. Donatian, patron of the church he hopes to be buried in.

Canon Joris, who hired Van Eyck, is not a pretty sight. He's old and wrinkled, with a double chin, weird earlobes, and bloodshot eyes. But the portrait isn't unflattering; it just shows unvarnished reality with crystal clarity.

Van Eyck brings Mary and the saints down from heaven and into a typical (rich) Bruges home. He strips off their haloes, banishes all angels, and pulls the plug on heavenly radiance. If this is a religious painting, then where's God?

God's in the details. From the bishop's damask robe and Mary's wispy hair to the folds in Jesus' baby fat and the oriental carpet to "Adonai" (Lord) written on St. George's breastplate, the painting is as complex and beautiful as God's creation. The color scheme—red Mary, white canon, and blue-and-gold saints—are Bruges' city colors, from its coat of arms.

Mary, crowned with a jeweled "halo" and surrounded by beautiful things, makes an appearance in 1400s Bruges, where she can be adored in all her human beauty by Canon Joris...and by us, reflected in the mirror-like shield on St. George's back.

Jan van Eyck—*Portrait of Margareta van Eyck* (1439)

At 35, shortly after moving to Bruges, Jan van Eyck married 20-year-old Margareta. They had two kids, and after Jan died,

Margareta took charge of his studio of assistants and kept it running until her death. This portrait (age 33), when paired with a matching self-portrait of Jan, was one of Europe's first husband-and-wife companion sets.

She sits half-turned, looking out of the frame. (Jan might have seen this "where-have-you-been?" expression in the window late one night.) She's dressed in a red, fur-lined coat, and we catch a glimpse of her wedding ring. Her hair is invisible—very fashionable at the time—pulled back tightly, bunched into horn-like hairnets, and draped with a headdress. Stray hairs along the perimeter were plucked to achieve the high forehead look.

This simple portrait is revolutionary—one of history's first individual portraits that wasn't of a saint, a king, a duke, or a pope, and wasn't part of a religious work. It signals the advent of humanism, celebrating the glory of ordinary people. Van Eyck proudly signed the work on the original frame, with his motto saying he painted it *"als ik kan" (ALC IXH KAN)...*"as good as I can."

Rogier van der Weyden— *St. Luke Drawing the Virgin's Portrait* (c. 1435)

Rogier van der Weyden (c. 1399-1464), the other giant among the Flemish Primitives, adds the human touch to Van Eyck's rather detached precision.

Flemish Primitives

Despite the "Primitive" label, the Low Countries of the 1400s (along with Venice and Florence) produced the most refined art in Europe. Here are some common features of Flemish Primitive art:

- **Primitive 3-D Perspective:** Expect unnaturally cramped-looking rooms; oddly slanted tables; and flat, cardboard-cutout people with stiff posture. Yes, these works are more primitive (hence the label) than those with the later Italian Renaissance perspective.
- **Realism:** Everyday bankers and clothmakers in their Sunday best are painted with clinical, warts-and-all precision. Even saints and heavenly visions are brought down to earth.
- **Details:** Like meticulous Bruges craftsmen, painters used fine-point brushes to capture almost microscopic details—flower petals, wrinkled foreheads, intricately patterned clothes, the sparkle in a ruby. The closer you get to a painting, the better it looks.
- **Oil Painted on Wood:** They were the pioneers of newfangled oil-based paint (while Italy still used egg-yolk tempera), working on wood before canvas became popular.
- **Portraits and Altarpieces:** Wealthy merchants and clergymen paid to have themselves painted either alone or mingling with saints.
- **Symbolism:** In earlier times, everyone understood that a dog symbolized fidelity, a lily meant chastity, and a rose was love.
- **Materialism:** Rich Flanders celebrated the beauty of luxury goods—the latest Italian dresses, jewels, carpets, oak tables—and the ordinary beauty that radiates from flesh-and-blood people.

As Mary prepares to nurse, Baby Jesus can't contain his glee, wiggling his fingers and toes, anticipating lunch. Mary, dressed in everyday clothes, doesn't try to hide her love as she tilts her head down with a proud smile. Meanwhile, St. Luke (the patron saint of painters, who was said to have experienced this vision) looks on intently with a sketch pad in his hand, trying to catch the scene. These small gestures, movements, and facial expressions add an element of human emotion that later artists would amplify.

The painting is neatly divided by a spacious view out the window, showing a river stretching off to a spacious horizon. Van der Weyden experimented with 3-D effects like this one (though ultimately it's just window-dressing).

Rogier van der Weyden—*Duke Philip the Good* (c. 1450)

Tall, lean, and elegant, this charismatic duke transformed Bruges from a commercial powerhouse to a cultural one. In 1425, Philip

moved his court to Bruges, making it the de facto capital of a Burgundian empire stretching from Amsterdam to Switzerland.

Philip wears a big hat to hide his hair, a fashion trend he himself began. He's also wearing the gold-chain necklace of the Order of the Golden Fleece, a distinguished knightly honor he gave himself. He inaugurated the Golden Fleece in a lavish ceremony at the Bruges City Hall, complete with parades, jousting, and festive pies that contained live people hiding inside to surprise his guests.

As a lover of painting, hunting, fine clothes, and many mistresses, Philip was a role model for Italian princes, such as Lorenzo the Magnificent—the *uomo universale,* the Renaissance Man.

Hugo van der Goes—*Death of the Virgin* (c. 1470)

The long deathwatch is over—their beloved Mary has passed on, and the disciples are bleary-eyed and dazed with grief, as though

GROENINGE MUSEUM

hit with a spiritual two-by-four. Each etched face is a study in sadness, as they all have their own way of coping—lighting a candle, fidgeting, praying, or just staring off into space. Blues and reds dominate, and there's little eye-catching ornamentation, which lets the lined faces and expressive hand gestures do the talking.

Hugo van der Goes (c. 1430-c. 1482) painted this, his last major work, the same year he attempted suicide. He had built a successful career in Ghent, then abruptly dropped out to join a monastery. His paintings became increasingly emotionally charged, his personality more troubled.

Above the bed floats a heavenly vision, as Jesus and the angels prepare to receive Mary's soul. Their smooth skin and serene expressions contrast with the gritty, wrinkled death pallor of those on earth. Caught up in their own grief, the disciples can't see the silver lining.

Oil Paint

Take vegetable oil pressed from linseeds (flax), blend in dry powdered pigments, whip to a paste the consistency of room-temperature butter, then brush onto a panel of whitewashed oak—you're painting in oils. First popularized in the early 1400s, oil eventually overshadowed egg-yolk-based tempera. Though tempera was great for making fine lines shaded with simple blocks of color, oil could blend colors together seamlessly.

Watch a master create a single dog's hair: He paints a dark stroke of brown, then lets it dry. Then comes a second layer painted over it, of translucent orange. The brown shows through, blending with the orange to match the color of a collie. Finally, he applies a third, transparent layer (a "glaze"), giving the collie her healthy sheen.

Many great artists were not necessarily great painters (e.g., Michelangelo). Van Eyck, Rembrandt, Hals, Velázquez, and Rubens were master painters, meticulously building objects with successive layers of paint...but they're not everyone's favorite artists.

Hans Memling—*The Moreel Triptych* (1484)

Memling (c. 1430-1494), though born in Germany, became Bruges' most famous painter. This triptych (three-paneled altarpiece) fuses the detail of Van Eyck with the balanced compositions of (his probable teacher) Rogier van der Weyden, while introducing his own innovations.

This is perhaps the art world's first group portrait, and everything about it celebrates the family of Willem Moreel, the wealthy two-term mayor of Bruges. In the center is St. Christopher—patron saint of seafarers—who brought wealth to the merchant Moreel family. He's shown (according to the traditional legend) as a gentle giant graciously carrying Baby Jesus across a river. Christopher is flanked by St. Maurus (the black-robed monk with staff and book) and St. Giles (a hermit whose only companion was a red deer). These two saints represent the family names of Moreel (from Maurus) and his wife.

The true stars of the triptych are not the saints but the earthbound mortals who paid for it. Moreel (left panel) kneels in devotion along with his five sons (and St. William, who was Willem's patron saint). Barbara (right) kneels with their 13 daughters (and her patron saint, Barbara). Memling's skills as a portraitist capture 20 different personalities in this large family. He sets all the figures in a single landscape—note that the horizon line stretches across all three panels. Saints and mortals mingle in this unique backdrop that's both down-to-earth (the castle, plants, and St. Barbara's stunning dress) and ethereal (the weird rock formations and unnaturally pristine light). The glowing Christ child sits at the peak of this balanced composition. Memling creates a motionless, peaceful world that invites meditation. It was perfect for where the triptych originally stood—in the Moreel burial chapel.

Jan Provoost—*Death and the Miser* (c. 1515)

A Bruges businessman in his office strikes a deal with Death. The grinning skeleton lays coins on the table and, in return, the man—

looking unhealthy and with fear in his eyes—reaches across the divide in the panels to give Death a promissory note, then marks the transaction in his ledger book. He's trading away a few years of his life for a little more money. The worried man on the right (the artist's self-portrait) says, "Don't do it."

Jan Provoost (also known as Provost; c. 1465-1529) worked for businessmen like this. He knew their offices, full of moneybags, paperwork, and books. Bruges' materialistic capitalism was at odds with Christian poverty, and society was divided over whether to praise or condemn it. Ironically, this painting's flip side is a religious work bought and paid for by...rich merchants.

THE REST OF THE MUSEUM

Breeze through the final rooms to get a quick once-over of Flemish art after Bruges' Golden Age. As Bruges declined into a cultural backwater, its artists simply copied the trends going on elsewhere: Italian-style Madonnas, British-style aristocrat portraits, French-Realist landscapes, Impressionism, and thick-paint Expressionism.

• *After fast-forwarding through the centuries, pause (in Rooms 9 and 10) to appreciate a couple of Belgium's 20th-century masters.*

GROENINGE MUSEUM

Paul Delvaux—
Serenity (1970)

Perhaps there's some vague connection between Van Eyck's medieval symbols and the Surrealist images of Paul Delvaux (1897-1994). Delvaux gained fame for his nudes sleepwalking through moonlit, video-game landscapes.

René Magritte—*The Assault* (c. 1932)

Magritte (1898-1967) had his own private reserve of symbolic images. The cloudy sky, the female torso, windows, and a horsebell (the

ball with the slit) appear in other works as well. They're arranged here side by side as if they should mean something, but they—as well as the title—only serve to short-circuit your thoughts when you try to make sense of them. Magritte paints real objects with photographic clarity, then jumbles them together in new and provocative ways.

• *When you're done touring the museum, consider a visit to the nearby Arentshuis Museum (same ticket and hours as the Groeninge Museum).*

ARENTSHUIS MUSEUM

This museum features the art of Frank Brangwyn (1867-1956; see his self-portrait in the first room), who was born in Bruges and built an international career in several fields. Brangwyn's style is accessible and varied. Ponder the dark, brooding engravings of Belgian street scenes (including the Begijnhof), his *Stations of the Cross*, some large colorful Art Nouveau canvases, and even some furniture he designed. He made Bruges proud.

GROENINGE MUSEUM

MEMLING MUSEUM TOUR

Memling in Sint Janshospitaal

Located in the former hospital wards and church of St. John's Hospital (Sint Janshospitaal), the Memling Museum offers a glimpse into medieval medicine, displaying surgical instruments, documents, and visual aids as you work your way to the museum's climax: several of Hans Memling's glowing masterpieces.

Orientation

Cost: €8, includes good audioguide and loaner folding chairs (if you'd like to sit and study the paintings).

Hours: Tue-Sun 9:30-17:00, closed Mon, last entry 30 minutes before closing.

Getting There: The museum is at Mariastraat 38, across the street from the Church of Our Lady.

Information: Posted descriptions are in Flemish, but many rooms have English descriptions to borrow. Tel. 050-448-713, www.brugge.be/musea.

Length of This Tour: Allow one hour.

Starring: The expansive hospital hall (with displays on medieval medicine) and Memling's *St. John Altarpiece*.

OVERVIEW

Hans Memling's art was the culmination of Bruges' Flemish Primitive style. His serene, soft-focus, motionless scenes capture a medieval piety that was quickly fading. The popular style made Memling (c. 1430-1494) one of Bruges' wealthiest citizens, and his work was gobbled up by visiting Italian merchants, who took it home with them, cross-pollinating European art.

The displays on medieval medicine are all on one floor of the former sick hall, with the Memlings in a chapel at the far end.

The Tour Begins

• After showing your ticket, enter a vast hall. In former days, this was...

THE HOSPITAL

Some 500 years ago, Bruges was a major destination for pilgrims. People both healthy and frail trekked here from all over this part of Europe to see the relic of the blood of Christ (at the Church of the Holy Blood). Many were or became ill and had to be cared for. And that's what this building was all about.

The building itself, which has housed a hospital since 1188, is impressive, with stout wood pillars and brick walls. It grew in importance as the precious relic of the holy blood grew in notoriety. This hall was lined with beds filled with the sick and dying. Nuns served as nurses. At the far end was the high altar, which once displayed Memling's *St. John Altarpiece* (which we'll see). Bedrid-

den patients could gaze on this peaceful, colorful vision and gain a moment's comfort from their agonies.

A painting by Jan Beer-block—*Zicht op de Oude Ziek-enzalen* (1778, see photo)—gives an intimate peek at "the old sick hall" in action. Study it for a sense of what it was like. The soup's on, dogs are wel-come, a nun administers last rites, the sedan chair ambulance taxi awaits a patient (an actual sedan chair ambulance still stands near-by). Snacks and drinks are served in bed. The floor needs mopping. A VIP clergyman drops in to see that all's OK.

Browse the hall's displays of medical implements. It's clear that medicine of the day was well-intentioned but very crude. In

many ways, this was less a hos-pital than a hospice, helping the dying make the transition from this world to the next. Reli-gious art (displayed throughout the museum) was therapeutic, addressing the patients' mental and spiritual health. The nu-merous Crucifixions reminded the sufferers that Christ could

feel their pain, having lived it himself.

• Continue through the displays (which make you glad for modern med-icine), past the ominous slabs marking graves of prominent nuns and

Some Memling Trademarks

- Serene symmetry, with little motion or emotion
- Serious faces that are realistic but timeless, with blemishes airbrushed out
- Eye-catching details such as precious carpets, mirrors, and brocaded clothes
- Glowing colors, even lighting, no shadows
- Cityscape backgrounds

friars who worked here. Head through the wooden doorway to the black-and-white tiled room where Memling's paintings are displayed. A large triptych (three-paneled altarpiece) dominates the space. (A replica stands nearby—less authentic, but less crowded.)

St. John Altarpiece
(a.k.a. *The Mystical Marriage of St. Catherine,* 1474)

Sick and dying patients lay in their beds in the hospital and looked at this colorful, three-part work, which sat atop the hospital/

church's high altar. The piece was dedicated to the hospital's patron saints, John the Baptist and John the Evangelist (see the inscription along the bottom of the frame), but Memling broadened the focus to take in a vision of heaven and the end of the world.

Central Panel: Mary, with Baby Jesus on her lap, sits in a canopied chair, crowned by hovering blue angels. It's an imaginary gathering of conversing saints *(Sacra Conversazione),* though nobody in this meditative group is saying a word or even exchanging meaningful eye contact.

Mary is flanked symmetrically by the other saints: John the Baptist (to the left) and John the Evangelist (in red); an organist angel (left) matched by a book-holding acolyte; St. Catherine (left) balanced by book-reading St. Barbara. Behind them, classical columns are also perfectly balanced left and right.

At the center of it all, Baby Jesus tips the balance by leaning over to place a ring on Catherine's finger, sealing the "mystical marriage" between them.

St. Catherine of Alexandria, born rich, smart, and pagan to Roman parents, joined the outlawed Christian faith. She spoke out against pagan Rome, attracting the attention of the emperor, Maxentius, who sent 50 philosophers to talk some sense into her—but she countered every argument, even converting the emperor's own wife. Maxentius killed his wife, then asked Catherine to marry him. She refused, determined to remain true to the man she'd already "married" in a mystical vision—Christ.

Frustrated, Maxentius ordered Catherine to be stretched across a large, spiked wheel (the rather quaint-looking object at her feet), but the wheel broke, so they just cut her head off, which is why she has a sword, along with her "Catherine Wheel."

Looking through the columns, we see scenes of Bruges. Just to the right of the chair's canopy, the wooden contraption is a crane used to hoist barrels from barges on Kraanplein.

Left Panel—The Beheading of John the Baptist: Even this gruesome scene, with blood still spurting from John's severed neck,

becomes serene under Memling's gentle brush. Everyone is solemn, graceful, and emotionless—including both parts of the decapitated John. Salomé (in green) receives the head on her silver platter with a humble servant's downcast eyes, as if accepting her role in God's wonderful, if sometimes painful, plan.

Right Panel—John the Evangelist's Vision of the Apocalypse: John sits on a high, rocky bluff on the island of Patmos and sees the end of the world as we know it...and he feels fine.

Overhead, in a rainbow bubble, God appears on his throne, resting his hand on a sealed book. A lamb steps up to open the seals, unleashing the awful events at the end of time. Standing at the bottom of the rainbow, an angel in green gestures to John and says, "Write this down." John picks up his quill, but he pauses, absolutely transfixed, experiencing the Apocalypse now.

He sees wars, fires, and plagues on the horizon, the Virgin in the sky rebuking a red dragon, and many other wonders. In the center ride the dreaded Four Horsemen, wreaking havoc on the cos-

mos (galloping over either islands or clouds). Horseman number four is a skeleton, followed by a human-eating monster head. Helpless mortals on the right seek shelter in the rocks, but find none.

Memling has been criticized for building a career by copying the formulas of his predecessors, but this panel is a complete original. Its theme had never been so fully expressed, and the bright, contrasting colors and vivid imagery are almost modern. In the *St. John Altarpiece,* Memling shows us the full range of his palette, from medieval grace to Renaissance symmetry, from the real to the surreal.

• *In a glass case nearby, you'll find another Memling masterpiece, the...*

St. Ursula Shrine (c. 1489)
On October 21, 1489, the mortal remains of St. Ursula were brought here to the church and placed in this gilded oak shrine, built specially for the occasion and decorated with paintings by Memling. Ursula, yet another Christian martyred by the ancient Romans, became a sensation in the Middle Ages when builders in Germany's Cologne unearthed a huge pile of bones believed to belong to her and her 11,000 slaughtered cohorts.

The church-shaped shrine, carved of wood and covered with gold, has "stained-glass windows" of Memling paintings describing Ursula's well-known legend.

• *"Read" the shrine's story counterclockwise, beginning with the...*

Left Panel: Ursula—in white and blue—arrives by boat at the city of Cologne and enters through the city gate. She's on a pilgrimage to Rome, accompanied by 11,000 (female) virgins. That night (look in the two windows of the house in the background, right), an angel appears and tells her this trip will mean her death, but she is undaunted.

Center Panel: Continuing up the Rhine (which Memling knew well, having grown up on it), they arrive in Basel and prepare to cross the Alps (background, right). Memling condenses the 11,000 virgins to a more manageable 11, making each one pure enough for a thousand.

Right Panel: They arrive at the gates of Rome where Ursula falls to her knees before the pope. Kneeling behind Ursula is her fiancé. Ursula has agreed to marry him only if he becomes a Christian and refrains from the marriage bed long enough for her to make this three-year pilgrimage as a virgin (making him, I guess, virgin number 11,001).

Opposite Side—Left Panel: They board ships to head back home, now joined by the pope. Memling's crowd scenes are hardly realistic—more like a collage of individual poses and faces—but they capture the pomp and ceremony Memling would have seen in Bruges parades.

Middle Panel: Back in Cologne, a surprise awaits them—the city has been taken over by vicious Huns. They grab Ursula's hubby, stab him, and he dies in Ursula's arms.

Right Panel: The Hun king (in red with turban and beard) woos Ursula, placing his hand over his heart, but she says, "No way." So a Hun soldier draws his arrow and prepares to shoot her dead. Even here, at the climax of the story, there are no histrionics. Even the dog just sits down, crosses his paws, and watches. The whole shrine cycle is as posed, motionless, and colorful as the *tableaux vivants* that may have inaugurated the shrine here in this church in 1489.

In the background, behind Ursula, a Bruges couple looks on sympathetically. This may be Memling himself (in red coat with fur lining) and his wife, Anna, who bore their three children.

• *In the small adjoining room, find more Memlings.*

Diptych of Martin van Nieuwenhove (1489)

Three-dimensional effects—borrowed from the Italian Renaissance style—enliven this two-panel devotional painting. Both Mary and Child and the 23-year-old Martin, though in different panels, inhabit the same space within the painting.

Stand right in front of Mary, facing her directly. If you line up the paintings' horizons (seen in the distance, out the room's windows), you'll see that both panels depict the same room—with two windows at the back and two along the right wall.

Want proof? In the convex mirror on the back wall (just to the left of Mary), the scene is reflected back at us, showing Mary and Martin from behind, silhouetted in the two "windows" of the picture frames. Apparently, Mary makes house calls, appearing right in the living room of the young donor Martin, the wealthy, unique-looking heir to his father's business.

• *Before leaving this area, find, to your right, a...*

MEMLING MUSEUM

Portrait of a Young Woman (1480)

Memling's bread-and-butter was portraits created for families of wealthy businessmen (especially visiting Italians and Portuguese). This portrait takes us right back to that time.

The young woman looks out of the frame as if she were looking out a window. Her hands rest on the "sill," with the fingertips

sticking over. The frame is original, but the banner and Van Eyck-like lettering are not.

Her clothes look somewhat simple, but they were high-class in their day. A dark damask dress is brightened by a red sash and a detachable white collar. She's pulled her hair into a tight bun at the back, pinned there with a fez-like cap and draped with a transparent veil. She's shaved her hairline and plucked her brows to get that clean, high-forehead look. Her ensemble is animated by a well-placed necklace of small stones.

Memling accentuates her fashionably pale complexion and gives her a pensive, sober expression, portraying her like a medieval saint. Still, she keeps her personality, with distinct features like her broad nose, neck tendons, and realistic hands. She peers out from her subtly painted veil, which sweeps down over the side of her face. What's she thinking? (My guess: "It's time for a waffle.")

• *Special exhibitions are sometimes displayed in a room up the stairs from the main hall. But it's hard to compete with a waffle.*

BRUGES SLEEPING, EATING & MORE

Contents

Bruges is the most inviting town in Belgium for an overnight. This chapter describes the town's top accommodations, eateries, shopping, and nightlife options, as well as train connections to other cities.

Sleeping in Bruges

Bruges is a great place to sleep, with Gothic spires out your window, little traffic noise, and the cheerily out-of-tune carillon heralding each new day at 8:00 sharp. (Thankfully, the bell tower is silent from 22:00 to 8:00.) Most Bruges accommodations are located between the train station and the old center, with the most distant (and best) being a few blocks to the north and east of the Markt (Market Square).

B&Bs offer the best value (listed on page 83), but hoteliers have lobbied City Hall to make it harder to have more than two "official" rooms. Creative B&B owners have found ways to get around the restrictions. All are on quiet streets and (with a few exceptions) keep the same prices throughout the year.

Bruges is most crowded Friday and Saturday evenings from Easter through October—July and August weekends are the worst.

Sleep Code

Abbreviations   **(€1 = about $1.40, country code: 32)**
S = Single, **D** = Double/Twin, **T** = Triple, **Q** = Quad, **b** = bath-
room, **s** = shower only
Price Rankings
  $$$ **Higher Priced**—Most rooms €125 or more
   $$ **Moderately Priced**—Most rooms between €80-125
    $ **Lower Priced**—Most rooms €80 or less
Unless otherwise noted, English is spoken, credit cards are
accepted, breakfast is included, and Wi-Fi is generally free.
Bruges levies a hotel tax of a few euros per person, per night
(typically not included in the prices here). Prices change; verify current rates online or by email. For the best prices, always
book directly with the hotel.

Many hotels charge a bit more on Friday and Saturday, and won't
let you stay just one night if it's a Saturday.

HOTELS

$$$ Hotel Heritage offers 22 rooms, with chandeliers that seem
hung especially for you, in a solid and completely modernized old
building with luxurious public spaces. Tastefully decorated and of-
fering all the amenities, it's one of those places that does everything
just right yet still feels warm and inviting—if you can afford it (Db-
€178, superior Db-€229, deluxe Db-€283, extra bed-€60, wonder-
ful buffet breakfast-€24, continental breakfast-€12, iPad and Ne-
spresso machine in every room, air-con, elevator, guest computer,
Wi-Fi, sauna, tanning bed, fitness room, bike rental, free 2-hour
guided city tour, parking-€35/day, Niklaas Desparsstraat 11, a
block north of the Markt, tel. 050-444-444, www.hotel-heritage.
com, info@hotel-heritage.com). It's run by cheery and hardwork-
ing Johan and Isabelle Creytens.

   $$$ Hotel Adornes is small and classy—a great value situ-
ated in the most charming part of town. This 17th-century canal-
side house has 20 rooms with full modern bathrooms, free parking (reserve in advance), free loaner bikes, and a cellar lounge with
games and videos (small Db-€135, larger Db-€155-165, Tb-€180,
Qb-€195, elevator, Wi-Fi in lobby, some street noise, near Carmersstraat at St. Annarei 26, tel. 050-341-336, www.adornes.be,
info@adornes.be). Nathalie runs the family business with the help
of courteous Rik.

   $$ Hotel Patritius, family-run and centrally located, is
a grand, circa-1830 Neoclassical mansion with hardwood oak
floors in its 16 stately, high-ceilinged rooms. It features a plush
lounge, a chandeliered breakfast room, and a courtyard garden. If

Bruges Accommodations

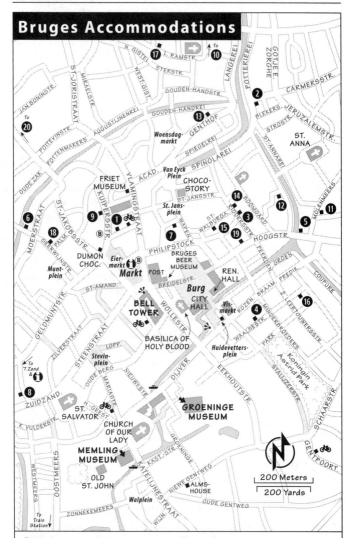

1. Hotel Heritage & Hotel Marcel
2. Hotel Adornes
3. Hotel Patritius
4. Hotel Botaniek
5. Canalview Hotel ter Reien
6. Walwyck Cool Down Hotel
7. Hotel Cordoeanier
8. Hotel Bla Bla & Passage Hostel
9. Hotel Cavalier
10. To Hotel de Pauw
11. Absoluut Verhulst B&B
12. Gastenhuis Sint-Andriescruyse
13. Hamiltons B&B
14. B&B Gheeraert
15. B&B Setola
16. Koen & Annemie Dieltiens B&B
17. Debruyne B&B
18. 't Geerwijn B&B
19. Charlie Rockets Hostel
20. To Snuffel Backpacker Hostel

you get a room at the lower end of the price range, this can be a great value (Db-€100-150, Tb-€140-175, Qb-€165-220, cheaper in off-season, rates depend on room size and demand—check site for best price, extra bed-€25, air-con, elevator, guest computer, Wi-Fi, coin-op laundry, parking-€17/day, garage parking-€15/day, Riddersstraat 11, tel. 050-338-454, www.hotelpatritius.be, info@ hotelpatritius.be, cordial Garrett and Elvi Spaey).

$$ Hotel Egmond is a creaky mansion located in the middle of the quietly idyllic Minnewater. Its eight 18th-century rooms are plain, with small modern baths shoehorned in, and the guests-only garden is just waiting for a tea party. This hotel is ideal for romantics who want a countryside setting—where you sleep surrounded by a park, not a city (Sb-€89-125, small twin Db-€98, larger Db-€140, Tb-€150, cheaper in winter, Wi-Fi, parking-€10/ day, Minnewater 15, for location see map on page 18, tel. 050-341-445, www.egmond.be, info@egmond.be, Steven).

$$ Hotel Botaniek, quietly located a block from Astrid Park, is a pint-sized hotel with a comfy lounge, renting nine slightly worn rooms—some of them quite big (Db-€95 weekday special for my readers, €99 Fri-Sat; Qb-€145, €149 Fri-Sat; less for longer and off-season stays, elevator, Waalsestraat 23, tel. 050-341-424, www. botaniek.be, info@botaniek.be, Veronika and Brend).

$$ Canalview Hotel ter Reien is big and basic, with 26 rooms overlooking a canal in the town center (Db-€70-110, Tb-€95-130, Qb-€140-160, rates vary widely with demand—check website for best prices; cheapest rates for weekdays, stays of at least 3 nights, or rooms without canal views; extra bed-€24-29, pay guest computer and Wi-Fi, Langestraat 1, tel. 050-349-100, www.hotelterreien. be, info@hotelterreien.be, owned by Diederik and Stephanie Pille-Maes).

$$ Walwyck Cool Down Hotel—a bit of modern comfort, chic design, and English verbiage in a medieval shell—is a nicely located hotel with 21 spacious rooms. If you're getting tired of Bruges cute, this is the place (small Db-€100, standard Db-€110, "superior" Db-€120, Tb-€150, family room-€155, "superior" family room-€180, Wi-Fi, Leeuwstraat 8, tel. 050-616-360, www. walwyck.com, rooms@walwyck.com).

$$ Hotel Cordoeanier, a charming family-run hotel, rents 22 simple, compact, hardwood-floor rooms on a quiet street two blocks off the Markt. It's one of the best deals in town (Sb-€85-105, Db-€90-120, twin Db-€100-120, Tb-€120-150, Qb-€155, cheaper with cash if you show this book and book directly through the hotel, breakfast buffet served in their pleasant Café Rose Red, no elevator, pay guest computer, Wi-Fi, patio, Cordoeanierstraat 16, tel. 050-339-051, www.cordoeanier.be, info@cordoeanier.be, Kris).

$$ Hotel Marcel has 20 big, boutique rooms with oversized photos of sights around Bruges plastering their ceilings and walls. Breakfast features fresh juice and baked goods served in the hip ground-level café. The location is ideal—on a quiet street a block off the Markt (Db-€100-110, elevator, Wi-Fi, Niklaas Desparsstraat 7, tel. 050-335-502, www.hotelmarcel.be, info@hotelmarcel.be, Sophie).

$$ Hotel Bla Bla is a modern hotel in a charming old-school building with eight airy rooms and a backyard annex. Uppermost-level rooms reward guests with vaulted ceilings and big bathrooms. It's homey and well-run on a central yet quiet street (Sb-€75-85, Db-€85, larger Db-€95, Tb-€130, Qb-€165, includes breakfast when you book directly with hotel, Wi-Fi, Dweersstraat 24, tel. 050-339-014, www.hotelblabla.com, info@hotelblalbla.com, David).

$ Hotel Cavalier, with lots of stairs and lots of character, rents eight rooms decorated with quirky knickknacks. The staff serves a hearty buffet breakfast in a once-royal setting (Sb-€65, Db-€75, Tb-€102, Qb-€108, 2 lofty en-suite "backpackers' doubles" on fourth floor-€50-55, book directly with the hotel and mention this book for special Rick Steves price and free Wi-Fi, Kuipersstraat 25, tel. 050-330-207, www.hotelcavalier.be, info@hotelcavalier.be, run by friendly Viviane De Clerck).

$ Hotel de Pauw is tall, skinny, flower-bedecked, and family-run, with eight straightforward rooms on a quiet street next to a church (Sb-€70-75, Db-€75-95, no elevator, Wi-Fi, free and easy street parking, Sint Gilliskerkhof 8, tel. 050-337-118, www.hoteldepauw.be, info@hoteldepauw.be, Philippe and Hilde).

$ Hotel 't Keizershof is a dollhouse of a hotel that lives by its motto, "Spend a night...not a fortune." (Its other motto: "When you're asleep, we look just like those big fancy hotels.") It's simple and tidy, with seven small, cheery, old-time rooms split between two floors, with a shower and toilet on each (S-€35-47, D-€47, T-€69, Q-€88, cash only, Wi-Fi, free and easy parking, laundry service-€7.50, Oostmeers 126, a block in front of station, for location see map on page 18, tel. 050-338-728, www.hotelkeizershof.be, info@hotelkeizershof.be). The hotel is run by Stefaan and Hilde, with decor by their children, Lorie and Fien; it's situated in a pleasant area near the train station and Minnewater, a 15-minute walk from the Markt.

BED-AND-BREAKFASTS

These B&Bs, run by people who enjoy their work, offer a better value than hotels. Most families rent out their entire top floor—several rooms and a small sitting area. And most are mod and stylish—they're just in medieval shells. Each is central, with lots of stairs and €70-80 doubles you'd pay €100 or more for in a hotel. Many places charge €10-15 extra for one-night stays. It's possible to find parking on the street in the evening (pay 9:00-19:00, 2-hour maximum for metered parking during the day, free overnight).

$$ Absoluut Verhulst is a great, modern-feeling B&B with three rooms in a 400-year-old house, run by friendly Frieda and Benno (Db-€95; huge and lofty suite-€130 for 2, €160 for 3, €180 for 4; €10 more for one-night stays, cash only, Wi-Fi, 5-minute walk east of the Markt at Verbrand Nieuwland 1, tel. 050-334-515, www.b-bverhulst.com, b-b.verhulst@pandora.be).

$$ Gastenhuis Sint-Andriescruyse offers warmly decorated rooms with high ceilings in a spacious, cheerfully red canalside house a short walk from the Old Town action. Owners Luc and Christiane treat guests like long-lost family, and proudly share their photo albums with pictures of previous guests (S-€75, D/Db-€100, T-€125, Q-€150, family room for up to 5 comes with board games, cash only, free soft drinks, guest computer, free pick-up at station, Verversdijk 15A, tel. 050-789-168, mobile 0477-973-933, www.gastenhuisst-andriescruyse.be, luc.cloet@telenet.be).

$$ Hamiltons B&B, formerly Royal Stewart B&B, offers two elegant luxury suites in a quiet, convent-style, 17th-century house (D/Db-€110, get this price if you book directly with the hotel and mention Rick Steves, cash preferred, homemade English breakfast in garden room, Genthof 27, 5-minute walk from the Markt, mobile 0479-445-134, www.hamiltons.be, nicola@hamiltons.be, English Nicola and Olivier).

$$ B&B Gheeraert is a Neoclassical mansion where Inne rents three huge, bright, comfy rooms (Sb-€75, Db-€85, Tb-€95, two-night minimum stay required, cash only but credit card required to hold reservation, fridges in rooms, guest computer, Wi-Fi, Riddersstraat 9, 5-minute walk east of the Markt, tel. 050-335-627, www.bb-bruges.be, bb-bruges@skynet.be).

$ B&B Setola, run by Lut and Bruno Setola, offers three expansive rooms and a spacious breakfast/living room on the top floor of their house. Wooden ceiling beams give the modern rooms a touch of Old World flair (Sb-€70, Db-€80, extra person-€25, add €10 for one-night stays, Wi-Fi, 5-minute walk from the Markt, Sint Walburgastraat 12, tel. 050-334-977, www.bedandbreakfast-bruges.com, setola@bedandbreakfast-bruges.com).

$ Koen and Annemie Dieltiens are a friendly couple who enjoy getting to know their guests while sharing a wealth of information on Bruges. You'll eat a hearty breakfast around a big table in their comfortable house (Sb-€60-80, Db-€70-90, Tb-€90-115, €10 more for one-night stays, cash only, guest computer, Wi-Fi, parking-€8.50/night, Waalsestraat 40, three blocks southeast of

Burg Square, tel. 050-334-294, www.bedandbreakfastbruges.be, dieltiens@bedandbreakfastbruges.be).

$ Debruyne B&B, run by Marie-Rose and her architect husband, Ronny, offers three rooms with artsy, modern decor (check out the elephant-size yellow doors—Ronny's design). The glass walls in the breakfast room open to a cloister-like garden. The architecture is cool but the hosts have genuine warmth (Sb-€65, Db-€70, Tb-€90, €10 more for one-night stays, cash only, guest computer, Wi-Fi, 7-minute walk north of the Markt, 2 blocks from the little church at Lange Raamstraat 18, tel. 050-347-606, www. bedandbreakfastbruges.com, mietjedebruyne@yahoo.co.uk).

$ 't Geerwijn B&B, run by Chris de Loof, offers homey rooms in the old center. Check out the fun, lofty A-frame room upstairs (Ds/Db-€75-80 depending on season, Tb-€85-90, cash only, pleasant breakfast room and royal lounge, Wi-Fi, Geerwijn-straat 14, tel. 050-340-544, www.geerwijn.be, info@geerwijn.be). Chris also rents an apartment that sleeps five.

$ Waterside B&B has two fresh, Zen-like rooms, one floor above a peaceful canal south of the town center (D-€80-85, €5 more on Sat, continental breakfast, Wi-Fi, 15-minute walk from Burg Square at Kazernevest 88, for location see map on page 18, tel. 050-616-686, mobile 0476-744-525, www.waterside.be, waterside@telenet.be, run by Mieke of recommended Pink Bear Bike Tours).

$ B&B AM/PM sports three ultra-modern rooms in a residential neighborhood just west of the old town (Sb-€65, Db-€70, Tb-€90, €10 more for one-night stay, cash only, guest computer—mornings only, Wi-Fi, 5-minute walk from 't Zand at Singel 10, for location see map on page 18, mobile 0485-071-003, www.bruges-bedandbreakfast.com, info@bruges-bedandbreakfast.com, artsy young couple Tiny and Kevin). From the train station, head left down busy Buiten Begijnevest to the roundabout. Stay to the left, take the pedestrian underpass, then follow the busy road (now on your left). Just before the next bridge, turn right onto the footpath called Buiten Boeverievest, then turn left onto Singel; the B&B is at #10.

HOSTELS

Bruges has several good hostels offering beds for around €20 in 4- to 12-bed rooms. Breakfast is about €3 extra. The American-style **$ Charlie Rockets** hostel (and bar), a backpacker dive, is the live-liest and most central. The ground floor feels like a 19th-century sports bar, with a foosball-and-movie-posters party ambience. Upstairs is an industrial-strength pile of hostel dorms (90 beds, €18/bed with sheets, €22/bed with sheets and breakfast, 4-6 beds/ room, D-€55 breakfast-€4, lockers, Wi-Fi, Hoogstraat 19, tel.

050-330-660, www.charlierockets.com). Other small and loose places are the minimal, funky, and central **$ Passage** (€25/bed with sheets, 4-7 beds/room, D-€52, Db-€67, Dweerstraat 26, tel. 050-340-232, www.passagebruges.com, info@passagebruges.com) and **$ Snuffel Backpacker Hostel,** which is less central and pretty grungy, but friendly and laid-back (60 beds, €16-18/bed includes sheets and breakfast, 4-12 beds/room, Ezelstraat 47, tel. 050-333-133, www.snuffel.be).

Eating in Bruges

Bruges doesn't really have any specialties all its own, but restaurants here excel at all the predictable Belgian dishes: mussels cooked a

variety of ways (one order can feed two), fish dishes, grilled meats, and french fries (for more on Belgian cuisine, see page 334). The town's two indigenous beers are the prizewinning Brugse Zot ("Bruges Fool"), a golden ale, and Straffe Hendrik, a potent, bitter triple ale.

You'll find plenty of affordable, touristy restaurants on floodlit squares and along dreamy canals. Bruges feeds 3.5 million tourists a year, and most are seduced by a high-profile location. These can be great experiences for the magical setting and views, but the quality of food and service will likely be mediocre. I wouldn't blame you for eating at one of these places, but I won't recommend any in particular. I prefer the candle-cool bistros that flicker on back streets or atmospheric beer halls where the pub grub takes a backseat to those famous Belgian brews.

Notice that many places are closed for a day or two midweek. On Wednesdays and Thursdays in particular, more places seem to be closed than open. Check before you make a special trip.

RESTAURANTS

Rock Fort is a chic spot with a modern, fresh coziness and a high-powered respect for good food. Two young chefs, Peter Laloo and Hermes Vanliefde, give their French cuisine a creative, gourmet twist. At the bar they serve a separate tapas menu. This place is a winner (€6-12 tapas, great pastas and salads, €15 lunch special, beautifully presented €17-34 dinner plates, €40 five-tapas special, fancy €49 fixed-price four-course meal, open Mon-Fri 12:00-14:30 & 18:30-23:00, closed Sat-Sun, reservations recommended, Langestraat 15, tel. 050-334-113, www.rock-fort.be).

Bistro in den Wittenkop, very Flemish, is a stylishly small, laid-back, old-time place specializing in local favorites, where

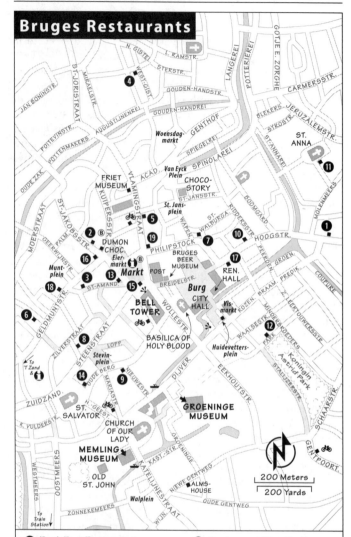

Bruges Restaurants

1. Rock Fort Restaurant
2. Bistro in den Wittenkop
3. Bistro den Amand & Medard Brasserie
4. Tom's Diner
5. Bistro Den Huzaar
6. The Flemish Pot
7. Lotus Vegetarian Restaurant
8. De Hobbit
9. Restaurant de Koetse
10. Carlito's
11. Restaurant Sint-Barbe
12. L'Estaminet Restaurant
13. Café-Brasserie Craenenburg
14. Chez Vincent
15. Frituur Stands
16. 't Brugsch Friethuys
17. Chez Albert
18. Gelateria Da Vinci & Grocery
19. Carrefour Express

Lindsey serves while Patrick cooks. It's a classy spot to enjoy hand-cut fries, which go particularly well with Straffe Hendrik beer (€37 three-course meal, €21-26 plates, Mon-Sat 18:00-21:30, closed Sun, reserve ahead, terrace in summer, Sint Jakobsstraat 14, tel. 050-332-059, www.indenwittenkop.be).

Bistro den Amand, with a plain interior and a few outdoor tables, exudes unpretentious quality the moment you step in. In this mussels-free zone, Chef An is enthusiastic about stir-fry and vegetables, as her busy wok and fun salads prove. Portions are split-table and there are always good vegetarian options. The creative dishes—some with a hint of Asian influence—are a welcome departure from Bruges' mostly predictable traditional restaurants. It's on a bustling pedestrian lane a half-block off the Markt (€35 three-course meal, €18-25 plates; Mon-Tue and Thu-Sat 12:00-14:15 & 18:00-21:00, closed Wed and Sun; reservations smart for dinner, Sint-Amandstraat 4, tel. 050-340-122, www.denamand.be, An Vissers and Arnout Beyaert).

Tom's Diner is a trendy, cozy little candlelit bistro in a quiet, cobbled residential area a 10-minute walk from the center. Young chef Tom gives traditional dishes a delightful modern twist, such as his signature Flemish meat loaf with rhubarb sauce. If you want to flee the tourists and experience a popular neighborhood joint, this is it—the locals love it. Reserve before you make the trip (€16-23 plates, Tue-Sat 12:00-14:00 & 18:00-23:00, closed Sun-Mon, north of the Markt near Sint-Gilliskerk at West-Gistelhof 23, tel. 050-333-382, www.tomsdiner.be).

Bistro Den Huzaar is classy but affordable, serving big portions of Belgian classics. The long dining room stretches back on well-worn wooden floors with white-tablecloth elegance. It's dignified but relaxed (€17-20 main dishes, €35 fixed-price meal, Fri-Tue 12:00-14:30 & 18:00-20:30, closed Wed-Thu, 5-minute walk north of the Markt at Vlamingstraat 36, tel. 050-333-797).

The Flemish Pot is a busy eatery where enthusiastic chefs Mario and Rik cook up a traditional menu of vintage Flemish specialties—from beef and rabbit stew to eel—served in little iron pots and skillets. Seating is tight and cluttered, the tourist-oriented menu can be pricey, and service can be spotty. But you'll enjoy huge portions, refills from the hovering "fries angel," a cozy atmosphere, and a good selection of local beers (€32-35 three-course meals, €22-29 plates, daily 12:00-22:00, reservations smart, just off Geldmuntstraat at Helmstraat 3, tel. 050-340-086, www.devlaamschepot.be).

Lotus Vegetarian Restaurant serves serious lunch plates (€14 *plat du jour* offered daily), salads, and homemade chocolate cake in a pleasantly small, bustling, and upscale setting. To keep carnivorous companions happy, they also serve several very good, organic meat dishes (Mon-Fri from 11:45, last orders at 14:00, closed Sat-Sun, just north of Burg Square at Wapenmakersstraat 5, tel. 050-331-078).

Balls & Glory is part of a small Belgian chain serving one thing: meatballs. Each day, two varieties are available from a rotating menu. One meatball is huge—nearly big enough to fill two light eaters. Pay €9.50 to take one away or €12 to eat in (choose mashed potatoes or salad on the side). The hip, youthful space has sleek unfinished-plywood decor and free water at shared tables. Locals stop in to buy smaller €5 meatballs from the cold case to take home (Mon-Sat 10:00-17:00, Wed-Fri until 19:00, closed Sun, 10-minute walk east of the Markt at Langestraat 93—for location see map on page 18, tel. 0486-444-127).

De Hobbit, featuring an entertaining menu, is always busy with happy eaters. For a swinging deal, try the all-you-can-eat spareribs with bread and salad (€25). It's nothing fancy, just good, basic food served in a fun, crowded, traditional grill house (daily 18:00-23:00, family-friendly, Kemelstraat 8, reservations smart, tel. 050-335-520, www.hobbitgrill.be).

Restaurant de Koetse is handy for central, good-quality, local-style food. The feeling is traditional, a bit formal (stuffy even), and dressy, yet accessible. The cuisine is Belgian and French, with an emphasis on grilled meat, seafood, and mussels (€25 lunch menu Mon-Sat, €36 three-course meals, €20-30 plates include vegetables and a salad, Fri-Wed 12:00-14:30 & 18:00-22:00, closed Thu, non-smoking section, Oude Burg 31, tel. 050-337-680, Piet).

Carlito's is a good choice for basic Italian fare. Their informal space, with whitewashed walls and tealight candles, is two blocks from Burg Square (€9-15 pizzas and pastas, daily 12:00-14:30 & 18:00-22:30, patio seating in back, Hoogstraat 21, tel. 050-490-075).

Restaurant Sint-Barbe, on the eastern edge of town, is a homey little neighborhood place where Evi serves classy Flemish dishes made from local ingredients in a fresh, modern space on two floors (€12 soup-and-main lunch, €14-22 main courses, Thu-Mon 11:30-14:00 & 18:00-22:00, closed Tue-Wed, food served until 21:00, St. Annaplein 29, tel. 050-330-999).

L'Estaminet is a youthful, jazz-filled eatery, similar to one of Amsterdam's brown cafés. Don't be intimidated by its lack of tourists. Local students flock here for the Tolkien-chic ambience, hearty €10 spaghetti, and big dinner salads. This is Belgium—it serves more beer than wine. For outdoor dining under an all-weather canopy, enjoy the relaxed patio facing peaceful Astrid Park (Fri-Wed 11:30-24:00, Thu 16:00-24:00, Park 5, tel. 050-330-916).

Restaurants on the Markt: Most tourists seem to be eating on the Markt with the bell tower high overhead and horse carriages clip-clopping by. The square is ringed by tourist traps with aggressive waiters expert at getting you to consume more than you intended. Still, if you order smartly, you can have a memorable meal or drink here on one of the finest squares in Europe at a reasonable price. Consider **Café-Brasserie Craenenburg,** with a straightforward menu, where you can get pasta and beer for €15 and spend all the time you want ogling the magic of Bruges (daily 7:30-23:00, Markt 16, tel. 050-333-402). While it's overpriced for dining, it can be a fine place to savor a before- or after-meal drink with the view.

Cheaper Restaurants Just Off the Markt: For a similar but less expensive array of interchangeable, tourist-focused eateries, head a few steps off the Markt up **Sint-Amandstraat** (through the gap between Café Craenenburg and the clock tower). You'll pop out into a pleasant little square with lots of choices. The best of these is **Bistro den Amand** (recommended earlier), but if that's full or closed, this is a fine place to browse for something else. **Medard Brasserie,** also on this square, serves the cheapest hot meal in town—hearty meat spaghetti (big plate-€4, huge plate-€6.50, sit inside or out, Mon-Tue and Thu-Sat 12:00-20:00, closed Wed and Sun, Sint Amandstraat 18, tel. 050-348-684).

PUBS AND BEER HALLS

My best budget-eating tip for Bruges: Stop into one of the city's bars for a simple meal and a couple of world-class beers with great Bruges ambience. Among these listings, Cambrinus puts more emphasis on its food; Café Terrastje, Herberg Vlissinghe, and Pub 't Gezelleke have a small selection of still-substantial meals; and 't Brugs Beertje and De Garre have lighter food and snacks. Note that the last few listings—Comptoir des Arts, the bar at 2Be, and the Duvelorium Grand Beer Café—aren't good places to eat; go to these to focus on the beer.

Kemelstraat: On this street, just west of the Markt, you'll find three nice options: **De Hobbit** (described earlier, under "Restaurants"), **The Habit** (hearty Belgian food, beer, and Belgians), and the convivial **'t Brugs Beertje,** where fun-loving manager Daisy is on a mission to sell the world on the wonders of beer and cheese rather than wine and cheese. You're welcome to sit at the bar and talk with the staff (more than 300 beers, including seasonal brews; very short menu of light meals—spaghetti, toasted sandwiches, and €12 cheese plate with 5 cheeses, bread, and salad; Thu-Mon 16:00-24:00, later on weekends, closed Tue-Wed but open Tue in Aug, Kemelstraat 5, tel. 050-339-616).

Just off the Markt: **De Garre** (deh-*H*AHR-reh) is another good place to gain an appreciation for Belgian beer culture. Rather

Bruges Beer Halls & Nightlife

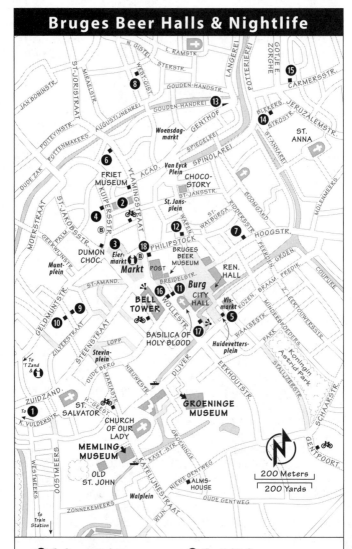

- **1** To Concertgebouw
- **2** Municipal Theater
- **3** Eiermarkt Bars
- **4** 't Zwart Huis &
  't Under Ground
- **5** Wijnbar Est
- **6** Comptoir des Arts
- **7** Charlie Rockets
- **8** 't Opkikkertje
- **9** De Hobbit
- **10** The Habit &
  't Brugs Beertje Pub
- **11** De Garre Pub
- **12** Cambrinus
- **13** Café Terrastje
- **14** Herberg Vlissinghe Pub
- **15** Pub 't Gezelleke
- **16** The Bottle Shop
- **17** 2Be Bar
- **18** Duvelorium Grand Beer Café

than a noisy pub scene, it has a dressy, sit-down-and-focus-on-your-friend-and-the-fine-beer vibe. It's mature and cozy, with light meals (cold cuts, pâtés, and toasted sandwiches) and a huge selection of beers. Heavy beers are the forte: Beer pilgrims flock here, as it's the only place on earth that sells the Tripel van de Garre beer on tap. As it's 12 percent alcohol, there's a three-Tripel limit...and many tourists find that the narrow alley out front provides much-needed support as they start their stumble back home (daily 12:00-24:00, later on weekends, additional seating up tiny staircase, off Breidelstraat between Burg and the Markt, on tiny Garre alley, tel. 050-341-029).

Rollicking Beer Brasserie: Cambrinus is a touristy but enjoyable *bierbrasserie*. Bright, tight, and boisterous, it serves 400 types of beer and good pub grub. Come here for a lively evening out; it's more high-spirited and accessible than some of Bruges' traditional, creaky old beer halls (€15-22 main dishes, daily 11:00-23:00, reservations smart, Philipstockstraat 19, tel. 050-332-328, www.cambrinus.eu/english.htm).

In the Gezellig Quarter, Northeast of the Markt: These three pubs are tucked in the wonderfully *gezellig* (cozy) quarter that follows the canal past Jan Van Eyckplein, northeast of the Markt. Just walking out here is a treat, as it gets you away from the tourists. **Café Terrastje** is a cozy pub serving light meals. Enjoy the subdued ambience inside, or relax on the front terrace overlooking the canal and heart of the *gezellig* district (€6-8 sandwiches, €10-18 dishes; food served Fri-Mon 12:00-15:00 & 18:00-21:00, open until 23:30; Tue 12:00-18:00; closed Wed-Thu; corner of Genthof and Langerei, tel. 050-330-919, Ian and Patricia). **Herberg Vlissinghe** is the oldest pub in town (1515). Bruno keeps things basic and laid-back, serving simple plates (lasagna, grilled cheese sandwiches, and famous €10 angel-hair spaghetti) and great beer in the best old-time tavern atmosphere in town. This must have been the Dutch Masters' rec room. The garden outside comes with a *boules* court—free for guests to watch or play (Wed-Sat 11:00-24:00, Sun 11:00-19:00, closed Mon-Tue, Blekersstraat 2, tel. 050-343-737). **Pub 't Gezelleke** lacks the mystique of the Vlissinghe, but it's a true neighborhood pub offering spaghetti and a few basic plates and a good chance to drink with locals (if you sit at the bar). Its name is an appropriate play on the word for "cozy" and the name of a great local poet (Mon-Tue and Thu-Sat 16:00-24:00, closed Wed and Sun, Carmersstraat 15, tel. 470-122-183, Jean de Bruges). Don't come here to eat outdoors.

Beer Cellar North of the Markt: Comptoir des Arts fills a warm, welcoming cellar with 90 types of Belgian beer, a fine selection of whisky, knowledgeable barkeeps, a big fireplace, and occasional live music (typically on Sunday evenings, but not in the peak of summer). It's a short walk from the Markt, away from the worst tourist crowds (not much in the way of food, Wed-Mon 18:00-late, closed Tue, Vlamingstraat 53, tel. 0494-387-961, www. comptoirdesarts.be).

Beer with a View: Though it's tucked in back of a tacky tourist shop, the bar at **2Be** serves several local beers on tap and boasts a fine scenic terrace over a canal (see page 95). **Duvelorium Grand Beer Café** is pricey but picturesque. It's located upstairs from the Historium, with a spiny Gothic terrace overlooking the bustle on the Markt. As it's operated by the big beer producer Duvel, choices are more limited than some local watering holes (eight beers on tap, plus lots of bottles), and the prices are high—but it's worth paying extra for the view (same hours as Historium—see listing on page 28, you can enter the pub without paying for the museum, last orders at 19:00, may be open later in summer). I wouldn't bother eating at either of these—they're all about the beer and the views.

SWEETS AND QUICK EATS
Belgian Fries
Belgian french fries *(frieten)* are a treat. Proud and traditional *frituur*s serve tubs of fries and various local-style shish kebabs. Bel-

gians dip their *frieten* in mayonnaise or other flavored sauces, but ketchup is there for the Yankees. I encourage you to skip the ketchup and have a sauce adventure (for more on fries see page 336).

On the Markt: For a quick, cheap, and scenic snack, hit a *frituur* and sit on the steps or benches overlooking the Markt (convenient benches are about 50 yards past the post office). Twin takeaway fry carts are on the square at the base of the bell tower (daily 10:00-24:00). I find the cart on the left better quality and more user-friendly.

Elsewhere: **Chez Vincent,** with pleasant outdoor tables on a terrace facing St. Salvator's Cathedral along the lively Steenstraat shopping drag, is a cut above. It's understandably popular for using fresh, local ingredients to turn out tasty fries and all manner of other fried and grilled Belgian tasties: burgers, sausages, meatballs, croquettes, and so on. Join the mob at the counter inside to order and pay, then find a table and wait for your pager to buzz (€3-5 fries and basics; "menu" option adds salad, fries, and a drink for a few euros more; 15 percent cheaper for takeaway, Wed-Fri 12:00-

14:30 & 17:30-20:00, Sat-Sun 12:00-20:00, closed Mon-Tue, Sint-Salvatorskerkhof 1, tel. 050-684-395).

't Brugsch Friethuys, a block off the Markt, is handy for fries you can sit down and enjoy. Its forte is greasy, deep-fried Flemish fast food. The €13.30 "Big Hunger menu" comes with all the traditional gut bombs (daily 11:00-late, at the corner of Geldmuntstraat and Sint Jakobsstraat, Luc will explain your options).

Picnics

A handy location for groceries is the **Carrefour Express** mini-supermarket, just off the Markt on Vlamingstraat (daily 8:00-19:00); for a slightly wider selection, **Delhaize-Proxy** is just up Geldmuntstraat (Mon-Sat 9:00-19:00, closed Sun, Noordzandstraat 4). For midnight snacks, you'll find Indian-run corner grocery stores scattered around town.

Belgian Waffles and Ice Cream

You'll see waffles sold at restaurants and takeaway stands (for more on waffles, see page 337). One of Bruges' best is also one of its most obvious: **Chez Albert,** on Breidelstraat connecting the Markt and Burg Square, is pricey, but the quality is good and—thanks to the tourist crowds—turnover is quick, so the waffles are fresh (daily 10:00-18:00, at #18).

Gelateria Da Vinci, the local favorite for homemade ice cream, has creative flavors and a lively atmosphere. As you approach, you'll see a line of happy lickers. Before ordering, ask to sample the Ferrero Rocher (chocolate, nuts, and crunchy cookie) and plain yogurt (daily 11:00-22:00, later in summer, Geldmuntstraat 34, tel. 050-333-650, run by Sylvia from Austria).

Shopping in Bruges

As a largely touristy town, Bruges isn't the place to shop for authenticity or bargains. (Brussels, Antwerp, and Ghent have more real-world stores and are more satisfying places to browse for fashion, design, or other non-clichéd Belgian fortes.) But souvenir shoppers find plenty of options. Shops are generally open from 10:00 to 18:00 and closed Sundays. Grocery stores are usually closed on Sunday.

WHAT TO BUY

Chocolate: A box of Belgian pralines is at the top of most souvenir shoppers' lists; see my tips and recommended chocolate shops on page 39.

Beer: Another consumable souvenir is Belgian beer—either a bottle (or three) for later in your trip, or a prized brew checked carefully in your luggage home. In addition to the pubs listed earlier—a few of which sell bottles to go—the streets of Bruges are lined with bottle shops. At some, you can buy the correct glass that's designed to go with each type of beer (it's a fragile item to pack, but purists insist). Options include the touristy souvenir store **2Be** (described below) or **The Bottle Shop,** which sells 600 different beers by the bottle and has a staff that enjoys helping visitors navigate the many choices (daily 10:00-18:30, just south of the Markt at Wollestraat 13, tel. 050-349-980).

Lace: This is a popular item, but very expensive; 't Apostelientje, described on page 36, is one good option (and conveniently located across the street from the Lace Center). For more on lace, see the sidebar on page 36.

WHERE TO SHOP

Souvenir shops abound on the streets that fan out from the Markt and the ones heading southwest, toward the Church of Our Lady. **2Be,** in a classic old brick mansion overlooking a canal a block south of the Markt, is huge, obvious, and grotesquely touristy...but well-stocked with a wide variety of tacky and not-so-tacky Belgian souvenirs: Tintin, Smurfs, beer, and chocolates. The "beerwall" at the entrance shows off over a thousand types of Belgian brew; their cellar is filled with a remarkably well-stocked bottle shop; and their pub has several rotating draft beers you can enjoy on a relaxing terrace floating over a perfect canal (daily 10:00-19:00, Wollestraat 53, tel. 050-611-222, www.2-be.biz).

Two parallel streets, running southwest between the Markt and 't Zand squares, are lined with shops that cater both to tourists and to workaday Bruggians. **Steenstraat,** which becomes **Zuidzandstraat** closer to 't Zand, has lots of affordable clothing chains (H&M, Zara), department stores (Hema), and mobile phone shops (handy if you need to buy a Belgian SIM card). At the Markt end of the street, a few tourist/souvenir shops are mixed in, but the farther you go, the more local it becomes.

More colorful are the shops a block to the north, along **Geldmuntstraat** (which becomes **Noordzandstraat**). Along this atmospheric drag—with perhaps Bruges' most enjoyable window-shopping—are smaller, more expensive chains and upscale boutiques (including L'Heroine, highlighting Belgian designers with Antwerp cred at Noordzandstraat 32); housewares shops (such as Cook & Serve, a fun kitchen gadgets shop, at Geldmuntstraat 16); and the popular Da Vinci gelato shop (see listing on page 94).

The **old fish market (Vismarkt)** just over the bridge from Burg Square still sells fresh fish most mornings, while souvenir stands fill some of its arcades all day long and into the evening. It's a central place to browse toys, jewelry, accessories, starving artists' depictions of Bruges, and more.

For the highest concentration of tourists (and, consequently, the highest concentration of souvenir, chocolate, lace, and *wafel* shops), head down **Katelijnestraat,** which runs south from the Church of Our Lady and Memling Museum. While you'll find no great values here, it's convenient for souvenir shopping.

Nightlife in Bruges

After dark, Bruges is sleepy but enchanting. While there's entertainment to be found, perhaps the city's most rewarding nighttime experience is strolling its floodlit cobbles and monuments. My favorite way to spend a late-summer evening in Bruges is in the twilight on a rental bike, savoring the cobbled wonders of its back streets, far from the touristic commotion. Another good option is to settle into a characteristic pub (or hop between a few) to enjoy some beer; of the several pubs listed earlier under "Eating in Bruges," **Herberg Vlissinghe** and **De Garre** are particularly memorable places to nurse a beer and enjoy new friends.

I've suggested some other options for entertainment below (for locations, see map on page 91). For live music, also check www.agendabrugge.be; it's in Dutch only, but easy enough to interpret (especially if you use Google's Translate function).

CONCERTS
The tiny courtyard behind the bell tower has a few benches where people can enjoy free evening **carillon concerts** (generally mid-June-mid-Sept Mon and Wed at 21:00; schedule posted on courtyard wall).

Otherwise, see what's on at one of the city's main venues: The **Concertgebouw,** a cutting-edge facility on the spacious square called 't Zand, features esoteric dance, classy orchestral music, and other high culture (tel. 070-223-302, www.concertgebouw.be). The **Municipal Theater** (Brugse Stadsschouwburg), two blocks north of the Markt on Vlamingstraat, features an eclectic lineup of classical and modern presentations, from ballet to contemporary dance to musical theater to big-name jazz performers (www.ccbrugge.be; check location carefully—some performances take place in smaller venues around town). The TI can give you information for any of these; the booking office inside the TI also sells tickets for most events in town.

Luc Vanlaere presents 40-minute **harp concerts** most days in summer at Old St. John's Church (Oud Sint Jan, across from the Church of Our Lady and tucked behind Memling Museum; free but donations appreciated, generally Tue-Sat 15:00, 17:00, and 18:30, no concerts Sun-Mon, fewer concerts off-season, Mariastraat 38, www.lucvanlaere-harp.be).

Other churches sometimes host concerts, including **Salvator's Cathedral** (organ concerts many Friday and some Tuesday evenings in summer, just southwest of the Markt along the busy Steenstraat shopping drag, www.kathedraalconcerten.be), **St. Walburga** (Jesuit church on Sint-Maartensplein east of the Markt), or **St. Jacob's** (on Sint-Jakobsplein, just northwest of the Markt).

LIVELY AFTER-HOURS STREETS

Check out the following areas for lively bars, many of which have loud music or DJs late at night:

Eiermarkt ("Egg Market"), a tiny, table-clogged lane a few steps off the Markt (follow Geernaartstraat, straight across the square from the bell tower), is a rollicking scene that gets younger as the night gets older; Café Pick anchors the scene with frequent live DJs.

Just to the north, **Kupiersstraat** runs behind the City Theater (Stadsschouwburg), with a smattering of bars that cater to various demographics—from funky dives for teens to elegant cellars with well-dressed retirees. Along here, **'t Zwart Huis** is the elegant trendsetter, with a classy bar/restaurant upstairs and **'t Under Ground** cellar bar below (described later).

Farther out to the west, the long, broad square called **'t Zand** (dominated by the Concertgebouw) is packed with outdoor tables. The bar at the north end of the square, around Ma Rica Rokk, is the most youthful scene.

East of the Markt, **Langestraat** is lined with young, borderline-rowdy bars and clubs; **de Kelk** (at #69) is a characteristic bar along here with a wide variety of Belgian beers.

BARS WITH LIVE MUSIC

In addition to the general areas noted earlier, these places have occasional live music.

Wijnbar Est, a classy and cozy little wine bar right in the middle of the tourist zone, has live music most Sundays at 20:00 (jazz and mellow covers, no cover charge, closed Tue-Wed, Braambergstraat 7, www.wijnbarest.be).

't Zwart Huis ("The Black House") is a vast, atmospheric space with an upscale vibe. Having appeared in the film *In Bruges*, it's popular with tourists. While you can get a meal here (€10-19 pastas, €17-25 main dishes), the main appeal is the chance to enjoy live jazz and blues music in a fine setting (performances every other

Sun at 21:00, usually €5 cover for music, closed Mon-Tue, Kuiperrsstraat 23, tel. 050-691-140, www.bistrozwarthuis.be). **'t Under Ground,** in the cellar, is a more casual and cozy place for drinks, but lacks live music; they sometimes have dance music late.

Comptoir des Arts, the cozy beer cellar described on page 92, offers live music on many Sunday evenings.

Charlie Rockets is an American-style bar—lively and central—with foosball, darts, and five pool tables (€9/hour) in the inviting back room. It also runs a youth hostel upstairs and therefore is filled with a young, international crowd who take full advantage of the guest-only happy hour prices (a block off the Markt at Hoogstraat 19). It's open nightly with nonstop rock 'n' roll (mostly recorded, sometimes live).

't Opkikkertje is a grubby dive bar with live rock music (mostly cover bands) every other Saturday at 20:30 (no cover charge, closed Sun, West-Gistelhof 13, www.opkikkertje.be).

Bruges Connections

BY TRAIN

For information on rail travel in Belgium, see www.belgiumrail.be; see also page 352.

From Bruges by Train to: Brussels (2/hour, usually at :31 and :58, 1 hour), **Brussels Airport** (2/hour, 1.5 hours, transfer at Brussels Nord), **Ghent** (4/hour, 30 minutes), **Antwerp** (2/hour, 1.5 hours, half the trains change in Ghent), **Ypres/Ieper** (hourly, 2 hours, change in Kortrijk), **Ostend** (3/hour, 15 minutes), **Delft** (hourly, 3 hours, change in Ghent, Antwerp, and Rotterdam), **The Hague** (hourly, 3 hours, change in Brussels and Rotterdam), **Cologne** (8/day, 3.5 hours, change to fast Thalys train or InterCity Express at Brussels Midi), **Paris** (roughly hourly via Brussels, 2.5 hours on fast Thalys trains—it's best to book by 20:00 the day before), **Amsterdam** (hourly, 3-4.5 hours, transfer at Brussels Midi; transfer can be tight—be alert and check with conductor; some trips via Thalys train, which requires supplement), **Amsterdam's Schiphol Airport** (hourly, 4 hours, change in Brussels; faster connection possible with Thalys, 3 hours but with 2 transfers), **Haarlem** (hourly, 3.5-4 hours, 2-3 changes—avoid Thalys if traveling with a rail pass).

Trains from London: Bruges is an ideal "Welcome to Europe" stop after London. Take the Eurostar train from London to Brussels (10/day, 2.5 hours), then transfer, backtracking to Bruges (2/hour, 1 hour, entire trip just a few dollars more with Eurostar ticket; see Eurostar details on page 215).

BY CRUISE SHIP

The tiny town of **Zeebrugge,** just 10 miles north of Bruges, has a gigantic port. From the cruise port, it's an easy tram-plus-train connection (with a little walking) to reach Bruges or Brussels.

Zeebrugge's port has two cruise berths (but no TIs or real terminal buildings—though there are plans to build one): Larger ships generally use **Swedish Quay** (Zweedse Kaai), which pokes straight up into the main harbor; smaller ships use **Maritime Station** (Zeestation), across the harbor along Leopold II-Dam. From either place, you'll ride a free shuttle bus out of the port area.

From Swedish Quay, your shuttle bus drops you at the port gate. Exit the port area to the right, following the busy road with the sea on your right. Walk about 10 minutes until you reach the big church, and the Zeebrugge Kerk stop for the coastal tram (explained below). From Maritime Station, your shuttle bus drops you off right at the Zeebrugge Strandwijk stop for the coastal tram.

The coastal tram (Kusttram) zips from Zeebrugge and Blankenberge, and beyond. From either of the stops described earlier, hop on a tram going in the direction of Ostend (Oostande) or De Panne, and ride it to Blankenberge Station (€2, buy ticket from driver and validate in yellow machine, 2-3/hour, 14 minutes). Stepping off the tram in Blankenberge, simply cross the street to the train station, with a handy hourly train that zips to **Bruges** (€3, 15 minutes), then on to **Ghent** (€8.50, 50 minutes total) and **Brussels** (€16.10, 1.5 hours total)—most trains leave at :10 past each hour.

NEAR BRUGES: FLANDERS FIELDS

These World War I battlefields, about 40 miles southwest of Bruges, remain infamous in military history. In Flanders Fields, the second decade of the 20th century saw the invention of modern warfare: machine guns, trenches, poison gas, and a war of attrition. The most intense fighting occurred in the area called the Ypres Salient, a nondescript but hilly—and therefore strategic—bulge of land just east of the medieval trading town of Ypres (which the Flemish call "Ieper"). Over a period of three and a half years, hundreds of thousands of soldiers from fifty nations and five continents drew their last breath here. Fields and forests were turned first to trenches and battlefields, and then to desolate wastelands with mud several feet deep, entirely devoid of life.

Poppies are the first flowers to bloom in a desolate battlefield once the dust (and mustard gas) clears. And today, this far-western corner of Belgium is blooming once more, having adopted that flower as its symbol. It represents sacrifice and renewal.

Today visitors can't drive through this part of Flanders without passing countless artillery craters, monuments and memorials, stones marking this advance or that conquest, and war cemeteries standing stoically between the cow-speckled pastures. Farmers here pull rusty relics of World War I from the earth when they till their fields. Many locals have their own garage collection of "Great War" debris fished out of a field. Human remains are also regularly disinterred, with every effort made to identify the fallen soldier and notify any surviving family.

If you're interested in this chapter of history, you can visit several Flanders Fields

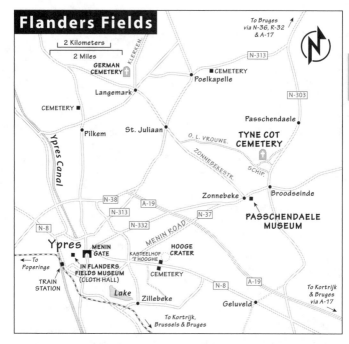

Flanders Fields

To Bruges
via N-36, R-32
& A-17

N-313

2 Kilometers

2 Miles

GERMAN
CEMETERY

KLERKEN

■ CEMETERY
Poelkapelle

N-303

Langemark

CEMETERY ■

Pilkem

St. Juliaan

O. L. VROUWE.

Passchendaele

TYNE COT
CEMETERY

ZONNEBEKESTR.

SCHIP.

Ypres Canal

N-38

N-313

Zonnebeke

Broodseinde

A-19

N-37

PASSCHENDAELE
MUSEUM

N-332

MENIN ROAD

N-8

Ypres

MENIN
GATE

HOOGE
CRATER

←—To
Poperinge

KASTEELHOF
'T HOOGHE

IN FLANDERS
FIELDS MUSEUM
(CLOTH HALL)

CEMETERY

N-8

A-19

To Kortrijk
& Bruges
via A-17

TRAIN
STATION

Lake

Zillebeke

Geluveld

To Kortrijk,
Brussels & Bruges

sights in a one-day side-trip from Bruges (best by car or guided tour). The most important and accessible sights are the pleasant, rebuilt market town of Ypres, with its impressive In Flanders Fields Museum; the town of Passchendaele (a.k.a. "Passiondale"), with a nearby, more humble, but still interesting museum; and Tyne Cot Cemetery, where thousands of enlisted men from the British Commonwealth are buried and honored. Because most of the fighting here involved British Commonwealth troops, the vast majority of visitors are Brits, Canadians, Australians, and New Zealanders, for whom the stories of Flanders Fields are etched, like names on gravestones, into their national consciousness. You'll notice on maps that many places have English names—often anglicized approximations of the Flemish names (Passiondale for Passchendaele) or evocative new names (Mount Sorrow, Hellfire Corner).

The years 2014 through 2018 are a banner time in this area,

as the centennial of various battles and other events are commemorated—book tours early and expect crowds during special events (listed at www.flandersfields.be).

Between the sights, you'll drive through idyllic Belgian countryside, streaked with corn-

In Flanders Fields

In Flanders fields the poppies blow
Between the crosses, row on row,
That mark our place; and in the sky
The larks, still bravely singing, fly
Scarce heard amid the guns below.

We are the Dead. Short days ago
We lived, felt dawn, saw sunset glow,
Loved and were loved, and now we lie,
In Flanders fields.

Take up our quarrel with the foe:
To you from failing hands we throw
The torch; be yours to hold it high.
If ye break faith with us who die
We shall not sleep, though poppies grow
In Flanders fields.

—John McCrae

fields, dotted with pudgy cows, and punctuated by the occasional artillery crater—now overgrown with grass or trees, or serving as a handy little pond. On your Flanders Fields journey, be sure to take time to slow down and smell the cabbage.

PLANNING YOUR TIME

By Tour: If you really want to delve into Flanders Fields, your best bet is to take a tour. These come with a rolling history lecture, taking you to off-the-beaten-path sights you'd likely not find on your own. Several companies based in Ypres run tours of the area (for information, check with the TI listed on page 108); if you're coming from Bruges, it's more convenient to take the Quasimodo big-bus tour (described on page 25).

By Car: Drivers can easily link the three main sights in a day. Be aware that road signs use the Flemish "Ieper," not "Ypres." Shop around locally for a good guidebook to point you to additional options. The tourist board publishes a free guidebooklet called *The Flanders Fields Country & The Great War*, which is a good starting place (download a PDF at www.visitflanders.co.uk).

Here's a one-day plan for seeing the sights listed in this chapter. If you're a WWI battlefield buff, invest in a good local guidebook and map to hunt down the many additional sights beyond what I list.

From Bruges, head south on the A-17 expressway. To make a beeline to Ypres, take this all the way to A-19 heading east and follow *Ieper Centrum* signs. For a slower, more scenic route that takes you past more sights, exit the A-17 expressway at R-32 and circle around the northern edge of Roeselare, then head west on N-36, then south on N-313. This leads you to Langemark and the German cemetery there. Then take Zonnebekestraat southeast to the village of Zonnebeke and the Passchendaele Museum. From there follow the Menin Road (N-37) into Ypres, crossing under the Menin Gate as you enter town. After touring Ypres' museum, you can explore more countryside sights or head back to Bruges (fastest route between Ypres and Bruges: A-19 expressway east to the A-17 interchange near Kortrijk, then zip north on A-17).

By Public Transportation: Non-drivers will find it time-consuming to get from Bruges to Ypres (2 hours one-way with a transfer in Kortrijk; note that Ypres is "Ieper" on timetables). Once at Ypres, it's very difficult to see the scattered sights using public transit. Taking a tour (from Ypres or Bruges) or renting a car is a must.

Flanders Fields and the Ypres Salient

Because American forces played a relatively minor role in the fighting at Flanders Fields, its history is obscure to many visitors from the US. This section will get you up to speed.

From 1830, Belgium was established as an independent and neutral state—an essential buffer zone to protect European peace,

surrounded by four big powers: France, Prussia, the Netherlands, and Britain. After defeating France and unifying in 1870, Germany was on the rise—an upstart powerhouse hungry for overseas colonies to fuel its growing economy. Germany amassed an intimidating army, and the rest of Europe worriedly watched flickering newsreel footage of wave after wave of German soldiers, goose-stepping past the camera in perfect sync, followed by gleaming, state-of-the-art cannons. Some of Europe's nations scrambled to ally with their neighbors against potential German encroachment; others allied with Germany. Because many alliances were secret, and often conflicting, no one knew for sure exactly where anyone else stood. As H. G. Wells said, "Every intelligent person in the world knew that disaster was impending and knew no way to avoid it."

On June 28, 1914, while on a visit to Sarajevo, the heir to the Austro-Hungarian throne, Archduke Franz Ferdinand, and his wife were assassinated by a teenage terrorist working for Bosnian Serb separatists. The Austrians held Serbia responsible and declared war. Germany joined Austria, and Russia (allied with France) backed Serbia. Through an intricate web of alliances—which ironically had been created to prevent war—soon all of Europe was drawn into the conflict. On August 4, 1914, Germany sent some 800,000 troops across the border into neutral Belgium en route to France. By August 20, they had already taken Brussels, and four days later they were in western Flanders.

The Germans expected to blow through the country quickly. However, the small but determined Belgian army—less than a quarter the size of the German army—pushed back hard, as they waited for British reinforcements to come from across the Channel. In the **Battle of the Yser (Ijzer) River,** the Belgians opened a sea gate at a pivotal moment to flood a low-lying plain just before a German advance. This diverted the German effort slightly to the south, around the town of Ypres.

Ypres was just an ordinary town. But its location, surrounding terrain, and modern weaponry turned it into a perpetual battlefield. This conflict saw the advent of the machine gun—a new invention that, before the war, had been called "the peacekeeper," because it was assumed that no sane commander would ever send his boys into its fire. The flat terrain of Flanders Fields, combined with these new battlefield techniques, made even the slightest gain in elevation strategically important. From any ridge, machine guns and artillery could be used to mow down enemy troops—advancing armies would be sitting ducks. (The names of some of the land features here—such as "Hill 60," as in 60 meters above sea level—indicate how notable even the most modest gain in elevation was.) Consequently, the low-lying ridges just east of Ypres—which came to be known as the **Ypres Salient** (the French term for "bulge")—saw some of the fiercest, most devastating fighting of World War I.

The **First Battle of Ypres** began on October 20, 1914, when German troops attempted to invade the town. It became a priority of the Allies—Belgians, French, and British Commonwealth troops—to hold the Germans at bay. Both sides sustained huge losses, but the German troops—mostly inexperienced young conscripts who had underestimated the opposition—were devastated; to this day, Germans call the battle *Kindermord,* "Massacre of the Innocents."

Both sides regrouped and prepared for a harsh winter. They dug trenches, as it was human nature for soldiers ducking machine-gun bullets to burrow down. Separated by as little as 50 yards, enemy armies were close enough to offer each other a *Gesundheit!* after each sneeze. It was during this time that the famous "Christmas Truce" took place, in which German soldiers erected little candlelit

*Tanenbaum*s beside their trenches and even approached the English trenches with gifts, kind words, and a pick-up soccer game.

During the **Second Battle of Ypres,** in the spring of 1915, the Germans used poison gas for the first time on a large scale, catching the Allies off-guard. Chlorine gas (a.k.a. bertholite) reacts with moisture in the lungs to form hydrochloric acid—choking soldiers from the inside out. It was also one of the first times flamethrowers were used in battle. Still, Germany was unable to take the town. By May of 1915, the opposing forces were deadlocked near the town of Passchendaele, seven miles east of Ypres; for two years, little progress was made in either direction.

Although the Western Front appeared to be "all quiet," each side fortified its positions. The Germans established an elaborate network of five successive trenches, connected to and supplied by one another with perpendicular "switches." They built stout fortresses with flat tops, designed to protect troops from British artillery while allowing them to quickly emerge to man nearby machine-gun nests. These flat-top German fortresses—which you'll still see everywhere—were dubbed "pillboxes." The British opted for underground wooden tunnels called "dugouts" and reserved concrete bunkers for more specialized use, as command posts and shelters for the wounded. (Their rounded-top bunkers proved to be a more effective deterrent to artillery blasts than the flat-top design—leading the Germans to adopt the round style in World War II.)

In the summer of 1917, the Allies attempted their own offensive against the newly strengthened German threat, the **Third Battle of Ypres** (a.k.a. the Battle of Passchendaele). After a sustained two-week artillery bombardment of German positions, some four million projectiles turned the countryside into a desolate wasteland. One solider said that "the earth had been churned and rechurned"; another termed it "as featureless as the Sahara."

Then British infantry took to the battlefield...going "over the top" (giving us that phrase), rather than staying in the trenches. They faced barbed wire, machine-gun fire, dangerously exposed high ground, and liquid mud. The devastation of the shelling, combined with historic rainfall (the most in the history of Flanders), turned the Ypres Salient into a sea of mud. The low ground became quicksand while fields flooded with stagnant water. Troops' boots and tank treads could barely move, causing the British to gain only two of the four miles they needed to conquer. This battle was also the first time the Germans used mustard gas, which causes exposed skin to blister on contact.

As the summer of 1917 turned to fall, and the heavy rains continued to deluge the area, British soldiers made more and more inroads, bunker by bunker. Their goal was the destroyed village of

Dulce et Decorum Est

Bent double, like old beggars under sacks,
Knock-kneed, coughing like hags, we cursed
   through sludge,
Till on the haunting flares we turned our backs
And towards our distant rest began to trudge.
Men marched asleep. Many had lost their boots
But limped on, blood-shod. All went lame;
   all blind;
Drunk with fatigue; deaf even to the hoots
Of tired, outstripped Five-Nines that dropped
   behind.

Gas! Gas! Quick, boys!—An ecstasy of fumbling,
Fitting the clumsy helmets just in time;
But someone still was yelling out and stumbling,
And flound'ring like a man in fire or lime...
Dim, through the misty panes and thick green
   light,
As under a green sea, I saw him drowning.

In all my dreams, before my helpless sight,
He plunges at me, guttering, choking, drowning.

If in some smothering dreams you too could
   pace
Behind the wagon that we flung him in,
And watch the white eyes writhing in his face,
His hanging face, like a devil's sick of sin;
If you could hear, at every jolt, the blood
Come gargling from the froth-corrupted lungs,
Obscene as cancer, bitter as the cud
Of vile, incurable sores on innocent tongues, —
My friend, you would not tell with such high zest
To children ardent for some desperate glory,
The old Lie: Dulce et decorum est
Pro patria mori.

—Wilfred Owen

Passchendaele, perched on a modest ridge with a strategic view over the flat lands below. The village's name literally meant "passing the valley," but the Brits dubbed it "Passiondale"...the valley of suffering. Menin Road, which connected Ypres to Passchendaele (now road N-37), was the focus of much warfare—especially the intersection dubbed "Hellfire Corner."

But British forces never succeeded in taking Passchendaele (Canadian forces finally took it in November of 1917). By this point, this was a war of attrition. Each side had lost about a quarter of a million men. And, as both sides poured troops and resources into the fighting, neither could actually make a definitive breakthrough—they simply wanted to be the last man standing.

Two pivotal events took place over the winter of 1917-1918: The United States entered the war on the side of the Allies; and Germany agreed to a separate peace with Russia, allowing it to steer more resources to the Ypres Salient. In spring of 1918, the **Fourth Battle of Ypres** (a.k.a. the Battle of the Lys) saw German forces trying to push through to the town of Ypres before US troops could arrive. They were emboldened by the collapse of Russia in the Bolshevik Revolution, which freed up more German troops and resources to direct at this front. Always innovative on the battlefield, the Germans introduced an elite squad of storm troopers (*Stosstruppen,* literally "shock troops")—lightly armed but well-trained and highly mobile special units tasked with breaking through enemy lines.

But by late April, the German advance stalled for lack of supplies; meanwhile, American troops had come to the rescue. By summer it was evident that Germany was losing the war of attrition, and by fall of 1918, in the **Fifth Battle of Ypres,** Allied forces made huge gains. Less than a month later, Armistice Day (Nov 11, 1918) brought an end to the war to end all wars...until the next war.

World War I claimed the lives of an estimated nine million people; about a million were killed, wounded, or declared missing in action here in the Ypres Salient. By war's end, the British Commonwealth forces had suffered 720,000 casualties, including (officially) 185,000 dead. In the century since, Flanders Fields has recovered, and has become a compelling tourist attraction for the descendants of the victims and survivors of the fighting here. As you tour the place, keep in mind that everything you see—every building, every tree—dates from after 1918.

Sights in Flanders Fields

IN YPRES TOWN

About 40 miles southwest of Bruges is the town most English  speakers call Ypres (EE-preh, though some pronounce it "Wipers"); its official Flemish name is Ieper (YEE-per). By the end of the war, Ypres was so devastated that Winston Churchill advocated keeping it in ruins as a monument to the travesty of warfare. But locals did rebuild, resurrecting its charming main market square (Grote Markt), watched over by the grand and impressive Cloth Hall (which houses the In Flanders Fields Museum). Today's Ypres is a pleasant market town (Saturday morning is market day), with a steady stream of mostly British tourists interested in the WWI sights.

Tourist Information: The TI, downstairs in the Cloth Hall, has information on tours (below the museum; Mon-Fri 9:00-18:00, Sat-Sun 10:00-18:00, off-season until 17:00; tel. 057-239-220, www.toerisme-ieper.be).

Getting There: If you're based in Bruges without a car, take a tour (see recommended tours on page 25). Less than an hour away, Ypres is easy for drivers (see route tips under "Planning Your Time," earlier). There's parking right on the main market square, next to the giant Cloth Hall that houses the museum (€1/first hour, €2/3 hours, 3-hour limit).

▲▲In Flanders Fields Museum

This excellent museum provides a moving look at the battles fought near Ypres, covering the entire Belgian front. The focus is not on the strategy and the commanders, but on the people who fought and died here. The descriptions personalize the miserable day-to-day existence in the trenches, and interactive computer displays trace the wartime lives of individual soldiers and citizens. Artifacts and thoughtful presentations all bring the war-torn places to life. The museum also ties exhibits to the actual sites in the surrounding countryside, and looks at the century of remembrances that have passed since the war's end.

The Cloth Hall's **belfry** (231 steps to the top, €2 extra) offers a panoramic view of the surrounding countryside.

Cost and Hours: €9; April-mid-Nov daily 10:00-18:00; mid-Nov-March Tue-Sun 10:00-17:00, closed Mon and for three weeks in Jan; last entry one hour before closing, in Ypres' huge Cloth Hall at Grote Markt 34, tel. 057-239-220, www.inflandersfields.be.

▲Menin Gate

This impressive Victorian archway is an easy two-block walk from the museum (past the end of Grote Markt). Built into the old town wall of Ypres, it's etched with the names of British Commonwealth victims who fought here. It marks the Menin Road, where many Brits, Canadians, Aussies, and Kiwis left this town for the battlefields and trenches, never to return. The gate is formally a mausoleum for "the Missing," 54,896 troops who likely perished at Flanders Fields but whose remains

were never found. To honor the hundreds of thousands of British subjects who gave their lives, every night under the arch at 20:00, a Belgian bugle corps plays the "Last Post" to honor the dead.

SIGHTS NEAR YPRES

Most of these sights are on or near Menin Road between Ypres and Passchendaele (to the northeast), where the most famous battles took place. The German Cemetery is a bit to the north (but still within a few miles).

The sights listed here are just the beginning. You can't drive a mile or two without passing a monument or memorial. Tranquil forests open into clearings with eerily rippled contours—overgrown trenches, pockmarks, and craters. Certain nondescript ponds and lakes are actually flooded artillery craters. Joining a tour helps you find some of the more out-of-the-way remnants of the war. If you're exploring on your own, get a guidebook on the region (several are available at local bookstores and tourist offices). If you have a special interest—for example, a nationality or a specific battle an ancestor participated in—just ask around to find related sites.

▲Passchendaele Museum

Although not as extensive or well-presented as the In Flanders Fields Museum, this good exhibit supplements it nicely, with a focus on strategy and battles. Presented chronologically on the top floor of a chalet-like mansion, it details each advance and retreat from the first German boot on Belgian soil to Armistice Day. You'll see displays of uniforms, medical instruments, and objects illustrating day-to-day life at the front. One exhibit explains—and lets you sniff—the four basic types of poison gas used here. You'll exit through a simulation of the wooden underground "dugout" tunnels used by British forces as their headquarters, after the ground level was so scorched by artillery that nothing was left up above.

Cost and Hours: €7.50, daily 9:00-18:00, closed mid-Dec-Jan, Ieperstraat 5, in Zonnebeke about 5 miles east of Ypres and 2 miles west of Passchendaele, tel. 051-770-441, www.passchendaele.be.

▲Tyne Cot Cemetery

This evocative cemetery is the final resting place of 11,956 British, Canadian, Australian, New Zealander, South African, and other British Commonwealth soldiers. It was named for a blockhouse on this site that was taken by British forces, who nicknamed it "Tyne Cottage" after the river

in North England. The cemetery grounds also hold three German pillbox bunkers. Between those are seemingly endless rows of white headstones, marked with a soldier's name and his unit's emblem (many of these are regional, such as the maple leaf of Canada). Many graves are marked simply "A soldier of the Great War, known to God."

In the center of the cemetery, near the tallest cross (marking the location of Tyne Cottage), notice the higgledy-piggledy arrangement of graves. During the war, when this cottage was a makeshift medic station, this area became an impromptu burial ground. (In contrast, any cemetery that's neat and symmetrical—like the surrounding headstones—dates from after the war.) Running along the top of the cemetery is a wall inscribed with the names of 34,857 "officers and men to whom the fortune of war denied the known and honoured burial given to their comrades in death." The visitors center has a few artifacts and exhibits about the fighting here.

Cost and Hours: Free, visitors center open daily 10:00-18:00, closed Dec-Jan, just northeast of Zonnebeke, off of N-37 toward Passchendaele, about 6.5 miles east of Ypres, www.cwgc.org.

Hooge Crater

This giant flooded crater, about three miles east of Ypres, was created when British forces detonated a vast store of artillery that destroyed the château they had been using as a headquarters. This desperate act was only partly successful, as the strategic high ground around the château (now a crater) switched hands repeatedly throughout the war.

Today the Hooge Crater area has a large British Commonwealth **cemetery;** the **Hooge Crater Museum,** a touristy exhibit with historic information about the fighting here (€4.50, Tue-Sat 10:00-18:00, Sun 10:00-21:00, closed Mon, www.hoogecrater. com); and—hiding out in the woods just down the road—a hotel/ restaurant called **Kasteelhof 't Hooghe,** where you can pay €1 to stroll around the adjacent crater-pond and see some old bunkers and trenches (restaurant closed Sun, www.hotelkasteelhofthooghe. be).

German Military Cemetery (Deutscher Soldatenfriedhof) at Langemark

A relatively rare site dedicated to the invaders of this region, this is the where 44,324 Central Powers soldiers are buried (along with two Brits who were originally misidentified). Compared with the gleaming British Commonwealth cemeteries nearby, it's dull and drab. That's because the Treaty of Versailles (which concluded World War I) forbade German WWI cemeteries from using white

BRUSSELS

ORIENTATION TO BRUSSELS

Brussel • Bruxelles

Six hundred years ago, Brussels was just a nice place to stop and buy a waffle on the way to Bruges. With no strategic importance, it was allowed to grow as a free trading town. Today it's the capital of Belgium, the headquarters of NATO, and the seat of the European Union. It's also a fascinating and vibrant city in its own right, with fun-to-explore neighborhoods, good sightseeing, an impressive selection of restaurants, and a quirky Flemish/French mix.

The Brussels of today reflects its past. The city enjoyed a Golden Age of peace and prosperity (1400-1550) when many of its signature structures were built. In the late 1800s, Brussels had another growth spurt, fueled by industrialization, wealth taken from the Belgian Congo, and the exhilaration of the country's recent independence (1830). The "Builder King" Leopold II erected grand monuments and palaces. Then, in 1992, EU countries signed the Treaty of Maastricht, and sleepy Brussels suddenly was thrust into the spotlight as the unofficial capital of the new Europe. It started a frenzy of renovation, infrastructure projects, foreign visitors, and world attention.

As a tourist destination, Brussels captivates some visitors and exasperates others. At its best, Brussels mingles French class and Belgian spunk. At its worst, it's a crowded, jaded city of demanding tourists, stuffy bureaucrats, and down-and-out immigrants. Its museums are endearing, but not quite befitting its status as a world capital. But if you make an effort to escape the tourists and explore some outlying neighborhoods, you'll experience another side of Brussels. The more you see, the more you'll like it.

In Brussels, people speak French. Bone up on *bonjour* and *s'il vous plait* (see the French survival phrases on page 373). The Bruxellois are cultured and genteel—even a bit snobby compared to their more earthy Flemish cousins. The whole feel of the town is

stones; instead, it uses basalt and even oak. As you wander the cemetery, notice that many of these "German" troops have Slavic names, as they were imported here to fight from the far-eastern corners of the multi-ethnic Austro-Hungarian Empire. In the center is a mass grave with 25,000 soldiers.

Cost and Hours: Free, always open, on the northern outskirts of Langemark, about five miles north/northeast of Ypres.

urban French, not rural Flemish. And yet you may notice an impish sparkle and joie de vivre, as evidenced by their love of comic strips (giant comic-strip panels are painted on buildings all over town) and their civic symbol: a statue of a little boy peeing.

Brussels is the cutting edge of modern Europe, but still clothed in its Old World garments. Stroll the Grand Place, snap a selfie with the *Manneken-Pis,* and watch diplomats at work at the EU assembly halls. Then grab some mussels, fries, and a hearty Belgian beer, and watch the sun set behind the Town Hall's lacy steeple.

BRUSSELS: A VERBAL MAP

Central Brussels is surrounded by a ring of roads (which replaced the old city wall) called the Pentagon. (Romantics think it looks more like a heart.) All hotels and nearly all the sights I mention are within this ring. The epicenter holds the main square (the Grand Place), the TI, and Central Station (all within three blocks of one another).

What isn't so apparent from maps is that Brussels is a city divided by altitude. A ridgeline that runs north-south splits the town into the Upper Town (east half, elevation 200 feet) and Lower Town (west, at sea level), with Central Station in between.

Brussels' bilingual street signs, combined with the near-complete lack of a regular grid plan, can make navigating the city confusing. It's easy to get turned around. I rely heavily on a good map (such as the TI's €0.50 map) when exploring this town.

It's helpful to think of the city as a series of neighborhoods, each with its own character.

The Lower Town: This crowded touristy district—with the Grand Place (grahn plahs; in Dutch: Grote Markt, *H*ROH-teh markt), narrow streets, old buildings, modern shops, tourist-trap eateries, and famous *Manneken-Pis* peeing-boy statue—is squeezed between Central Station and Boulevard Anspach.

West of Boulevard Anspach (Anspachlaan): This bustling boulevard, which runs over the city's forgotten river, marks the boundary between Brussels' touristy core and some more characteristic neighborhoods. Just beyond Boulevard Anspach—past a block or two of high-rise ugliness—is the lively and youthful market square called **Place St-Géry** (Sint-Goriksplein). The **Dansaert** district (just past Place St-Géry, along Rue Antoine Dansaert) is emerging as a high-fashion district, with a creative "bobo" (bourgeois-bohème) ambience. Just to the north is the **Ste. Catherine** neighborhood, a charming village-within-a-city huddled around the old fish market, and home to several recommended hotels and restaurants.

The Upper Town: This uphill, upper-crust, stuck-up district

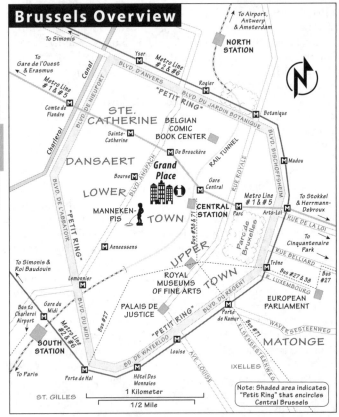

surrounds the Royal Palace. Traditionally the home of nobility and the rich, this area has big marble palaces, broad boulevards, and the major museums. Compared to other parts of the city, it feels stately and sterile. The zone between the Upper and Lower towns, called **Sablon,** feels French and urbane.

Beyond the Core: Everything described previously is walkable. Outside the pentagon-shaped center, sprawling suburbs and vast green zones contain other tourist attractions, which are more easily reached by public transportation or taxi. To the east are the **European Parliament** and, beyond that, the **Park of the Cinquantenaire** (Royal Museum of the Army and Military History, Autoworld, and a lesser art museum). Tucked between the Eurocrat campus and the Upper Town is **Matongé,** an African immigrant neighborhood that has become high-rent. And far to the north is the **1958 World's Fair site,** with the Atomium and Mini-Europe.

PLANNING YOUR TIME

For a city of its size and prominence, Brussels can be seen quickly: Its main attraction, the Grand Place, is a short walk from the central train station; several good museums and neighborhoods are also easily walkable. On a quick trip, a day and a night are enough for a good first taste (but if you have more time, Brussels has enjoyable ways to fill it). Or—if you're in a hurry—Brussels can be done as a day trip by train from Bruges, Ghent, or Antwerp (frequent trains, less than an hour from any of these) or a stopover on the Amsterdam-Paris or Amsterdam-Bruges ride (hourly trains).

Below, I've outlined two approaches: One covers a quick stopover and the other is for those who want to linger.

Brussels in Three to Five Hours

Toss your bag in a locker at Central Station and confirm your departure time and station (if you're catching a fast international train, factor in any necessary transit time to the Midi/Zuid/South Station—described on page 122). Then walk about five minutes into town and do this Brussels blitz:

Head directly for the Grand Place and take my Grand Place Walk. To streamline, skip the *Manneken-Pis* until later, and end the walk at the Bourse (stock-exchange building), where you can catch a taxi to Place Royale (Koningsplein). Enjoy the Royal Museums of Fine Arts. If you're rushing to get back to your train, make a beeline to the station; if you have another hour or two to kill, do my Upper Town Walk, which ends near the *Manneken-Pis* and the Grand Place. Buy a box of chocolates and a bottle of Belgian beer, and pop the top as your train pulls out of the station. You did the Brussels blitz.

Brussels in One to Two Days

A full day (with one or two overnights) is about right to get a more complete taste of Brussels. With a second day, you can slow down and really delve into the city.

Day 1

10:00	Get your bearings with my Grand Place Walk.
12:00	Walk up to the Ste. Catherine neighborhood for an early, quick lunch (fresh seafood at Mer du Nord or a sandwich from Crèmerie de Linkebeek).
13:30	Tour the Musical Instruments Museum on your way to the Upper Town.
15:00	Tour the Royal Museums of Fine Arts.
17:00	Follow my Upper Town Walk.
Evening	Relax with a pre-dinner drink on the Grand Place. Then explore some of the interesting neighborhoods

away from the touristy core, and find a good place for dinner: Poke around the fun and colorful streets around Place St-Géry and Ste. Catherine, or venture out to Matongé.

Day 2

If staying for two days, you could do the Grand Place Walk on the first day, and save the art museums and Upper Town Walk for the second day. To fill in the remaining time each day, consider the following options. Very near the Royal Museums, historians enjoy the excellent story of Belgium at the BELvue Museum. In the Lower Town, aficionados of the funny pages head for the Belgian Comic Strip Center (a 15-minute walk from the Grand Place). And political-science majors visit the European Parliament complex for a lesson in Euro-civics (best on weekdays). With more time or a special interest, head out to the museums at the Park of the Cinquantenaire, visit the kitschy former fairgrounds at the giant Atomium, or venture to the adjacent town of Tervuren to tour the Royal Museum of the Belgian Congo and relax in a big park (because of renovations, check to make sure the museum is open).

Brussels Overview

TOURIST INFORMATION

Brussels has two competing TIs (indicative of Belgium's latent Walloon-Flemish tension). The TI at Rue du Marché aux Herbes 63 covers **Brussels and Flanders** (April-Sept Mon-Sat 9:00-18:00, Sun 10:00-17:00, shorter hours off-season; three blocks downhill from Central Station, tel. 02-504-0390, www.visitflanders.com, fun Europe store nearby). They offer free Wi-Fi and several Internet terminals where you can get online for free for up to 15 minutes (and print a few pages—handy for checking in for a flight and printing boarding passes).

The other TI, which focuses on just the **city of Brussels,** is inside the Town Hall on the Grand Place (daily April-Nov 9:00-18:00, shorter hours off-season; tel. 02-513-8940, www.visitbrussels.be).

Both TIs have countless fliers. Day-trippers should pick up a free public transit map. The city map costs €0.50. The €3 *Brussels Guide* booklet is an overview of the city, including a more complete explanation of the city's many museums, and a series of neighborhood walks (including ones focusing on Art Nouveau, comic strips, and shopping). For current listings of concerts and other entertainment options, look for the free weekly magazines *Agenda* (in English, French, and Dutch) and *Brussels Unlimited* (only in English).

Alternative Tourist Information: The excellent, welcoming

USE-IT information office, which is geared toward backpackers, offers free Internet access and Wi-Fi, free coffee and tea, and in-the-know advice about Brussels and other Belgian destinations, including Bruges, Antwerp, and Ghent (Mon-Sat 10:00-13:00 & 14:00-18:00, closed Sun, Quai à la Houille 9B, Metro: Sainte-Catherine/Sint-Katelijne, www.use-it.be). They also publish free user-friendly maps of Brussels and several other Belgian cities; all of their maps are packed with homegrown insight.

Sightseeing Deals: Brussels does not offer a must-have sight-seeing pass. The **Brussels Card,** sold at TIs, provides unlimited public transportation and free entrance to nearly all the major museums (€24/24 hours, €34/48 hours, €40/72 hours, also sold at museums, public transportation offices, and some hotels, www.brusselscard.be). If you're in town for less than a day, it's unlikely this pass will pay for itself. Those using public transit and doing a bit more sightseeing—for example, touring the Royal Museums of Fine Arts, plus a couple of other museums—could get their money's worth. The TIs also offer a deal called **Must of Brussels**—you pay €19 for 10 vouchers that you can mix and match for discounted entries into top sights. Though complicated to figure out, it could save you a few euros (www.mustofbrussels.com).

ARRIVAL IN BRUSSELS
By Train

Brussels has three stations (none of which is officially the "main" train station): Centraal/Central, Midi/Zuid/South, and Nord/Noord/North. Most Brussels-bound trains (except high-speed international trains) stop at all three stations. Central Station is a short walk from the Grand Place and is by far the easiest for arriving sightseers. Pay close attention and ask your conductor for help to ensure you get off at the right stop. If your train doesn't go to Central Station, it's easy to get there by hopping one of the many trains (leaving about every five minutes) that connect the three stations.

Centraal/Central Station

This station, nearest to the sights and my recommended hotels, has handy services: a small grocery store, fast food, waiting rooms, and luggage lockers (between tracks 3 and 4).

You can walk from Central Station to the Grand Place in about five minutes: Following signs inside the station for *Marché aux Herbes/Grasmarkt,* you'll be directed through the Galerie Horta shopping mall, where you'll ride an escalator down, pass a Smurf shop, and pop out 50 yards from the little square nicknamed "Agora." At the far end of this square, turn left to reach the Grand Place, or continue straight ahead to find the big Brussels and Flanders TI on

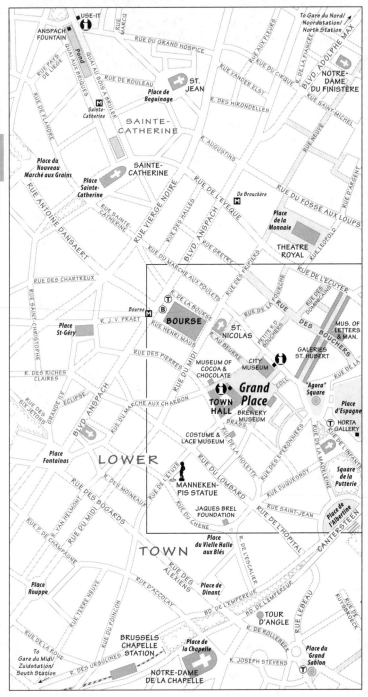

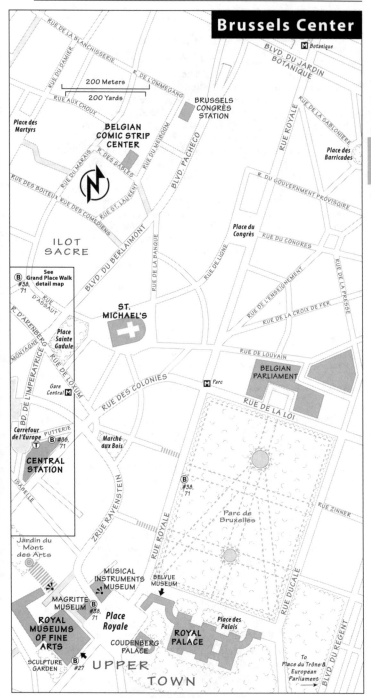

Brussels Center

RUE DE LA BLANCHISSERIE

RUE DU DAMIER

R. DE L'OMMEGANG

BLVD DU JARDIN BOTANIQUE

M Botanique

200 Meters

200 Yards

RUE AUX CHOUX

RUE ROYALE

RUE DE LA SABLONIÈRE

Place des Martyrs

BRUSSELS CONGRÈS STATION

BELGIAN COMIC STRIP CENTER

R. DES SABLES

RUE DU MARAIS

RUE DU MEIBOOM

BLVD. PACHECO

Place des Barricades

RUE DES BOITEUX   RUE DES COMÉDIENS

RUE DU GOUVERNEMENT PROVISOIRE

R. ST. LAURENT

ILOT SACRE

BLVD. DU BERLAIMONT

RUE DE LA BANQUE

RUE DE LIGNE

Place du Congrès   RUE DU CONGRÈS

RUE DE L'ENSEIGNEMENT

RUE DE LA PRESSE

B Grand Place Walk #38, 71
See detail map

RUE D'ASSAUT

R. D'ARENBERG

MONTAGNE

ST. MICHAEL'S

RUE DE LA CROIX DE FER

Place Sainte Gudule

RUE DE LOXUM

RUE DE LOUVAIN

BELGIAN PARLIAMENT

BD. DE L'IMPÉRATRICE

Gare Central M

RUE DES COLONIES

M Parc

RUE DE LA LOI

Carrefour de l'Europe

PUTTERIE

B #38, 71

Marché aux Bois

T

CENTRAL STATION

ISABELLE

B #38, 71

RUE ZINNER

2 RUE RAVENSTEIN

Parc de Bruxelles

Jardin du Mont des Arts

RUE ROYALE

MUSICAL INSTRUMENTS MUSEUM

BELVUE MUSEUM

RUE DUCALE

MAGRITTE MUSEUM

B #38, 71

Place Royale

Place des Palais

ROYAL MUSEUMS OF FINE ARTS

COUDENBERG PALACE

ROYAL PALACE

To Place du Trône & European Parliament

SCULPTURE GARDEN

B #27

UPPER TOWN

BLVD. DU RÉGENT

Brussels Waffles...Linguistically

Brussels is the one part of Belgium that's neither fully French, nor fully Flemish. (It occupies its own bicultural mini-province, near the border between Wallonia and Flanders.) While residents spoke mostly Dutch until 1900, today Brussels is officially bilingual and bicultural. In practice, 65 percent of "Bruxellois" speak French as their first language, and only 5 percent speak Dutch (and call themselves "Brusselaar").

The remaining third of people who call Brussels home aren't Bruxellois, or even Belgian. They are non-natives who speak their own languages. As the unofficial capital of Europe, Brussels is multicultural—it hosts politicians and businesspeople (not to mention immigrants) from around the globe and features a world of ethnic restaurants. The city is home to 400 embassies (the US has three here, one each to the EU, NATO, and Belgium). Every sizable corporation has a lobbyist in Brussels. Most businesspeople, diplomats, and politicians use English as their default. Many predict that in 20 years, English will be the city's de facto first language.

Because the city is officially bilingual, Brussels' street signs and maps are in both French and Dutch. In this book—due to space constraints—I've generally given only the French name. Because the languages are so different (French is a Romance language, Dutch is Germanic), many places have two names that barely resemble each other (for example, Marché aux Herbes/Grasmarkt, or Place Royale/Koningsplein).

your left. If you arrive after 20:00 (18:00 on Sun), when the shopping gallery is closed, you may have to exit through the station's main door upstairs and head downhill on Rue de l'Infante Isabelle to "Agora" square.

Hop-on, hop-off tourist buses depart from Central Station—handy if you want an easy way to get oriented to the city (see "Tours in Brussels," later).

Midi/Zuid/South Station

About a mile and a half southwest of the city center, South Station serves the fastest high-speed international connections, such as Eurostar, Thalys, and TGV (for more on these connections, see page 215). These trains stop only at South Station. (All other trains that stop at South Station also stop at Central and North.)

It's a good idea to know both the French and Dutch names for this station. Instead of one bilingual sign, the names are posted on two different signs, several feet apart from one another. If you see a sign that says *Bruxelles-Midi* or a sign that says *Brussel-Zuid*, don't be confused—you're in the same place.

South Station's tracks are connected by a long, gloomy, gray-steel concourse with ample computer screens showing upcoming trains. High-speed trains use tracks 1-6 (1-2 for Eurostar and 3-6 for the others). The station has plenty of luggage lockers (between tracks 6 and 7), as well as three separate Travel Centre ticket offices (for domestic, international, and international/immediate departures). The area around South Station is a rough-and-tumble immigrant neighborhood (marked by its towering Ferris wheel).

Getting from Midi/Zuid/South Station to Central Station: If you must disembark at South Station, it's easy to make your way to Central Station.

Trains zip under the city, connecting all three stations every few minutes or so. The fare is covered by any train ticket into or out of Brussels (or an activated rail pass). Scan the departure boards for trains leaving in the next few minutes. Even if it doesn't specifically list "Centraal" as a destination, trains headed for many places (the airport, Alost/Aalst, Antwerp, Leuven, Liège, Namur, etc.) will stop there. Once you find a train going to "Centraal" (or the above places), just head to that track. (But note that trains headed in the opposite direction—including those to Ghent and Bruges—have *already* stopped at Central Station.)

Alternatively, you can take a **taxi** from South Station into the city center. It should cost you no more than €10, but cabbies from this station are notorious for taking a roundabout route to overcharge arriving tourists. So insist on the meter, follow the route on a map, and if the total fare seems too high, enlist the help of your hotel receptionist.

Nord/Noord/North Station

Any train that goes through North Station (surrounded by a seedy red light district, far from any significant sightseeing) will also stop at the other two. Don't bother getting off at North Station—disembark at Central Station instead.

By Plane

Brussels is served by two airports. Most flights use the primary Brussels Airport, a.k.a. Zaventem. No-frills carriers use the Brussels South Charleroi Airport. For details on both, see "Brussels Connections" on page 214.

HELPFUL HINTS

Theft Alert: Though the tourist zone—the area within the pentagon-shaped ring road—is basically safe at any hour of day or night, muggings do occur in some rough-and-tumble areas farther afield. (Here's a local joke: The Midi/Zuid/South Station is in a Muslim immigrant neighborhood. The North Station is near a red light district. So they say that as you walk from one end of town to the other, you go from seeing women entirely covered to women entirely uncovered.)

Sightseeing Schedules: Brussels' most important museums are closed on Monday. Of course, the city's single best sight—the Grand Place—is always open. You can also enjoy a bus tour any day of the week, or visit the more far-flung sights (which *are* open on Monday), such as the Atomium/Mini-Europe and the European Parliament's museum. Most importantly, this is a city to browse and wander.

Internet Access: The **Brussels and Flanders TI** and the **USE-IT** information office (both listed earlier) offer free Wi-Fi, as well as free use of their Internet terminals (15-minute limit at the TI). There's also an **Internet café** in a dreary urban area between the Grand Place and Ste. Catherine (€1.50/hour, also cheap calls and printing, calling cabins downstairs, computer terminals upstairs, daily 9:30-23:15, 18 Rue Marché aux Poulets).

Travel Bookstore: Anticyclone des Açores has a wide selection of maps and travel books, including many in English (Mon-Sat 11:00-18:00, closed Sun, Rue Fossé aux Loups 34, tel. 02-217-5246, www.anticyclonedesacores.be).

Laundry: Coin-op launderettes aren't too hard to find. Two are near the Grand Place: one along the lively café and shopping street Rue du Marché au Charbon (Wash Club, at #68, daily 7:00-22:00), and another just around the corner at Rue du Midi 65 (daily 7:00-21:00, change machine). Those sleeping in the Ste. Catherine neighborhood will find one at Rue Flandres 51 (daily 7:00-22:00, no change machine).

Updates to This Book: For updates to this book, check www.ricksteves.com/update.

GETTING AROUND BRUSSELS

Most of central Brussels' sights can be reached on foot. But public transport is handy for connecting the train stations, climbing to the Upper Town, visiting sights outside the central core (the EU, Autoworld, Atomium, or Matongé neighborhood), and getting to Ste. Catherine neighborhood hotels. You might see some public bike stations around town, but for now, the system (called Villo) is designed for locals.

By Public Transportation

A single €2.10 ticket is good for one hour on all public transportation—Métro, buses, trams, and even trains shuttling between Brussels' three train stations. If you're staying long enough to take multiple rides, you can save money with a discounted five-ride card (€8) or 10-ride card (€14). An all-day pass (Discover Brussels 24H) is €7—cheaper than four single tickets—and on Sat-Sun and holidays, this pass covers two people. (Skip the prepaid MOBIB card, which is practical only for locals.)

Buy individual tickets at newsstands, in Métro stations (vending machines accept credit cards or coins), or (for €0.40 extra) from the bus driver. Get multiride cards and passes from the Brussels and Flanders TI or at Métro stations. The excellent, free *Métro Tram Bus Plan* is available at either TI or any Métro station.

Validate your ticket when you enter a bus or tram by feeding it into one of the breadbox-size machines. In the Métro (where locals can scan their electronic tickets directly at the turnstiles), you may need to look around a bit to find the orange machine where you validate your paper ticket. Transit info: tel. 02-515-2000, www.mivb.be.

Brussels' transit stops are labeled in both French and Dutch (though sometimes just one name works in both languages); I've followed suit in this book.

Here are some of the more helpful lines for users of this book:

Métro: Lines 1 and 5 travel east-west through the city, with stops at Sainte-Catherine/Sint-Katelijne (recommended hotels), De Brouckère (more hotels near the Bourse and Grand Place), Gare Central/Centraal Station (trains), Parc/Park (Upper Town), and continuing east to Merode (Cinquantenaire). The other Métro lines are less helpful for travelers. Lines 3 and 4 run north and south through the city, with stops at De Brouckère, Bourse/Beurs, and Gare du Midi/Zuidstation. Métro line 6 takes you to sights far north of downtown (Atomium, near Métro stop Heysel/Heizel).

Buses: Buses #38 and #71 travel roughly east-west, connecting the Lower Town (near Central Station), the Upper Town (Royal Museums), and sights farther east (#38 to the EU, #78 to Matongé). Bus #27 connects the Royal Museums with the European Parliament and the Park of the Cinquantenaire. The hop-on, hop-off buses (described later) can be helpful to get to some outlying sights.

By Taxi

Cabbies charge a €2.40 drop fee, as well as €1.70 per additional kilometer. After 22:00, they hit you with a €2 surcharge. You'll pay about €7 for a ride from the Bourse to the Royal Museums of Fine Arts or from Central Station to the Ste. Catherine neighborhood. Figure €12 to ride from the center to the European Parliament. Convenient taxi stands near the Grand Place are at the Bourse and at the "Agora" square (Rue du Marché aux Herbes). In the Upper Town, try Place du Grand Sablon. To call a cab, ring **Taxi Bleu** (tel. 02-268-0000) or **Autolux** (tel. 02-512-3123).

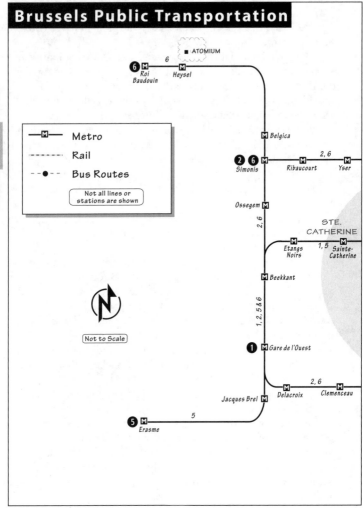

Tours in Brussels

Hop-On, Hop-Off Bus Tours

Two companies—**City Tours** and **CitySightseeing/Open Tours**—offer nearly identical 1.5-hour loops with (mediocre) recorded narration on double-decker buses that go topless on sunny days. You can hop on and off for 24 hours with one ticket. You could use either as a way to get around the city (especially to visit the far-flung European Parliament and Park of the Cinquantenaire), but schedules are sparse. I prefer to just kick back, ride the entire loop, and enjoy

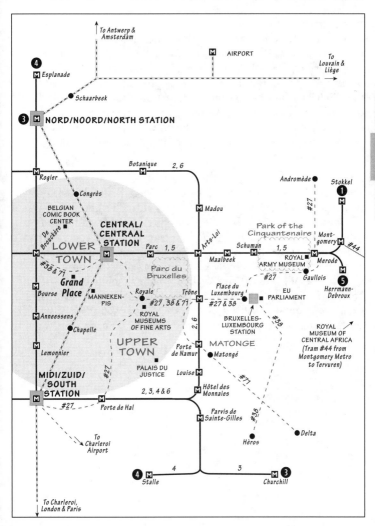

the views. The handiest starting points are at Central Station and the Bourse.

The companies often have hustlers at Central Station trying to get you on board (offering "student" discounts to customers of all ages). Each runs a similar route (check their fliers to find what suits you). Each charges about €20-22 and runs about twice hourly (roughly April-Oct daily 10:00-16:00, Sat until 17:00; Nov-March daily 10:00-15:00, Sat until 16:00; City Tours—tel. 02-513-7744, www.brussels-city-tours.com; CitySightseeing/Open Tours—tel. 02-466-1111, www.citysightseeingbrussel.be).

Bus Tours

City Tours also offers a typical three-hour guided bus tour (in up to five languages), providing you an easy way to get the grand perspective on Brussels. You start with a walk around the Grand Place, then jump on a tour bus (€26, year-round daily at 10:00, they'll pick you up at your hotel or depart from their office a block off Grand Place at Rue du Marché aux Herbes 82; you can buy tickets there, at a TI, or in your hotel; tel. 02-513-7744, www. brussels-city-tours.com). You'll get off the bus at the Atomium for a quick photo stop.

Local Guides

You can hire a private guide through **Visit Brussels** (€117/3 hours, €216/full day, tel. 02-548-0448, guides@visitbrussles.be; I enjoyed the guiding of Didier Rochette). **Claude and Dominique Janssens** are a father-and-son team who lead tours both in Brussels and to other Belgian cities, including Bruges, Ghent, and Antwerp (€120/3 hours, €240/full day plus €25 for lunch, Claude's mobile 0485-025-423, Dominique's mobile 0486-451-155, www.discover-b.be, claude@discover-b.be). **Daniëlle Janssens,** who is based in Bruges, offers a full-day tour of Brussels for €210 (for contact info, see "Local Guides" on page 24).

SIGHTS IN BRUSSELS

The Grand Place may be Brussels' top sight, but the city offers a variety of museums, big and small, to fill your time here. I've divided the sights between the Lower Town, the Upper Town, and the outskirts.

Lower Town

ON THE GRAND PLACE

Brussels' Grand Place—as well as some of the sights fronting it, including the Town Hall, City Museum, and chocolate shops—are described in more detail in the ✪ Grand Place Walk chapter.

▲▲▲Grand Place

Brussels' main square, aptly called the Grand Place (grahn plahs; in Dutch: Grote Markt, *H*ROH-teh markt), is the heart of the old town and Brussels' greatest sight. Any time of day, it's worth swinging by to see what's going on. Concerts, flower markets, sound-and-light shows, endless people-watching—it entertains (as do the streets around it). The museums on the square are well-advertised but dull.

Town Hall (Hôtel de Ville)

With the Grand Place's tallest spire, this is the square's centerpiece, but its interior is no big deal. Admission is only possible with a 45-minute English tour, which also covers city history and the building's tapestries and architecture. Only 25 people are allowed per tour; assure a spot by buying tickets from the guide exactly 40 minutes before the tour starts (in the courtyard behind the spire).

Cost and Hours: €5, English tours offered Wed at 15:00, Sun at 10:00 and 14:00, no Sun tours Oct-March.

▲City Museum (Musée de la Ville de Bruxelles)

Inside the King's House (Maison du Roi) building on the Grand Place, this mildly interesting museum has city history, a roomful of goofy costumes the *Manneken* statue has pissed through, models of old Brussels, and some old tapestries, altarpieces, and paintings. Posted information is in Dutch and French only, but there are English info sheets throughout. Note: For Belgian history, the best choice is not this museum, but the BELvue Museum in the Upper Town (described later).

Cost and Hours: €4, Tue-Sun 10:00-17:00, Thu until 20:00, closed Mon, Grand Place, tel. 02-279-4350, www.museedelavilledebruxelles.be.

Visiting the Museum: Begin your visit on the top floor, and work your way down.

Top Floor: Start with the *Manneken-Pis* outfits. For three centuries, it's been a tradition for the statue to be outfitted in cloth-

ing—the little guy goes through several costume changes each week. Many of the costumes you'll see here were donated by other countries—you'll see everything from a Civil War Union soldier to an El Salvadorian farmer, from a Polish hussar to a Japanese samurai, an Indian maharajah, a Spanish bullfighter, a Russian cosmonaut, and a Fiji islander. There are some 800 costumes in the archives.

A history exhibit explains that Brussels has had a tradition of fountains that spurted through various body parts perhaps dating back a thousand years. Don't bypass the entertaining video showing visitors' reactions to the ridiculous little statue.

The top floor's main hall—under an interesting wood-carved roof—generally has temporary exhibits highlighting the city's history.

Middle Floor: A 20-minute (English) video is a more bite-sized introduction to Brussels history. Find the model of the city in the 13th century. (Get oriented: Uphill is east.) The largest structure back then was St. Michael's Cathedral (northeast). At the top of the model is the Upper Town—which, at this point, hasn't even a

hint of its monumental future. At the bottom of the hill is the (former) River Senne, which was the city's trading lifeline. In between stands the fledgling Grand Place—only a small clearing amid a cluster of houses.

The city was a port town—see the crane unloading barges—since it was at this point that the shallow Senne became navigable. Grain from the area was processed in the watermills, then shipped downstream to Antwerp and on to the North Sea.

By the 1200s, Brussels—though tiny by today's standards—was an important commercial center, and St. Michael's was the region's religious hub. Still, most of the area inside the 2.5-mile-long city wall was farmland, dotted with a few churches, towers, markets, and convents (such as the Carmelite convent hugging the south wall).

Another model (at the far end of the room) shows the city a couple of centuries later—much bigger, but still within the same wall. By this time, the Upper and Lower Towns are clearly defined. In the Upper Town, the huge palace of the dukes of Burgundy marks the site of today's Royal Palace (described on page 172).

Ground Floor: You'll see the original statues that once adorned the Town Hall. The limestone is no match for the corrosive acidic air, so they were brought inside for protection. Also on this floor are a few old paintings (one may be by Jan Brueghel the Elder), fine carved altarpieces, and porcelain. Spend some time with a Brussels specialty—tapestries. With access to great materials (via the thriving cloth trade) and great artists (like Peter Paul Rubens), Brussels cranked out these wall hangings that adorned Europe's homes as both functional insulators and artistic masterpieces.

▲Chocolate Shops on the Grand Place

For many, the best thing about the Grand Place is the chocolate sold at its venerable chocolate shops: Godiva, Neuhaus, Galler, and Leonidas (shops generally open Mon-Sat 9:00-22:00, Sun 10:00-22:00). It takes a lot of sampling to judge. For more info, see the sidebar on page 158.

Brewery Museum

This little basement-level, bar-like place has one room of old brewing paraphernalia and one room of new, plus a beer video in English. It's pretty lame...but a good excuse for a beer.

Cost and Hours: €5 includes an unnamed local beer, daily 10:00-17:00, Grand Place 10, tel. 02-511-4987, www.belgianbrewers.be.

Brussels at a Glance

▲▲▲**Grand Place** Main square and spirited heart of the Lower Town, surrounded by mediocre museums and delectable chocolate shops. **Hours:** Always open. See page 129.

▲▲▲**Royal Museums of Fine Arts of Belgium** Museums displaying Old Masters (14th-18th century), turn-of-the-century art (19th-20th centuries), and works by the prominent Belgian Surrealist painter René Magritte. **Hours:** Tue-Sun 10:00-17:00, closed Mon, Magritte Museum open Wed until 20:00. See page 139.

▲▲*Manneken-Pis* World-famous statue of a leaky little boy. **Hours:** Always peeing. See page 134.

▲▲**BELvue Museum** Interesting Belgian history museum with a focus on the popular royal family. **Hours:** Tue-Fri 9:30-17:00, July-Aug until 18:00, Sat-Sun 10:00-18:00, closed Mon. See page 140.

▲▲**European Parliament** Soaring home of Europe's governing body. **Hours:** Parlamentarium exhibit open Mon 13:00-18:00, Tue-Fri 9:00-18:00, Sat-Sun 10:00-18:00; Parliament tours offered Sept-June Mon-Thu at 10:00 and 15:00, Fri at 10:00; July-Aug Mon-Thu at 10:00, 11:00, 14:00, and 15:00, Fri at 10:00 and 11:00. See page 143.

▲**City Museum** Costumes worn by the *Manneken-Pis* statue and models of Brussels' history. **Hours:** Tue-Sun 10:00-17:00, Thu until 20:00, closed Mon. See page 130.

▲**Costume and Lace Museum** World-famous Brussels lace, as well as outfits, embroidery, and accessories from the 17th-20th centuries. **Hours:** Tue-Sun 10:00-17:00, closed Mon. See page 134.

▲**Museum of Letters and Manuscripts** Modest museum preserving papers from popes to Picasso. **Hours:** Tue-Fri 10:00-18:00, Sat-Sun 11:00-18:00, closed Mon. See page 135.

▲**St. Michael's Cathedral** White-stone Gothic church where Belgian royals are married and buried. **Hours:** Mon-Fri 7:00-18:00, Sat-Sun 8:30-18:00. See page 136.

▲**Belgian Comic Strip Center** Homage to hometown heroes including the Smurfs, Tintin, and Lucky Luke. **Hours:** Tue-Sun 10:00-18:00, closed Mon. See page 136.

▲**Musical Instruments Museum** Exhibits with more than 1,500 instruments, complete with audio. **Hours:** Tue-Fri 9:30-17:00, Sat-Sun 10:00-17:00, closed Mon. See page 140.

▲**Autoworld** Hundreds of historic vehicles, including Mr. Benz's 1886 motorized tricycle. **Hours:** Daily April-Sept 10:00-18:00, shorter hours off-season. See page 148.

▲**Royal Army and Military History Museum** Vast collection of weaponry and uniforms. **Hours:** Tue-Fri 9:00-17:00, Sat-Sun 10:00-18:00, closed Mon. See page 149.

▲**Matongé** African immigrant district, with international eateries and fine turn-of-the-century architecture. **Hours:** Always open. See page 151.

▲**Royal Museum of Central Africa** Excellent but far-flung exhibit about the former Belgian Congo, featuring ethnology, artifacts, and wildlife (closed for renovation until mid-2017). See page 154.

Town Hall Focal point of the Grand Place, with arresting spire but boring interior. **Hours:** Tours depart Wed at 15:00, Sun at 10:00 and 14:00, no Sun tours Oct-March. See page 129.

Royal Belgian Institute of Natural Sciences Europe's largest dinosaur gallery. **Hours:** Tue-Fri 9:30-17:00, Sat-Sun 10:00-18:00, closed Mon. See page 148.

Cinquantenaire Museum Eclectic but unexciting art and archaeology museum. **Hours:** Tue-Fri 9:30-17:00, Sat-Sun 10:00-17:00, closed Mon. See page 150.

Atomium Giant homage to the atomic age with fun exhibit and panorama deck. **Hours:** Exterior always viewable; interior open daily 10:00-18:00. See page 153.

Mini-Europe Models of 350 famous European landmarks. **Hours:** Daily mid-March-Sept 9:30-18:00, July-Aug until 20:00, Oct-Dec 10:00-18:00, closed Jan-mid-March. See page 154.

Museum of Cocoa and Chocolate

This touristy exhibit, just off the Grand Place to the right of Town Hall, is a delightful concept and tries hard, but it's overpriced. Its three floors feature meager displays, a ho-hum video, a look at a "chocolate master" at work (live demos 2/hour), and a choco-sample.

Cost and Hours: €5.50, Tue-Sun 10:00-16:30, closed Mon, Rue de la Tête d'Or 9, tel. 02-514-2048, www.mucc.be.

SOUTH OF THE GRAND PLACE

▲▲*Manneken-Pis*

Brussels is a great city with a cheesy mascot: a statue of a little boy urinating (apparently symbolizing the city's irreverence and love of the good life). Read up on his story at any postcard stand. He's three short blocks off the Grand Place: For directions, take my Grand Place Walk; look for small, white *Manneken-Pis* signs; or just ask a local, *"Où est le Manneken-Pis?"* (oo ay luh man-ay-kehn peese). The little squirt may be wearing some clever outfit, as costumes are sent to Brussels from around the world. Cases full of these are on display in the City Museum (described earlier). Be warned: Some people adore the wee tyke, while others abhor him. Take a peek and make up your own mind. The tourist hubbub and frantic selfie derby on this street corner is as much of a sight as the statue itself.

▲Costume and Lace Museum
(Musée du Costume et de la Dentelle)

This fine little museum, a block off the Grand Place, showcases rotating exhibits of historic costumes and fashion as well as the art of lace. You'll enjoy exquisite costumes, feathery fans, and baby baptismal gowns. As the lace is fragile, much of it is stored in drawers—be sure to pull them out. At the entry, borrow the necessary English booklet that describes each showpiece.

Cost and Hours: €4, Tue-Sun 10:00-17:00, closed Mon, Rue de la Violette 12, a block off the Grand Place, tel. 02-213-4450, www.museeducostumeetdeladentelle.be.

WEST OF THE GRAND PLACE

These two fun-to-explore neighborhoods, just across the busy Boulevard Anspach from the Bourse, offer some of Brussels' most appealing restaurants (far less touristy than those near the Grand Place). Ste. Catherine is also a fine place to sleep. If you're looking for a bustling nighttime neighborhood full of inviting eateries and bars, you'll enjoy strolling these two areas and the five-minute walk between them.

Ste. Catherine and the Old Fish Market
(Vieux Marché aux Poissons)

Two blocks northwest of the Bourse is the ragtag Church of Ste. Catherine, which marks an inviting "village in the city" area with great eating options. The church itself is falling apart—during its construction, the architect got the commission for the Place of Justice in the Upper Town, and rushed to complete this church so he could begin the more lucrative new job as quickly as possible. In front of the church stretches the long, skinny former fish market, lined with a range of upscale fish restaurants. Alongside the church is Place Ste. Catherine (Sint-Katelijneplein), with more restaurants, bars, and the city's best cheap-and-fast lunch options (see page 206 for recommended eateries in this area).

Place St-Géry

This square—called Sint-Goriksplein in Dutch—was actually once an island. The market hall in the middle of the square evokes a

time when goods—which were offloaded a few blocks away, at the old fish market—were brought here for sale. Today the hall houses a café and special exhibits. On Sunday mornings, the surrounding square is filled with a comics market. Across from the southwest corner of the hall, at #23 (next to the *Au Lion d'Or* information board), duck through the little gateway to find a relaxing courtyard. You might see businesspeople dozing on their lunch break here in this oasis in the heart of the city. At the far end of the courtyard you'll see a small stretch of the river that used to be Brussels' trading lifeline, but was long ago covered over and forgotten.

EAST OF THE GRAND PLACE
▲Museum of Letters and Manuscripts
(Musée des Lettres et Manuscrits)

Located inside the Galeries Hubert, this small museum contains letters, books, and memorabilia from famous artists, writers, scientists, and composers. The permanent collection is on the top floor, and temporary exhibits are on the ground floor. There's enough English info to get you started.

Find your favorite celebrities from history. See a letter from Van Gogh, a postcard by Picasso, and doodles by Dalí. There's a papal bull of Pope Alexander III (1179) and competing edicts from French King Louis XVI and his nemesis Robespierre. You'll see Mozart's music, Einstein's equations, books by Hemingway and Voltaire, and scientific texts from Newton to Freud to Curie. Belgians are represented by artist René Magritte, the cartoonist Hergé, and singer Jacques Brel.

Cost and Hours: €7, includes temporary exhibition, Tue-Fri 10:00-18:00, Sat-Sun 11:00-18:00, closed Mon, Galerie du Roi 1, tel. 02-514-7187, www.mlmb.be.

▲St. Michael's Cathedral

One of Europe's classic Gothic churches, built between roughly 1200 and 1500, Brussels' cathedral is made from white stone and topped by twin towers. For nearly 1,000 years, it's been the most important church in this largely Catholic country. (Whereas the Netherlands went in a Protestant direction in the 1500s, Belgium remains 80 percent Catholic—although only about 20 percent attend Mass.)

Cost and Hours: Free, but small fees to visit the underwhelming crypt and treasury, Mon-Fri 7:00-18:00, Sat-Sun 8:30-18:00.

Visiting the Cathedral: The white-themed nave is bare but impressive, with a few nice stained-glass windows and a marvelous carved pulpit of Adam and Eve supporting the preacher. On top, St. Michael stabs Satan in serpent form.

This church is where royal weddings and funerals take place. Photographs (to the right of the entrance) show the funeral of the popular King Baudouin, who died in 1993. He was succeeded by his younger brother, Albert II, who abdicated in 2014 to allow his son, Philippe, to become king. (Belgium's newest euro coins show Philippe, but older ones with Albert will stay in circulation for years.) Traditionally, the ruler was always a male, but in 1992 the constitution was changed to allow the oldest child of either gender—boy or girl—to take the throne. King Philippe and Queen Mathilde's first child was a daughter—Elisabeth, born in 2001—so she is next in line for the throne.

Before leaving, pause on the outer porch to enjoy the great view of the Town Hall spire with its gold statue of St. Michael.

▲Belgian Comic Strip Center
(Centre Belge de la Bande Dessinée)

Belgians are as proud of their comics as they are of their beer, lace, and chocolates. Something about the comic medium resonates with the wry and artistic-yet-unpretentious Belgian sensibility. Belgium has produced some of the world's most popular comic characters, including the Smurfs, Tintin, and Lucky Luke. You'll find these, and many less famous local comics, at the Comic Strip Center. It's

Tintin 101

The Belgian comic character Tintin is beloved to several generations of Europeans. He's increasingly known in the US,

thanks to translations of his adventures and Steven Spielberg's 2011 Tintin film, which won the Golden Globe for best animated feature.

In 1929, Brussels cartoonist Georges Rémi (1907-1983), using the pseudonym Hergé, created a dedicated young reporter with a shock of blond hair who's constantly getting into and out of misadventures. A precise artist, Hergé used a simple, uncluttered style with clear lines and appealing color.

Combining fantasy, mystery, and sci-fi with a dash of humor, the Tintin stories quickly found an appreciative audience. *The Adventures of Tintin* spanned 47 years and 24 books (selling some 200 million copies—and counting—in 50 languages). Tintin's popularity continues even today, as nostalgic parents buy the comics they grew up on for their own kids.

Tintin is the smart, upbeat, inquisitive, noble, brave-but-not-foolhardy young man whose adventures propel the plot. His newspaper sends him on assignments all over the world. Snowy, Tintin's loyal fox terrier, is his constant canine companion—and often saves the day. The grizzled, grouchy, heavy-drinking Captain Haddock is as cynical as Tintin is optimistic, with a penchant for colorful curses ("Blistering barnacles!"). Professor Calculus is as brilliant as he is absentminded and hard of hearing, and comic relief is provided by the bumbling, nearly identical detectives called Thomson and Thompson.

Throughout his swashbuckling adventures, Tintin travels far and wide to many exotic destinations. Hergé has been acclaimed for his meticulous research—he studied up on the actual places he portrayed and tried to avoid basing his stories on assumptions or stereotypes (though by today's standards, some of the comics still betray an ugly Eurocentrism—one of the earliest, *Tintin in the Congo,* Hergé himself later acknowledged was regrettably racist).

And though the supporting characters are dynamic and colorful, Tintin himself has a rather bland personality. His expressions are usually indistinct (Hergé wanted the young reader to project his or her own emotions onto Tintin's blank-canvas face). While presumably a teenager, Tintin's age is unclear—at times we imagine him to be a young boy, while others he's seen drinking a beer, piloting a plane, or living in his own apartment (we never meet his family, if he has one). All of this is intentional: Hergé's style subconsciously encourages readers to put themselves in Tintin's everyman shoes.

not a wacky, lighthearted place, but a serious museum about a legitimate artistic medium.

Even if you don't have time or interest to visit the museum's collection, pop in to the lobby to see the groundbreaking Art Nouveau building (a former department store  designed in 1903 by Belgian architect Victor Horta), browse through comics in the bookshop, and snap a photo with a three-foot-tall Smurf. That's enough for many people. Kids might find the museum, like, totally boring, but those who appreciate art in general will enjoy this sometimes humorous, sometimes probing, often beautiful medium. Most of the cartoons are in French and Dutch, but descriptions come in English. Borrow the free, English guide-booklet to read short bios of famous cartoonists.

Cost and Hours: €8, Tue-Sun 10:00-18:00, closed Mon, 10-minute walk from the Grand Place to Rue des Sables 20, tel. 02-219-1980, www.comicscenter.net.

Getting There: From Central Station, walk north along the big boulevard, then turn left down the stairs at the giant comic character (Gaston Lagaffe).

Visiting the Museum: The collection changes often, but no matter what's on you'll see how comics are made and watch early animated films. The heart of the collection is the golden age of comics in the 1950s and 1960s. You'll likely see a sprawling exhibit on Tintin, the intrepid young reporter with the button eyes and wavy shock of hair, launched in 1929 by Hergé and much loved by older Europeans (see sidebar). Brussels' own Peyo (a.k.a. Pierre Culliford, 1928-1992) invented the Smurfs—the little blue forest creatures that stand "three apples high." First popular across much of Europe, especially in Belgium (where they're known as Les Schtroumpfs), the Smurfs became well-known to a generation of Americans after they starred in Hanna-Barbera's 1980s televised cartoons. In this century, they've won over a new generation with a series of major movies. The cowboy Lucky Luke (by Morris, a.k.a. Maurice De Bevere, 1923-2001) exemplifies Belgians' fascination for exotic locales, especially America's Wild West.

The top floor's temporary exhibits are often dedicated to "serious" comics, where more adult themes and high-quality drawing aspire to turn kids' stuff into that "Ninth Art." These works can be grimly realistic, openly erotic or graphic, or darker in tone, often featuring flawed antiheroes. The museum's bookstore is nearly as interesting, giving you the chance to page through reproductions of classic comics.

Nearby: The related **Marc Sleen Museum,** across the street, is dedicated to the oh-so-typically Belgian cartoonist whose big-nosed, caricatured drawings are recognizable even to many Americans. Sleen's *Adventures of Nero and Co.,* which he churned out in two strips a day for a staggering 55 years, holds the record for the longest-running comic by a single artist. Still, the collection is worth a visit only to his fans (€1 extra with Comic Strip Center entry, or €2.50 alone; Tue-Sun 11:00-18:00, closed Mon; tel. 02-219-1980, www.marc-sleen.be).

Other Comic Sights: If you're a Belgian comics completist, consider visiting the **Museum of Original Figurines (MOOF),** at the entrance to the Horta Gallery at the lower end of Central Station (a few steps from "Agora" square). They feature changing exhibits of colorful figurines of your favorite Belgian characters (closed Mon, www.moofmuseum.be). A handy **Smurf Store** is next door.

Upper Town

Brussels' grandiose Upper Town, with its huge palace, is described in the ✪ Upper Town Walk chapter. Along that walk, you'll pass the following sights (for locations, see map on page 171).

▲▲▲Royal Museums of Fine Arts of Belgium (Musées Royaux des Beaux-Arts de Belgique)

This sprawling complex houses a trio of museums showing off the country's best all-around art collection. The **Old Masters Muse-**

um—featuring Flemish and Belgian art of the 14th through 18th centuries—is packed with a dazzling collection of masterpieces by Van der Weyden, Bruegel, Bosch, and Rubens. The **Fin-de-Siècle Museum** covers art of the late 19th and early 20th centuries, including an extensive Art Nouveau collection. The **Magritte Museum** contains more than 200 works by the Surrealist painter René Magritte. Although you won't see many of Magritte's most famous pieces, this lovingly presented museum offers an unusually intimate look at the life and work of one of Belgium's top artists.

Cost and Hours: €8 for each museum, €13 combo-ticket covers all three, free first Wed of month after 13:00; open Tue-Sun 10:00-17:00, closed Mon, Magritte Museum open Wed until 20:00, last entry 30 minutes before closing; audioguides cost €4-5 depending on museum, tour booklet-€2.50, pricey cafeteria with salad bar, Rue de la Régence 3, tel. 02-508-3211, www.fine-arts-museum.be or www.musee-magritte-museum.be.

▲Musical Instruments Museum
(Musée des Instruments de Musique)

One of Europe's best music museums (nicknamed "MIM") is housed in one of Brussels' most impressive Art Nouveau buildings, the beautifully renovated Old England department store. This museum has more than 1,500 instruments—from Egyptian harps, to medieval lutes, to groundbreaking harpsichords, to the Brussels-built saxophone.

Inside you'll be given an included audioguide and set free to wander several levels: musical mechanics like radios and organs on the lower floor, folk instruments from around the world on the first floor, a history of Western musical instruments on the second, and rotating special exhibits on the fourth. As you approach an instrument, you hear it playing on your headphones. On the fifth floor is an exhibit about the history of the building and Brussels Art Nouveau in general. The displays lack complete English descriptions, but the music you'll hear is an international language.

Cost and Hours: €8, Tue-Fri 9:30-17:00, Sat-Sun 10:00-17:00, closed Mon, last entry 45 minutes before closing, mandatory free coat and bag check, Rue Montagne de la Cour 2, just downhill and toward Grand Place from the Royal Museums, tel. 02-545-0130, www.mim.be.

Eating with City Views: The 10th floor has a restaurant, a terrace, and a great view of Brussels (€10-15 *plats du jour,* same hours as museum, pick up free access pass at museum entrance). The corner alcoves on each level (accessible as you tour the museum) have even better views.

▲▲BELvue Museum

This earnest museum is the best introduction to modern Belgian history (1830-2000) you'll find in Brussels. It's chronological, self-

contained, well-described in English, and spiced up with a few videos. But it's also Belgian history—so it is what it is.

Cost and Hours: €6, €10 combo-ticket includes Coudenberg Palace; Tue-Fri 9:30-17:00, July-Aug until 18:00, Sat-Sun 10:00-18:00, closed Mon; audioguide-€2.50, to the right of the palace at Place des Palais 7, tel. 070-220-492, www.belvue.be.

Eating: Healthy lunches are served

in the cool "Green Kitchen" café in the lobby and leafy courtyard of this former princess' palace (€10-15 plates, same hours as museum).

Visiting the Museum: To make the most of your visit, focus on the highlights I describe here. Then get additional details on individual exhibits from the excellent English brochure or rent the (almost identical) audioguide.

First Floor: A video sets the stage by showing the changing map of Europe from 1000 to 1830. Room 1 takes you back to September 1830: Revolution was in the air, and mobs and soldiers were squaring off right outside (today's) BELvue Museum. Belgium won its independence from the Netherlands and chose a new king to move into the palace next door.

Rooms 2-4 show the young nation's growing pains: rapid industrialization, the expansion of Brussels, its World's Fairs and colony in the Congo, as well as the struggle between its Francophone-dominated ruling class and its generally Flemish peasant class. Room 5 chronicles the devastation of World War I, when tiny Belgium was swamped by a brutal German invasion.

Second Floor: Belgium recovered but faced the growing menace of fascism (Room 6). Hitler invaded (Room 7), and Belgium surrendered 18 days later. The nation hunkered down under Nazi occupation: Jews were rounded up, but resistance fighters kept the hope alive. Next, in Room 8, comes postwar Belgium's recovery—the optimism of the 1950s, the World's Fair that produced the Atomium, a flood of consumer goods, and the arrival of rock music (now in glorious color).

Later, Brussels emerged as the unofficial capital of Europe, a symbol of international cooperation. A video in Room 9 traces the growth of the EU from Benelux in 1948 to today. But Belgium remained divided within. Even now, the Flemish-Walloon conflict festers, and there is a struggle to prevent Belgium from splitting completely in half.

Royal Family Exhibits: Throughout the museum, the hallways feature the royal family with paintings, photos, and biographical sketches. It's clear the dynasty is generally appreciated, even loved. Since these imported German monarchs arrived in 1830, each of the seven "Kings of the Belgians" (as they're officially known) has had his own style and claim to fame. Leopold I was the visionary who united the young nation. Leopold II was the "Builder King" and Congo exploiter. Albert I guided Belgium through World War I—only 30,000 Belgian troops died. Controversial World War II-era Leopold III was tainted after his attempt to negotiate with Hitler, and later abdicated in disgrace. Baudouin (r. 1950-1993) restored respect for the monarchy. His equally popular brother became King Albert II. Albert's son Philippe now reigns as king; the royal family includes his wife Mathilde, two princes (Gabriel and Emmanuel), and two princesses (Elisabeth and Eléonore).

Coudenberg Palace

The BELvue Museum stands atop the barren archaeological remains of a 12th-century Brussels palace. Though well-lit and well-described, these long, vaulted cellars require too much imagination to make them meaningful. A small museum explains artifacts from the palace. The best thing is the free orientation video you see before descending. If you do tour the palace ruins, do so after you're finished at the BELvue Museum, because you'll exit the Coudenberg downhill, near the Musical Instruments Museum.

Cost and Hours: €6, €10 combo-ticket includes BELvue Museum; €2.50 audioguide does not cover BELvue Museum, yet must be (inconveniently) returned to BELvue entrance; same hours as BELvue Museum.

East of Downtown

Two clusters of sights lie just east of the city center: the European Parliament (where you can learn about the European Union and tour the complex) and the Park of the Cinquantenaire (with three museums: cars, the military, and art). Between these areas and central Brussels is the neighborhood called Matongé—a fascinating blend of African immigrants and trendy Eurocrats, and a fun place to grab a bite to eat post-sightseeing.

Planning Your Time: Before making the trip out here, read ahead to decide what interests you and where to spend your time. (Frankly, for some people, none of these sights is worth the trip.) Because the areas are connected by a quick bus ride, it's easy to visit both in one excursion (about 4-5 hours).

Here's a suggested itinerary for seeing them both:

Start with the Park of the Cinquantenaire. Take Métro line 1 or 5 from the city center (e.g., from Métro stop De Brouckère or Sainte-Catherine/Sint-Katelijne) to the Park of the Cinquantenaire (Métro stop: Merode). Ascending from the Merode stop, you'll see the grand arch of the Cinquantenaire complex, which houses the three museums.

After visiting the museums, take a bus to the European Parliament. Catch bus #27 behind the Autoworld building on Avenue des Gaulois (bus stop: Gaulois/Galliërs, direction: Gare du Midi/Zuidstation, 4-5/hour Mon-Fri, 2-3/hour Sat-Sun) to the Luxembourg stop. Arriving at Place du Luxembourg, you immediately see a group of modern gray-and-glass buildings—the EU complex. After your European Parliament visit, catch bus #38 to the city center (or walk to the Matongé district). You're back. It was cheap and easy, and you'll feel quite clever doing it.

The best days to visit both areas are Tuesdays through Fridays, as some Cinquantenaire museums are closed on Mondays, and the European Parliament is pretty dead on weekends.

▲▲EUROPEAN PARLIAMENT

Europe's governing body welcomes visitors with an exhibit about the EU, an entertaining information center, and audioguide tours.

This sprawling complex of modern glass buildings is a babel of black-suited politicians speaking 24 different Euro-languages. It's exciting just to be here—a fly on the wall of a place that aspires to chart the future of Europe "with respect for all political thinking...consolidating democracy in the spirit of peace and solidarity." The 766 parliament members, representing 28 countries and more than 500 million citizens, shape Europe with a €140 billion budget.

Getting There: The European Parliament is next to Place du Luxembourg. Bus #38 heads here from Central Station or the Royal Museums while bus #27 comes from the Royal Museums or the museums at the Park of the Cinquantenaire. Place du Luxembourg is also a seven-minute walk from the Trône/Troon Métro stop (straight ahead up Luxembourg street—Europe's K Street which teems with lobbyists). Once at Place du Luxembourg, the sprawling gray-and-glass EU complex is right there—approach it and you'll find signs directing you to its three main visitor sights: the Parlamentarium, Info Point, and Visit EP (touring the actual Parliament building). To return to the old center, catch bus #38 departing from in front of the Gare de Bruxelles-Luxembourg/Station Brussels-Luxemburg just to the right as you leave the EU center.

Parlamentarium

This high-tech, fun, informative museum is designed to let you meet the EU and understand how it works. Pick up your free audioguide headset and wander through its many exhibits. You'll learn about how the EU came to be and the many challenges it has faced; "meet" virtual EU parliamentarians; find out about some of Europe's most powerful, transnational political parties and movements; cast your own vote regarding recent hot-button EU issues; and get a rundown of each EU country's culture, commerce, and

contemporary challenges. The touchscreens, audioguide, videos, and other interactive exhibits bring the story of the EU to life. While this is a convenient place to kill time waiting for your tour of the Parliament, consider returning afterwards to delve deeper into all it has to offer.

Cost and Hours: Free, Mon 13:00-18:00, Tue-Fri 9:00-18:00, Sat-Sun 10:00-18:00, www.europarl.europa.eu/visiting.

Info Point Visitors Center

This welcoming visitors center has racks of entertaining freebies—including maps outlining the member states, the free *Troubled Waters* comic book that explains how the parliament works, and bins of miniature *My Fundamental Rights in the EU* booklets—everything in 24 different languages, of course.

Cost and Hours: Free, Mon-Thu 9:00-17:15, Fri 9:00-13:00, closed Sat-Sun.

Parliament Tours

The only way to get inside the European Parliament itself is to join a free 45-minute audioguide tour. While you can't make an advance reservation, you can drop by the starting point up to 30 minutes before the tour to pick up your free ticket. You can spend

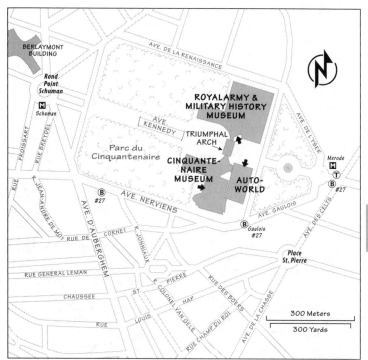

your waiting time at the Parlamentarium or check out the slice of the Berlin Wall in the scruffy park a few steps from the tour point.

Cost and Hours: Free, tours offered Sept-June Mon-Thu at 10:00 and 15:00, Fri at 10:00; July-Aug Mon-Thu at 10:00, 11:00, 14:00, and 15:00, Fri at 10:00 and 11:00; busiest on Mon.

Getting There: The Parliament building is behind the main complex, a five-minute walk from the Info Point—follow *Visit EP* signs.

Visiting the Parliament: When you check in, you'll be sent through security and given an audioguide. Head up the stairs and wait for your tour to begin in the atrium, with exhibits and a gift shop. At the appointed time, your escort leads you to various view-points in the complex where you'll be instructed to listen to the related audioguide commentary.

The informative but slow-paced audioguide—with helpful video illustrations—takes you through the history of the EU, as well as its current structure and procedures. You'll learn how early visionary utopians (like Churchill, who in 1946 called for a "United States of Europe" to avoid future wars) led the way as Europe grad-ually evolved into the European Union (1992).

From the balcony overlooking the building's lobby, you can see

BRUSSELS SIGHTS

The European Union

Brussels is the capital of one of the biggest, most powerful, and most idealistic states in the world (and, arguably, in history): the European Union (EU). In just one generation, more than two dozen European countries have gone from being bitter rivals to compatriots. This union of such a diverse collection of separate nations—with different languages, cultures, and soccer teams—is almost unprecedented. And it all started in the rubble of a devastating war.

World War II left 40 million dead and a continent in ruins, and it convinced Europeans that they had to work together to maintain peace. Poised between competing superpowers (the US and the USSR), they also needed to cooperate economically to survive in an increasingly globalized economy. Just after the war ended, visionary "Eurocrats" began the task of convincing reluctant European nations to relinquish elements of their sovereignty and merge into a united body.

The transition happened very gradually, in fits and starts. It began in 1948, when Belgium, the Netherlands, and Luxembourg—jointly called "BeNeLux"—established a free-trade zone. That evolved into an ever-broadening alliance of states (the European Coal and Steel Union, then the European Economic Community, or "Common Market"). In 1992, with the Treaty of Maastricht, the 12 member countries of the Common Market made a leap of faith: They created a "European Union" that would eventually allow for free movement of capital, goods, services, and labor (that is, people).

In 2002, most EU members adopted a single currency (the euro), and for all practical purposes, economic unity was a reality. Additional member states now bring the total to 28—encompassing the British Isles, nearly all of Western Europe, and much of Eastern Europe and Scandinavia. Almost all EU members have joined the open-borders Schengen Agreement, making passport checkpoints obsolete. This makes the EU the world's seventh-

the giant *Confluence* sculpture with moving metal-wire pieces—representing people coming together for a common purpose. The audio-guide tells you all about the building itself: In line with EU idealism, it's functional, transparent, and very "green."

The grand finale is the vast

largest "country" (1.7 million square miles), with the third-largest population (more than 500 million people), and an economy that matches the US's as the world's biggest (around $16 trillion GDP).

The EU is governed from Brussels. While it has a parliament, the EU is primarily led by the European Commission (with commissioners appointed by individual member governments and approved by its parliament) and the Council of Ministers. Daily business is conducted by an army of bureaucrats and policy wonks.

Unlike America's federation of 50 states, Europe's member states retain the right to opt out of some EU policies. Britain, for example, belongs to the EU but hasn't adopted the euro as its currency. While the 2009 Lisbon Treaty streamlines EU responses to conflicts and issues, there's no unified foreign or economic policy among the member countries. The EU also lacks a powerful chief executive—the president of the European Council, appointed for a two-and-a-half-year term, is much weaker than the US president, as EU laws require consensus on taxes, foreign policy, defense, and social programs.

The EU is currently financing an ambitious 21st-century infrastructure of roads, high-speed trains, high-tech industries, and communication networks. The goal is to create a competitive, sustainable, environmentally friendly economy that improves the quality of life for all Europeans.

Still, many "Euroskeptics" remain unconvinced that the EU is a good thing. Some chafe at the highly regulated business environment and high taxes. They complain about the bureaucracy and worry that their national cultures will be swallowed up and Euro-fied. The wealthier member countries (mostly in the north) are reluctant to bail out their economically unsound compatriots (mostly in the south) in order to prop up the euro, while the troubled countries resent the cuts demanded by the richer ones.

Despite the problems facing them, Europeans don't want to go back to the days of division and strife. Most recognize that a strong, unified Europe is necessary to keep the peace and compete in a global economy.

BRUSSELS SIGHTS

"hemicycle," where the members of the European Parliament sit. Here you'll listen to a political-science lesson about the all-Europe system of governance. Parliamentarians representing 160 different national political parties, organized into seven different voting blocs based on political ideals (rather than nationality), hash out pan-European issues in this hall.

With the president facing them, they're seated from left to right—both literally and politically—which means that from their own perspective, they sit on the "wrong" side of the hall. This is done to foster empathy. Although most parliamentarians can speak English, in this setting they are encouraged to talk in their mother tongues—ensuring they will be fully comfortable in expressing their thoughts. That makes this the largest multilingual operation on the planet, with a very busy army of translators, who simultaneously translate every word into all 24 official languages. Yet somehow things get done; recent pieces of legislation include preserving "Internet neutrality," creating a European banking union, and imposing a cap on carbon dioxide emissions.

Nearby: The worthwhile **Royal Belgian Institute of Natural Sciences** (Institut Royal des Sciences Naturelles de Belgique) sits practically next door to the European Parliament. Dinosaur enthusiasts come here for the world's largest collection of iguanodon skeletons (€7, Tue-Fri 9:30-17:00, Sat-Sun 10:00-18:00, closed Mon, last entry 30 minutes before closing, Rue Vautier 29, tel. 02-627-4211, www.naturalsciences.be).

PARK OF THE CINQUANTENAIRE MUSEUMS

Standing proudly in a big park in eastern Brussels is a trio of sprawling museums housed in cavernous halls: the Royal Army and Military History Museum, Autoworld, and the Cinquantenaire Museum. These attractions thrill specialists but bore most others.

The complex itself is interesting to see. There's a huge Neoclassical triumphal arch, and the place is surrounded by a spacious park (Parc du Cinquantenaire). It has a grandiose history: The ambitious 19th-century Belgian King Leopold II wanted Brussels to rival Paris. In 1880, he celebrated the 50th anniversary *(cinquantenaire)* of Belgian independence by building the arch flanked by massive exhibition halls, which today house the museums.

Getting There: Take Métro line 1 or 5 from the city center to Métro stop Merode. Exit the Métro station following signs to *Yser/IJzer,* then cross the street toward the big arch. Other options: Take bus #27 from the Upper Town (Royale/Koning) to the Gaulois/Galliërs stop or consider a hop-on-hop-off bus (see page 126).

▲Autoworld

A cavernous hall filled with 400 historic cars shows the vast array of motorized vehicles built over the last century-plus. The place is made for just browsing—each car is clearly labeled. There's an audioguide and some English descriptions, but for much of it, you're left to either bring your own knowledge or simply admire the high-polish gleam.

Cost and Hours: €9, includes audioguide, daily April-Sept 10:00-18:00, shorter hours off-season, in Palais Mondial, Parc du Cinquantenaire 11, tel. 02-736-4165, www.autoworld.be.

Visiting the Museum: Start by tracing the history of automobiles, decade-by-decade, along the right wall. (But first up, admire the humongous green 1929 Minerva sedan at the entrance—a rarity by Belgium's best-known automaker.)

As you work your way counterclockwise through the ground floor, you'll see the first handmade cars—basically converted horse carriages. Then comes mass production (introduced by America's Henry Ford) and the big luxury cars of the 1920s. During the Great Depression, small economy cars were in vogue—France's Citroën and Hitler's brainchild, the Volkswagen. It was Hitler and Mussolini who built the first freeways to quickly mobilize troops in wartime. The postwar years produced monstrous gas-guzzling cars for the suburban masses—particularly in America.

Head upstairs to the sporty '60s, the fuel-efficient '70s (after the Arab oil embargo of 1973), and the international brands of the '80s and '90s. Then just browse the rest of this vast collection. Besides historic cars, Autoworld always features some of the latest and hottest designs. Vroom.

▲Royal Army and Military History Museum (Musée Royal de l'Armée et d'Histoire Militaire)

Wander through this enormous collection of weaponry, uniforms, tanks, warplanes, and endless exhibits about military history, focusing on the 19th and 20th centuries. The museum is filled with real, tangible history. This impressively complete museum made me want to watch my favorite war movies all over again. It's a nirvana for

fans of military history and aviation, but skippable for those who think a "panzer" is a pretty flower. Current renovation work might close some sections—especially parts of the aviation wing—during your visit, and staff cuts may temporarily close some sections midday.

Cost and Hours: Free; Tue-Fri 9:00-17:00, Sat-Sun 10:00-18:00, closed Mon; audioguide-€3 (available

9:00-11:30 & 13:00-16:30), Parc du Cinquantenaire 3, tel. 02-737-7811, www.klm-mra.be. Much of the museum (except for the aviation section) closes from 12:00 to 13:00.

Visiting the Museum: Exploring the whole place is exhausting, so be selective and use the floor plan and directional signs to navigate. Each item is labeled in French and Dutch, but some good English descriptions are available; to get the most out of your visit, renting the audioguide is essential.

Here's how I'd tour the place. From the entrance, go straight ahead, through the Belgian military history section—seeing Belgian flags, cannons, uniforms, and Leopold II's tricycle (midway along). This leads to exhibits on World War I and World War II (which, naturally, are strong on the role of Belgium). The grand finale is the vast (and I mean vast) aviation hall filled with warplanes. (During the renovation, it's best to just follow *Aviation* signs.) You'll see WWI biplanes and WWII fighters, plus a Soviet MiG fighter (with camouflage paint) that crashed in Belgium in 1989 (one of the last airspace violations of the Cold War). Some of these planes are one-of-a-kind relics—including a French Nieuport fighter, a Schreck seaplane, and two German observation planes from World War I. There's much more to the museum, including the arms and armor section (access it through the gift shop near the entrance).

Finish your visit at the Panorama—the stunning viewpoint atop the Cinquantenaire arch (free, open in summer only). The elevator is near the museum's entrance lobby and gift shop—follow signs to *Arcades* and *Panorama* (or just ask for directions). You'll enjoy Napoleonic views over the park complex and the Brussels skyline—some of the best views in the city. Find the distant Atomium and the curved glass arch of the European Parliament.

Cinquantenaire Museum

This varied, decent (but not spectacular) collection features artifacts from many cultures—both European and non-European— ranging from prehistoric times to the present. As you wander the almost-empty halls, you'll see fine tapestries, exquisite altarpieces, impressive Islamic and Antiquities collections, gorgeous Art Nouveau and Art Deco, and a "museum of the heart" (featuring various creative depictions of everyone's favorite organ, donated by a local heart  doctor). The collection is arranged somewhat haphazardly; pick up the brochure at the entry to figure out which items you'd like to find, then follow the signposts.

Cost and Hours: €5, free first Wed of each month after 13:00; Tue-Fri 9:30-17:00, Sat-Sun 10:00-17:00, closed Mon; audio-guide-€4, limited English information posted; hiding behind Autoworld at Jubelpark 10, Parc du Cinquantenaire, tel. 02-741-7211, www.kmkg-mrah.be.

Visiting the Museum: As you enter and stand under the rotunda, to the left is the Non-European wing (American Indian, Mayan, Asia), and to the right is European (Gothic-Renaissance-Baroque tapestries, altarpieces, and jewels).

A highlight is the Antiquities wing: From the rotunda, head left, then turn left at the totem pole. Start in Rome, in a spacious hall with a vast floor mosaic of an animal hunt, overseen by a bronze statue of Emperor Severus Septimus. There's a room-sized model of ancient Rome (on the same level as the floor mosaic)—find the Colosseum, the Circus Maximus chariot-race course, and the grand buildings of the Forum in between. (Ask when the next model demonstration takes place.) On other floors, you'll find Greek pottery and a reconstructed Egyptian tomb you can walk inside.

▲MATONGÉ NEIGHBORHOOD

About one out of every 10 Brussels residents claims African ancestry. Wedged between the Eurocrat campus of the European Parliament and the royal sights of the Upper Town is the Matongé (mah-tong-gay) district, a mélange of African immigrant culture, fine turn-of-the-century architecture, and young Bruxellois in search of a trendy scene in an "emerging" neighborhood. Consider riding the Métro to Matongé, exploring the neighborhood, and staying for lunch or dinner (for eating recommendations, see page 210).

Getting Here: Take the Métro to Porte de Namur/Naam-sepoort. If you're starting at the European Parliament, it's a 15-minute walk to Porte de Namur.

Background: Matongé, part of the Ixelles district of Brussels, had ties to Africa even before any Africans lived here. Back when the Belgian Congo was still a colony, many of its administrative offices were located in this part of Brussels. A Congolese choir was invited to perform at the 1958 World's Fair, and soon after, several of the performers decided to return to Belgium to study at the university. A local aristocrat bought them a residential building in this neighborhood. More and more immigrants arrived—from Congo and throughout Africa—and soon the neighborhood was nicknamed Matongé (after a market district in the Congolese capital, Kinshasa). For decades, Matongé was a center of "Belgican" (Belgian African) culture, although more recently it also has large Indian, Pakistani, and Latin American communities. While it remains a popular place for Brussels' African population to socialize, the cost of living in this high-rent district (with fine old buildings and a central location near the European Parliament) has pushed out many residents. As with gentrification anywhere, the people whose gritty creativity made this place fertile for development are harvesting a bumper crop of relocation notices.

❍ Self-Guided Walk: From the Porte de Namur/Naamsepoort Métro station, exit toward *Chaussée d'Ixelles/Elsensesteenweg* and *Chaussée de Wavre/Waversteenweg.* Riding the escalator up into the square, head up Chaussée d'Ixelles (with your back to the giant traffic circle and modern monument), then take the first left down **Chaussée de Wavre.** You'll pass the landmark Cinéma Vendôme art house movie theater on your left. Soon after, on your right, look for the entrance to the bustling African market. The sign *Souriez, vous êtes à Matongé* means "Smile! You are in Matongé." You can enter the market, or if that's too intense, simply keep strolling down the street—passing exotic taste-of-Africa grocery shops (displaying cassava, plantain, and other ingredients utterly unknown to Belgian chefs), call shops offering cheap rates for phone calls to Africa, boutiques selling colorful batik fabric, and neighborhood-gathering-place barber shops and hair salons.

After two blocks, you reach a little crossroads. Turn right down Rue Ernest Solvay to find the **Afrikamäli** shop, a cooperative selling fair-trade, high-quality, African-made handicrafts (closed Sun-Mon, Rue Ernest Solvay 19, tel. 02-503-0074).

Just past Afrikamäli, you'll arrive at the cross-street of **Rue Saint-Boniface.** This energetic café row, which dead-ends at the front door of St. Boniface Church, is the spine of the neighborhood and one of Matongé's most gentrified drags. Rather than African, this strip has a decidedly urbane-Bruxellois vibe, with busy brasseries and cafés, and an eclectic range of eateries. Explore a bit, and don't miss the exquisite, skinny **Art Nouveau facades** at #17 (housing the Comptoir Florian tea house) and #19.

Wander slowly up toward the church—window-shopping for a drink or meal—and just before you reach the door, turn left on **Rue de la Paix.** Halfway down the block on the right is **Kuumba,** a café that also serves as a sort of cultural center for the neighborhood, with occasional live music (Rue de la Paix 35, tel. 02-503-5730, www.kuumba.be).

At the end of the block, you'll run into **Rue Longue Vie.** To the left (back the way you came) is a pair of African-food-for-Europeans eateries, offering a taste of this neighborhood's adopted culture.

From here, you can head back to the Métro station (up Rue Longue Vie, which runs into Chaussée de Wavre). Or, to discover another fun neighborhood with some trendy nightspots, keep going. Turn right down Rue Longue Vie, then immediately right again on Rue Bouré. At the cute little square behind the church (where L'Athénée's pub tables spill out onto the street), take a left, then a right, to find your way to charming **Place**

Fernand Cocq. This leafy, triangular square—facing the Town Hall of the district of Ixelles—feels a world away from the African vibe of streets just a few steps away. A dozen cafés, bars, and restaurants compete for your attention, all with inviting sidewalk tables.

When you're ready to head back, you can retrace your steps through the heart of Matongé. Or, for a more direct route, head up Chaussée d'Ixelles all the way back to the Métro.

North of Downtown

1958 WORLD'S FAIR GROUNDS SIGHTS

These sights are next to each other about four miles north of the Grand Place at Bruparck, a complex of tacky-but-fun attractions at the old 1958 World's Fair grounds.

Getting There: It's easy but fairly time-consuming to reach from the center. Ride the Métro to Heysel/Heizel and walk about five minutes toward the can't-miss-it Atomium. You'll come to a little pavilion with a walkway going over the train tracks; to reach Mini-Europe, take this walkway and enter "The Village," a corny food circus (with a giant cineplex and a water park) done up like a European village. Entering this area, turn left and head down the stairs to reach the Mini-Europe entrance. If you're only going to the Atomium, simply go straight through the pavilion and head for the big silver balls.

Atomium

This giant, silvery iron molecule, with escalators and stairs connecting the various "atoms" and a view from the top sphere, was the über-optimistic symbol of the 1958 World's Fair. It's Brussels' answer to Paris' Eiffel Tower, Seattle's Space Needle, and St. Louis' Gateway Arch. Reopened after an extensive renovation, the Atomium celebrates its kitschy past with fun space-age videos and displays.

Your ticket includes an elevator ride to the panorama deck, with views over the fairgrounds and Mini-Europe (which looks *really* mini from up here)—but, disappointingly, you can't actually see the landmarks of downtown Brussels. From there, you'll meander on endless escalators and stairs through five of the nine balls on your way back down. Renting the audioguide provides a good explanation of the building and the 1958 World's Fair, including sound clips from people who actually attended the festivities. If you don't like heights or tight spaces, tell your friends you'll wave to them...from the ground.

Cost and Hours: €11, €23.50 combo-ticket with Mini-Europe, daily 10:00-18:00, last entry 30 minutes before closing, audioguide-€2, overpriced restaurant inside, tel. 02-475-4775, www.atomium.be.

Mini-Europe

This kid-pleasing sight, sharing a park with the Atomium, has 1:25-scale models of 350 famous European landmarks, such as Big Ben, the Eiffel Tower, and Venice's canals. The "Spirit of Europe" section is an interactive educational exhibit about the European Union.

Cost and Hours: €14.30, €23.50 combo-ticket with Atomium; daily mid-March-Sept 9:30-18:00, July-Aug until 20:00, Oct-Dec 10:00-18:00, closed Jan-mid-March; last entry one hour before closing, tel. 02-474-1313, www.minieurope.com.

Outside Brussels

This museum is in the town of Tervuren, about an hour by public transit east of Brussels.

▲Royal Museum of Central Africa
(Musée Royal de l'Afrique Centrale)

Remember the Belgian Congo? This worthwhile museum covers the Congo and much more of Africa, including ethnography, sculpture, jewelry, colonial history, flora, and fauna (note that the museum is closed for renovation until mid-2017). It's a great place to learn about both the history of Belgian adventure in the Congo (when it was the king's private plantation) and the region's natural wonders. Unfortunately, there's barely a word of English.

The museum, housed in an immense palace, is surrounded by a vast, well-kept park. A trip out here puts you in a lush, wooded oasis a world away from the big, noisy city. The palace was built by the king in 1907 to promote the beauties of living and working in the Congo.

Cost and Hours: When it reopens, likely €4, more for special exhibits; Tue-Fri 10:00-17:00, Sat-Sun 10:00-18:00, closed Mon; audioguide-€2, Leuvensesteenweg 13 in the town of Tervuren, tel. 02-769-5211, www.africamuseum.be.

Getting There: Take Métro line 1 (direction: Stockel/Stok-kel) to Montgomery, and then catch tram #44 and ride it about 20 minutes to its final stop, Tervuren. From there, walk 300 yards through the park to the palace.

BRUSSELS SIGHTS

GRAND PLACE WALK

Like most European cities, Brussels has a main square, but few are as "Grand" as this one. From its medieval origins as a market for a small village, the Grand Place has grown into a vast public space enclosed by Old World buildings with stately gables. Today, the "Place" is the place to see Europe on parade. Visitors come to bask in the ambience, sample chocolate, and relax with a beer at an outdoor café.

This walk allows all that, but also goes a bit beyond. We'll take in the spectacular (if heavily touristed) square, browse an elegant shopping arcade, run the frenetic gauntlet of "Restaurant Row," stand at the center of modern Brussels at the Bourse, and end at the grand finale (he said with a wink): the one-of-a-kind *Manneken-Pis*.

Orientation

Length of This Walk: Allow two hours.
Town Hall: €5, English tours offered Wed at 15:00, Sun at 10:00 and 14:00 except no Sun tours Oct-March.
City Museum: €4, Tue-Sun 10:00-17:00, Thu until 20:00, closed Mon.
Brewery Museum: €5, daily 10:00-17:00.
Chocolate Shops on the Grand Place: Generally open Mon-Sat 9:00-22:00, Sun 10:00-22:00.

The Walk Begins

❶ The Grand Place

This colorful cobblestone square is the heart—historically and geographically—of heart-shaped Brussels. As the town's market square for 1,000 years, this was where farmers and merchants sold their wares in open-air stalls, enticing travelers from the main east-west highway across Belgium, which ran a block north of the square. Today, shops and cafés sell chocolates, *gaufres* (waffles), beer, mussels, fries, *dentelles* (lace), and flowers (for details on cafés and chocolate shops on the Grand Place, see the sidebar on page 158).

Brussels was born about 1,000 years ago at a strategic spot on the banks of the Senne (not Seine) River, which today is completely bricked over. The river crossed the main road from Cologne to Bruges.

Pan the square to get oriented. Face the Town Hall with its skyscraping spire. One TI is on your right, under the Town Hall's arches, while another TI is one block behind you; "Restaurant Row" is another block beyond that. To your right, a block away (downhill), is the Bourse building. The Upper Town is to your left, rising up the hill beyond the Central Station. Over your left shoulder a few blocks away is St. Michael's Cathedral. And most important? The *Manneken-Pis* is three blocks ahead, down the street that runs along the left side of the Town Hall.

The **Town Hall** (Hôtel de Ville) dominates the square with its 300-foot-tall tower, topped by a golden statue of St. Michael slaying a devil. Built in the 1400s, this

was where the city council met to rule this free trading town. Brussels proudly maintained its self-governing independence while dukes, kings, and clergymen ruled much of Europe. These days, the Town Hall hosts weddings—it's where King Philippe got married in 1999. (The Belgian government demands that all marriages first be performed in simple civil ceremonies.) You can step into the Town Hall courtyard for a little peace (but the building's interior is only open by tour—see page 129).

Opposite the Town Hall is the impressive, gray **King's House** (Maison du Roi), which now houses the **City Museum.** It's gone through several incarnations in its 800-year history. First it was the medieval square's bread market—hence, the building's Dutch name—Broodhuis. Then (early 1500s) it became the regional office for the vast Habsburg empire of Charles V—hence, its French name—Maison du Roi. The lacy, prickly Gothic facade dates from the late-1800s, when it was renovated to be the City Museum. (For details on visiting the museum, see the listing on page 130.)

The fancy smaller buildings giving the square its uniquely grand medieval character are former **guild halls** (now mostly shops

Tasty Treats Around the Grand Place

Brussels' grand square (and the surrounding area) offers plenty of places to sample Belgium's culinary specialties.

Cafés: Mussels in Brussels, Belgian-style fries, yeasty local beers, waffles...if all you do here is plop down at a café on the square, try some of these specialties, and watch the world go by—hey, that's a great afternoon in Brussels.

The outdoor cafés are casual and come with fair prices (a decent Belgian beer costs €4.50, and a really good one is more like €5-7—with no cover or service charge). Have a seat, and a waiter will serve you. The half-dozen or so cafés on the downhill side of the square are all roughly equal in price and quality for simple drinks and foods—check the posted menus. As they are generally owned by breweries, you won't have a big selection of beers.

Choco-Crawl: The best chocolate shops all lie along the north (uphill) side of the square, starting with Godiva at the high end (higher in both altitude and price). The cost goes down slightly as you descend to the other shops. Each shop has a mouth-watering display case of chocolates and sells 100-gram mixes (six or so pieces) for about €5, or individual pieces for about €1 (for more on buying chocolate in Belgium, see page 39).

Godiva is synonymous with fine Belgian chocolate. Now owned by a Turkish company, Godiva still has its management and the original factory (built in 1926) in Belgium. This store, at Grand Place 22, was Godiva's first (est. 1937). The almond and honey goes way beyond almond roca.

Neuhaus, a few doors down at #27, has been encouraging local chocoholics since 1857. Their main store is in the Galeries Royales St. Hubert. Neuhaus publishes a good little pamphlet explaining its products. The "caprice" (toffee with vanilla crème) tastes like Easter. Neuhaus claims to be the inventor of the praline.

Galler, just off the square at Rue au Beurre 44, is homier and less famous because it doesn't export. Still family-run, it proudly serves the less sugary dark chocolate. The new top-end choice, 85 percent pure chocolate, is called simply "Black 85"—and worth a sample if you like chocolate without the sweetness. Galler's products are well-described in English.

Leonidas, four doors down at Rue au Beurre 34, is where cost-conscious Bruxellois get their fix, sacrificing 10 percent in quality to nearly triple their take (machine-made, only €2.20/100 grams). White chocolate is their specialty. If all the chocolate has made you thirsty, wash it down with **250 Beers,** next to Leonidas.

and restaurants), their impressive gabled roofs topped with statues. Once the home offices for the town's different professions (brewers, bakers, and *Manneken-Pis* corkscrew makers), they all date from shortly after 1695—the year French king Louis XIV's troops took the high ground east of the city, sighted their cannons on the Town Hall spire,

and managed to level everything around it (4,000 mostly wooden buildings) without ever hitting the spire itself. As a matter of pride, these Brussels businessmen rebuilt their offices better than ever, completing everything within seven years. They're in stone, taller, and with ornamented gables and classical statues. While they were all built at about the same time, the many differences in styles reflect the independent spirit of the people and the many cultural influences that converged in this crossroads trading center.

The **Swan House** (#9, just to the left of the Town Hall) once housed a bar where Karl Marx and Friedrich Engels met in February of 1848 to write their *Communist Manifesto*. Later that year, when the treatise sparked socialist revolution around Europe, Belgium exiled Marx and Engels. Today, the once-proletarian bar is one of the city's most expensive restaurants. Next door (#10) and still is the brewers' guild, now housing the **Brewery Museum** (see listing on page 131).

Imagine this already glorious square filled with a carpet of flowers. Every other year (next in August of 2016; www.flowercarpet.be), florists create a colorful 19,000-square-foot pattern of tightly packed begonias—that's about three-quarters of a million individual flowers. Begun in 1971 by a begonia salesman as a way to promote his wares, this gorgeous display has become a biennial Brussels fixture that makes this grand space even grander. If you're here in August on the off-year, there is a massive floral display inside the Town Hall (see www.floralientime.be).

Each **rooftop statue** comes with its own uninteresting legend, but the Bruxellois have an earthier explanation: "What's that

smell?" say the statues on the roof of the Swan House. "Someone farted." "Yeah," says the golden man riding a horse atop the Brewery Museum next door, "it was that guy over there," and he points north across the square to another statue. "It wasn't me," says that statue, "it was him—way over there." Follow his gaze to the middle

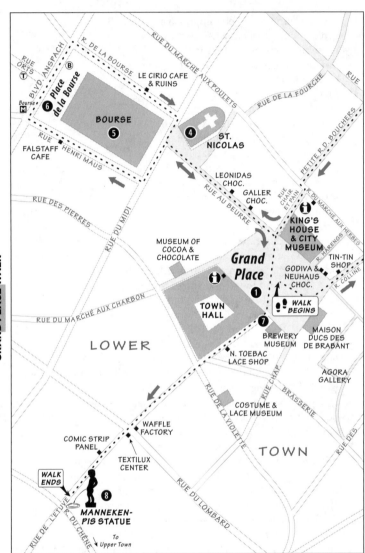

GRAND PLACE WALK

of the northwest side of the square, where the statue of a saint with a shepherd's staff hangs his head in shame. (By the way, the shepherd saint may be missing. Some say he's being restored, while others say he fled the square out of embarrassment.)

• Exit the Grand Place next to Godiva (from the northeast, or uphill, corner of the square), and go north one block on Rue de la Colline. Along the way, you'll pass a popular **Tintin boutique** (at #9). It sells merchandise of the popular Belgian comic-strip hero to both kids and adults who

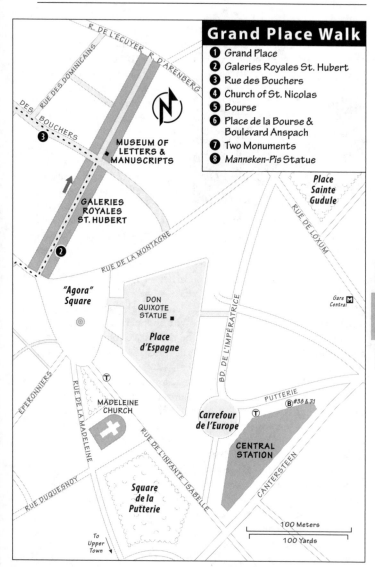

Grand Place Walk

1. Grand Place
2. Galeries Royales St. Hubert
3. Rue des Bouchers
4. Church of St. Nicolas
5. Bourse
6. Place de la Bourse & Boulevard Anspach
7. Two Monuments
8. Manneken-Pis Statue

GRAND PLACE WALK

grew up with him. Continue to Rue du Marché aux Herbes, which was once the main east-west highway through Belgium. The little park-like square just to your right—a modest gathering place with market stalls— is nicknamed "Agora" (after the nearby covered shopping area). Looking to the right, notice that it's all uphill from here to the Upper Town, another four blocks (and 200-foot elevation gain) beyond. Straight ahead, you enter the arcaded shopping mall called...

❷ Galeries Royales St. Hubert

Built in 1847, Europe's oldest still-operating shopping mall served as the glass-covered model that inspired many other shopping gal-

leries in Paris, London, and beyond. It celebrated the town's new modern attitude (having recently gained its independence from the Netherlands). Built in an age of expansion and industrialization, the mall demonstrated efficient modern living, with elegant apartments upstairs above trendy shops, theaters, and cafés. It was center of upwardly mobile Brussels—progressive newspapers, French expats (Hugo, Dumas, Baudelaire), and where the first Belgian motion picture was screened. Originally, you had to pay to get in to see its fancy shops, and that elite sensibility still survives. Even today, people live in the upstairs apartments.

Looking down the arcade (233 yards long), you'll notice that it bends halfway down, designed to lure shoppers farther. Its iron-and-glass look is still popular, but the decorative columns, cameos, and pastel colors evoke a more elegant time. It's Neo-Renaissance, like a pastel Florentine palace.

There's no Gap (yet), no Foot Locker, no Cinnabon. Instead, you'll find hat, cane, and, umbrella stores that sell...hats, canes, and umbrellas—that's it, all made on the premises. **Philippe** (halfway down the first section, on the left) carries shoes made especially for the curves of your feet, handcrafted by a family that's been doing it for generations. Since 1857, **Neuhaus** (near the end of the first section, on the right) has sold chocolates from here at its flagship store, where many Brussels natives buy their pralines—invented in this very house in 1912. Across from Neuhaus, the **Taverne du Passage** restaurant serves the same local special-

ties that singer Jacques Brel used to come here for: *croquettes de crevettes* (shrimp croquettes), *tête de veau* (calf's head), *anguilles au vert* (eels with herb sauce), and *fondue au fromage* (cheese croquettes; €25 meals, daily 12:00-24:00).

• *Midway down the mall, where the two sections bend (and where you'll find the Museum of Letters and Manuscripts—see page 135), turn left and exit the mall onto...*

❸ Rue des Bouchers

Yikes! During meal times, this street is absolutely crawling with tourists browsing through wall-to-wall, mid-level-quality restaurants. Brussels is known worldwide for its food, serving all kinds of cuisine, but specializing in seafood (particularly mussels). You'll have plenty to choose from along the table-clogged "Restaurant Row." To get an idea of prices, compare their posted *menùs*—the fixed-price, several-course meal offered by most restaurants. But don't count on getting a good value—better restaurants are just a few steps away (for specifics, see page 205).

Many diners here are day-trippers. Colin from London, Marie from Paris, Martje from Holland, and Dietrich from Frankfurt could easily all "do lunch" together in Brussels—just three hours away.

The first intersection, with Petite Rue des Bouchers, is the heart of the restaurant quarter, which sprawls for several blocks around. The street names reveal what sorts of shops used to stand here—butchers *(bouchers)*, herbs, chickens, and cheese.

• *At this intersection, turn left onto Petite Rue des Bouchers and walk straight back to the Grand Place. (You'll see the Town Hall tower ahead.) At the Grand Place, turn right (west) on Rue au Beurre. Comparison-shop a little more at the Galler and Leonidas chocolate stores and pass by the little "Is it raining?" fountain. At the intersection with Rue du Midi is the...*

❹ Church of St. Nicolas

Since the 12th century, there's been a church here. Inside, along the left aisle, see rough stones in some of the arches from the early church. Outside, notice the barnacle-like shops, such as De Witte Jewelers, built right into the church. The church was rebuilt 300 years ago with money provided by the town's jewelers. As thanks, they were given these shops with apartments upstairs. Close to God, this was prime real estate. And jewelers are still here.

• *Just beyond the church, you run into the back entrance of a big Neoclassical building.*

❺ The Bourse (Stock Exchange) and Art Nouveau Cafés

The stock exchange was built in the 1870s in the Historicist style—a mix-and-match, Neo-everything architectural movement. Plans are in the works for the former stock exchange to host a big beer museum. The **ruins** under glass on the right side of the Bourse are from a 13th-century convent; there's a small museum inside.

Several **historic cafés** huddle around the Bourse. To the right (next to the covered ruins) is the woody **Le Cirio,** with its delightful circa-1900 interior. Around the left side of the Bourse is the **Falstaff Café,** which is worth a peek inside. Some Brussels cafés, like the Falstaff, are still decorated in the early 20th-century Art

Nouveau style. Ironwork columns twist and bend like flower stems, and lots of Tiffany-style stained glass and mirrors make them light and spacious. Slender, elegant, willowy Gibson Girls decorate the wallpaper, while waiters in bowties glide by.

• *Circle around to the front of the Bourse, toward the busy Boulevard Anspach.*

⑥ Place de la Bourse and Boulevard Anspach

Brussels is the political nerve center of Europe (with as many lobbyists as Washington, DC), and the city sees several hundred demonstrations a year. When the

local team wins a soccer match or some political group wants to make a statement, this is where people flock to wave flags and honk horns.

It's also where the old town meets the new. To the right along Boulevard Anspach are two shopping malls and several first-run movie theaters. Rue Neuve, which parallels Anspach, is a bustling pedestrian-only shopping street.

Boulevard Anspach covers the still-flowing Senne River (which was open until 1870). Remember that Brussels was once a port, with North Sea boats coming as far as this point to unload their goods. But with frequent cholera epidemics killing thousands of its citizens, the city decided to cover up its stinky river.

Beyond Boulevard Anspach—two blocks past the black, blocky skyscraper—is the charming **Ste. Catherine** neighborhood, clustered around the former fish market and the Church of Ste. Catherine. This village-like zone is the easiest escape from the bustle of downtown Brussels, and features two recommended lunch stops: the Mer du Nord/Nordzee fish bar and the delightful Belgian cheese shop Crèmerie de Linkebeek (both worth a detour and described on page 209).

• *For efficient sightseeing, consider catching a taxi across the street from the Bourse to the Place Royale, where you can follow my Upper Town Walk (see next chapter), which ends near the* Manneken-Pis. *But if you'd rather stay in the Lower Town, return to the Grand Place.*

From the Grand Place to the *Manneken-Pis*

• *Leave the Grand Place kitty-corner, heading south down the street running along the left side of the Town Hall, Rue Charles Buls (which soon changes its name to Stoofstraat). Just five yards off the square, under the arch, are* ⑦ *two monuments honoring illustrious Brussels notables:*

The first monument features a beautiful young man—an Art

Nouveau allegory of knowledge and science (which brings illumination, as indicated by the Roman oil lamp)—designed by Victor Horta. It honors **Charles Buls,** mayor from 1888 to 1899. If you enjoyed the Grand Place, thank him for saving it. He stopped King Leopold II from blasting a grand esplanade from Grand Place up the hill to the palace.

A few steps farther you'll see tourists and locals rubbing a **brass statue** of a reclining man. This was Alderman Evrard 't Serclaes, who in 1356 bravely refused to surrender the keys of the city to invaders, and so was tortured and killed. Touch him, and his misfortune becomes your good luck. Judging by the reverence with which locals treat this ritual, I figure there must be something to it.

From here, the street serves up a sampler of typical Belgian products. A half-block farther (on the left), the **N. Toebac Lace Shop** shows off some fine lace. Brussels is perhaps the best-known city for traditional lacemaking, and this shop still sells handmade pieces in the old style: lace clothing, doilies, tablecloths, and ornamental pieces. The shop gives travelers with this book a 15 percent discount. For more on lace, see the sidebar on page 36 or visit the Costume and Lace Museum, which is a block away and just around the corner (closed Mon, see page 134).

GRAND PLACE WALK

A block farther down the street is the recommended, always-popular **Waffle Factory,** where €2-3 gets you a freshly made takeaway "Belgian" waffle (the different varieties are explained on page 204).

Cross busy Rue du Lombard and step into the **Textilux Center** (Rue du Lombard 41, on the left) for a good look at Belgian tapestries—both traditional wall-hangings and modern goods, such as tapestry purses and luggage in traditional designs.

Continuing down the street, notice a **mural** on the wall ahead, depicting that favorite of Belgian comic heroes, Tintin, escaping down a fire escape. Tintin is known and beloved by virtually all Europeans. His dog is named Snowy, Captain Haddock keeps an eye out for him, and the trio is always getting

Tapestries

In 1500, tapestry workshops in Brussels were famous, cranking out high-quality tapestries for the walls of Europe's palaces. They were functional (as insulation and propaganda for a church, king, or nobleman) and beautiful—an intricate design formed by colored thread. Even great painters, such as Rubens and Raphael, designed tapestries, which rivaled Renaissance canvases. The best Belgian tapestries are in Madrid, because the Golden Age of Belgian tapestries was under Spanish rule in the 16th and 17th centuries. Also impressive are the Brussels-made tapestries of the Sistine Chapel, which some say were so extraordinary that they sparked the Northern Renaissance.

To make a tapestry, neutral-colored threads are stretched vertically over a loom. (In Renaissance Belgium, the threads were made from imported English wool.) The design of the tapestry is created with the horizontal weave, from the colored threads that (mostly) overlay the vertical threads. Tapestry making is much more difficult than basic weaving, as each horizontal thread is only as long as the detail it's meant to create. A single horizontal row can be made up of many individual pieces of thread. Before weaving begins, an artist designs a pattern for the larger picture, called a "cartoon," which weavers follow for guidance as they work.

Flanders and Paris (in the Gobelins workshop) were the two centers of tapestrymaking until the art died out, mirroring the decline of Europe's noble class.

into misadventures. (For more on Tintin, see page 137.) Dozens of these building-sized comic-strip panels decorate Brussels (marked on the TI's €0.50 map), celebrating the Belgians' favorite medium. Just as Ireland has its writers, Italy its painters, and France its chefs, Belgium has a knack for turning out world-class comic artists.

• *Follow the crowds, noticing the excitement build, because in another block you reach the...*

❽ *Manneken-Pis*

Even with low expectations, this bronze statue is smaller than you'd think—the little squirt's under two feet tall, practically the size of a newborn. Still, the little peeing boy is an appropriately low-key symbol for the unpretentious Bruxellois. The statue was made in 1619 to provide drinking water for the neighborhood. Notice that the baby, sculpted in Renaissance style, actually has the musculature of a man instead of the

pudgy limbs of a child. The statue was knighted by the occupying King Louis XV—so French soldiers had to salute the eternally pissing lad when they passed.

As it's tradition for visiting VIPs to bring the statue an outfit, and he also dresses up for special occasions, you can often see the *Manneken* peeing through a colorful costume. A sign on the fence lists the month's festival days and how he'll be dressed. For example, on January 8, Elvis Presley's birthday, he's an Elvis impersonator; on Prostate Awareness Day, his flow is down to a slow drip. He can also be hooked up to a keg to pee wine or beer.

There are several different legends about the story behind *Manneken*—take your pick: He was a naughty boy who peed inside a witch's house, so she froze him. A rich man lost his son and declared, "Find my son, and we'll make a statue of him doing what he did when found." Or—the locals' favorite version—the little tyke loved his beer, which came in handy when a fire threatened the wooden city: He bravely put it out. Want the truth? The city commissioned the *Manneken* to show the freedom and joie de vivre of living in Brussels—where happy people eat, drink...and drink...and then pee.

The gathering crowds make the scene more interesting. Hang out for a while and watch the commotion this little guy makes as tour groups come and go. When I was there, a Russian man marveled at the statue, shook his head, and said, "He never stop!"

UPPER TOWN WALK

The Upper Town has always had a more aristocratic feel than the medieval, commercial streets of the Lower Town. With broad boulevards, big marble buildings, palaces, museums, and so many things called "royal," it also seems much newer and a bit more sterile. But the Upper Town has plenty to offer.

Use this walk to get acquainted with this less-touristed part of town, sample some world-class museums, see the palace, explore art galleries, and get the lay of the land from a panoramic viewpoint. The tour starts at Place Royale, a half-block from the one essential art sight in town, the Royal Museums of Fine Arts of Belgium (Old Masters, Fin-de-Siècle, and the Magritte Museum). Consider a visit while you're here (see next chapter). The Musical Instruments Museum is also in the neighborhood.

From Place Royale, we'll walk south along the ridge, pop into a stained-glass-filled Gothic church, continue on to the towering Palace of Justice (next to the best view of the city), descend through the well-worn tapestry of the Sablon Quarter's antique stores, art galleries, and cafés, and end at a homey little square right near the *Manneken-Pis,* the pride and joy of Brussels.

Orientation

Length of This Walk: Allow 1.5 hours.

Getting There: The walk begins at Place Royale in the Upper Town. You have several ways to get there:

    1. From the Grand Place, walk uphill for 15 minutes (follow your map).

    2. Catch a taxi (figure €7 from the Bourse).

    3. From Putterie street just north of Central Station, take buses #38 or #71 (direction: Héros/Helden or Delta), which leave

every few minutes for Place Royale (the bus stop is Royale/ Koning, 2 stops on either route; buy €2.50 ticket from driver, validate in machine).

4. Hop off here during a hop-on, hop-off bus tour (see page 126).

Royal Museums of Fine Arts of Belgium: €8 for each museum, €13 combo-ticket covers all three, free first Wed of month after 13:00; open Tue-Sun 10:00-17:00, closed Mon, Magritte Museum open Wed until 20:00, last entry 30 minutes before closing; audioguides cost €4-5 depending on museum.

Musical Instruments Museum: €8, Tue-Fri 9:30-17:00, Sat-Sun 10:00-17:00, closed Mon, last entry 45 minutes before closing.

BELvue Museum: €6, €10 combo-ticket includes Coudenberg Palace; Tue-Fri 9:30-17:00, July-Aug until 18:00, Sat-Sun 10:00-18:00, closed Mon; audioguide-€2.50.

Coudenberg Palace: Same cost and hours as BELvue Museum.

Mercedes House: Free, Mon-Sat 10:00-20:00, Sun 10:00-16:00, Rue Bodenbroek 22-24, café, tel. 02-400-4250, www. mercedeshouse.be.

Notre-Dame du Sablon Church: Free, daily 9:00-18:30.

Eating: Near the end of this walk you'll find Rue de Rollebeek, with several options for a meal.

Starring: Brussels' genteel Upper Town, with its best museums, top views, and a bit of personality poking out from behind its stuffy veneer.

The Walk Begins

❶ Place Royale

At the crest of the hill sits Place Royale (a.k.a. Koningsplein), en-circled by cars and trams and enclosed by white Neoclassical build-ings forming a mirror image across a cobblestone square. A big, green statue of a horseman stands in the center.

The **statue** depicts the local hero, Godfrey de Bouillon, who led the First Crusade (in 1096). The ultimate Catholic knight, he

rides forward with his flag, gazing down on the Town Hall spire. If Godfrey turned and looked left down Rue de la Régence, he'd see the domed Palace of Justice at the end of the boulevard. Over his right shoulder, just outside the square, is the Royal Palace, the king's residence.

In the 1870s, as Belgium exerted itself to industrialize and modernize, this tight ensemble of planned buildings and squares

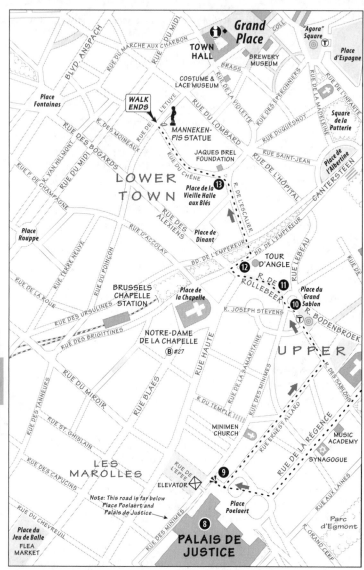

was rebuilt as a sign that Brussels had arrived as a world capital. Broad vistas down wide boulevards end at gleaming white, Greek-columned monuments—this look was all the rage, seen in Paris, London, Washington, DC...and here.

The cupola of the **Church of St. Jacques sur Coudenberg**—the central portion of the square's ring of buildings—makes the church look more like a bank building. But St. Jacques' church goes

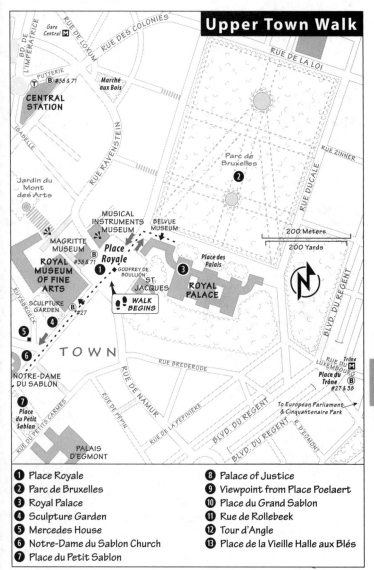

Upper Town Walk

- **1** Place Royale
- **2** Parc de Bruxelles
- **3** Royal Palace
- **4** Sculpture Garden
- **5** Mercedes House
- **6** Notre-Dame du Sablon Church
- **7** Place du Petit Sablon
- **8** Palace of Justice
- **9** Viewpoint from Place Poelaert
- **10** Place du Grand Sablon
- **11** Rue de Rollebeek
- **12** Tour d'Angle
- **13** Place de la Vieille Halle aux Blés

back much further than this building (from 1787); the original was built here in the 13th century near a 12th-century castle. Nobles chose to build their mansions in the neighborhood—and, later, so did the king. And when locals stand here, they remember that it was on the porch of this building, on July 21, 1831, that their first king took the oath that established modern Belgium.

The square has several worthwhile museums. The main entrance to the **Royal Museums of Fine Arts of Belgium** is a half-block to the right (❍ see the Royal Museums of Fine Arts Tour chapter). The **Musical Instruments Museum** is straight downhill from the square—if Godfrey spurred his horse straight ahead, he'd pass it on his right. It's housed in an early 20th-century iron-and-glass former department store. Its Art Nouveau facade was a deliberate attempt to get beyond the retro-looking Greek columns and domes of the Place Royale. Even if you don't visit the Musical Instruments Museum, you can ride the elevator up to the museum café for a superb Lower Town view.

• *Before heading south, exit Place Royale on the north side (to the left as you face Godfrey), which opens up to the large, tree-lined...*

❷ Parc de Bruxelles

Copying Versailles, the Habsburg empress Maria Theresa of Austria (Marie-Antoinette's mom) had this symmetrical park laid out

in 1776, when she ruled (but never visited) the city. This is just one of many large parks in Brussels, which started with an awareness of the importance of city planning.

At the far (north) end of the park (directly opposite the Royal Palace, no need to actually walk there) is the Parliament building. Which parliament? The city hosts several: the European Parliament, the Belgian Parliament, and several local, city-council-type parliaments. This is the Belgian Parliament, seen on nightly newscasts as a backdrop for talking heads and politicians.

In 1830, Belgian patriots rose up and converged on the park, where they attacked the troops of the Dutch king. This was the first blow in a short, almost bloodless revolution that drove out the foreign-born king and gave the Belgians independence...and a different foreign-born king.

• *The long building facing the park is the...*

❸ Royal Palace (Palais Royale)

Belgium struck out twice trying to convince someone to be its new king. Finally, Leopold I (r. 1831-1865), a nobleman from Germany, agreed to become "King of the Belgians." Leopold was a steadying influence as the country modernized. His son rebuilt this palace—near the site of earlier palaces, dating back to the 10th century—by linking a row of townhouse mansions with a unifying facade (around 1870).

Leopold's great-great-great-great-grandnephew, King Philippe, today uses the palace as an office. (His head is on Belgium's euro coins.)

Philippe and his wife, Queen Mathilde, live in a palace north of here (near the Atomium), at several country estates, and on the French Riviera. If the Belgian flag (black-yellow-red) is flying from the palace, the king is somewhere in Belgium.

Philippe (born 1960) is a figurehead king, as in many European democracies, but he serves an important function as a common bond between bickering Flemish and Walloon citizens. The king—regarded by some as awkward and standoffish—is not as popular as Queen Mathilde, also a Belgian native. Their daughter, Elisabeth, born in 2001, is first in line to become the next Belgian monarch.

The bulk of the palace is off-limits to tourists except from late July through early September (see www.opt.be for the latest schedule; gardens open April-May). The adjacent **BELvue Museum** has a well-presented exhibit on Belgian history and the royal family, but I'd skip the ho-hum **Coudenberg Palace** ruins (see listings on pages 140-142).

• *Return to Place Royale, then continue south along Rue de la Régence, noticing the main entrance to the Royal Museums of Fine Arts of Belgium complex. Just past the museums, on the right, you'll see a...*

❹ Sculpture Garden (Jardin de Sculpture)

This pleasant public garden features a statue by Rodin's contemporary, Aristide Maillol, a master of the female form. In *The River*

(1938-1943), the moving water is personified as a woman sprawled on her side (and looking terrified, or at least stressed—the statue was originally conceived to represent a victim of war). The wave-like figure teeters on the edge of a pool of water, about to pour in. Is she a symbol of the mystery of water, the trauma of war...or is she just washing her hair? Another copy of this bronze statue sprawls near a pool in the courtyard of New York's Museum of Modern Art.

The garden looks like a great way to descend into the Sablon Quarter, but the gates at the bottom are often locked.

• *About 75 yards farther along Rue de la Régence, on your right at the intersection, is the...*

❺ Mercedes House

This sleek, modern showroom (with gift shop) hosts temporary car exhibits that change every six months. There's usually a bit of history for classic-car enthusiasts, plus a peek at the latest Mercedes models. The venue also hosts cultural events such as chamber music and jazz.

• *A few yards farther along, you reach the top of the Sablon neighborhood, dominated by the...*

❻ Notre-Dame du Sablon Church

The round, rose, stained-glass windows in the clerestory of this 14th-century Flamboyant Gothic church are nice by day, but are thrilling at night, when the church is lit from inside and glows like a lantern, enjoyed by locals at the cafés in the surrounding square. Either way, it's worth a stop inside.

Visiting the Church: An artistically carved pulpit stands midway up the nave. The stained-glass windows in the nave (which  date from the 19th and 20th centuries) are notable for their symmetry—rows of saints in Gothic niches topped by coats of arms. The glorious apse behind the altar—bathed in colorful light from original 15th-century windows—is what Gothic is all about. The left transept has relics of Karl I, the last Habsburg emperor (1887-1922), who was deposed when Austria became a republic after World War I. Karl's Catholic devotion was legendary, and he was beatified in 2004. Many devoted people pray here, inspired by his patient suffering in exile.

Next to the altar, see a small wooden **statue of Mary** dressed in white with a lace veil. This is a copy, made after iconoclastic Protestant vandals destroyed the original. The original statue was thought to have had miraculous powers that saved the town from plagues. In 1348, when the statue was in Antwerp, it spoke to a godly woman named Beatrix, prompting her to snatch Mary, board a boat, and steal the statue away from Antwerp. (That's why the church is decorated with several images of boats, including the small **wooden boat** high up in the right transept.) When the citizens of Antwerp tried to stop Beatrix, the Mary statue froze them in their tracks.

UPPER TOWN WALK

When Beatrix and the statue arrived here, the Bruxellois welcomed Mary with a joyous parade. Not long after, this large church was erected in her honor. Every summer, in Brussels' famous Ommegang procession, locals in tights and flamboyant costumes re-create the joyous arrival with colorful banners and large puppets. Imagine the scene as they carry Mary from here through the city streets to the parade's climax on the Grand Place.

• *We'll return to the colorful Place du Grand Sablon (below the church) later in the walk. For now, head to the other side of Rue de la Régence from the church, where you'll find a leafy, fenced-off garden called the...*

❼ Place du Petit Sablon

Step into this charming little park, a pleasant refuge from the busy street and part of why this neighborhood is considered so livable.

Its central fountain, a fine example of 19th-century Romanticism, honors two local nobles who were executed because they promoted tolerance during the Inquisition. Good friends, one Catholic and the other Protestant, they were beheaded on the Grand Place in 1568.

Check out the other statues. The 48 small statues atop the wrought-iron fence represent the craftsman guilds—weavers, brewers, and butchers—of 16th-century Brussels. And inside the garden, the 10 large statues represent hometown thinkers of the 16th century—a time of great intellectual accomplishments in Brussels. Gerardus Mercator (1512-1594), the Belgian mapmaker who devised a way to more accurately show the spherical Earth on a flat surface, holds a globe.

This collection of statues functions as a reminder that, even though Belgium was never a great power, Belgians have much to be proud of as a people. From here, look back at the church and enjoy its flamboyant late Gothic lines.

• *We'll visit the Sablon neighborhood below the church later, but before losing elevation, let's continue along Rue de la Régence. You'll pass (on the left) the Music Academy and Brussels' main synagogue—its sidewalk fortified with concrete posts to keep car bombs at a distance—and an ugly, prefab, concrete Lego-style building of the 1960s (on the right). Soon you'll reach the long-scaffolded...*

❽ Palace of Justice (Palais de Justice)

This domed mountain of marble sits on the edge of the Upper Town ridge, dominating the Brussels skyline. Built in wedding-cake layers of Greek columns, it's topped with a dome taller than St. Peter's in Rome, rising 340 feet. Covering more than six acres, it's the size of a baseball stadium. Extending seven floors underground, it's so big it has its own postal code.

The palace was built in the time of King Leopold II (son of Leo I, r. 1865-1909) and epitomizes the brassy, showy grandeur of his reign. Leopold became obscenely wealthy by turning Africa's Congo region—80 times the size of Belgium—into his personal colony. Whip-wielding Belgian masters forced Congolese slaves to tend lucrative rubber plantations, exploiting the new craze for car tires. Leopold spent much of this wealth expanding and beautifying the city of Brussels.

The building, (which stands on the historic site of the town gallows) serves as a Hall of Justice, where major court cases are tried. If you pop in to the lobby, you may see lawyers in black robes buzzing about.

Notice the rack of city bikes. Like many other European cities, Brussels subsidizes a public-bike system. The program, called "Villo," is designed for locals, who, for a token fee, can pick up a bike in one part of town and drop it off anywhere else. But the scheme doesn't always work as well as intended: These bike racks are often empty, since this is a popular place to grab a bike for the easy ride back down to the Lower Town.

• One of the best views of Brussels is immediately to the right of the Palace of Justice.

❾ Viewpoint from Place Poelaert

You're standing 200 feet above the former Senne River Valley. Gazing west over the Lower Town, pan the valley from right (north) to left:

Near you is the stubby **clock tower** of the Minimen Church (which hosts lunchtime concerts in the summer). To the left of that, in the distance past a tall square skyscraper, is the lacy, white Town Hall **spire** (marking the Grand Place).

Twinkling in the far distance, six miles away, you can see one of the city's landmarks, the **Atomium.** (No doubt, someone atop it is looking back at you.) The Atomium's nine shiny steel balls form the shape of an iron molecule that's the size of the Palace of Justice behind you. Built for the 1958 World's Fair, it's now a middle-aged symbol of the dawn of the Atomic Era.

Next (closer to you) rises the **black clock tower** of the Notre-Dame de la Chapelle church, the city's oldest (from 1134, with a tower that starts Gothic and ends Baroque). On the distant horizon, see **four boxy skyscrapers,** part of the residential sprawl of this city of over a million, which now covers 62 square miles. Breaking the horizon to the left is a **green dome,** which belongs to the Basilica of Koekelberg (fourth-biggest in the world). And finally (panning quickly to the left), you see a **black glass skyscraper** marking the Midi/Zuid/South train station, where you can catch special high-speed train lines, such as the Eurostar, to London.

At your feet lies the **Marolles neighborhood.** Once a funky, poor place where locals developed their own quirky dialogue, today it can be either seedy or colorful, depending on the time of day and your perception. The area is famous for its sprawling flea market (daily 7:00-14:00, best on weekends). Two of the streets just below you—Rue Haute and Rue Blaes—are lined with secondhand shops. A free **elevator** connects Place Poelaert with the Marolles neighborhood, which is worth a 10-minute detour to descend to the café-lined square. People who brake for garage sales may want to cut out of this walk early and head to the Marolles from here.

Gazing off into the distance to the far left (south), you can't quite see the suburb of **Waterloo,** 10 miles away. But try to imagine it, because it was there that the tide of European history turned. On the morning of June 18, 1815, Napoleon waited two hours for the ground to dry before sending his troops into battle. That time lag may have cost him the battle. His 72,000 soldiers could have defeated Wellington's 68,000, but the two-hour delay was just enough time for Wellington's reinforcements to arrive—45,000 Prussian troops. Napoleon had to surrender, his rule of Europe ended, and Belgium was placed under a Dutch king—until the Belgians won their independence in the 1830 revolution.

Behind you, in Place Poelaert, is a memorial to the two World Wars, both of which slashed through Belgium with deadly force.

• *Backtrack east, descending to Place du Grand Sablon by walking down Rue Ernest Allard. Passing lots of antique shops and galleries, you'll eventually reach a square below the Notre-Dame du Sablon Church. (For a light, healthy, and characteristic meal,* **Le Pain Quotidien**—*on the square at Rue des Sablons 11—offers a fine value with delightful seating and baked goods right out of the oven.)*

❿ Place du Grand Sablon

The Sablon neighborhood that surrounds this square and its church

UPPER TOWN WALK

features cafés and restaurants, antique stores, and art galleries. Every
weekend, there's an antique market
on the square. On warm summer
evenings, the square sparks magic,
as sophisticated locals sip *apéritifs*
at the café tables, admiring the
church's glowing stained glass.
Chocolatier Wittamer (on the far
side of the square, at #6) often has
elaborate window displays. And

at the bottom of the square is the shop of the innovative **Pierre
Marcolini**—who was declared the world's top chocolatier—with a
tempting buffet upstairs.

• *Sloping Place du Grand Sablon funnels downhill into the pedestrian-
only street called...*

⓫ Rue de Rollebeek

With a few surviving buildings, this street gives you a taste of
the city before its 1695 bombardment (which leveled the center of
town). Today it's a delightful traffic-free lane lined with sidewalk
cafés, art galleries, shops, midrange restaurants, and boutiques—a
pleasant place to press "Pause" before returning to the bustle of
Brussels. While the eateries here feel a bit touristy and overpriced,
it's an easy place to comparison-shop for a drink or meal. **Toscana
21** (at #21) feels like a slice of Italy, with fine pizzas and pastas. **Peï
& Meï** (at #15) is well-regarded for its creative Belgian/Mediterra-
nean/international fare in a bright and mod interior. **L'Estrille du
Vieux Bruxelles** (near the bottom, at #21) is a traditional, slightly
stuffy, classic French spot with an affordable lunch special. A block
south of Rue de Rollebeek is the more workaday Rue Joseph Ste-
vens—home to the appealing sandwich shop **Pistolet Original** (at
#24-26) and the hip, split-level bar **Skievelat Sablon** (at #16-18).

• *Rue de Rollebeek leads down to the busy Boulevard de l'Empereur. To
the right on the boulevard, just past the bowling alley, is the...*

⓬ Tour d'Angle

The "Corner Tower" is a rare surviving section
of Brussels' medieval city wall. It stood over
one of seven gates along the 2.5-mile-long
wall that enclosed one of Europe's great cities—13th-century Brussels. Notice the slash
through the city here that marks where underground train lines connect the Central Station
(to your right) and the South Station (to your
left). Six tracks under you are kept busy with

about a thousand trains a day. This ambitious bit of city infrastructure was a project started in 1902 and not finished until 1952—two occupations by Germany slowed things down.

• *Cross the street, head right, and take the first left at Rue de l'Escalier, which leads downhill to a pleasant square at the T-intersection.*

⓲ Place de la Vieille Halle aux Blés

Do a 360-degree sweep from the center of this little square—circled by nice apartments and lined with cafés that hum (on a sunny day). Imagine what a delight it would be to call this neighborhood home. Twenty years ago, this was a derelict slum—a good reason why Brussels was famous as a fine place to work but a lousy place to live. People were moving out, leaving the down-and-out downtown. But in 1989 Brussels became its own political region and got its own government. Since then, its policy has been to revitalize the center of town; tearing down homes to build office space is no longer allowed. Consequently, new construction is reserved for residences, and people are moving into the area again. As in so many European cities, government policies are spurring the revitalization of old town centers.

• *Your walk is finished. From here, the* Manneken-Pis *(described on page 166) is about a five-minute walk, and the Grand Place (see page 156) is about 10 minutes. You can reach either just by following the signs.*

ROYAL MUSEUMS OF FINE ARTS TOUR

Musées Royaux des Beaux-Arts de Belgique

This museum complex, spread throughout three large buildings, covers much of the history of Western painting. We'll visit a trio of interconnected museums: the Old Masters Museum (pre-1850); the Fin-de-Siècle Museum (1850-1910); and the Magritte Museum, which celebrates the work of the popular Belgian Surrealist painter. The collections, while enjoyable, can be overwhelming, so this chapter highlights the museums' strengths: Flemish and Belgian artists. But don't limit your visit to these works—let the museums surprise you.

Orientation

Cost: €8 for each individual museum, €13 combo-ticket covers all three. All are free the first Wed of the month after 13:00.

Hours: Tue-Sun 10:00-17:00, closed Mon, last entry 30 minutes before closing. The Magritte Museum stays open Wed until 20:00.

Getting There: The main entrance, with access to all three museums, is at Rue de la Régence 3 in the Upper Town, a five-minute walk uphill from Central Station (or take bus #38 or #71). Bus #38 or #27 connects this area with the European Parliament, with #27 continuing to the Park of the Cinquantenaire. These museums are also located at the beginning of my Upper Town Walk (see previous chapter).

Keep Your Magrittes Straight: Don't confuse this Magritte Museum with the much smaller René Magritte Museum, located in Magritte's former home on the outskirts of Brussels. This is clearly the place to enjoy his art.

Information: A €2.50 tour booklet, *Twenty Masterpieces of the Art of Painting: A Brief Guided Tour,* is sold in the museum shop.

Tel. 02-508-3211, www.fine-arts-museum.be or www.musee-magritte-museum.be.

Tours: Consider the €4 audioguide for the Old Masters Museum, the €5 videoguide for the Fin-de-Siècle Museum, or the €4 audioguide for the Magritte Museum.

Length of This Tour: Allow one hour for the Old Masters and Fin-de-Siècle museums, and another hour for the Magritte Museum.

Cuisine Art: The museums have a pricey café and a fancy brasserie on site. The Musical Instruments Museum, a block away, has a much-appreciated restaurant on its rooftop (see page 140).

Starring: Bruegel's *Census at Bethlehem;* Post-Impressionist works by Seurat, Gauguin, and Ensor; and Magritte's *The Treachery of Images.*

The Tour Begins

Enter at Rue de la Régence 3 and buy your ticket. It's smart to get a combo-ticket to see all three museums. Continue into the large

entrance hall and get oriented. The Old Masters Museum is on the second floor (in the galleries above you), reached by the staircase directly ahead. The Fin-de-Siècle Museum is through the passageway to the right, down several levels. The Magritte Museum is also to the right, through the passageway.

Pause at the information desk to pick up a free map and consider renting an audioguide. Now let's dive in. As you make your way through the maze of rooms, keep an eye out for this chapter's highlights.

Old Masters Museum

• *Go up to the second floor and start with the Flemish masters. Notice how the rooms on the second floor surround a central hall. The art is displayed in (roughly) chronological order, working counterclockwise around the central gallery. In the first room, look for a small canvas with a portrait...*

Rogier van der Weyden—
Portrait of Anthony of Burgundy, c. 1456-1465

Anthony was known in his day as the Great Bastard, the bravest and most distinguished of the many bastards fathered by prolific

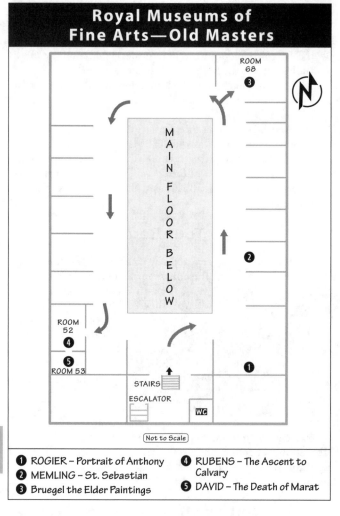

Royal Museums of Fine Arts—Old Masters

ROOM 68 ❸

MAIN FLOOR BELOW

ROOM 52 ❹

❺
ROOM 53

❷

❶

STAIRS

ESCALATOR

WC

Not to Scale

❶ ROGIER – Portrait of Anthony
❷ MEMLING – St. Sebastian
❸ Bruegel the Elder Paintings
❹ RUBENS – The Ascent to Calvary
❺ DAVID – The Death of Marat

ROYAL MUSEUMS

Duke Philip the Good (a Renaissance prince whose sense of style impressed Florence's young Lorenzo the Magnificent, patron of the arts).

Anthony, a member of the Archers Guild, fingers the arrow like a bowstring. From his gold necklace dangles a Golden Fleece, one of Europe's more prestigious knightly honors. Wearing a black cloak, a bowl-cut hairdo, and a dark-red cap, with his pale face and hand emerging from a dark background, the man who'd been called a bastard all his life gazes to the distance, his clear, sad eyes lit with a speckle of white paint.

Van der Weyden (c. 1399-1464), Brussels' official portrait

painter, faithfully rendered life-size, life-like portraits of wealthy traders, bankers, and craftsmen. Here he captures the wrinkles in Anthony's neck and the faint shadow his chin casts on his Adam's apple. Van der Weyden had also painted Philip the Good (in Bruges' Groeninge Museum—see page 68), and young Anthony's long, elegant face and full lips are a mirror image—pretty convincing DNA evidence in a paternity suit.

Capitalist Flanders in the 1400s was one of the richest, most cultured, and progressive areas in Europe, rivaling Florence and Venice.

• *Continue counterclockwise around the central gallery. As you head up the right side (in the third section), find...*

Hans Memling—*Martyrdom of St. Sebastian* (*Le Martyre de Saint Sébastien*), c. 1475

Serene Sebastian is filled with arrows by a serene firing squad in a serene landscape. Sebastian, a Roman captain who'd converted to Christianity, was ordered to be shot to death. (He miraculously survived, so they clubbed him to death.)

Ready, freeze! Like a *tableau vivant* (popular with Philip the Good's crowd), the well-dressed archers and saint freeze this mo-

ment in the martyrdom so the crowd can applaud the colorful costumes and painted cityscape backdrop.

Hans Memling (c. 1430-1494), along with his former employer, Rogier van der Weyden, are called Flemish Primitives. Why "Primitive"? The term comes from the lack of 3-D realism so admired in Italy at the time (for more on Flemish Primitives, see sidebar on page 67). Sebastian's arm is tied to a branch that's not arching overhead, as it should be, but instead is behind him. An archer aims slightly behind, not at, Sebastian. The other archer strings his bow in a stilted pose. But Memling is clearly a master of detail, and the faces, beautiful textiles, and hazy landscape combine to create a meditative mood appropriate to the church altar in Bruges where this painting was once placed.

• *Next, head for the far-right corner of the gallery and find Room 68, where paintings by Pieter Bruegel I often are displayed.*

ROYAL MUSEUMS

Pieter Bruegel I, the Elder—*The Census at Bethlehem* (*Le Dénombrement de Bethléem*), 1566

Perched at treetop level, you have a bird's-eye view over a snow-covered village near Brussels. The canals are frozen over, but life

goes on, with everyone doing something. Kids throw snowballs and sled across the ice. A crowd gathers at the inn (lower left), where a woman holds a pan to catch blood while a man slaughters a pig. Most everyone has his or her back to us or head covered, so the figures speak through poses and motions.

Into the scene rides a woman on a donkey led by a man—it's Mary and husband Joseph hoping to find a room at the inn (or at least a manger), because Mary's going into labor.

The year is 1566—the same year that Protestant extremists throughout the Low Countries vandalized Catholic churches, tearing down "idolatrous" statues and paintings of the Virgin Mary. Bruegel (more discreetly) brings Mary down to earth from her Triumphant Coronation in heaven, and places Jesus' birth in the humble here and now. The busy villagers put their heads down and work, oblivious to the future Mother of God and the wondrous birth about to take place.

Bruegel the Elder (c. 1527-1569) was famous for his landscapes filled with crowds of peasants in motion. His religious paintings place the miraculous in everyday settings.

In this room you'll see Bruegel's works, as well as those of his less famous sons. Pieter Brueghel II, the younger Pieter, copied his dad's style (and even some paintings, like the *Census at Bethlehem*—displayed to the left). Another son, Jan, was known as the "Velvet Brueghel" for his glossy still lifes of flower arrangements.

• *Continue your counterclockwise circuit around the gallery, through the rest of the Old Masters collection, until you finally reach works by Rubens in Rooms 52 and 53, including the wall-sized...*

Peter Paul Rubens—*The Ascent to Calvary* (*La Montée au Calvaire*), c. 1636

Life-size figures scale this 18-foot-tall canvas on the way to Christ's Crucifixion. The scene ripples with motion, from the windblown clothes to steroid-enhanced muscles to billowing flags and a troubled sky. Christ stumbles—he might get trampled by the surging crowd. Veronica kneels to gently wipe his bloody head.

This 200-square-foot canvas was manufactured by Rubens

(1577-1640) at his studio in Antwerp. Hiring top-notch assistants, Rubens could crank out large altarpieces for the area's Catholic churches. First, Rubens himself did a small-scale sketch in oil (like many of the studies in Room 52). He would then make other sketches, highlighting individual details. His assistants would reproduce them on the large canvas, and Rubens would then add the final touches.

This work is from late in Rubens' long and very successful career. He got a second wind in his fifties, when he married 16-year-old Hélène Fourment. She was the model for Veronica, who consoles the faltering Christ in this painting.

• *Exit the Rubens room to the left, go into the perpendicular Room 53, and look right to find...*

Jacques-Louis David—*The Death of Marat* (*Marat Assassiné*), 1793

In a scene ripped from the day's headlines, Jean-Paul Marat—a well-known crusading French journalist—has been stabbed to death in his bathtub by Char-lotte Corday, a conservative fanatic. Marat's life drains out of him, turning the bathwater red. With his last strength, he pens a final, patriotic, *"Vive la Révolution"* message to his fellow patriots. Corday, a young noblewoman angered by Marat's campaign to behead the French king, was arrested and guillotined three days later.

Jacques-Louis David (1748-1825), one of Marat's fellow revolutionaries, set to work painting a tribute to his fallen comrade right after the 1793 assassination. (He signed the painting: *"À Marat"*—"To Marat.")

David makes it a secular *pietà*, with the brave writer portrayed as a martyred Christ in a classic dangling-arm pose. Still, the deathly pallor and harsh lighting pull no punches, creating in-your-face realism.

David, the official art director of the French Revolution, supervised propaganda and the costumes worn for patriotic parades. A year after finishing this painting, in 1794, his extreme brand of revolution (which included guillotining thousands of supposed enemies) was squelched by moderates, and David was jailed. He emerged later as Napoleon's court painter. When Napoleon was exiled in 1815, so was David, spending his last years in Brussels.

• *To get to the Fin-de-Siècle Museum, return to the ground floor and the large main entrance hall of the Old Masters Museum and rent the videoguide here if you like. From the entry hall a passageway leads you to the Fin-de-Siècle and Magritte museums. Immediately after entering the passageway, you'll pass by the tiny fourth museum in this complex (included in the combo-ticket)—the Modern Museum. Continue down the passageway (noting the entrance to the Magritte Museum), then continue on into the Fin-de-Siècle wing (entering on level –3).*

Fin-de-Siècle Museum

Brussels likes to think of itself as the capital of Art Nouveau and the crossroads of Europe, and this newly remodeled space presents a convincing case. Covering the period from the mid-19th century to the early 20th century, it shows the many cultural trends that converged in Brussels to create great art. The collection features a handful of high-powered paintings by notable Impressionists, Post-Impressionists, Realists, and Symbolists. It also houses a dazzling assemblage of Art Nouveau glassware, jewelry, and furniture.

Don't expect to see this art in chronological order. Galleries are organized thematically, to show the art in context with the period's literature, opera, architecture, and photography.

• *You enter on level –3. On your visit, you'll go down, down, down through several levels. (Pray the elevator is working for the trip back up.) Keep the big picture. I've pointed out a few specific paintings, but don't worry so much about finding them all. Enlist the help of nearby guards if you must find a particular piece.*

WELCOME TO THE FIN-DE-SIÈCLE (LEVEL -5)

Paintings of distinguished men in suits and ladies in gowns introduce you to the era. The last half of the 19th century was a time of great technological progress—the train, camera, and telegraph—but also one where traditional beauty and elegance was valued. As you browse the rest of the museum, keep in mind that the art was paid for and consumed by these wealthy industrialists and their trophy wives.

• *Continue down to the next level, which often displays the museum's best-known masterpieces.*

IMPRESSIONISM AND POST-IMPRESSIONISM (LEVEL -6)

In the late 1800s, there was a revolution in painting. The starting point was Realism. Rather than painting Madonnas and Greek gods in the comfort of the studio, painters went out to paint the "real" world. They hung out in cafés, sketchbook in hand, capturing the bustle of modern life. The Impressionists took it a step further, actually setting their canvases up in the open air to paint a land-

scape or city scene. On level -6 you'll find classic examples.

Georges Seurat (1859-1891) paints a Sunday-in-the-park view from his favorite Parisian island in *The Seine at Grande-Jatte (La Seine à la Grande-Jatte)*. Taking Impressionism to its extreme, he builds the scene out of small points of primary colors that blend at a distance to form objects. The bright colors capture the dazzling, sunlit atmosphere of this hazy day.

Paul Gauguin (1848–1903), schooled in Impressionism, de-veloped his own unique style. In *Breton Calvary (Calvaire Breton*; a.k.a. *The Green Christ/Le Christ Vert)*, he returned to the bold, black, coloring-book outlines of more Primitive (pre-3-D) art. The Chris-tian statue and countryside look less like Brittany and more like primitive Tahiti, where Gauguin would soon settle.

Finally, find paintings by Belgium's own **James Ensor** (1860-1949). At 22, Ensor, an acclaimed child prodigy,

proudly presented his lively Impressionist-style works to the Brussels Salon for exhibi-tion. They were flatly rejected.

The artist withdrew from public view and, in seclusion, painted *Shocked Masks (Les Masques Scandalisés)*, a dark and murky scene set in a small room of an ordinary couple wear-ing grotesque masks. Once again, everyone disliked this disturbing canvas and heaped more criticism on him. For the next six decades, Ensor painted the world as he saw it—full of bizarre, carnival-masked, stupid-looking crowds of cruel strangers who mock the viewer.

• *Descend to the next floor, enjoying exhibits on the central role opera played in turn-of-the-century life (level -7). Then head for the bottom floor.*

ART NOUVEAU (LEVEL -8)

The Gillion Crowet Collection is a stunning €36 million assem-blage of Art Nouveau paintings, jewelry, woodwork furniture, and flowery vases (by the likes of Emile Gallé). You'll also see pieces by Victor Horta, whose influential architecture (such as the Belgian Comic Strip Center, see page 136) steered the curvaceous Art Nouveau style toward simpler Art Deco and Modernism.

Among the paintings, it's hard not to notice *The Caress of the Sphinx (Des Caresses)*, where a young man cozies up to a cheetah-girl. The painter, **Fernand Khnopff** (1858-1921), was James Ensor's college buddy. Khnopff championed the Symbolist movement, presenting arresting images (often of women as femme fatales) intended to provoke primeval emotions.

Which is the perfect segue to the...

Magritte Museum

Magritte's works are perhaps best described in his own words: "My paintings are visible images which conceal nothing; they evoke mystery and, indeed, when one sees one of my pictures, one asks oneself this simple question, 'What does that mean'? It does not mean anything, because mystery means nothing either, it is unknowable." If that brainteaser titillates you, you'll love this museum.

The exhibits take you on a chronological route through René Magritte's life and art. The museum divides his life into three sections, with one floor devoted to each. In each section, a detailed timeline (in English) puts the work you'll see in a biographical and historical context. Fascinating quotes from Magritte are posted around the museum, but only in French and Dutch; pick up the English translation as you enter. The audioguide is helpful.

The following tour follows the layout of the museum, but it's not really intended as a room-by-room analysis. It's best to read this tour ahead of time. Or, at the museum, take a seat and read each section before you enter that level. Armed with a little background, enter the darkened rooms and let Magritte transport you to his world.

• *From the entrance, you'll board an elevator that takes you up to level +3.*

1898-1929 (LEVEL +3)

Born to a middle-class Belgian family, Magritte moved to Brussels at age 17 to study at the Academy, where he learned to draw meticulously and got a broad liberal arts education. In the 1920s, he eked out a living designing advertisements, posters, and sheet music, and wrote for the avant-garde *7 Arts* magazine (you'll see samples posted). Meanwhile, he dabbled in various styles—Post-Impressionism, Futurism, Cubism—in search of his own voice.

In 1922, he married his childhood sweetheart, Georgette,

The Art of René Magritte

René Magritte (1898-1967) trained and worked in Brussels. Though he's world-famous now, it took decades before his peculiar brand of Surrealism caught on. He painted real objects with photographic clarity, and then jumbled them together in new and provocative ways.

Magritte had his own private reserve of symbolic images. You'll see clouds, blue sky, windows, the female torso, men in bowler hats, rocks, pipes, sleigh bells, birds, turtles, and castles arranged side by side as if the arrangement means something. He heightens the mystery by making objects unnaturally large or small. People morph into animals or inanimate objects. The juxtaposition short-circuits your brain only when you try to make sense of it. Magritte's works are at once playful and disorienting...and, at times, disturbing.

who became his lifelong companion and muse. It's said that all the women he would paint (and you'll see many of them in this collection) were versions of Georgette.

Influenced by the Dada and Surrealist movements coming out of Paris (Salvador Dalí, Marcel Duchamp, Giorgio de Chirico), Magritte became intrigued with the idea of painting dreamscapes that capture an air of mystery. He painted mysterious figures on beaches, inspired by de Chirico's similar canvases.

For Magritte, 1927 was a watershed year, when he painted his first truly Surrealist works. *The Man of the Sea* featured a man on a beach with a wood-block head, pulling a lever. *The Secret Player* perplexed the public (then and now) with a man swinging a bat and missing a flying turtle.

Together, René and Georgette mingled in sophisticated, bohemian circles. Georgette posed for René's canvases—often nude—and also for black-and-white photographs. It's touching to think that he had found a soul mate who seemed to truly understand and encourage his weirdness. In the photo series called *The Fidelity of the Image*, René, Georgette, and their friends struck wacky tableaux that intentionally distorted normal poses.

Magritte experimented with writing words on his paintings. This culminated in his most famous work, *The Treachery of Images*, painted in the late '20s. (The original is in the Los Angeles County Museum of Art, but you may see a later version displayed.) It's a photorealistic painting of a pipe with the words (in French) "This is not a pipe." Of course it's not a pipe, Magritte always insisted—it's a *painting* of a pipe. Magritte's wordplay forces the viewer to ponder the relationship between the object and its name—between the "signified" and the "signifier," to quote the deconstructionist philosophy that Magritte's paradoxical paintings inspired. Some credit this work for planting the seeds of Postmodernism. Two decades later, Magritte did another version with the message (also in French): "This continues not to be a pipe."

• *Head downstairs to...*

1930-1950 (LEVEL +2)

After a few years in Paris, Magritte survived the Depression in Brussels by doing ad work and painting portraits of friends.

By the late 1930s, he'd refined his signature style: combining two arresting images to disrupt rational thought and produce an emotion of mystery. The paintings' weird titles—*Forbidden Literature, God is No Saint*—added another layer of disruption. These were intentional nonsequiturs, which he and his Surrealist friends concocted at Sunday-night naming soirees.

During the WWII years—spent under Nazi occupation—Magritte used birds as a metaphor for the longing to be free *(The Companions of Fear, Treasure Island).*

In the 1940s, Magritte dabbled in different styles: Impressionistic colors and rough brushwork, tongue-in-cheek "portraits" of animals, and Technicolorized female nudes (often starring Georgette). He went through a *vache* ("cow") period of comic-book-inspired paintings (including the green man with rifle-barrel nose, called *The Ellipsis*). Almost childlike, these are a dramatic departure from his normally photorealistic style.

But he also found time for plenty of his signature paintings where the background and foreground seem to shift, with plenty of familiar motifs such as clouds and bowler hats.

1951-1967 (LEVEL +1)

This floor is divided into two sections (don't overlook the easy-to-miss second one). It's like a victory lap for all of the symbols and styles we've seen. Nearing the end of his prolific life, Magritte had a quiver full of artistic arrows to shoot at the canvas. He mixed his trademark symbols—doves, clouds, balls, open windows, forlorn landscapes—in recombinant ways.

The collection culminates at his *Empire of Lights*, which shows how even well-scrubbed suburbia can possess an ominous air of mystery. Magritte loved night-sky tones. He often created several versions of the same work, which explains why there are several *Empire of Lights* canvases in the world.

ROYAL MUSEUMS

By the end of his life, Magritte was well-known, especially in America. His use of everyday objects and poster-art style inspired Pop Art. His mix of words and images inspired Postmodernist philosophers. His bizarre imagery inspired the psychedelia of the '60s. And the mystery his canvases evoke is timeless.

• *Exit through level -1, which has a bookshop and an appropriately perplexing 50-minute film about Magritte (plays constantly, English subtitles). Descend to level -2 to find the passageway back to the Royal Museums entry...and reality.*

BRUSSELS SLEEPING, EATING & MORE

Contents

As the capital of Belgium—and of the European Union—Brussels is a great place to spend some time. This chapter provides suggestions for the best places to sleep and eat; tips for shopping and after-hours fun; and a rundown of the connections to points throughout Belgium, the Netherlands, and beyond, as well as tips for getting to and from the city's two airports.

Sleeping in Brussels

Normal hotel prices are high in central Brussels. A popular business destination, it tends to be busiest and most expensive on weekdays, especially in April, May, September, and October, when finding a room without a reservation can be impossible. The busiest time of year is during the European Seafood Exhibition, which generally takes place in late April or early May (check www.euroseafood.com for dates). Conversely, Bruges—a pleasure destination—has higher demand on weekends. If your trip is flexible, consider arranging your overnights in these two towns with these patterns in mind.

On the flip side, Brussels' fancy business-class hotels can be desperately empty most of July and August (sometimes June, too) and on most weekends (Fri, Sat, and, to a lesser extent, Sun nights).

Sleep Code

Abbreviations   (€1 = about $1.40, country code: 32)
S = Single, **D** = Double/Twin, **T** = Triple, **Q** = Quad, **b** = bathroom, **s** = shower only

$$$ **Higher Priced**—Most rooms €125 or more
$$ **Moderately Priced**—Most rooms between €80-125
$ **Lower Priced**—Most rooms €80 or less

Unless otherwise noted, English is spoken, credit cards are accepted, breakfast is included, and Wi-Fi is generally free. Brussels levies a hotel tax of a few euros per person, per night (typically not included in the prices here). Prices change; verify current rates online or by email. For the best prices, always book directly with the hotel.

During these slow times, rates can drop by a third to two-thirds, making them your best budget bet. Three-star hotels in the center, which generally cost about €150-200 for a double, abound with low summer rates—you may be able to rent a double room with enough comforts to keep a diplomat happy, including a fancy breakfast, for about €70-80.

For the best rates, always check the hotel website first, but also look at booking websites like Booking.com, Expedia, or Orbitz. Because some hotels hold out until the last minute to cut their rates, prices tend to plummet as the date approaches. Note that these seasonal discounts apply only to business-class hotels.

NEAR THE GRAND PLACE

$$$ Hotel Le Dixseptième, with rather nondescript rooms behind its luxurious lounges and entryway, is ideally located a block below Central Station. Prim, proper, and peaceful, with chandeliers and squeaky hardwood floors, the hotel has 34 rooms, each themed after a different painter (Db-€150-200, Db suites-€270, extra bed-€30, 25 percent off Fri-Sat, often Db-€100 with no breakfast included in July-Aug, see their website for deals, aircon, elevator, free guest computer, Wi-Fi, Rue de la Madeleine 25, tel. 02-517-1717, www.ledixseptieme.be, info@ledixseptieme.be).

$$$ Art de Séjour is a classy splurge B&B a few blocks from the Grand Place (farther than the others listed here...but worth it). Well-run by Mario, it fills a gorgeously restored old building with three thoughtfully appointed rooms that are an engaging mix of new and old (Db-€150, more for spacious studio, air-con, elevator and a few stairs, Wi-Fi, free minibar, Rue des Bogards 12, tel. 02-513-9755, www.artdesejour.com, concierge@artdesejour.com).

$$$ Hotel Ibis off Grand Place, well-situated halfway between Central Station and the Grand Place, is the best of six Ibis

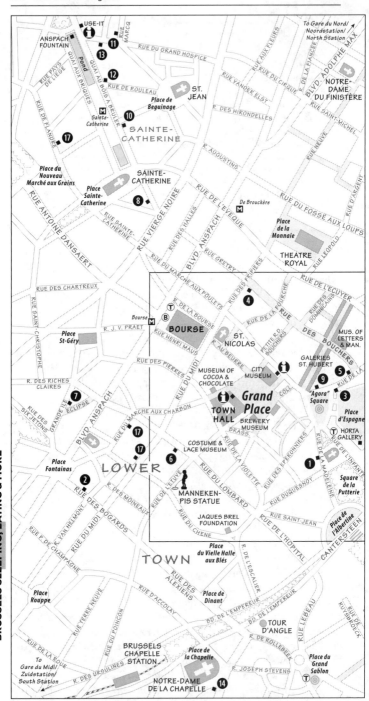

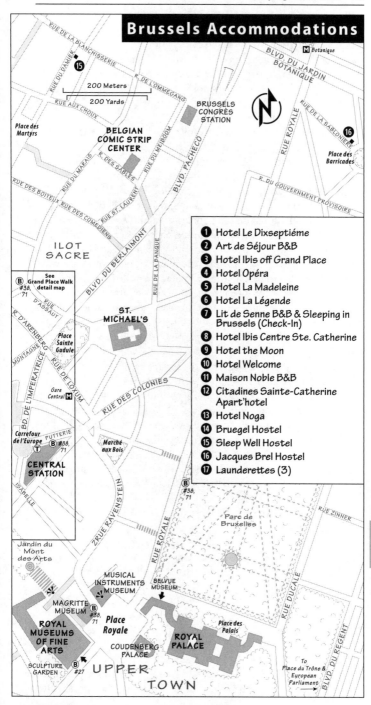

Brussels Accommodations

1. Hotel Le Dixseptiéme
2. Art de Séjour B&B
3. Hotel Ibis off Grand Place
4. Hotel Opéra
5. Hotel La Madeleine
6. Hotel La Légende
7. Lit de Senne B&B & Sleeping in Brussels (Check-In)
8. Hotel Ibis Centre Ste. Catherine
9. Hotel the Moon
10. Hotel Welcome
11. Maison Noble B&B
12. Citadines Sainte-Catherine Apart'hotel
13. Hotel Noga
14. Bruegel Hostel
15. Sleep Well Hostel
16. Jacques Brel Hostel
17. Launderettes (3)

BRUSSELS SLEEPING, EATING & MORE

locations in or near Brussels. It's a big, modern hotel offering 184 simple, industrial-strength-yet-comfy rooms. Prices change almost daily with demand, so check the website (Sb/Db-€145-169 Mon-Thu, generally around €79 Fri-Sun and daily July-Aug, extra bed-€20, breakfast-€14, non-smoking, air-con, elevator, free guest computer, Wi-Fi, Marché aux Herbes 100, tel. 02-514-4040, www. ibishotel.com, h1046@accor.com).

$$$ **Hotel Opéra,** on a people-filled street near the Grand Place, is professional but standardized, with lots of street noise and 49 well-worn rooms (Sb-€99, Db-€129 or €79 in July-Aug, Tb-€149, Qb-€169, 10 percent less with this book if you reserve direct, request a quieter courtyard room, elevator, Wi-Fi, Rue Grétry 53, tel. 02-219-4343, www.hotel-opera.be, reception@hotel-opera.be).

$$ **Hotel La Madeleine,** on the small "Agora" square between Central Station and the Grand Place, rents 56 plain, dimly lit rooms. It has a great location and a friendly staff (S-€57; Ss-€79, Sb-€109, Db-€117; bigger "executive" rooms: Sb-€122, Db-€132, Tb-€139, family Qb-€180; 20 percent off Fri-Sat, 30 percent off July-Aug—see website for deals, book directly with the hotel and mention Rick Steves to get the best rates; request a quieter back room when you reserve, breakfast-€8.50, elevator, pay guest computer, Wi-Fi, Rue de la Montagne 22, tel. 02-513-2973, www. hotel-la-madeleine.be, info@hotel-la-madeleine.be, Philippe).

$$ **Hotel La Légende** rents 26 small, straightforward rooms a block from the *Manneken-Pis* statue. Although it's on a busy road, its classic lobby sits back on a pleasant courtyard. The furnishings are basic, but the location and price are right and the rooms are comfortable enough (prices very flexible—generally Sb-€75, Db-€85 for a standard "classic" room, €10-40 extra for a bigger "executive" room, often cheaper on weekends and July-Aug, request a quieter courtyard room, elevator, Wi-Fi, Rue du Lombard 35, tel. 02-512-8290, www.hotellalegende.com, info@hotellalegende. com).

$$ **Lit de Senne B&B,** lovingly described by owner Fabien as a well-preserved "old lady," has three vintage rooms, each on its own floor, reached by climbing windy, uneven stairs. The uppermost room oozes homey ambience with a pitched wooden roof and book-laden shelves. Guests share a small second-floor terrace and a cluttered ground-level kitchen (Sb-€85, Db-€100, includes breakfast, Wi-Fi, Rue de la Grande Ile 38, mobile 0472-474-795, www.litdesenne.be, fabiengaudry@gmail.com).

$$ **Sleeping in Brussels** runs two cozy B&Bs, **Les Clarisses** and **La Petite Éclipse,** with a total of 12 straightforward, slightly scruffy rooms a few blocks from the Grand Place, just far enough from the Place St-Géry liveliness. Arrange a meeting time in advance, and check in at the Winehouse Osteria on the corner (Db-

€95, bigger Db or studio apartment-€105, can be less in slower times, breakfast included with rooms but costs extra for apartments, Wi-Fi, Rue de la Grande Ile 42, tel. 02-350-0921, mobile 0488-920-093, www.sleepinginbrussels.com, sleepinginbrussels@gmail.com).

$$ Hotel the Moon is a concrete and efficient last resort, with 17 bare-bones rooms and no public spaces. It has absolutely no character and the thin walls and doors, along with noise from the square out front, can make for a noisy night. But the location is super-convenient—just steps from the Grand Place—and it's the cheapest centrally located hotel this side of a youth hostel (Sb-€55-70, Db-€65-90, Tb-€81-110, lower prices are for slow times including July-Aug, 10 percent discount if you book directly with the hotel with the latest edition of this book, ask for a quieter room in the back, stairs but no elevator, on the small "Agora" square at Rue de la Montagne 4, tel. 02-508-1580, www.hotelthemoon.com, info@hotelthemoon.com).

IN STE. CATHERINE, NEAR THE OLD FISH MARKET

The following listings are a 10-minute walk from the intensity of the old center, near the Sainte-Catherine/Sint-Katelijne Métro stop. This charming neighborhood, called "the village in Brussels," faces the canalside fish market and has many of the town's best restaurants. When you get good with the Métro, this area is a simple, two-stop ride from the Central Station and super convenient.

$$$ Hotel Welcome, run by an energetic bundle of hospitality named Michel Smeesters and his wife Sophie, offers outrageous-

ly creative rooms, exuberantly decorated with artifacts they've picked up in their world travels. Each of the 17 rooms has a different geographic theme, from India to Japan to Bali: Take a virtual tour of the rooms on their website (Sb-€120, standard Db-€75-175, deluxe Db-€105-195, family room, discounted on weekends and with direct Rick Steves bookings in Aug, air-con in most rooms, elevator, free guest computer, Wi-Fi, reasonably priced laundry service, parking-€15/day, Quai au Bois à Brûler 23, tel. 02-219-9546, www.hotelwelcome.com, info@hotelwelcome.com).

$$$ Maison Noble is a charming boutique B&B run by Matthieu and Brendon. This gay-friendly place (the well-hung art gravitates toward male nudes) has three classy, mod rooms, a gorgeous Art Nouveau/Art Deco stained-glass window over the breakfast table, and a free steam room. It's on a dull street just a block off the old fish market (D-€129, big Db-€149, 1-night stay-€20 extra, €10 less for 4 nights or longer, €20 less mid-July-Aug, includes breakfast, free guest computer, Wi-Fi, Rue Marcq 10, tel. 02-219-2339, www.maison-noble.eu, info@maison-noble.eu).

$$$ Citadines Sainte-Catherine Apart'hotel, part of a Europe-wide chain, is a huge apartment-style hotel with modern, shipshape rooms. Choose from efficiency studios with foldout double beds or two-room apartments with a bedroom and a foldout couch in the living room. All 169 units come with a kitchen, stocked cupboards, a stereo, and everything you need to settle right in—even a dishwasher. This may be the best place if you're bringing your family and staying three to four nights (official rates: one- or two-person studio-€135, apartment for up to four people-€170, but rates very flexible—check online, much less July-Aug, 15 percent cheaper by the week, breakfast-€14, free guest computer, Wi-Fi, parking-€18/day, Quai au Bois à Brûler 51, tel. 02-221-1411, www.citadines.com, stecatherine@citadines.com).

$$ Hotel Noga feels extremely homey, with 19 rooms, a welcoming game room, and old photos of Belgian royalty lining the hallways. It's carefully run by Frederich Faucher and his son, Mourad (Sb-€75, Db-€110, Tb-€135, Qb-€160, low rates Fri-Sat and in Aug, 5 percent discount if you pay in cash, very quiet, pay guest computer, Wi-Fi, garage parking-€15/day, Rue du Beguinage 38, tel. 02-218-6763, www.nogahotel.com, info@nogahotel.com).

$$ Hotel Ibis Centre Ste. Catherine is a big, impersonal, perfectly comfortable place with 236 rooms in a great location that offers discounts during its slow times (Db-€150 during the week, €85 on weekends, breakfast-€14, air-con, elevator, Wi-Fi, Rue Joseph Plateau 2 at Place Ste. Catherine, tel. 02-513-7620, www.ibishotel.com, h1454@accor.com).

HOSTELS

Three classy and modern hostels—in buildings that could double as small, state-of-the-art, minimum-security prisons—are within a 10-minute walk of Central Station. Each accepts people of all ages, serves cheap and hot meals, takes credit cards, and is budget-priced. All rates include sheets, breakfast, and showers down the hall.

$ Bruegel Hostel, an "official" hostel and fortress of cleanliness, is handiest and most comfortable, with 135 beds. Of its many rooms, 22 are bunk-bed doubles (D-€55, beds in quads or dorms-€25, nonmembers and guests over age 26 pay €3 extra/night, open 7:00-10:00 & 14:00-1:00 in the morning, Wi-Fi, midway between Midi/Zuid/South and Central stations, behind Chapelle church at Rue de St. Esprit 2, tel. 02-511-0436, www.youthhostels.be, brussel@vjh.be).

$ Sleep Well Hostel, surrounded by high-rise parking structures, is also comfortable (bunks in 4-6-bed rooms-€23-25, Sb-€42/50, Db-€63/71, Tb-€84/96, lower price for dorm-style rooms, higher price for hotelesque rooms, guest computer, Wi-Fi, lockout 11:00-15:00, Rue de Damier 23, tel. 02-218-5050, www.sleepwell. be, info@sleepwell.be).

$ Jacques Brel Hostel, with 171 beds, is a little farther out, but it's still a reasonable walk from everything (dorm bed-€20-23, S-€39, D-€46-54, T-€60-68, nonmembers and guests over age 26 pay €3 extra/night, no curfew, laundry, Rue de la Sablonnière 30, tel. 02-218-0187, www.laj.be, brussels.brel@laj.be).

Eating in Brussels

Brussels is known for both its high-quality, French-style cuisine and for multicultural variety. Seafood—fish, eel, shrimp, and oys-

ters—is especially well-prepared here. As in France, if you ask for the *menù* (muh-noo) at a restaurant, you won't get a list of dishes; you'll get a fixed-price meal. *Menùs,* which include three or four courses, are generally a good value if you're hungry. Ask for *la carte* (lah kart) if you want to see a printed menu and order à la carte. For more on Belgian cuisine, see page 334.

When it comes to choosing a restaurant, many tourists congregate on the Grand Place or at the Rue des Bouchers, "Restaurant Row." While the Grand Place is undeniably mag-

nificent, locals suggest enjoying dessert or a drink there, but going elsewhere to eat well, such as the ethnic and trendy zone past the Bourse near Place St-Géry or the colorful Matongé neighborhood. Compare the ambience, check posted menus, and choose your favorite.

IN THE OLD CENTER
Dining on the Grand Place

My vote for northern Europe's grandest medieval square is lined with hardworking eateries that serve predictable dishes to tourist crowds. Of course, you won't get the best quality or prices—but, after all, it's the Grand Place.

For an atmospheric cellar or a table right on the Grand Place, **La Rose Blanche** and **L'Estaminet du Kelderke** each has the same formula, with tables outside overlooking the action. L'Estaminet du Kelderke—with its one steamy vault under the square packed with both natives and tourists—is a real Brussels fixture. It serves local specialties, including mussels (a splittable kilo bucket for

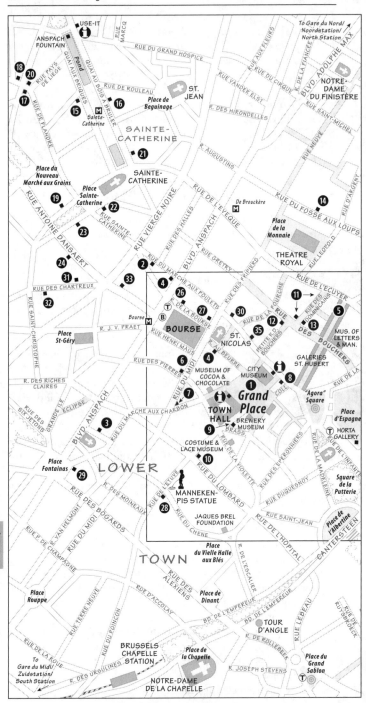

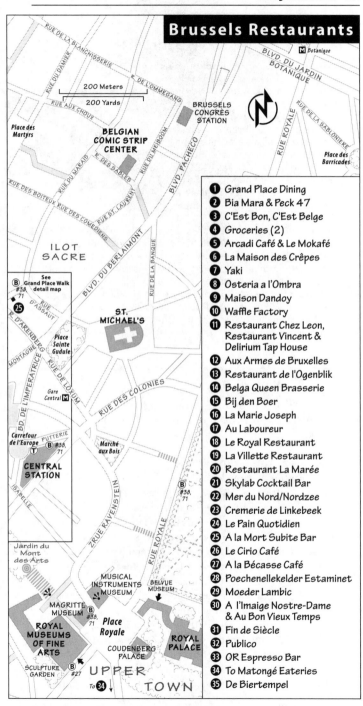

Brussels Restaurants

1 Grand Place Dining
2 Bia Mara & Peck 47
3 C'Est Bon, C'Est Belge
4 Groceries (2)
5 Arcadi Café & Le Mokafé
6 La Maison des Crêpes
7 Yaki
8 Osteria a l'Ombra
9 Maison Dandoy
10 Waffle Factory
11 Restaurant Chez Leon, Restaurant Vincent & Delirium Tap House
12 Aux Armes de Bruxelles
13 Restaurant de l'Ogenblik
14 Belga Queen Brasserie
15 Bij den Boer
16 La Marie Joseph
17 Au Laboureur
18 Le Royal Restaurant
19 La Villette Restaurant
20 Restaurant La Marée
21 Skylab Cocktail Bar
22 Mer du Nord/Nordzee
23 Cremerie de Linkebeek
24 Le Pain Quotidien
25 A la Mort Subite Bar
26 Le Cirio Café
27 A la Bécasse Café
28 Poechenellekelder Estaminet
29 Moeder Lambic
30 A l'Imaige Nostre-Dame & Au Bon Vieux Temps
31 Fin de Siècle
32 Publico
33 OR Espresso Bar
34 To Matongé Eateries
35 De Biertempel

BRUSSELS SLEEPING, EATING & MORE

Mussels in Brussels

Mussels *(moules)* are available all over town. Mostly harvested from aqua farms along the North Sea, they are available for most of the year (except from about May through mid-July, when they're brought in from Denmark). The classic Belgian preparation is *à la marinière,* cooked in white wine, onions, celery, parsley, and butter. Or, instead of wine, cooks use light Belgian beer for the stock. For a high-calorie version, try *moules à la crème,* where the stock is thickened with heavy cream.

You order by the kilo (just more than 2 pounds), which is a pretty big bucket. While restaurants don't promote these as splittable, they certainly are. Your mussels come with Belgian fries (what we think of as "French fries"—dip them in mayo). To accompany your mussels, try a French white wine such as Muscadet or Chablis, or a Belgian blonde ale such as Duvel or La Chouffe. When eating mussels, you can feel a little more local by nonchalantly using an empty mussel shell as a pincher to pull the meat out of other shells. It actually works quite nicely.

€22-25; daily 12:00-24:00, no reservations taken, Grand Place 15, tel. 02-511-0956). **Brasserie L'Ommegang,** with a fancier restaurant upstairs, offers perhaps the classiest seating and best food on the square.

Lunches near the Grand Place

The super-central square dubbed the "Agora" (officially Marché aux Herbes, just between the Grand Place and Central Station) is lined with low-end eateries—Quick, Subway, Panos sandwich shop, Exki health-food store—and is especially fun on sunny days. On the other side of the Grand Place is a "restaurant row" street called Rue du Marché aux Fromages, jammed with mostly Greek and gyros places, with diners sitting elbow-to-elbow at cramped tables out front. But for something fresher and more interesting, stroll a few blocks to one of the following alternatives, or consider the nearby Ste. Catherine neighborhood (see listings, later).

Bia Mara ("Sea Food" in Irish Gaelic) offers five different styles of fish-and-chips made with sustainable ingredients (plus a chicken option and a rotating special with creative international flavors). Around the corner from the Grand Place, this place serves up convenient, affordable, unique meals with a foodie emphasis.

Considering Belgium's affinity for fried food and its proximity to the sea, it's a wonder that it took an Irishman—gregarious owner Barry—to introduce this innovative concept, which started as a food cart in Dublin. The industrial-mod interior is small, so lines can be long at peak times (€10-12 fish-and-chips, daily 12:00-14:30 & 17:30-22:30, Fri-Sun open throughout the day, Rue du Marché aux Poulets 41, tel. 02-502-0061).

C'Est Bon, C'Est Belge ("It's good, it's Belgian") is a cheery little café tucked on a side street a few blocks from the Grand Place. They serve a simple lunch menu of Belgian specials in their very tight, funhouse-floors dining room or at a few sidewalk tables. They also run a small shop selling Belgian food products (€8-12 lunches, Thu-Mon 10:30-18:00, closed Tue-Wed, Rue du Bon Sec-ours 14, tel. 02-512-1999).

Peck 47—named for its location along "Chicken Market" street—is a mod café with artistic decor and white subway tile. They offer €5-8 breakfasts and €5 sandwiches with fresh and in-novative style (Mon-Fri 7:30-17:00, Sat-Sun 11:00-18:00, Rue du Marché aux Poulets 47, tel. 02-513-0287).

Groceries: Mini-markets dot the city. Marked "night shop" and often run by Pakistani and Indian immigrants, they're pricier than supermarkets but handy and often open late. A convenient **Carrefour Express** is along the street between the Grand Place and the Bourse, near the "Is it raining?" fountain (daily 8:00-22:00, Rue au Beurre 27). **AD Delhaize** is another mini-market, at the intersection of Rue du Marché aux Poulets and Boulevard Anspach (Mon-Sat 9:00-20:00, Sun 9:00-18:00, Boulevard Anspach 63).

More Eateries near the Grand Place

These restaurants are good for a sit-down meal day or night.

Arcadi Café is a delightful little eatery serving daily plates (€10-15), salads, and a selection of quiche-like tortes (€7.50/slice). The interior comes with a fun, circa-1900 ambience; grab a table there, on the street, or at the end of Galeries St. Hubert (daily 7:00-23:30, 1 Rue d'Arenberg, tel. 02-511-3343).

Le Mokafé is inexpensive but feels splurgy. They dish up light café fare at the quiet end of the elegant Galeries St. Hubert, with great people-watching outdoor tables. This is also a good spot to try a Brussels waffle or to order a *café-filtre*—a rare, old-fashioned method where the coffee drips directly into your cup (€3-6 sand-wiches, €7-11 salads, €8-10 pastas, €9-12 main dishes, daily 8:00-24:00, Galerie du Roi 9, tel. 02-511-7870).

La Maison des Crêpes, a little eatery a half-block south of the Bourse, looks underwhelming but serves delicious €8-10 crêpes (both savory and sweet varieties) and salads. Even though it's just a few steps away from the tourist bustle, it feels laid-back and local (good beers, fresh mint tea, sidewalk seating, daily 12:00-23:00, Rue du Midi 13, mobile 0475-957-368).

Yaki is a tempting Vietnamese and Thai noodle bar in a stately old flatiron building tucked between the Grand Place and the Rue du Marché au Charbon café/nightlife zone. Choose between the tight interior and the outdoor tables (€10-13 meals, daily 12:00-23:00, Rue du Midi 52, tel. 02-503-3409).

Osteria a l'Ombra, a true Italian joint, is good for a quality bowl of pasta with a glass of fine Italian wine. A block off the Grand Place, it's pricey, but the woody bistro ambience and tasty food make it a good value. If you choose a main dish (€15-18), your choice of pasta or salad is included in the price (otherwise €10-15 pasta meals). The ground-floor seating on high stools is fine, but also consider sitting upstairs (Mon-Sat 12:00-15:00 & 18:30-23:30, closed Sun, Rue des Harengs 2, tel. 02-511-6710).

Waffles near the Grand Place

Dozens of waffle windows clog the streets surrounding the Grand Place. Most of them sell suspiciously cheap €1 waffles—but the big stack of stale waffles in the window clues you in that these are far from top-quality. Below I've listed a couple of good options that sell both Liège-style and Brussels-style waffles (for details on both types, see page 337).

Maison Dandoy, which has been making waffles since the 19th century, is the pricey, elegant choice. You can take the waffles to go or enjoy them at a table surrounded by an upscale Parisian atmosphere (daily 9:30-19:00, just off the Grand Place at Rue Charles Buls 14, tel. 02-512-6588).

Waffle Factory, near the *Manneken-Pis,* is cheaper but still good. While it has an American fast-food ambience, it's efficient and popular—and thanks to the high turnover, you'll usually get a waffle that's grilled while you wait. Get your waffle to go, or sit upstairs to enjoy some peace and quiet (and free Wi-Fi). Besides the standard waffle styles, they also serve their own innovations: the *waffine* (a thin waffle filled with Nutella or jam) or a *lunchwaf* (with savory fillings). For a very Belgian taste treat, top your waffle with *speculoos*—a decadent spread with a peanut butter-like consistency but made with ground-up gingerbread cookies (€2-3 waffles plus toppings, open long hours daily, look for green-and-red-striped awning at corner of Rue du Lombard and Rue de l'Etuve).

Rue des Bouchers ("Restaurant Row")

Brussels' restaurant streets, two blocks north of the Grand Place, are touristy and notorious for touts who aggressively suck you in and predatory servers who greedily rip you off. It's hard to justify dining here when far better options sit just a block or two away (see

later listings). If you are seduced into a meal here, order carefully, understand the prices thoroughly, and watch your wallet.

Restaurant Chez Leon is a touristy mussels factory, slamming out piles of cheap buckets since 1893. The €16 "Formula Leon" is a light meal consisting of a small bucket of mussels, fries, and a beer (daily 12:00-23:00, kids under 12 eat free, Rue des Bouchers 18, tel. 02-511-1415).

Aux Armes de Bruxelles is a venerable restaurant that has been serving reliably good food to locals in a dressy setting for generations. You'll pay for the formality (€8-23 starters, €19-57 main dishes, €22 fixed-price lunch, €40 fixed-price dinner, daily 12:00-22:45, indoor seating only, Rue des Bouchers 13, tel. 02-511-5550, www.auxarmesdebruxelles.com).

Restaurant Vincent has you enter through the kitchen to enjoy their 1905-era ambience. This place is better for meat dishes than for seafood (€15-20 starters, €20-32 main dishes, daily 12:00-14:30 & 18:30-23:30, Rue des Dominicains 8-10, tel. 02-511-2607, Michel and Jacques).

Finer Dining near Rue des Bouchers

These options, though just steps away from those listed above, are more authentic and a better value.

Restaurant de l'Ogenblik, a remarkably peaceful eddy just off the raging restaurant row, fills an early 20th-century space in the corner of an arcade. The waiters serve well-presented, near-gourmet French cuisine. This mussels-free zone has a great, splittable rack of lamb with 10 vegetables. Their sea bass with risotto and truffle oil, at €27, is a hit with return eaters. Reservations are smart (€20 first courses, €30 plates, Mon-Sat 12:00-14:30 & 19:00-24:00, closed Sun, across from Restaurant Vincent—listed earlier—at Galerie des Princes 1, tel. 02-511-6151, www.ogenblik.be, Yves).

Belga Queen Brasserie, a huge, dressy brasserie filling a palatial former bank building, is crowded with Brussels' beautiful people and visiting European diplomats. It's more expensive than most of my alternatives, but their "creative Belgian cuisine" is admirable, the service is sharp, and the experience is memorable—from the fries served in silver cones, to the double-decker platters of iced shellfish (€65/person for the Belga Queen platter), to the transparent toilet stalls, which become opaque only after you nervously lock the door (€15-25 starters, €20-30 main dishes, €30-50 fixed-price meals, daily 12:00-14:30 & 19:00-24:00, reservations smart, Rue

BRUSSELS SLEEPING, EATING & MORE

Sampling Belgian Beer in Brussels

Brussels is full of atmospheric cafés to savor the local brew. The places lining the Grand Place are touristy, but the setting—plush, old medieval guildhalls fronting all that cobbled wonder—is hard to beat.

All varieties of Belgian beer are available, but Brussels' most distinctive beers are *lambic*-based. Look for *lambic doux, lambic blanche, gueuze* (pronounced "kurrs"), and *faro,* as well as fruit-flavored *lambics,* such as *kriek* (cherry) and *framboise* (raspberry—*frambozen* in Dutch). These beers look and taste more like a dry, somewhat bitter cider. The brewer doesn't add yeast—the beer ferments naturally from wild yeast floating in the marshy air around Brussels. For more on Belgian beer, see page 338.

The following places are generally open daily from about 11:00 until late but aren't really good for a full meal—though you can usually get lighter fare, such as a cold-meat plate, a *tartine* (open-face sandwich), or a salad.

A la Mort Subite, a few steps above the top end of the Galeries St. Hubert, is a classic old bar that has retained its 1928 decor...

and its loyal customers seem to go back just about as far. Named after the "sudden death" playoff that workingmen used to end their lunchtime dice games, it still has an unpretentious, working-class feel. The decor is simple, with wood tables, grimy yellow wallpaper, and some-other-era garland trim. Tiny metal plates on the walls mark spots where gas-powered flames once flickered—used by patrons to light their cigars. A typical lunch or snack here is an omelet with a salad or a *tartine* spread with *fromage blanc* (cream cheese) or pressed meat. Eat it with one of the home-brewed, *lambic*-based beers. This is a good place to try the *kriek* beer. While their beer list is limited, they do have Chimay on tap (Rue Montagne aux Herbes Potagères 7, tel. 02-513-1318).

Le Cirio, across from the Bourse, feels a bit more upscale,

Fosse-aux-Loups 32, tel. 02-217-2187, www.belgaqueen.be). The vault downstairs is a plush cigar and cocktail lounge.

IN STE. CATHERINE, NEAR THE OLD FISH MARKET

A 10-minute walk from the old center puts you in "the village within the city" area of Ste. Catherine (Métro: Sainte-Catherine/Sint-Katelijne). The historic fish market here has spawned a tradition of fine restaurants specializing mostly in seafood. The old fish canal survives, and if you walk around it, you'll see plenty of entic-

with a faded yet still luxurious gilded-wood interior, booths with velvet padding, and dark tables that bear the skid marks of over a century's worth of beer glasses. The service is jaded—perhaps understandably given its touristy location (Rue de la Bourse 18-20, tel. 02-512-1395).

A la Bécasse is lower profile than Le Cirio, with less pretense and a simple wood-panel and wood-table decor that appeals to both poor students and lunching businessmen. The *lambic doux* has been served in clay jars since 1825. This place is just around the corner from Le Cirio, toward the Grand Place, hidden away at the end of a tight lane (Tabora 11, tel. 02-511-0006).

Poechenellekelder Estaminet is a great bar with lots of real character located conveniently, if oddly, right across the street from the *Manneken-Pis*. As the word *estaminet* (tavern) indicates, it's not brewery-owned, so they have a great selection of beers. Inside tables are immersed in *Pis* kitsch and puppets. Outside tables offer some fine people-watching (Rue du Chêne 5, tel. 02-511-9262).

Moeder Lambic has a modern industrial feel, with owners who are maniacs about craft beer and sell only traditional brews from independent producers. With a knowledgeable staff, this is an excellent place to start exploring the acquired tastes of *lambic, gueuze,* and *kriek.* For a snack, try the toast with *pottekaas,* a spread made with local white cheese and beer (on a square off Boulevard Anspach at Place Fontainas 8, tel. 02-503-6068).

Two tiny and extremely characteristic bars are tucked away down long entry corridors just off Rue du Marché aux Herbes. **A l'Imaige Nostre-Dame** (closed Sun, at #8) and **Au Bon Vieux Temps** (at #12) both treat fine beer with great reverence and seem to have extremely local clientele, which you're bound to meet if you grab a stool.

Delirium Tap House is a sloppy frat party nightly with no ambience, a noisy young crowd, beer-soaked wooden floors, rock 'n' roll, and a famous variety of great Belgian beers on tap (near "Restaurant Row," not far from Chez Leon at Impasse de la Fidélité 4).

ing places to eat. Make the circuit, considering these very good, yet very different, options.

Bij den Boer, a fun, noisy eatery popular with locals and tourists, has inviting tables out on the esplanade and feels like a traditional and very successful brasserie. Their specialty: fish (€14-16 starters, €22-30 main dishes, €30 four-course fixed-price meal, Mon-Sat 12:00-14:30 & 18:00-22:30, closed Sun, Quai aux Briques 60, tel. 02-512-6122, www.bijdenboer.com).

La Marie Joseph, stylish and modern—both the food and

the clientele—serves fancy fish and fries, and earns raves from the natives (€15-22 starters, €24-34 plates, Tue-Sun 12:00-15:00 & 18:30-23:00, closed Mon, no reservations taken, Quai au Bois à Brûler 47-49, tel. 02-218-0596, Sara is the fourth generation to run the place).

Au Laboureur, where charming Filip churns out handmade shrimp croquettes from a stand attached to the café, attracts a wide cross-section of Bruxellois—from posh lawyers to laborers to young alternative types. For €10 you get two croquettes worthy of a light lunch or a shared snack. Look out for rotating alternatives: calamari, haddock, or some other fried ocean dweller. Order food at the stand and grab a seat at any table. The bar staff will come around for drink orders. Pay for drinks with the waiters and seafood to Filip (daily 16:00-22:00, later on weekends, open for lunch on Sat, Rue de Flandre 108, tel. 02-512-1382).

Le Royal is a cool-feeling brasserie serving tasty and elegantly presented food that's worth the splurge. They offer both traditional (and well-executed) Belgian staples and modern fusion dishes—some with a hint of Asian influence. Sit in the trendy interior, or choose a sidewalk table. Reservations are smart (€7-20 starters, €20-26 main dishes, €3 sides, daily 12:00-15:00 & 18:00-23:00 except closed Tue for lunch, Rue de Flandre 103, tel. 02-217-8500, www.royalbrasseriebrussels.be).

La Villette Restaurant ("The Slaughterhouse") is a romantic, subdued alternative, serving traditional Belgian cuisine: heavy, meaty stews, eels, *stoemp* (mashed potatoes and vegetables), and dishes with beer. The chef proudly makes the sauces from scratch, and Agata can match your order to the right beer. The restaurant has a charming red-and-white-tablecloth interior and good outdoor seating facing a small square (€15 two-course fixed-price lunch, €20-25 plates, Mon-Sat 12:00-14:30 & 18:30-22:30, closed Sun, Rue du Vieux Marché-aux-Grains 3, tel. 02-512-7550).

Restaurant La Marée is a classic local scene a couple of blocks away from the trendy canalside places. An untouristy, less trendy bistro with an older clientele, an open kitchen, and an inviting menu, it specializes in mussels and seafood—their only pretense is their insistence that it's fresh (€19-26 meals, Tue-Sat 12:00-14:00 & 18:30-22:00, closed Sun-Mon, near Rue du Marché-aux-Porcs at Rue de Flandre 99, tel. 02-511-0040).

Drinks with a View: **Skylab Cocktail Bar** is perfect for a drink before or after dinner. It's a warm and welcoming bar with great outdoor tables right on the canal, and a casual, classy, mature ambience (Tue-Sun 16:00 until late, closed Mon, Quai au Bois à Brûler 9, tel. 02-203-0350).

Cheap, Fast, and Tasty Lunches in Ste. Catherine

Place Ste. Catherine, which branches off from the side of Ste. Catherine Church, is lined with enjoyable cafés with outdoor seating.

Mer du Nord/Nordzee is as delicious as it is inexpensive. This seafood bar—basically a grill attached to a fresh fish shop—cooks up whatever it catches and serves it on small tapas-like plates with glasses of wine to a very appreciative local crowd. Just belly up to the counter and place your order, then eat it standing at the tables. The €7 *scampi à la plancha* (grilled shrimp) is exquisite (€4-7 small dishes, Tue-Thu 11:00-17:00, Fri-Sat 11:00-18:00, Sun 11:00-20:00, closed Mon, Rue Ste. Catherine 45, at corner with Place Ste. Catherine, tel. 02-513-1192). The similar **Poissonerie/Vishandel ABC,** across the street, has a comparable operation.

Crèmerie de Linkebeek, owned by Jordan (who's part American) and Laurence, is the best place in town to shop for local Bel-  gian cheeses—rubbed and flavored with beer rather than wine or alcohol. The English-speaking staff is happy to help you explore the options and choose the perfect cheese for your picnic (they also sell baguettes, wine, and crackers—you could assemble a light meal or a snack right here). At midday, they also sell delicious €4 baguette sandwiches to go—grab one before they sell out (Mon 9:00-15:00, Tue-Sat 9:00-18:00, closed Sun, Rue du Vieux Marché-aux-Grains 4, tel. 02-512-3510).

Le Pain Quotidien ("The Daily Bread") is a popular, upscale, artisan bakery chain selling good sandwiches and other dishes in a rustic yet dignified setting (Mon-Sat 7:30-19:00, Sun 7:30-18:00, Rue Antoine Dansaert 16A, tel. 02-502-2361). Across the street is **Comocomo** (#19), serving mediocre Basque-style tapas with an innovative twist: on a conveyor belt, sushi bar-style.

ON OR NEAR PLACE ST-GÉRY

For a less touristy, more trendy and youthful scene, head to Place St-Géry (a.k.a. Sint-Goriksplein). The epicenter is at the intersection of Pont de la Carpe and Plétinckx street. This area is more about drinking than about dining, but several eateries are mixed in among the bars: sushi, Italian, Thai, Vietnamese, Indian, and so on. Rue Jules van Praet is lined mostly with interchangeable Asian and Indian restaurants. You could just take your pick. But for a more memorable meal, consider one of the following places.

On Rue des Chartreux: Just across Rue Van Artevelde from the Place St-Géry action, this street has several enticing options. **La Fin de Siècle** is a bohemian scene serving basic, unpretentious

Belgian/French fare. With appropriately turn-of-the-century atmosphere, mismatched secondhand furniture, and long, shared tables, it has a youthful energy (€14-19 meals, food served daily 18:00-24:00, at #9, tel. 02-512-5123). Next door at #7, **Le Greenwich** has an even more exquisite Art Nouveau facade. Just up the street, **Publico** is hip but accessible, with a black-subway-tile interior and well-priced Belgian and Mediterranean fare. Reservations are smart on weekends (€12 weekday lunch specials, €13-19 main courses, Mon-Sat 12:00-24:00, closed Sun, at #32, tel. 02-503-0430, www.publicobxl.be).

Caffeine: For excellent coffee, drop by **OR Espresso Bar,** the first specialty coffee roaster in Brussels (daily until 18:00, Rue Auguste Orts 9, tel. 02-511-7400).

IN MATONGÉ

The neighborhood of Matongé—just past the royal sights of the Upper Town—is a fun-to-explore mix of vivid African immigrant culture and Belgian trend seekers. If you have time, ride the Métro to Porte de Namur/Naamsepoort and follow my self-guided walk on page 151, then hang around for a meal.

On and near Rue Saint-Boniface: This broad street, leading up to St. Boniface Church, has some great trendy options—Belgian, French, Italian, Japanese, Greek, and more. Two inviting spots are just in front of the church: **Le Clan des Belges** is a high-energy hit, with a rustic, cozy interior and a lively, leafy outdoor dining zone with tables in the shadow of the church steeple (€14-18 Belgian classics, daily 12:00-14:30 & 19:00-23:00, Rue de la Paix 20, tel. 02-511-1121 www.leclandesbelges.com). **Le Comptoir,** a mod French bistro across the street, is a more affordable choice (€6 pitas, €13 burgers, daily 12:00-14:30 & 18:00-23:00, Sat-Sun open throughout the day, Rue de la Paix 22, tel. 02-503-2236). A few steps away from the middle of this drag, **Eccome No!** is a handy spot for pizza by the slice (Tue-Sat 12:00-22:00, closed Sun-Mon, Rue Ernest Solvay 10, tel. 02-502-1611).

On Rue Longue Vie: Around the corner from the church, you'll find a pair of fiercely competitive eateries—**Soleil d'Afrique** and **Cap Africa**—dishing up similar menus of African classics (both have €7-10 plates, open long hours daily).

Place Fernand Cocq: A few blocks from the heart of Matongé, this grassy square boasts a cluster of inviting bars and eateries with sidewalk tables. **Il Nobile** is a popular pizzeria (daily, at #24); **Volle Gas** is a classic, energetic brasserie with old-fashioned woody ambience and crank-'em-out Belgian classics (closed Sun, at #21); and—across the square—**L'Amour Fou** is a painfully hip, artsy bar proud of its burgers (daily except closed Mon lunch, Chaussée d'Ixelles 185).

Shopping in Brussels

The obvious temptations—available absolutely everywhere—are chocolate and lace. Other popular Brussels souvenirs include EU gear with the gold circle of stars on a blue background (flags, T-shirts, mugs, bottle openers, hats, pens, and so on) and miniature reproductions of the *Manneken-Pis* or the Atomium. Belgian beers are a fun, imbibable souvenir that you can either enjoy at a picnic while traveling, or pack (carefully) in your checked luggage to take home. Here's a rundown of where you can buy certain items:

Souvenirs near the Grand Place

The streets immediately surrounding the Grand Place are jammed with Belgium's tackiest souvenir stands, with a few good shops mixed in. In my Grand Place Walk, I've listed some good places to pick up chocolates (page 158) and to browse for tapestries and lace (page 165).

De Biertempel, facing the TI on the street that runs below the Grand Place, not only stocks hundreds of types of Belgian beer, but an entire wall of beer glasses—each one designed to highlight the qualities of a specific beer (Rue du Marché aux Herbes 56, tel. 02-502-1906).

Fashion on Rue Antoine Dansaert

While Antwerp is the epicenter of Belgian design, Brussels has worked hard in recent years to catch up. To browse the best selec-

tion of Belgian boutiques, start by heading up Rue Antoine Dansaert (from the big Bourse building, cross Boulevard Anspach and continue straight up Rue Auguste Orts, which becomes Rue Antoine Dansaert). Along here, you'll see an eclectic array of both Belgian and international apparel. While specific designers seem to come and go, the genteel vibe persists. Window-shopping this street, you'll pass fine parks. After Place du Nouveau Marché aux Grains, the high-fashion focus downshifts, and the rest of the street feels like an emerging neighborhood with some funkier, lower-rent shops. You could return the way you came, or cut a few blocks northeast to the long fish market square at Ste. Catherine, which runs roughly parallel to Rue Antoine Dansaert.

Funky Design Shops near Place St-Géry

Brussels has its own term for what we might call "hipsters": *bobo,* short for *bourgeois-bohème*...bohemian middle-class kids with enough money and free time for creative endeavors. You'll find *bobo* pockets around town, but these two streets are a good place to start.

Rue des Chartreux, which angles off of Rue Antoine Dansaert, has a decidedly lower-rent aura and a lineup of funky and creative shops, such as **Blender 01** (style and gadgets, at #18) and **Espace Bizarre** (home decor and furniture, #19).

A bit closer to the Grand Place, the lively, café-lined **Rue du Marché au Charbon** and the streets nearby (especially Plattesteen) are another good area to browse for creative shops.

Big Chains on Rue Neuve

This street, a few blocks north of the Grand Place, is where you'll find big department stores and other international shops. The giant City2 complex on this street is the downtown's primary modern shopping mall.

Secondhand Shops in Marolles

This somewhat seedy neighborhood is well-known for its secondhand shops. Rue Blaes and Rue Haute, which run southwest from near the old Tour d'Angle (described in the Upper Town Walk chapter) to the Midi/Zuid/South Train Station, are lined with several characteristic stores. There's a lively flea market each morning (7:00-14:00, best on weekends) on Place du Jeu de Balle, just off of Rue Blaes.

A Taste of Africa in Matongé

Browse the neighborhood of Matongé (described on page 151) for colorful fabrics and exotic ingredients at the many African grocery stores (you'll find the highest concentration along Chaussée de Wavre). A few blocks away, the **Afrikamäli** boutique sells fair-trade, traditional crafts from Africa (Tue-Sat 11:00-19:00, closed Sun-Mon, Rue Ernest Solvay 19, tel. 02-503-0074).

Nightlife in Brussels

Pick up the free *Agenda* and *Brussels Unlimited* magazines from the TI, which list events including opera, symphony, and ballet. Make a point to savor the Grand Place at night, when it becomes even more magical—as day-tripping tourists are gone and the Town Hall spire is floodlit.

Films

At one time, Brussels had a wide range of characteristic little cinemas. These days, most Bruxellois flock to the multiplexes; a handy one is the **UGC** cinema on De

Brouckère square (look for *v.o.* for the original version; *v.f.* means it's dubbed in French). There's also a small art-house cinema in the Galeries St. Hubert; movies here play in their original language (generally not English, as these are typically international films), with Dutch and French subtitles.

After-Dark Neighborhoods

The most interesting neighborhood to explore after-hours (or any time of day) is just a few steps west of the Grand Place. **Rue du Marché au Charbon** (Kolenmarkt) is the center of Brussels' gay scene, with many lively cafés and restaurants with outdoor seating. The trendy eateries, shops, and businesses along here change so fast, the locals can't keep track.

Across Boulevard Anspach is **Place St-Géry,** where you'll find a raucous collection of lively bars with rollicking interiors and a

sea of outdoor tables. Mappa Mondo anchors the area, with two levels of scenic tables. Zebra Bar, across the street by the market hall, is another fun scene. And inside the market hall is the Café des Halles, with chichi cocktails in an elegantly airy, open-feeling, steel-beamed space, and DJs on the weekends.

A five-minute walk northeast is the pleasant **Ste. Catherine** district, with lively local restaurants and hotels huddled around the Church of Ste. Catherine and the old fish market (and the cool and inviting Skylab Cocktail Bar, described earlier under "Eating in Brussels"). On Place Ste. Catherine, the little red wagon with the brightly painted macaw sells tropical drinks to an appreciative local crowd; in warm weather, young people sip mojitos while socializing on the square.

Farther from the center, the **Matongé** African immigrant neighborhood is lively after dark. Rue Saint-Boniface, leading up to the front door of the neighborhood church, is "café row"—with plenty of choices for an al fresco drink. Hiding behind the church is the lively L'Athénée bar, with appealing outdoor tables, a pubby interior, and a variety of Belgian beers (but no food). The widest selection of bars and cafés clusters around Place Fernand Cocq.

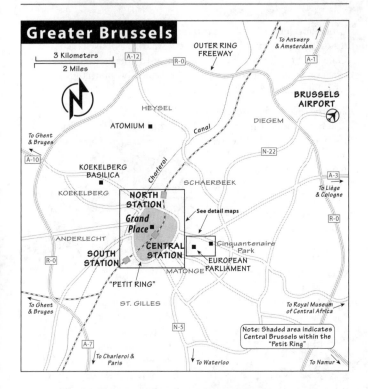

Greater Brussels

OUTER RING
FREEWAY

To Antwerp
& Amsterdam

3 Kilometers   A-12   R-0   A-1

2 Miles

BRUSSELS
AIRPORT

HEYSEL

ATOMIUM ■   DIEGEM

To Ghent
& Bruges

A-10

Canal   N-22

KOEKELBERG
BASILICA ■   SCHAERBEEK

A-3

To Liège
& Cologne

KOEKELBERG

NORTH
STATION

Grand   See detail maps
Place ■   R-0

ANDERLECHT   CENTRAL
STATION   ■ ■ Cinquantenaire
Park

SOUTH
STATION   EUROPEAN
R-0   MATONGE PARLIAMENT

"PETIT RING"

To Ghent
& Bruges   ST. GILLES   To Royal Museum
of Central Africa

A-7   N-5   Note: Shaded area indicates
Central Brussels within the
"Petit Ring"

To Charleroi &
Paris   To Waterloo   To Namur

Brussels Connections

BY TRAIN

Brussels has three train stations: Centraal/Central, Midi/Zuid/South, and Nord/Noord/North. Most trains stop at all three stations, but high-speed international trains serve only the Midi/Zuid/South Station. Any train ticket to any Brussels station includes a transfer to any other Brussels train station (but not the airport). For more details on all three stations—and tips on connecting between them—see page 119. For schedules, see www.belgiumrail.be or www.bahn.com. For general information on rail travel in Belgium, see page 352.

At any station, as you wait on the platform for your train, watch the track notice board that tells you which train is approaching. Trains zip in and out constantly, so a train with an open door on your train's track—three minutes before your departure time—may well be the wrong train. Anxious travelers, who think their train has arrived early, often board the wrong train on the right track.

Trains Within Belgium and the Netherlands

From All Brussels Stations by Train to: Bruges (2/hour, 1 hour, catch InterCity train—direction: Ostend or Knokke-Blanken-berge), **Antwerp** (3/hour, 40-50 minutes), **Ghent** (3/hour, 35 minutes), **Ypres/Ieper** (hourly, 2 hours, some change in Kortrijk). The following destinations are in the Netherlands: **Haarlem** (hourly, 3 hours, transfer in Roosendaal and Leiden), **Delft** (almost hourly, 2.5 hours, change in Roosendaal), **The Hague** (almost hourly, 2.5 hours).

Getting Between Brussels and Amsterdam: Slower, regional trains leave for Amsterdam and Amsterdam's Schiphol Airport from all three Brussels stations about hourly (3 hours to Schiphol, 3.5 hours to Amsterdam's Central Station). For a faster (but more expensive) connection, the high-speed Thalys train goes direct from Brussels' Midi/Zuid/South Station to Amsterdam's Central Station and Schiphol Airport (about hourly, 2 hours).

High-Speed Trains Outside Belgium and the Netherlands

The following special, high-speed train lines depart only from the Midi/Zuid/South Station, tracks 1-6 (station described in detail on page 122; for more on high-speed trains, see page 354). For schedules, see www.bahn.com or www.b-europe.com (the Belgian rail website for cross-border trains).

From Brussels by Thalys Train to: Paris (2/hour, 1.5 hours, €40-100 second class), **Cologne** (9/day, 2 hours). For the best fares, buy Thalys tickets early. Rail-pass holders must prebook an expensive seat reservation—and they can sell out fast. Train info: Toll tel. 07-066-7788 (long wait), www.thalys.com.

By TGV Train to France: French TGV trains connect to **Paris' Charles de Gaulle Airport** (5/day, 1.5-2 hours, www.tgv-europe.com) and then continue on to various destinations in France, including Marseille, Nice, Rennes, and Bordeaux. TGV trains from Brussels do not go to downtown Paris—to get there, you must transfer at the airport. All TGV seats are reserved, and rail-pass holders pay extra for a reservation (very limited availability).

By ICE Train to Germany: Germany's InterCity Express trains zip to **Cologne** (3/day, 2 hours) and **Frankfurt** (3/day, 3 hours), with onward connections to the rest of the country. Reservations are not required except for advance-ticket discounts.

By Eurostar to/from London: Brussels and London are 2.5 hours apart by Eurostar train (10/day). Trains to London leave from tracks 1 and 2 at Brussels' South Station. Arrive 30 minutes early to get your ticket validated and your luggage and passport checked by British authorities (similar to airport check-in for an international flight).

BRUSSELS SLEEPING, EATING & MORE

Fares vary depending on how far ahead you reserve (up to nine months out), whether you can live with restrictions, and whether you're eligible for any discounts (children, youths, seniors, and rail-pass holders all qualify). Typically a **one-way, full-fare ticket** (with no restrictions on refundability) runs about $450 for first class and $240 for second class. Accepting more restrictions lowers the price substantially, but these **cheaper rates** can sell out quickly.

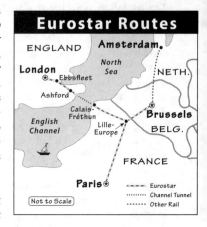

Rail passes qualify you for a discount on a Eurostar ticket. Those traveling with a rail pass that covers Belgium, France, or Britain should look first at the **passholder** fare (about $85-150 for second-class, one-way Eurostar trips, sold through most agents but not through Eurostar website).

See more general info at www.ricksteves.com/eurostar or buy most ticket types at www.eurostar.com (Belgian tel. 02-528-2828).

Discounts on Connecting Trains: A Thalys ticket between Brussels and Paris or a Eurostar ticket between Brussels and London can also cover a regional train connection to/from any Belgian station for a few dollars more, if you choose the "ABS option" at the time of purchase. Just show your ticket when boarding the connecting train(s) within 24 hours of the reserved Brussels arrival or departure (as long as the connecting train is not a Thalys).

BY BUS

You can save money—but not time—by traveling by Eurolines bus from Brussels to Paris or London (Eurolines tel. 02-274-1350 in Brussels, www.eurolines.be).

From Brussels by Bus to: Paris (around €35 one-way, 11/day, 4 hours), **London** (around €45 one-way, 3/day, 2/night, 6 hours).

BY PLANE

Brussels Airport

Brussels' big but well-organized main airport is nine miles north of downtown (many arriving flights pass over the giant, silver molecule-shaped Atomium). The airport is sometimes called "Zaventem," for the nearby town. Terminals A and B are connected by an underground walkway; the train station is in the basement at level -1 (airport code: BRU, tel. 0900-70000, www.brusselsairport.be).

The clear winner for getting to and from the airport is the **train** that runs between the airport and all three Brussels train stations (€8.50, rail-pass holders must pay a €5 airport tax, 4/hour, 25 minutes, daily 6:00-23:00). If you're connecting the airport with Bruges, take this shuttle train and transfer at Brussels' North Station (about 1.5 hours total). For a **taxi,** figure on spending around €40 between downtown Brussels and the airport.

Thrifty Brussels Airlines flies between Brussels and several European cities, including Athens, London, Milan, Florence, Zürich, Nice, Lisbon, Barcelona, Madrid, and more (Belgian tel. 07-035-1111, www.brusselsairlines.com).

Brussels South Charleroi Airport

Discount airlines Ryanair (www.ryanair.com) and Wizz Air (www.wizzair.com) use this smaller airport, located about 30 miles from downtown Brussels in the town of Gosselies, on the outskirts of the city of Charleroi (airport code: CRL, tel. 09-020-2490, www.charleroi-airport.com).

The easiest way to connect to downtown Brussels is to take the **shuttle bus** to Brussels' Midi/Zuid/South Station (likely 2/hour, about 1 hour, runs 4:00-22:30; stops right in front of airport terminal; if you're taking the bus from Brussels' South Station, look for it outside at the corner of Rue de France and Rue de l'Instruction—the bus stop is not clearly marked and can be confusing, but locals are generally happy to help, www.voyages-lelan.be). You can also take a **bus-plus-train** connection: Bus #A connects Charleroi Airport and Charleroi Station (2/hour, 20 minutes, €3 covers both bus and train), where you can take the train to all three Brussels train stations (2/hour, 40 minutes). It's costly by taxi (figure around €85-90); depending on traffic, it can take between 45 minutes and 1.5 hours to drive between downtown Brussels and Charleroi Airport.

BY CRUISE SHIP

The cruise port of Zeebrugge—near Bruges—is often billed by cruise lines as "Brussels." While Bruges is the easier choice for an excursion from that port, Brussels is also doable. For tips on how to get from Zeebrugge's dock to Brussels, see page 99.

BRUSSELS SLEEPING, EATING & MORE

.

ANTWERP

ORIENTATION TO ANTWERP

Antwerpen • Anvers

Antwerp (Antwerpen in Dutch, Anvers in French) is the biggest city and de facto capital of Flanders, with an illustrious history: once Europe's most important trading city, later the hometown of accomplished painter Peter Paul Rubens, destroyed by World War II and then reborn, and recently emerging as a European fashion capital. Today it's one of Europe's finest once-drab, now-reborn "second cities" (like Barcelona, Liverpool, or Rotterdam), where a focus on heavy industry has been supplanted by an edgy, creative spirit of rejuvenation.

Antwerpenaars (as locals are called) have a love of life. If funky urbanity is your thing, Antwerp is one of Europe's most intriguing cities. Antwerp's big-city bustle is the yang to Bruges' cutesy-village yin. And while Brussels has become international, Antwerp has retained more of a local identity—it's an honest, what-you-see-is-what-you-get place that feels more Flemish.

The sights here are easily on par with the best in Belgium. Antwerp is renowned for the art of Rubens (and fellow Flemish artists Anthony van Dyck and Pieter Bruegel), a soaring cathedral, several other interesting churches packed with great art, and a red light district that boxes puritan ears. Historians enjoy the Museum Plantin-Moretus, art lovers savor the Rockox House, fashionistas love the ModeMuseum and nearby window-shopping, children of immigrants are moved by the Red Star Line Museum, and architecture fans drool over the building housing the Museum aan de Stroom (Museum on the River, or MAS for short). And yet, Antwerp is equally enjoyable without a sightseeing agenda, offering fun-to-explore neighborhoods, abundant al fresco café tables, and an inviting main market square with a carillon that jingles the hour.

PLANNING YOUR TIME

While Antwerp could easily fill a day or two, it's worth at least a few hours. You could even see it as a day trip from Brussels—less than an hour away by train—or on the way between Brussels and Amsterdam. With a few hours, take Parts 1 and 2 of my Antwerp City Walk from the train station to the Old Town (by way of the Rubens House), tour the cathedral, ogle the Grote Markt, and pay a quick visit to other sights that intrigue you (if you're really short on time, skip straight to Part 2). Then zip back to the train station on underground trams known as the "metro." If you have more time, Antwerp's diverse restaurant scene and lively nightlife make it well worth considering for an overnight. With a variety of quirky boutiques and cafés on each street, it's a delightful place to linger. As in most of Belgium, be aware that most Antwerp museums are closed on Mondays.

Antwerp Overview

Belgium's "second city" (with a half-million people), Antwerp sits along the east bank of the Scheldt River (Schelde in Dutch). The main tourist area is fairly compact. On a quick trip, narrow your focus to these main zones: the **Old Town** along the river; the **train station area** and **Diamond Quarter** to the east, and the **Meir** shopping district between the Old Town and train station; the newly rejuvenated **Little Island** (Eilandje) zone and the red light district to the north; and, to the south, the **Sint-Andries** fashion district and, beyond that, the happening nightlife zone aptly called **'t Zuid** ("The South"). All of these areas are within about a 30-minute walk (or a quick tram or taxi ride) of one another.

TOURIST INFORMATION

Antwerp's TI has two branches: in the train station (at the head of the tracks, on level 0) and right on the Grote Markt (both open Mon-Sat 9:00-17:45, Sun 9:00-16:45; tel. 03-232-0103, phone answered Mon-Fri only; www.visitantwerp.be). Peruse their racks of fliers and pick up a free town map. The **City Card,** which covers entry to most museums and churches (plus discounts on special exhibits), pays for itself if you visit at least four major museums (€28/48 hours, sold at TI, clock starts running when you visit your first sight).

The Grote Markt TI also has a desk where you can get information and buy tickets for musical events and half-price tickets for weekend performances (possible €1 service charge—depends on event, Tue-Fri 10:00-17:45, Sat 12:00-17:00, closed Sun-Mon, half-price tickets go on sale at 12:00 Fri and Sat only).

Antwerp's History

Owning a prime location where the major Scheldt River meets the North Sea, Antwerp established itself in Roman times as a river-trade town. In the late 15th century, as Bruges' harbor silted up, Antwerp became a major trading center and the Low Countries' top city of the Baroque period. As the Age of Exploration dawned, Portuguese and Spanish ships returning from the New World laden with exotic goods docked here in Antwerp, making it a center of world trade. During Antwerp's 16th-century Golden Age, it became Europe's wealthiest city, with a population of about 100,000.

In the mid-16th century, Antwerp was pulled into the Eighty Years' War between the Dutch rebel Protestants and the ruling Spanish Catholics. In 1576, after growing impatient at not being paid by Habsburg King Philip II, Spanish troops relentlessly sacked Antwerp for three days—massacring thousands of its residents and destroying hundreds of homes. The outraged public response to this so-called "Spanish Fury" elevated Antwerp to the capital of the Dutch Revolt. (The event also irrevocably damaged Antwerp's trade ties with partners who wanted no business with a war zone.) But the crushing, Spanish-led Siege of Antwerp (July 1584 through August 1585) wore down the independence movement, and the city fell under Spanish/Catholic control. In a postwar "brain drain," more than half of the city's population fled to Amsterdam... and took the Golden Age with them.

Seeking to rehabilitate its image in the aftermath of the bloody warfare, the Catholic Church invested mightily in building and decorating churches in Antwerp. A local artist named Peter Paul Rubens (1577-1640)—while arguably less talented than some of his contemporaries—found himself in the right place at the right time, and was a brilliant salesman who allied himself with the Church to win big commission after big commission. Rubens' style epitomized exactly what the Church was looking for: bold, bombastic images trumpeting the glory of God (and his Church on earth).

The treaty that ended the Eighty Years' War in 1648 imposed rigid regulations on shipping on the Scheldt River, restricting Antwerp's outlet to the North Sea. The city devolved from an international port to a regional one. Antwerp's industry, led by an elite group of pro-Catholic traders, began to specialize in luxury goods—cabinets, paintings, tapestries, and so on. The city would languish as a Catholic backwater and second-rate shipping city for centuries, although its industry was kept alive by Napoleon, then by Belgian independence, and later by Belgium's colonization of the Congo. By the 20th century, Antwerp ranked as Europe's second-busiest port (just after Dutch rival Rotterdam). Damaged in both World Wars, Antwerp has recently begun to enjoy a new gentrification that's making it one of Europe's most exciting young cities.

ARRIVAL IN ANTWERP

By Train: Antwerp's Central Station (Antwerpen Centraal)—with a grand century-old shell recently refurbished and expanded with a modern underground zone—is one of Europe's most impressive. It's easy to navigate, with three well-signed levels of tracks connected by escalators and elevators.

Level 0 is the hub of activity, where you'll find a large TI and luggage lockers tucked under the stairs (€3-4, exact change only, swipe the printout when you're ready to open the locker). As you exit to the street, you pass through the great hall—a gorgeously restored temple of travel—with the ticket windows (for more on the history and architecture of the train station, see page 240 of my Antwerp City Walk). Exiting out the front door puts you in the vast and somewhat seedy Koningin Astridplein, with the city's zoo on your immediate right.

To get to the Old Town and most sights, you can **walk** (about 20 minutes to Grote Markt—see my Antwerp City Walk) or ride the **metro** (actually an underground tram line). From next to the TI, take the escalator marked *metro* to the underground tracks. Buy a ticket from the machines on the platform—they accept coins and bills. Take tram #9 or #15 in direction: Linkeroever. Be sure to validate your ticket in the yellow machine when you board. Get off at the Groenplaats stop for the Grote Markt and the historical center. Note: The train station's metro stop is named Diamant (for the surrounding Diamond Quarter).

HELPFUL HINTS

Sightseeing Strategies: Most sights are closed on Mondays, and many sights are free the last Wednesday of the month. You can save money with the City Card (described earlier) if you plan to visit at least four major museums.

Markets: At the charming Vrijdagmarkt—"Friday Market"—antiques and other secondhand items are auctioned off in Dutch. The Sunday morning Vogeltjesmarkt, or "Bird Market" (at Oudevaartplaats), features pets, clothes, food, and other items.

City Views: Museum aan de Stroom (MAS) has a free rooftop panorama with sprawling views of the city. A less impressive view of the harbor is available from the panorama tower of the Red Star Line Museum.

GETTING AROUND ANTWERP

Sprawling Antwerp is walkable, but using the city's public-transit network saves time and sweat. For visitors, the main downtown corridor, where underground tram ("metro") lines #9 and #15 connect, matters the most. You'll most likely use these four stops: Diamant (train station), Opera (at east end of Meir shopping street), Meir (at west end of Meir shopping street, a block from the Rubens House), and Groenplaats (with a handy underground grocery store, near the cathedral and Grote Markt). Other tram lines can be confusing, as lines going in a similar direction can be marked by different end stations: If you're heading from the train station to the Old Town, look for *Linkeroever* or *Zwijndrecht;* in the opposite direction, from the Old Town to the train station, look for *Merksem/Eksterlaar/Boechout.*

A ticket costs €1.30 and is good for a single ride (including a transfer, if necessary). It's easy to buy tickets at machines on the platform (select the "Zone 1-2" ticket); otherwise pay €2 on board. Other options: day pass-€5, three-day pass-€10, shareable 10-ride ticket-€9. Validate your ticket when you board—day passes need validation only once. Smart travelers buy their return ticket at the same time to avoid later hassles. Information: Toll tel. 070-220-200, www.delijn.be.

A simpler alternative on a short visit could be the hourly hop-on, hop-off **Citytour Shuttle,** an old-fashioned trolley bus that makes a loop connecting several harder-to-reach destinations; the 50-minute route includes the train station, the Grote Markt, the MAS museum, and the Red Star Line Museum (€10 for all-day ticket, April-Oct departs from the Grote Markt at the top of each hour 10:30-15:30, runs later Sat-Sun and July-Aug, www.hopnstop.eu, tel. 0479-113-974).

Tours in Antwerp

Walking Tours

The TI organizes a two-hour historical **walking tour** through town combining English and French (€8—or €6 if you book at least a day in advance, July-Aug daily at 14:00, Sept-June Sat-Sun only, departs from TI on Grote Markt).

Local Guide

The TI can arrange a private guide for an affordable city tour (€65/2 hours, tel. 03-338-9539, gidsenwerking@stad.antwerpen.be). One of their excellent guides, **Ariane van Duytekom,** tells Antwerp's story well, with a knack for psychoanalyzing its complicated history. If Ariane isn't available, the TI can book another good guide for you.

SIGHTS IN ANTWERP

Antwerp offers visitors an eclectic array of sightseeing. If you have just one day (or less), you'll need to be selective: art, churches, history, fashion, and so on. Most of these sights are stops on the city walk described in the next chapter. And every sight is either in the old center or within walking distance. Most sights are free the last Wednesday of the month.

IN THE OLD TOWN
▲▲Rubens House (Rubenshuis)

Here's Europe's best look at the artist Peter Paul Rubens. By touring the house he lived and worked in, you get a sense of both the man and his art. Be aware that, though the house looks old, it's been remodeled so many times over the years that what we see today is not so much Rubens' original house but more of a well-executed replica. There are better places in Antwerp to see old houses (such as the Rockox House and Museum Plantin-Moretus) and better places to see Rubens' paintings (the cathedral). But this exhibit shows his lifestyle and working methods—interesting even to people who think Peter Paul Rubens is the guy who plays Pee-Wee Herman.

Cost and Hours: €8, Tue-Sun 10:00-17:00, closed Mon, last entry 30 minutes before closing, audioguide-€2, Wapper 9, tel. 03-201-1555, www.rubenshuis.be.

✪ See the Rubens House Tour chapter.

▲▲Cathedral of Our Lady
(Onze-Lieve-Vrouwekathedraal)

Antwerp's biggest church has a spire that shoots 400 feet up from the middle of the Old Town, like a Gothic rocket. Its cavernous interior is packed with fine artwork, including several paintings by

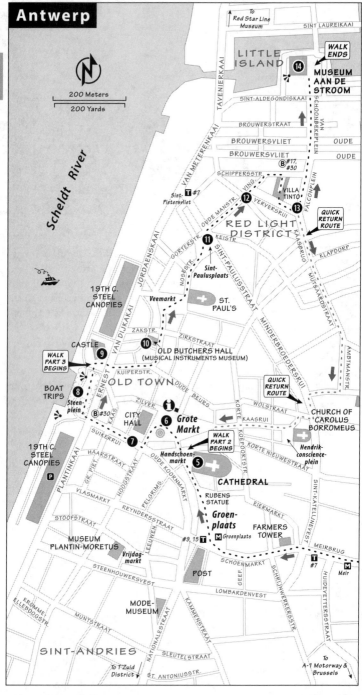

Antwerp

To Red Star Line Museum

SINT LAUREIKAAI

WALK ENDS

LITTLE ISLAND

MUSEUM AAN DE STROOM

⑭

SINT-ALDEGONDISKAAI

N

200 Meters
200 Yards

BROUWERSTRAAT

BROUWERSVLIET

BROUWERSVLIET

OUDE

OUDE

Scheldt River

⑬ #17, #30

SCHIPPERSSTR.

VILLA TINTO

QUICK RETURN ROUTE

Sint-Pietersvliet ⓣ #7

RED LIGHT DISTRICT

⑫

VERVERSRUI

KLAPDORP

⑪

Sint-Paulusplaats

19TH C. STEEL CANOPIES

Veemarkt

ST. PAUL'S

ZAKSTR.

ZIRKSTRAAT

MINDERBROEDERSRUI

CASTLE ⑨

⑩ OLD BUTCHERS HALL (MUSICAL INSTRUMENTS MUSEUM)

QUICK RETURN ROUTE

WALK PART 3 BEGINS

OLD TOWN

OUDE BEURS

WOLSTRAAT

CHURCH OF CAROLUS BORROMEUS

BOAT TRIPS ⑧

Steenplein

ⓑ #30

CITY HALL

ZILVER

KAASRUI

Hendrik-conscience-plein

⑥ Grote Markt

KOEPOORTSTR.

KORTE NIEUWESTRAAT

19TH C. STEEL CANOPIES

Ⓟ

⑦

Handschoenmarkt

WALK PART 2 BEGINS

⑤

CATHEDRAL

MUSEUM PLANTIN-MORETUS

#9, 15 ⓣ

RUBENS STATUE

Groen-plaats

Ⓜ Groenplaats

FARMERS TOWER

EIERMARKT

MEIRBRUG

Meir ⓣ #7 Ⓜ

Vrijdagmarkt

POST

SCHOENMARKT

LOMBARDENVEST

MODE-MUSEUM

SINT-ANDRIES

To 't Zuid District

To A-1 Motorway & Brussels

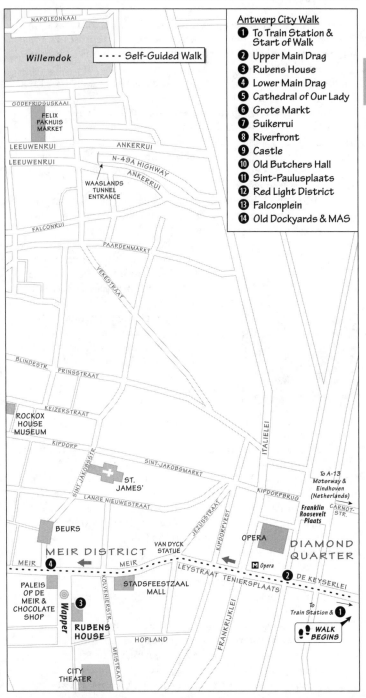

Antwerp City Walk

1 To Train Station & Start of Walk
2 Upper Main Drag
3 Rubens House
4 Lower Main Drag
5 Cathedral of Our Lady
6 Grote Markt
7 Suikerrui
8 Riverfront
9 Castle
10 Old Butchers Hall
11 Sint-Paulusplaats
12 Red Light District
13 Falconplein
14 Old Dockyards & MAS

---- Self-Guided Walk

Rubens. While the Museum of Fine Arts is closed for renovation (through late 2017), you'll see these fine original canvases in situ (in the setting for which they were intended) here in the cathedral.

Cost and Hours: €6, cash only, Mon-Fri 10:00-17:00, Sat 10:00-15:00, Sun 13:00-16:00, Handschoenmarkt, tel. 03-213-9951, www.dekathedraal.be.

Tours: Free English tours are offered most days when guides are available—ask. Some English info is located near Rubens' paintings. The €2 audioguide (along with a rack of free pamphlets) focuses on the church's three-paneled paintings that hang in their original positions, creating a private little garden of worship space at the base of each column.

Visiting the Church: Stepping inside, notice how remark-ably wide the cathedral is (250 feet), with three aisles on either side of the nave. Looking up, you'll see  that the Gothic design is also dramati-cally vertical—everything stretches up-ward (90 feet) toward heaven. In the Middle Ages, the interior was filled with countless candles, and this was the only place to find bright light after dark. The stained-glass windows (some of them still original) colorized the light emanat-ing from inside, drawing worshippers like moths to a flame. At the base of the pillars, notice that each local guild had its own private altar area, where mem-bers celebrated baptisms, weddings, and funerals—this was truly a community church.

The cathedral has a troubled history: It was gutted by the fire of 1533, then stripped of its medieval decoration (1566) by icono-clastic Protestants. (A few fragments of colorful murals remain on the underside of the vaults, where the iconoclasts couldn't reach.) After the Catholics came to power (1585), they redecorated the church in bubbly Baroque, including several pieces by Rubens. Na-poleon's troops (late 18th century) turned the church into a sta-ble and carried off several Rubens paintings (only returned later). Church leaders redecorated with a hodgepodge of ecclesiastical art brought here from elsewhere, including the Baroque pulpit (1713), a riot of birds, foliage, and cupids symbolizing the spread of the faith and the word.

The church's collection includes three huge Rubens paintings.

In the *Raising of the Cross* (left transept, 1610-1611), biblical bodybuilders strain to upright the cross, which is heavy with the swooning body of Christ. The painting is emotive, sumptuous, and almost sensual. Having just returned from eight years in Italy, the influence is obvious—Michelangelo's twisting poses and bulky musculature and Caravaggio's light-dark contrast. Notice how lifelike Jesus' skin appears—a Rubens forte. The bold diagonal composition, thickly muscled bodies in motion, bright (almost garish) colors, and illusion of movement are vintage Rubens. The painting is the inner panel of a hinged altarpiece; it was normally kept closed, and opened to reveal this scene only on special occasions—when its color and motion must have been even

more striking to churchgoers unaccustomed to this sort of spectacle.

The Assumption (choir area, over the main altar, 1626) shows the moment that Mary—the cathedral's namesake—was brought up to heaven. Beneath Mary are the 12 apostles (after the Resurrection, the faithful disciple Matthias replaced Judas) and the three women who were present at her death. The role of Mary in church doctrine was one of the major dividing lines between Catholics and Protestants; whereas the Catholic Church considered her a saint to be venerated, the Protestants embraced the notion that she was an ordinary woman called to do God's work. The gauzy heroine-worship of this canvas makes it clear who finally controlled the turf here.

Rubens' diagonal composition in **Descent from the Cross** (right transept, 1612-1614) is the mirror image of *Raising of the Cross,* the

painting across the nave. It's a freeze-frame of an action-packed moment...just as workers strained to erect the cross with Christ's limp body, now they struggle to lower him from it. But at this somber moment, the subjects seem to be moving more slowly, methodically. Notice the pallor of Christ's dead skin—a strong contrast to the lifelike luster of the other painting. The details make the poignancy of this moment come to life: the man in the top-right corner who's holding onto the shroud with his teeth; Mary's outstretched arm, in a tender matronly effort to comfort her son even in death; and, in the lower-right section, a blood-filled bronze basin holding the crown of thorns and the nails. This main canvas is flanked by side panels showing people "carrying" Christ in two very different ways: On the left, a pregnant Mary, and on the right, presenting

Antwerp at a Glance

▲▲**Rubens House** The richly decorated home, studio, and garden of Peter Paul Rubens, with a few of his paintings to boot. **Hours:** Tue-Sun 10:00-17:00, closed Mon. See page 225.

▲▲**Cathedral of Our Lady** Cavernous church packed with fine artwork, including paintings by Rubens. **Hours:** Mon-Fri 10:00-17:00, Sat 10:00-15:00, Sun 13:00-16:00. See page 225.

▲▲**Museum Plantin-Moretus** Early printing presses, workshops, and memorabilia from Antwerp's Golden Age. **Hours:** Tue-Sun 10:00-17:00, closed Mon. See page 233.

▲▲**Red Star Line Museum** Illustrates the "other end" of the Ellis Island experience, where emigrants were processed on their way to the New World. **Hours:** Tue-Sun 10:00-17:00, Easter-Oct Sat-Sun until 18:00, closed Mon. See page 236.

▲**Rockox House Museum** Aristocratic 17th-century home with impressive art, furniture, and delightful garden courtyard. **Hours:** Tue-Sun 10:00-17:00, closed Mon. See page 231.

▲**ModeMuseum (MoMu)** Rotating exhibits showcasing contemporary Belgian fashion and designers, and home of the Antwerp Fashion Academy. **Hours:** Tue-Sun 10:00-18:00, closed Mon. See page 234.

▲**Museum aan de Stroom (MAS)** Displays focusing on Antwerp's and Belgium's history of trade and cultural exchange—plus a rooftop viewpoint. **Hours:** Exhibits open Tue-Sun 10:00-17:00, closed Mon; building open Tue-Sun 9:30-24:00, until 22:30 in winter, closed Mon. See page 235.

Musical Instruments Museum Well-presented exhibits of instruments and old music manuscripts. **Hours:** Thu-Sun 10:00-17:00, closed Mon-Wed. See page 231.

the young Jesus at the temple. You may see Japanese tourists admiring this painting, as it figured into a novel that's popular in Japan.

Explore the rest of the church. The sacristy shows historic portraits of the church's 21 local bishops. In the apse, beyond the high altar, a video in a chapel shows the church in action on Easter and Christmas.

Musical Instruments Museum at the Old Butchers Hall (Museum Vleeshuis)

This restored brick palace, home to Antwerp's butchers during the city's glory days, now houses a collection of musical instruments.  The Klank van de Stad ("Sound of the City") exhibition presents two floors of instruments and old music manuscripts (don't miss the cellar). The collection is decent and well presented, but English information is limited (unless you buy a €3.50 booklet with descriptions). Even the included touchscreen audioguide is mostly in Dutch—but at least it lets you hear some of the instruments. And though the experience here can be a little underwhelming, it's fun to duck into the (free) entry area for a peek at the impressive brick vaults (or to use the WC).

Cost and Hours: €5, Thu-Sun 10:00-17:00, closed Mon-Wed, Vleeshouwersstraat 38, tel. 03-233-6404, www.museumvleeshuis. be. To get here from the Grote Markt, face the City Hall and turn right up Braderijstraat, take the first left on Kuipersstraat, then look right.

▲Rockox House Museum (Museum Rockoxhuis)

Nicolaas Rockox (1560-1640) was a mayor of Antwerp and a friend and sponsor of Peter Paul Rubens. Today his house—buried in a residential zone a 10-minute walk northeast of the cathedral and Grote Markt—is a lovely museum.

Here you can get a truly authentic look at an aristocratic home from the period (unlike the Rubens House, which was rebuilt), while viewing impressive artwork, furniture, and a beautiful garden courtyard. Exhibits draw from Rockox's vast personal art collection. People used art to decorate as a way of expressing themselves—their values, the people they knew, and so on—so viewing the collection lets you psychoanalyze Rockox.

The collection is particularly worth seeing now. Through 2016, the Rockox is filled with a temporary exhibit called The Golden Cabinet, featuring great paintings from Antwerp's Museum of Fine Arts, which is closed for renovation through late 2017.

Cost and Hours: €6, Tue-Sun 10:00-17:00, closed Mon, Keizerstraat 10, tel. 03-201-9250, www.rockoxhuis.be. No audioguide, but the museum is well described in a free English booklet. In the small auditorium, request the 25-minute video, "Antwerp in 1600," to set the context for your visit.

Visiting the Museum: To appreciate this art—mostly small dark canvases and precious objects—focus your attentive powers and treat this museum as a cabinet of curious miniatures. Here are some of the highlights:

Rooms 1-2: Jan van Eyck's teeny-tiny *Madonna at the Fountain* (1439) is the master's last signed work. Find his name on the frame, along with his trademark slogan *"Als Ich Xan"*—I paint "as best I can." Rogier van der Weyden's *Philippe de Croy* is an especially subtle portrait of the refined 25-year-old nobleman. Hans Memling's *Man with a Roman Coin* captures a Bruges-based businessman lost in thought.

Room 3: Spend some time with Pieter Brueghel the Younger's fun *The Proverbs,* one of 20 copies he made of his father's famous work. In it, Brueghel strives to make literal more than a hundred Flemish sayings and figures of speech, some of which we still use in English, such as: "banging your head against a wall" (lower left), "armed to the teeth" (lower left), "the die is cast" (in the window, upper left), "don't cry over spilled milk" (lower right), "the blind leading the blind" (upper right), and "cast pearls (roses) before swine" (lower middle). Others don't make literal sense but you get the drift: "He's so rich he tiles his roof with pies" (upper left) or, "He's so poor he's stretched between two bread loaves" (lower right). Many more make no literal sense at all, like the unfaithful wife (lower middle) who cuckolds her husband by "putting on the blue cloak." And, "Who knows why the geese go barefoot"?

Also in Room 3 is a rare painting by a female artist—Caterina van Hemessen's *Portrait of a Woman.*

Room 4—The Big Parlour: Rubens' shivering *Venus Frigida* brings to life an ancient Roman proverb: "Without Ceres (that is, bread) and Bacchus (wine), Venus (love) grows cold." In Rubens'

Doubting Thomas triptych, the left panel features a portrait of Nicolaas Rockox, who commissioned the work for his burial chapel. It's clear that Rubens really knew this man, as the portrait truly captures his personality. Anthony van Dyck shows his remarkable skill with a portrait of his fellow painter, *Marten Pepijn.* Before moving on, turn your attention to some of the beautiful objects in the room, especially two art cabinets for curios.

Room 5—The Study: A big art cabinet displays an odd variety of things, including a coin collection and a plaster cast of the foot of Emperor Constantine (atop the cabinet). It was trophies such as these that Rockox would bring out at dinner parties as conversation pieces.

▲▲Museum Plantin-Moretus

In the digital age, it's easy to forget how revolutionary printing books once was. Antwerp of the 1500s was a wide-open city, dis-

seminating ideas from its new-fangled presses. The museum is named for two influential Antwerp printers: Frenchman Christoffel Plantin, who began a printing business here in 1546; and his son-in-law Jan Moretus, who carried on the family business. (Eventually, they were the official court printer for the Spanish monarchs of the Low Countries.)

This building was both the family's home and their workshop. It's a remarkably well-preserved look at 16th- and 17th-century aristocratic life. It also shows several aspects of Antwerp's Golden Age. You'll see early printing presses, the printer's historic workshop and house, old books (including a Gutenberg Bible), and art and memorabilia owned by the prominent printing family. Every Flemish kid comes here on a field trip to understand their enlightened heritage.

Cost and Hours: €8, Tue-Sun 10:00-17:00, closed Mon, last entry 30 minutes before closing, audioguide-€2, Vrijdagmarkt 22, tel. 03-221-1450, www.museumplantinmoretus.be.

Visiting the Museum: There's a lot to see in this meandering maze of rooms. I'd suggest following my tour to hit the highlights, then using the excellent audioguide for the whole story. Allow at least one hour to appreciate the place. Though the building is large and sprawling, you follow an easy, one-way route.

Ground Floor: In Room 2, a large and elaborately decorated hall, find the portraits (to the right of the fireplace) of Mr. Plantin and his relatives. In Room 3, find rare manuscripts from before the age of printing (such as the ninth century), back when books were copied and illustrated by monks. The Plantin family treasured these.

In the courtyard, find Room 4, a reconstructed bookshop. On the wall is a list of books forbidden by the Catholic Church—the list was printed by, and includes books sold by, Christoffel Plantin. Room 7 has a printing press and displays on how it worked—one man inking it up, another lowering a blank paper onto it, then rinsing and repeating every 20 seconds. In the proofreaders' room (Room 9), you can imagine diligent editors huddled around the enormous shared oak desk, debating the 17th-century equivalent of whether "email" takes a hyphen. The publisher's private leather-bound office (Room 10) is classy.

Finally you reach the actual workshop (Rooms 13-14). Here you'll see a dozen presses and other printer's tools. At the far end

stand some of the oldest printing presses in the world (c. 1600). Neatly stacked in the entry room are some 10 tons of lead letters, with racks of complete sets of fonts and different type sizes.

Upstairs: At the top of the stairs, find Room "14 bis," which displays a (possible) Bible by the founder of modern printing, Johannes Gutenberg (c. 1461). Room 15 has some of Plantin's first books.

The rest of the upstairs (a dozen-plus rooms) is the residence, showing off how the upper crust lived a few centuries ago—tapestry wall hangings, high-beamed ceilings, leather-tooled walls, and so on. The 18th-century library displays a polyglot Bible, with five languages on one page, printed by Christoffel Plantin. The Rubens Room (Room 19) is a reminder that the famous painter was an old family friend. You'll wrap up your visit with shelves and shelves of books, which the family had a passion for collecting into the 20th century.

Nearby: The museum is on a charming square called Vrijdagmarkt, where there really is a "Friday market" (for more, see page 223).

▲ModeMuseum (MoMu)

The collection here, like fashion itself, is always changing...but it's also always good. Housed in the modern ModeNatie facility in the heart of the Sint-Andries fashion zone, this museum presents good rotating exhibits about fashion history or a big-name designer, with a new exhibit every six months. The building is also home to the Antwerp Fashion Academy, a library with books about fashion, a good bookshop, and—on the ground floor near the ticket desk—a gallery showcasing works by students. Everything is (no surprise) very stylishly presented. You stroll a one-floor, one-way circuit as you visit.

Cost and Hours: €8, Tue-Sun 10:00-18:00, closed Mon, last entry 30 minutes before closing, includes English guidebook, a five-minute walk south of Groenplaats at Nationalestraat 28, tel. 03-470-2770, www.momu.be.

AT THE OLD DOCKYARDS, NORTH OF DOWNTOWN

The dockyards—an easy 15-minute walk north from the Grote Markt—have been boldly redeveloped, and now house a pair of fine museums: the Museum aan de Stroom (MAS) and the Red Star Line Museum. For the most interesting approach here, through Antwerp's red light district, see Part 3 of my Antwerp City Walk (page 247). Otherwise, from the train station, take bus #17 (direction: Rijnkaai) to the Van Schoonbekeplein stop, a short walk from the MAS. If you're coming from the Grote Markt and riverfront, ride bus #30 north to Van Schoonbekeplein. If you're short on time, the Red Star Line Museum is more worthwhile than the Museum aan de Stroom.

▲Museum aan de Stroom (MAS—Museum on the River)

This strikingly modern building houses an eclectic collection—somehow fitting for this global-crossroads city. In addition to exhibits on Antwerp, you'll also see pre-Columbian stone heads (world-class, but probably not what you came to Antwerp to see), African masks, Polynesian fertility statues, weapons, and an array of temporary exhibits. In this city of excellent museums, this collection is nothing special, but the building itself and its roof terrace—which are free to enter—make it worth the trip.

Cost and Hours: Building free to enter and explore, Tue-Sun 9:30-24:00, until 22:30 in winter, closed Mon; exhibit rooms cost €5 for permanent collection or €10 to add any temporary exhibits, open Tue-Sun 10:00-17:00, closed Mon; limited English info in the exhibit rooms, but smartphone users can get more with QR code reader; top-floor top-class restaurant (by reservation only), 15-minute walk north of Groenplaats at Hanzestedenplaats 1, tel. 03-338-4434, www.mas.be.

Visiting the Museum: In the lobby, buy your ticket (if you want to enter the exhibits) and pick up information brochures, then ride the escalators up, up, up through 10 levels. Giant **photographs** tell the poignant story of the Belgians who fled the devastation of World War I, were taken in by other nations, and returned at war's end.

The museum's **permanent exhibits** are on floors 4-8. I'd focus

most of your attention on the two dedicated to Antwerp (floors 5 and 6). Display of Power (floor 4) analyzes status symbols from Japan to Africa to Polynesia—a fitting theme for this city built upon luxury goods. In Metropolis (floor 5), you follow the growth of the city in maps and paintings of the changing skyline, see big

Eating at the Dockyards

The gentrified harbor out in front of the MAS is lined with great options.

The fun **Felix Pakhuis** market hall in the large, brick, triple-arched building to the left (with the MAS at your back) houses several options (Tue-Sun 10:00-20:00, closed Mon, Godefriduskaai 30). There's a branch of the tasty **Balls & Glory** chain, serving splittable baseball-size meatballs and mashed potatoes or salad (€9.50 to go, €12 to eat in). **De Markt** is an upscale food court (€5 soups, €7-8 sandwiches, €13-15 salads and main dishes), or there's the fancy **Q&M** grocery. You can sit inside or take your food out to the harborfront tables.

If you're heading to the Red Star Line Museum, you'll spot several tempting cafés and a cheap-and-handy **Louis Delihaze supermarket** along the way, on Nassaustraat.

papier-mâché heads of Brabo and the Giant, and admire a gleaming made-in-Antwerp Minerva automobile. World Port (floor 6) displays models of the many kinds of ships that docked here and traces the evolution of the port through videos and photos. Life or Death (floor 7) considers how world cultures wrestle with these big questions—from Egyptian mummies to a roomful of Buddhas to Catholic symbols. And finally, Life or Death: On the Upper- and Underworld (floor 8) is an excuse to show off the museum's exquisite collection of pre-Columbian artifacts.

Finish your visit by ascending to the **rooftop panorama.** Find the soaring spire of the Cathedral of Our Lady. To the left of that is the unmistakable Farmers Tower skyscraper (see page 243). To the right of the cathedral, there's the Scheldt River. And around you is the harbor—the huge cranes, barges, container ships, tugs, and vast warehouses. It stretches into the distance and is one of the busiest ports in the world.

Nearby: The low-lying, long building just in front of the MAS houses three small, free exhibits: The best is the **Port of Antwerp exhibit,** where you can walk across a blown-up aerial view of the sprawling port area—giving you a sense of its astonishing scale (Tue-Sun 9:30-17:30, closed Mon). The **diamond exhibit** (Diamantpaviljoen) feels like a shill for the local diamond council, with a virtual diamond-cutting demonstration and a few gem-encrusted objects (Tue-Sun 10:00-17:00, closed Mon). The **Unicom** space hosts temporary exhibits.

▲▲Red Star Line Museum

Is there anything more poignant than a person willing to sacrifice everything in pursuit of a better life? This cutting-edge museum—filling the hall that processed many of the two million emigrants

who passed through Antwerp on their way to a New World of opportunity—combines personal stories with high-tech presentation to detail the "other end" of the Ellis Island experience. Particularly for North Americans who are descended from immigrants (read: almost all of us), it's well worth the five-minute walk beyond the MAS.

Cost and Hours: €8, Tue-Sun 10:00-17:00, Easter-Oct Sat-Sun until 18:00, closed Mon, Montevideostraat 3, tel. 03-298-2770, www.redstarline.be.

Getting There: From the MAS, cross the drawbridge and head up Nassaustraat, past the two-tone green skyscrapers. Just after those buildings, turn left down Montevideostraat. This part of Antwerp's docklands is still being redeveloped, so it's not easily accessible by public transportation (though eventually they plan to build a tram line to this area).

Background: In the late 19th century, Europe was changing. The Industrial Revolution, the end of traditional peasant lifestyles, and a tremendous population boom led to political instability and difficult lives. Across the Atlantic, the United States and Canada symbolized a hope for a better life. And during the great migration between 1873 and 1935, the Red Star shipping line brought some two million emigrants from Antwerp to New York City. This was the point of exit not only for Belgians, but for people from all over Europe—especially Germany and Eastern Europe—who rode in rickety trains all the way across the Continent to get here. (By the 1930s, many of the emigrants were Jews fleeing the Nazi regime in Germany.) The 10-day steamer journey transported cargo, luxury travelers, and "steerage-class" peasants alike. In these red-brick warehouses, emigrants underwent humiliating health exams and nervously waited while clerks processed their paperwork. (Because arriving passengers who were ill were immediately deported at the shipping line's expense, screening procedures were stringent.)

Visiting the Museum: The cavernous main hall has a café and temporary exhibits. As posted English information is limited, when buying your ticket ask to borrow the booklet that translates the descriptions, or log onto the free Wi-Fi hotspot to view them on your smartphone (www.rslm.be).

First up: a small exhibit on the history of the Red Star Line and the powerful **Always on the Move** exhibition—using wrap-around video screens to drive home the point that immigration is as common today as it was in the heyday of Ellis Island. Displays profile different kinds of immigrants through history—from the first humans who left Africa in 40,000 B.C. to the migrant workers of today.

The next section, **In the Footsteps of Emigrant Passengers,** highlights individuals who passed through this building as they gave up everything they knew for the prospect of a new start in the New World. A 10-minute video introduces you to some of the Red Star Line's passengers, and touchscreens let you zoom in on stories in the emigrants' own words. You'll see the (deceptively) glossy brochures that the shipping lines used to lure customers, a map demonstrating how far many immigrants traveled on the train even before stepping on the ship (many rode in from Russia), and period photos of Antwerp—the last European city many of these soon-to-be-former-Europeans would ever see.

The next section details the invasive processing procedures for passengers before they were allowed on board: They were stripped of their baggage and clothes—which were disinfected—then forced to shower and be inspected for lice and other disease (as illustrated by video clips). You'll learn about life on board (especially for the miserable below-decks steerage passengers) and about that stirring moment when immigrants first saw the Statue of Liberty. The final room emphasizes that Antwerp today is a city not of emigrants, but of immigrants—people from other countries flocking here to pursue their dreams.

Before leaving, you can ride the elevator up to the **panorama tower** for a glimpse at the last view many Europeans enjoyed of their home continent before leaving forever—but if you've been up to the top of the MAS, this view is a letdown.

ANTWERP CITY WALK

With this single walk, you can say you've "seen" Antwerp, as it laces together many of the city's main sights. It's ideal for day-trippers who want to see it all in a few hours' blitz from the train station.

Another option is to slice and dice Antwerp into savory bites, which you can enjoy at your leisure, and in any order: Part 1 of the walk is an easy stroll from the train station down a modern, pedestrian-friendly shopping street to the heart of town. Part 2 covers the historic core—the towering cathedral, the Grote Markt, and the riverfront where the city was born. Part 3 takes you where fewer tourists go—through a semi-residential neighborhood, the red light district (prostitution), and to the modern dockyards.

Along the way, you'll see the city's historic architecture, youthful citizens, trendy restaurants, and a high-tech brothel. You can also take this opportunity to stop in and tour several sights, including the Rubens House, the cathedral, or the Museum aan de Stroom (MAS). The walk ends with a view back over the towers, steeples, cranes, and skyscrapers of this teeming city. For a map of the route, see pages 226-227.

Orientation

Length of This Walk: The whole walk covers two miles. Allow at least 30 minutes for each of the three segments, plus another 20-30 minutes for getting back. Budget still more time if you go inside any sights along the way. With limited time, focus on Part 2.

Rubens House: €8, Tue-Sun 10:00-17:00, closed Mon, last entry 30 minutes before closing, audioguide-€2.

Cathedral of Our Lady: €6, cash only, Mon-Fri 10:00-17:00, Sat 10:00-15:00, Sun 13:00-16:00, audioguide-€2.

Musical Instruments Museum at the Old Butchers Hall: €5, Thu-Sun 10:00-17:00, closed Mon-Wed.

Museum aan de Stroom (MAS): Building free to enter, Tue-Sun 9:30-24:00, until 22:30 in winter, closed Mon; museum exhibits €5-10, Tue-Sun 10:00-17:00, closed Mon.

The Walk Begins

This L-shaped walk starts at the train station, turns right at the Old Town, and ends at the harbor to the north. For a map of the route, see page 226. If you're short on time, skip to Part 2 by riding the metro directly from the train station to the Old Town (see page 223). You could also skip Part 3 (with the in-your-face red light district), and consider the MAS a separate sight.

PART 1: FROM THE TRAIN STATION TO THE OLD TOWN

❶ Antwerp's Train Station

• *Start on level +1—under the ornate old-timey clock—and take in the view.*

The city's central train station is not merely a convenient transportation hub, it's a work of art and a loud-and-clear comment on a confident new age. Built around the turn of the 20th century, it's Industrial Age meets Art Nouveau, giddy with steel and glass. This eclectic mix of Historicism is a temple of time. Look down through the center of the station to see the various levels of train tracks. The origi-

nal station was all on one level—you'd walk from your wheezing steam train directly to the place you're standing now. But dead-end stations are just too slow for today's express trains, so they've excavated these several layers of tracks. Today's fastest trains, on the lowest level, pass straight through a tunnel beneath the station—connecting Antwerp with Amsterdam or Paris in just an hour or two.

Look up at the vintage clock in the center of the hall, towering high above the tracks. Timekeeping first became important in the age of train schedules, and the facade is a kind of triumphal arch crowned by the clock. The "builder king" Leopold II was a force for modernity—you'll see his double-cursive *L* monogram and *KB* for "King of Belgium" everywhere. The station was constructed in an era when Belgium was a new colonial power, with the vast and resource-rich Congo providing a wealth of ivory and rubber.

Antwerp's Diamond Quarter

The area around the train station is known as the Diamond Quarter—one of the world's top centers for commerce in these gems. Although the industry is highly secretive, experts guess that four out of every five of the world's rough diamonds pass through Antwerp at some point. The diamond industry is located in the train-station neighborhood for good reason: If you're carrying millions of dollars' worth of precious jewels in your briefcase through a strange city, you don't want to have to venture too far to reach a trader or diamond cutter.

Beginning in the 16th century, the diamond industry in Antwerp was dominated by Sephardic Jews from Spain, but under Catholic rule, they fled to Amsterdam. Then, in the late 19th century, Hasidic Orthodox Jews fleeing the pogroms in Russia settled here and took up the industry. In the streets around the train station, you'll likely see men wearing tall hats and black coats, with long beards and curly locks at their temples, and women with long dresses and hair covers. More recently, the diamond trade here is increasingly dominated by Indians.

The history of the diamond trade focuses on Africa, where diamond seekers dug the world's biggest man-made hole, the Kimberley Crater in South Africa. In some parts of Africa, the exploitative conditions for finding these gems haven't improved much since the early days of Belgian colonialism. A strict new diamond-certification process, introduced in Antwerp in 2000, attempts to block the sale of so-called "blood diamonds"—stones sold by rebels fighting governments in war zones in central and western Africa.

The Royal Café, at the original track level, is first-class, yet economical and elegant...a fine place for a quiet cup of coffee or light bite.

• *Go through the door right under the ornate clock.*

Here in the main lobby of the train station, you're surrounded by some of the most grandiose architecture found in any train station in Europe. Note that even though we are in the Dutch-speaking part of Belgium, the mottos inscribed in the elaborate shields are all in French.

• *Exit the main lobby of the station. Facing the train ticket office, turn left. Look for the sign that reads* Keyserlei/Meir/Centrum. *From here, we'll walk basically straight ahead on the Keyserlei pedestrian mall, past the ugly gold skyscraper, all the way to the Old Town (marked by the lacy spire of the cathedral in the distance).*

❷ Upper Main Drag: Train Station to Rubens House

Stroll three blocks gradually downhill on the bustling, sand-colored boulevard called **De Keyserlei,** lined with chain restaurants and shops. Following European trends, this boulevard, like much of the old center, is becoming a bike-and-pedestrian zone.

The area around the train station is known as the **Diamond Quarter**—one of the world's top centers where diamonds are sold and cleaved (split into smaller pieces to prepare them for cutting). Other than casual-looking people with briefcases handcuffed to their wrists, there's little to see.

This stretch of the walk is light on actual sights but great for people- and city-watching. You'll run into the big boulevard called Frankrijklei, which marks the former course of the town wall. Continue straight across the street, then stroll between the **twin grand facades** that exemplify the style called Historicism. All the rage in the late 19th century, this school of architectural thought borrowed the best, most bombastic bits and pieces from past styles to wow the viewer. Now turn around and look at the towering 1960s-era skyscraper, and compare the aesthetics of the ages.

Beyond the facades, you enter a delightful pedestrians-only shopping zone. Bear left as the road curves at the **statue of Anthony van Dyck** (1599-

1641), a talented Antwerp artist who became the court painter for English King Charles I, and whose works now appear in many local museums. This puts you on **the Meir** (pronounced "mare"), Antwerp's showcase shopping zone, built, like the train station, in the boom times around 1900. (Meir is the name of both the street and the neighborhood.) A block later, on the left, notice the grand **Stadsfeestzaal** shopping mall (with the gold niche over the door). Venture inside for a look at its astonishing interior.

Lower Main Drag: Rubens House to Cathedral

One block later, the big gap in the buildings with the fountain (on your left) marks Wapper square, featuring (a block down) one of the city's top sights, the ❸ **Rubens House.** This former home of Peter Paul Rubens introduces visitors to the artist's work and lifestyle. For more on Rubens' home, ✪ see the Rubens House Tour chapter.

Continuing on the ❹ lower main drag, just past Wapper square, the ornate building is the **Paleis op de Meir,** a gorgeous Rococo-style palace built in 1745 by a local aristocrat who died before he could actually move in. Later, Napoleon purchased the home and decorated the upstairs in Empire Style. With Belgium's independence in 1830, this became an official residence of the king of the Belgians. It was recently refurbished and opened to the public.

But what really matters is chocolate. At the Paleis entrance, step into the **Chocolate Line** shop (and notice the amazingly 3-D *grisailles*—the monochrome paintings above the doors). Here, you can see the creative work of the crazy "shock-o-latier" Dominique Persoone (€3.75 for your choice of three wacky flavors, daily until 18:30).

Ahead is the Art Deco, Gotham City-style skyscraper called the **Farmers Tower** (Boerentoren, marked for its current occupant,

KBC). Completed in 1932, this was considered the first American-style skyscraper in Europe, and held the title of Europe's tallest skyscraper for 20 years. Pass the Meir metro stop, built on the cheap under the road, and a rack of city loaner bikes. Then cross the tram tracks and continue straight, bearing left on Schoenmarkt around the Farmers Tower.

You eventually arrive at the square called **Groenplaats,** with its handy metro stop, statue of Rubens, and the cathedral spire hovering just beyond. The high-

fashion district is to your left, and the Old Town is beyond the cathedral. (If you're skipping the red light district, you can return to this metro stop after seeing the riverfront to catch a tram back to the train station.)

• *Stroll through the square. Bear left up "Little Italy Lane"—the narrow street at the top of the square (Jan Blomstraat), passing a row of Italian restaurants—you'll end up at Handschoenmarkt in front of the cathedral.*

PART 2: FROM THE CATHEDRAL TO THE RIVERFRONT

• *This part of the walk begins on the little square in front of the cathedral.*

❺ Cathedral of Our Lady

Antwerp's biggest church, with its lacy 400-foot-tall spire—still the tallest structure in the city—dominates the Old Town. Its mismatched towers tell Antwerp's story in a nutshell. The church was begun in 1352 and consecrated in 1521, when Antwerp was at its peak, and there were grandiose plans to make the already huge church even bigger—the biggest on earth. But then a fire gutted the church (1533), and in 1576, the city was sacked and Antwerp's fortunes plummeted. The church was left with only one completed tower—once the tallest in the Low Countries; the other is a stump of thwarted dreams.

Though much of the facade was left undecorated, the tympanum (archway) over the main door is remarkable. It's the Last Judgment, and Christ raises his hand to divide the righteous from the wicked. Below him, St. Michael weighs souls. One naughty lady is led away by a gleeful demon to be sexually harassed for eternity. Beneath the tympanum is a statue of Mary—"Our Lady"—who smiles, willing to save us from that grim fate.

The church's richly ornamented interior is packed with fine art, including several huge paintings by Peter Paul Rubens (for details, see page 225).

• Now, as you face the church, turn left and exit the square by squeezing through the little gap, walking down Maalderijstraat. Bearing right, you'll wind up in the...

❻ Grote Markt

Antwerp's main square is dominated by the looming tower of the cathedral at one end and the stately City Hall at the other.

With a facade dating from Antwerp's Golden Age (16th century), the **City Hall** (Stadhuis) is adorned with flags from many different countries—representing the importance of international trade to the city. The central tower sports the golden coats of arms of great medieval powers that shaped the city: the lion of the Duchy of Brabant, the Margraviate of Antwerp, and the two-headed eagle of the Habsburgs.

The other buildings fronting the square are **guild houses,** celebrating the trade associations of each of the city's industries. Each one is topped with a golden statue, which usually represents that guild's patron saint. There's a man on a rearing horse, a cat (or is it

a wolf?), and a saint with a migraine. Some of these are over-the-top, exaggerated rebuilt versions from the Romantic period in the 19th century. The many ground-floor cafés (especially the venerable Den Engel and Den Bengel) are inviting places for a drink with a view. Locals say that when the outdoor terraces open up, they know summer has arrived in Antwerp.

The **fountain** in the middle of Grote Markt illustrates a gruesome story from Flemish folklore. Supposedly, a giant named Druon Antigoon collected tolls along the Scheldt River. If someone was unable or unwilling to pay, the giant would sever their hand. His reign of terror finally ended when a brave young Roman soldier named Silvius Brabo defeated Antigoon, then cut off the giant's hand. Here we see Brabo in his wind-up, ready to toss Antigoon's blood-spouting hand into the river. (You can circle around behind to see the giant's bloody stump.) Tour guides love to explain that *hand werpen* ("to throw a hand") evolved into "Antwerpen"...though scholars prefer less glamorous alternatives: *an 't werf,* "on the wharf"; or *ando verpis,* "where land is thrown up against land" (the river has long deposited sludge along the bank here).

• *From the Grote Markt, circle around the left side of the City Hall. Now head toward the river up the big street called...*

❼ Suikerrui

Along Suikerrui you get your first sense of Antwerp's origins as a river-trading port town. Where the paved street is now was once an open canal that flowed to the river. You'll pass the much-loved statue to the unknown dockworker, whose insolent pose is both carefree and defiant. Created in 1890 (by Constantin Meunier), it instantly became a symbol of the city. Farther along, the building at

#5 is adorned with big green statues. This is the former Hansahuis, where the German guild of traders had their regional headquarters.

• *Suikerrui street leads to the river. The best place to view the water is up the ramp to the promenade.*

❽ Riverfront

Antwerp was born on the Scheldt River. The river flows northward 200 miles, from France to Belgium (passing through Ghent), to Antwerp, where it begins bearing northwest to the North Sea. The city began right along the riverbank back in Roman times. The port was always fortified, and today there's still a castle.

During Antwerp's Golden Age (early 1500s), the Scheldt brought more than a hundred ships a day, carrying goods from all over the world—sugar and silver from America, pepper and cinnamon from Asia. The city was completely cosmopolitan, full of international businessmen. When Antwerp fell in 1576, the Dutch gained control of the Scheldt's river trade, and Antwerp declined, until Belgium gained its independence in the 19th century.

Today, the port of Antwerp is Europe's second largest—but you'd hardly know it standing here, because the main docks have moved to the north (we'll see them later) and the focus of the city has shifted east. Now the original riverfront is dingy and drab—tucked behind a busy boulevard and basically ignored by the city. The steel canopies nearby are former warehouses, now used for covered parking or to shelter old boats (and a WC below). Cruise ships dock right here (along the canopies) to disgorge their passengers into town.

• *From the promenade, backtrack down the ramp, turn left and head north along the riverfront, through the park 100 yards, to the...*

❾ Castle

All that's left from those glory days is the forlorn and empty **castle.** It was once part of a city wall that fortified the heart of town. Enjoy the photogenic anchor out front and the statue of the legendary giant intimidating two poor traders (or is he harassing a medieval gay couple?).

Occasionally, the long-ignored river demands attention. Because the Scheldt is a tidal river, there's a huge risk of flooding—made more serious by rising sea levels. Notice the waist-high concrete **retaining wall** that runs along the busy street. It's equipped with orange steel doors that can roll along railroad tracks to open or close. This wall is a small part of a long-range plan (the Belgian-Dutch "Sigma Project") to raise seawalls to accommodate rising sea levels (and also transform this area into a lively people zone).

• *Part 2 of our walk is finished. If you're short on time and want to do some sightseeing in the Old Town or head south to the fashion district, feel free to bail out now. To return to the train station, make your way back to the cathedral and Groenplaats, and hop on tram line #9 or #15.*

If you stick with Part 3, you'll wander through Antwerp's somewhat jarring (but generally safe and well-patrolled) red light district before reaching the rejuvenated old dockyards, with super-modern buildings. (If you'd like to see the dockyards, but not the red lights, you can walk north along the riverbank for about 15 minutes, then turn right at the harbor; or hop on bus #30 for the short ride to Van Schoonbekeplein and the MAS.)

PART 3: FROM THE RIVERFRONT TO THE RED LIGHT DISTRICT AND OLD DOCKYARDS

• *From the castle, find the modest little staircase that takes you up and over the concrete retaining wall. Cross the busy street at the crosswalk, and then climb the stairs. At the top of the stairs, look left for a street sign that reads* Willem Ogier Plaats. *From there, head down the adjoining Kuipersstraat as it curves through brick row houses. After two blocks, turn left to find a big old building, the...*

❿ Old Butchers Hall

This hall was built in 1504 to house one of Antwerp's guilds—the butchers. The impressive red-and-white stone structure (which locals say reminds them of bacon) was the neighborhood meat market. It now houses the Musical Instruments Museum (see page 231).

Notice that the building stands on something quite rare in Antwerp—a small hill. As the hill was always a desirable place to live, this is one of the oldest neighborhoods. But the area today is mostly modern, sterile brick buildings. It was bombed heavily by Nazi V-2 rockets in World War II. Only the Old Butchers Hall survived. Then in the 1970s, whatever remained was replaced by these modern brick "projects"—subsidized housing. Notice there are no pubs or shops around here. But if you poke around you'll discover pleasant public courtyards tucked back inside many of these buildings, with benches that are inviting on a sunny day (and sinister on a cold, dark night).

• *From the Old Butchers Hall, head downhill on Vleeshouwersstraat. Walk two blocks. At a pleasant residential square (Veemarkt), cut diagonally across the basketball court and continue up Nosestraat, passing a church...and some sex-toy shops. You'll wind up at the square called...*

⓫ Sint-Paulusplaats

This used to be a medieval harbor, then a bustling sailors' quarter with red lights in the windows. The area now has its share of trendy, youth-oriented restaurants.

At this point, you could cut this walk short and opt out of the red light district. If you follow the tram tracks to the left, you'll come to the Sint-Pietersvliet stop, where tram #7 can take you back to the Old Town.

Prepare to enter the red light district. In fact, you may want to read ahead (especially the directions) before tucking your book away and walking boldly through.

• *Here's the route we'll follow through the red light district: Walk past the big anchor and over the tram tracks, up the pedestrian street Oudeman-straat, which becomes Vingerlingstraat, and into the heart of the red light district. Follow the road as it curves to the right (through another block of the red light district) and eventually spills out on peaceful Falconplein. See you there.*

⓬ Red Light District

Enter Antwerp's red light district—Belgium's biggest hub of legalized prostitution—with its streets lined with ladies shimmying in windows. City leaders believe that legalizing prostitution and concentrating it here makes things safer both for the sex workers and for city residents at large.

Antwerp's red light district lacks the touristy patina of Amsterdam's...which makes it feel that much creepier. You'll see fewer rowdy "stag parties" making a racket, but lots of lonely men silently prowling the pedestrian zone. The area is not as dangerous as it might seem—the mayor actually encourages visitors to stroll here—but it's also not entirely safe either. It feels more comfortable during the day and more lively after dark.

In the 19th century, Antwerp's red light district was known (or notorious) the world over; these days, it's a much tamer place...but still provocative, particularly so when you realize that about a third of the "girls" are men. Don't be surprised if you're flashed top and bottom by a transvestite.

Halfway down the block on the right is **Villa Tinto**—essentially a shopping mall of ladies in windows. Designed by prominent artist Arne Quinze, it's a state-of-the-art brothel. It has a high-tech system of "panic buttons" that sex workers can use to call for help and a police station right in the middle. If a prostitute needs help, it's better that a policeman comes than a pimp.

• *You'll pop out on a long, narrow square called...*

⓭ Falconplein

Whew, you made it. At this point, you could backtrack a half-block to explore more of Villa Tinto. If you enter the Villa Tinto mall, it eventually spills you out back here on Falconplein.

Falconplein used to be dubbed "Red Square," for its Russian mafia-style thugs selling designer knockoffs...and worse. City leaders recently cracked down, evicted the worst offenders, and gentrified the square.

At Falconplein, consider your options: Our walk continues 200 yards farther, to one final sight—the museum called MAS,

with a great rooftop panorama of the modern harbor. Had enough? No MAS? Then you could return from here to the center of town—on foot, by bus, or by tram (for details, see the end of the walk).

• *To continue the walk from Falconplein, cross busy Brouwersvliet. Notice how wide this street is. Once a canal accommodating cargo ships* that moored here to unload, it was paved over in the 19th century when the mightier docklands were constructed nearby.

Continue straight, strolling through Van Schoonbekeplein toward the towering red building up ahead.

⓮ Old Dockyards and MAS (Museum aan de Stroom)

Antwerp's formerly derelict and dangerous old port area has been rejuvenated and redeveloped. Built by Napoleon in the early 1800s, and filled with brick warehouses around the turn of the 20th century, this part of town became deserted in the 1950s and 1960s, when the city's shipping industry relocated to the larger ports farther north. In the mid-1980s, city leaders decided to reclaim and gentrify this prime real estate. Today it's home to a tidy little yacht marina, a row of desirable condos, some trendy restaurants, and a state-of-the-art museum housed in an eye-catching tower. Perched next to the museum is a towering black floating crane, to keep alive the memory of ships unloading in this first Industrial-Age harbor from the early 19th century.

The **Museum aan de Stroom** (Museum on the River), or **MAS** for short, is housed in a 210-foot-tall blocky tower, encased  in hand-cut red stone and speckled with silver hands (the symbol of Antwerp). Designed to resemble the spiraling stacks of goods in an old maritime warehouse, the museum emphasizes the way that Antwerp's status as a shipping center has made it a crossroads for people from around the world. Since you've made it this far, it would be a shame not to check it out. The building itself is free to enter and wander around in (but you need to buy a ticket if you want to enter the exhibition rooms). Take the (free) escalators up 10 stories to the museum's rooftop. It takes a while (and the elevators are restricted to visitors with disabilities), but the view is good. After this long walk, you've earned a look back over all you've traversed. (For a description of the view, the building, and the museum exhibits inside, see page 235.)

• You're done. To **walk** back to the Old Town, the quickest route (15 minutes, see the map on page 226) is to return to Falconplein and exit the square at the far end, heading south down Kaasbrug street, which quickly becomes Mutsaardstraat. After about four blocks, you reach an intersection at a small square. Turn right on Minderbroedersstraat and begin following signs to the Grote Markt (or jog straight from the intersection another block to reach the Rockox House—see page 231). An alternate route (15-20 minutes) is along the river back to the castle.

To return to the train station by **bus**, backtrack from the MAS to the wide Brouwersvliet, cross it, and look for the bus stop on your right. From here you can catch bus #17 (direction: UZA) to the train station.

To return to the Old Town or train station by **tram**, continue walking on Brouwersvliet to the river, turn left, and watch for the tram tracks that loop right next to the roadway on the left. This is the terminus for tram #7 (Sint-Pietersvliet metro stop). Hop on and get off three stops later at Meirbrug, where you can transfer to tram #9 or #15.

RUBENS HOUSE TOUR

Rubenshuis

One of the world's most famous artists called this place home. He transformed a traditional Flemish house into an architectural showpiece. Here he worked (in his spacious studio); enjoyed family life (with his young trophy wife); tinkered with his collection of curiosities; and entertained fellow artists, geniuses, and aristocrats.

The historic (if heavily restored) house has impressive wood-paneled and richly furnished rooms as well as a garden courtyard. You'll find a half-dozen high-quality paintings by Rubens (including a self-portrait and *Christ on the Cross*), plus a few by his talented student, Anthony van Dyck. By seeing the kitchen where Rubens' meals were cooked, the dining room where he ate, and the bedroom where he slept, you may walk out seeing this Old Master as a flesh-and-blood human being.

Orientation

Cost: €8.

Hours: Tue-Sun 10:00-17:00, closed Mon, last entry 30 minutes before closing.

Crowd Control: Because the place is small, enjoy it with fewer crowds by arriving right at opening time or late in the day.

Getting There: The house is at Wapper 9, between the train station and the Old Town—to walk here, follow my Antwerp City Walk. Or, ride the metro to the Meir stop, then walk one long block east (back toward the train station).

Information: A free guidebooklet in English is included with your ticket. Tel. 03-201-1555, www.rubenshuis.be.

Tours: The 1.5-hour audioguide (€2) is excellent and essential.

Optional Add-on: An extra €2 gets you admission to the nearby Museum Mayer van den Bergh, whose highlight is Pieter

Bruegel the Elder's enigmatic 1562 battle scene starring "Mad Meg." The museum is pleasant but is located several blocks away, and is skippable for most.

Length of This Tour: One hour—those in a hurry can see it in less.

Starring: His dining room (with portraits of Rubens and wife Hélène) and his studio (with *Christ on the Cross* and a handful of other Rubens paintings).

The Tour Begins

Buy your ticket at the glass pavilion in the middle of the square in front of the house, then head inside. The audioguide takes you on a detailed tour. Here are the highlights.

• *The visit begins in the open-air...*

Courtyard

In 1610, Rubens—age 33 and just hired as the country's official court painter—bought this house and moved in with his wife. Rubens would live here the rest of his long life. In the courtyard, you can see the original Flemish-style 16th-century house (on the left), the Italian palazzo-style studio that Rubens added on to the complex (on the right), the elaborate Michelangelo-flavored portico that connects them, and the Italian-style garden (directly ahead). An architect as well as a painter, Rubens designed the additions himself. The influence of his time in Italy is evident: Notice the dramatic contrast between the traditional Flemish home and the flamboyant Italian palazzo-style studio.

• *Now go inside the house and follow the one-way route through the various rooms.*

Ground Floor

Pass quickly through the parlor (with its fireplace) and kitchen (with rich decorative tile work from Spain). Many of the paintings are not by Rubens, but by artists he admired; in fact, his personal art collection was the biggest in the Low Countries.

In the dining room, admire the rich period furniture, leather-tooled walls, carved mantel, and wood ceiling. There's a rare self-portrait of Rubens in his fifties—one of only four known Rubens self-portraits. Facing him from across the room is a portrait (not by Rubens) of his second wife, Hélène Fourment. After his first wife died, Rubens married 16-year-old Hélène for love instead of entering into a strategic marriage with a noblewoman. In the library, see some of his curios (especially his bust of Seneca), many of which were displayed in his mini-Pantheon rotunda.

Upstairs

Find a portrait of the *Bishop of Antwerp* by Rubens' star pupil, Anthony van Dyck. Van Dyck's ability to capture a personality on

canvas made him invaluable to Rubens (whose forte was not faces). After several years working here in Rubens' studio, Van Dyck went on to fame painting for the king of England. In the bedroom is a short, carved-wood bed like the one Rubens likely used—people slept sitting up in those days. Also, keep an eye out for Van Dyck's portrait of a cute little prince and his dog.

RUBENS HOUSE

• *Continue downstairs to the studio. You'll find the following paintings in either the large studio or in the small adjoining room by the entrance.*

Studio

Here Rubens and his students produced thousands of paintings. Lingering over the selection of canvases here, appreciate how they were made. For an important commission, Rubens would paint the entire work himself. If it was successful, he'd have his school make copies to sell on a wide scale. Once the copy was 99 percent completed, Rubens would step in to add a few finishing touches...only Rubens himself could create just the perfect twinkle in an eye or glimmer of light on that cellulite. Other times, Rubens would simply do a rough oil sketch of what he wanted, then enlist experts in certain areas (such as flowers or portraits) to fill in the blanks. Then he'd sweep through at the end to finalize the work.

In the main hall, start with the large ***Christ on the Cross*** (on

loan while the Museum of Fine Arts is closed through late 2017). It's typical Rubens: large-scale and dramatic, with rippling flesh, a wind-whipped loincloth, and strong emotions. It captures Christ at His lowest moment on the cross—a lone figure amid the gathering gloom gazing up asking, "God, why have you forsaken me?"

The *Christ* is flanked by twin portraits of the Spanish monarchs of the Netherlands, **Archduke Albert** and **Infanta Isabella,** in their

Peter Paul Rubens (1577-1640)

Born in Germany in 1577, Rubens at age 12 moved with his family to Antwerp, where he was apprenticed to a local painter. During his twenties, he studied in Rome, where he picked up the Italian fad of painting giant compositions on huge canvases. He returned to Antwerp in 1608, married, and settled down, buying today's Rubens House in 1610. He would live and work there for the remainder of his life, churning out painting after painting.

Rubens' paintings run the gamut, from realistic portraits to lounging nudes, Greek myths to Catholic altarpieces, pious devotion to rough sex. Rubens painted anything that would raise your pulse: battles, miracles, hunts, rapes, and especially, fleshy "Rubenesque" women with dimples on all four cheeks.

An expert of composition, Rubens could arrange a pig pile of many figures into a harmonious unit. Each painting was powered with an energy that people called his "fury of the brush." Rubens turns the wind machine on high.

Everything is on a larger-than-life scale in Rubens' work. Many canvases almost fill entire walls—you can see the seams

elaborate ruffed collars. Rubens was this couple's official court painter, and these original works were copied in large numbers by

his assistants. The monarchs' time was valuable, so Rubens worked quickly. To pose for her portrait, Isabella reportedly came to Antwerp for only one night; Rubens sketched her face quickly, just enough to capture her likeness, then filled in the details later. Elsewhere in the main hall (or nearby) is another portrait of Isabella—this time dressed in a nun's habit, which she donned after her husband died and she joined the Poor Clare order, mourning him for the rest of her life.

Adam and Eve is an early (pre-Italy) work, done when Rubens was barely 21. The poses are a bit stiff, the colors subdued, and the bodies lack the rippling muscles and folds of fat that would later become Rubens' trademark.

St. Sebastian is an early Rubens take on a common Italian subject. In his version, the angel tries to delicately pluck an arrow from the martyr's supple flesh.

where the cloth pieces were stitched together—and approximately 2,500 canvases bear his name. How could he paint so many enormous canvases in one lifetime? He didn't. His house was an art factory, designed to mass-produce masterpieces. As was standard at the time, his assistants did much of the work: After he laid out a painting, his apprentices painted the background and filled in minor details. Rubens orchestrated the production from a balcony, and before a painting was carried out his tall, narrow door, he would put on the finishing touches, whipping each figure to life with a flick of his furious brush.

Rubens' fascination with plus-size models, and his skill at capturing their rippling folds of fat, are the reasons we now describe certain figures as "Rubenesque." The sweet faces and ample proportions of the damsels he painted were inspired by Hélène Fourment, 37 years Rubens' junior, whom the artist married after his first wife died.

Rubens distinguished himself as a smart businessman who knew how to provide wealthy benefactors with exactly what they wanted. In his long career, he was rich, famous, well-traveled, and the friend of kings and princes. A true Renaissance Man in the Baroque Age, Rubens was even an accomplished diplomat—he helped to negotiate peace between England and Spain (and was knighted by the kings of both countries in appreciation).

The Annunciation shows the angel barging into Mary's home (notice the sleeping kitten) to bring the news of Jesus' impending birth. Rubens was frantically soaking up Italian-style dynamism, but here he crams a bit too much action into a tiny apartment.

Henry IV at the Battle of Ivry, with the unfinished battle scene, illustrates Rubens' collaborative process. Rubens sketched the main outlines in oil, then turned it over to assistants to fill in the detail. You can see (at the top of the canvas) where the battle specialist

has already filled in his section. But the foreground remains a cloud of unfinished possibilities—the main soldier on horseback has three arms.

The Feast of St. Martin—with its bonfire in the midst of revelers—is not by Rubens, so why is it here? Rubens had a hobby of buying paintings like this so he could add touches to make it his own. He'd add whitener to the teeth, paint a sparkle in the eyes, and transform a peasant into a society lady.

The **portrait of Anthony van Dyck**

shows Rubens' most talented pupil. The canvas is probably by Rubens, but some think it's a self-portrait by Van Dyck himself. While Rubens got the lion's share of the fame, some of his students were even more talented than he was—and Van Dyck was a verifiable genius, who prodded Rubens to become a better painter. And yet Van Dyck was just a painter...whereas Rubens was also an architect, an aristocrat, and a diplomat—a true jack-of-all-trades who carved a large legacy.

ANTWERP SLEEPING, EATING & MORE

Contents

Sleeping in Antwerp

$$$ Hotel Julien, an extremely chic boutique hotel, is Antwerp's most enticing splurge. Located in a renovated 16th-century building on a drab street just outside the Old Town, its 22 rooms are a perfectly executed combination of old and new. The public areas, with high ceilings and lots of unfinished wood, feel like an art gallery (Db-€170-290 depending on size and amenities, air-con in most rooms, elevator, free guest computer, Wi-Fi, spa in basement, Korte Nieuwstraat 24, tel. 03-229-0600, www.hotel-julien.com, info@hotel-julien.com).

$$$ Matelote Hotel ("Fisherman") enjoys an extremely central location on a characteristic street deep in the Old Town, just a few steps from...everything. Its 10 rooms mix heavy old beams with sleek, sometimes boldly modern flourishes. While getting a bit worn, the place still feels stylish and has some nice touches, such as mini-fridges with free soft drinks (flexible pricing, but usually Db-€90-100, bigger deluxe Db-€110-120, typically about €20 more on Sat, breakfast-€12, Wi-Fi, Haarstraat 11a, tel. 03-201-8800, www.hotel-matelote.be, info@matelote.be).

$$$ APlace B&B offers two stylish suites and two apart-

Sleep Code

Abbreviations (€1 = about $1.40, country code: 32)
S = Single, **D** = Double/Twin, **T** = Triple, **Q** = Quad, **b** = bathroom, **s** = shower only

Price Rankings
  $$$ Higher Priced—Most rooms €105 or more
   $$ Moderately Priced—Most rooms between €60-105
    $ Lower Priced—Most rooms €60 or less

Unless otherwise noted, English is spoken, credit cards are accepted, breakfast is included, and Wi-Fi is generally free. Antwerp levies a hotel tax of a few euros per person, per night (typically not included in the prices here). Prices change; verify current rates online or by email. For the best prices, always book directly with the hotel.

---

ments overlooking charming Vrijdagmarkt and the Museum Plantin-Moretus. Expertly decorated with a lifetime's worth of vintage finds, the spacious suites have a shared kitchenette; the apartments offer full-size kitchens (Db-€125-130, apartments-€150, minimum 3 nights in apartments, Wi-Fi, Vrijdagmarkt 1, mobile 0473-735-650, www.aplaceantwerp.be, sleep@aplace.be, knowledgeable Karin).

$$$ Hotel O Kathedral is an ultramodern boutique hotel with a swanky wine bar and 33 rooms on the small square facing the Cathedral of Our Lady. Superior rooms are plastered with oversized Rubens prints and have sexy—but not exactly private—see-through showers (standard Db-€99, superior Db-€119, Tb-€158, €20 more on weekends, elevator, Wi-Fi, Handschoenmarkt 3, tel. 03-500-8950, www.hotelokathedral.com, kathedral@hotelhotelo.com).

$$ Enich Anders B&B is well-priced, unfussy, and nicely located above an art gallery around the corner from Vrijdagmarkt, in the heart of town. This is a great place for families, as most rooms come with lofts (Sb-€66, Db-€72, Tb-€88, Qb-€104, €5 cheaper per night with 2-night stay, includes a make-it-yourself breakfast served in your own kitchenette, cash only, Wi-Fi, tight and steep stairs, Leeuwenstraat 12, mobile 0476-998-601, www.enich-anders.be, charming Ine).

$$ Hotel Scheldezicht, a homey, well-worn inn with friendly service, has 21 airy rooms with high ceilings on a tree-lined square across from the river. Bathrooms are pint-sized; the "simple" options have shared toilets down the hall ("simple" D-€70, Db-€80, Db with views-€95, around €30 more per extra guest, Wi-Fi, Sint-Jansvliet 12, tel. 03-231-6602, www.hotelscheldezicht.eu, info@hotelscheldezicht.be).

$$ Ibis Antwerpen Centrum, the cookie-cutter standby, has 150 predictable rooms sharing the big Oudevaartplaats square with the modern City Theater, just south of the Meir and the Rubens House between the train station and Old Town (Sb/Db-€92-109 depending on demand, as low as €59 in slow times if you book online 3 weeks ahead, breakfast-€14/person, air-con, elevator, free guest computer, Wi-Fi, Meistraat 39, tel. 03-231-8830, www.ibishotel.com, h1453@accor.com).

$ 't Katshuis is a rough-around-the-edges budget option, with nine sketchy but affordable rooms in two buildings right in the center of town. This last resort has some of the best-located cheap beds in town, if you don't mind sharing a WC (Ss-€35, Ds-€55, Db-€60, includes coffee but not breakfast, Grote Pieter Potstraat 18 and 19—reception at #19, mobile 0476-206-947, www.katshuis.be, katshuis@gmail.com).

$ Pulcinella Youth Hostel is Antwerp's newest and best official hostel. With 21 doubles, it offers privacy and bargain prices (bed in 4-6 person dorm-€23, Sb-€37, Db-€54, nonmembers pay €3 fee, includes breakfast, no curfew, Wi-Fi, in the fashion district at Bogaardeplein 1, tel. 03-234-0314, www.vjh.be, antwerpen@vjh.be).

Eating in Antwerp

This trendy, youthful city is changing all the time, and the range of options is impressive. Because what's good one year is old news the next, it's risky to recommend any particular place. Instead, I suggest poking around the neighborhoods described here and choosing the menu and ambience that appeal to you the most. Exploring this evolving scene is actually enjoyable—a fun part of the Antwerp experience. Ask your hotelier for pointers.

If you're dining in the Old Town area, simply accept that anywhere you go will cater at least partly to tourists. But since Antwerp isn't overrun by visitors, these places also entertain their share of locals. For a more authentic Antwerp experience, head south to 't Zuid. While Antwerp is as crazy about obscure gourmet beers as anywhere else in Belgium, they also have an affinity for their mass-produced hometown brew, De Koninek.

IN AND NEAR THE OLD TOWN

About 95 percent of Antwerp's tourists dine on a handful of streets in the old center. Touristy restaurants with outdoor seating abound on the Grote Markt and Handschoenmarkt, the square in front of the cathedral; nearby streets are lined with mostly Italian and Greek/Turkish eateries. Choose your view and overpay for medio-

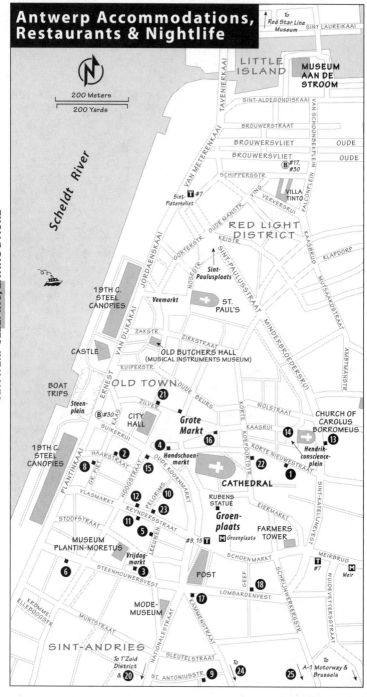

Antwerp Accommodations, Restaurants & Nightlife

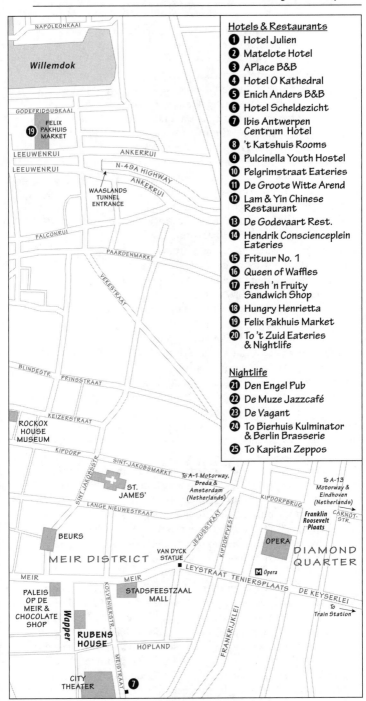

Hotels & Restaurants
1. Hotel Julien
2. Matelote Hotel
3. APlace B&B
4. Hotel O Kathedral
5. Enich Anders B&B
6. Hotel Scheldezicht
7. Ibis Antwerpen Centrum Hotel
8. 't Katshuis Rooms
9. Pulcinella Youth Hostel
10. Pelgrimstraat Eateries
11. De Groote Witte Arend
12. Lam & Yin Chinese Restaurant
13. De Godevaart Rest.
14. Hendrik Conscienceplein Eateries
15. Frituur No. 1
16. Queen of Waffles
17. Fresh 'n Fruity Sandwich Shop
18. Hungry Henrietta
19. Felix Pakhuis Market
20. To 't Zuid Eateries & Nightlife

Nightlife
21. Den Engel Pub
22. De Muze Jazzcafé
23. De Vagant
24. To Bierhuis Kulminator & Berlin Brasserie
25. To Kapitan Zeppos

cre food. The following central options are still touristy, but a bit less tacky than the main area.

Pelgrimstraat: Just a block south of the cathedral, this delightful, cobbled, traffic-free lane is a tourist zone—but a bit more respectable than the high-profile squares. You'll find a good variety along here: Italian, tapas, sushi, Thai, along with rustic taverns and chic bars. Keep an eye out for these (coming from the cathedral): **Pasta Hippo** has a reputation for good pasta. On the right at #4, go through the doorway to discover a series of narrow alleyways (called **Vlaeykensngang**) that twist through the middle of the block, passing a trio of well-regarded restaurants en route. Back on the main drag, on the left, is **Pelgrom,** a tavern in a cozy brick cellar that oozes atmosphere (but feels stuffy on a hot day). Farther down on the right is **Lollapalooza,** with a fun, eclectic menu; it comes with a charming little brick grotto across the street. Two nearby streets (Grote Pieter Potstraat and Haarstraat) are similar, but less developed and more bar-oriented.

De Groote Witte Arend, across from the far end of Pelgrimstraat, is a good place to try well-executed, stick-to-your-ribs Belgian classics—a relative rarity in this modern town. To wash things down, they have a wonderful list of 90 Belgian beers. Explore the sprawling complex (which was originally a merchant's house and then a monastery): You can sit in the cozy cobbled courtyard or in the high-ceilinged interior on two floors—and peek into the chapel (hearty €18-22 meals, daily 11:30-24:00, Reyndersstraat 18, tel. 03-233-5033).

Lam & Yin Chinese Restaurant has a tiny dining room, a small menu, great service, and wonderful traditional Chinese food served by Hong Kong immigrants. They have two seatings (18:00 and 20:30), and you'll choose from four starters (€12-16) and five main dishes (€20-30). This is a rare place, with a Michelin star and no pretense—but you'll need to reserve well in advance to snare one of its 36 seats (Wed-Sun only, closed Mon-Tue, Reyndersstraat 17, tel. 03-232-8838, www.lam-en-yin.be).

De Godevaart is another foodie splurge that's gaining international attention for chef Dave de Belder's innovative, molecular-gastronomy take on Belgian cuisine. The dining room is stately but not pretentious, and those willing to pay dearly for a unique experience will want to reserve ahead (€30-40 main dishes, €43/3-course menu available weekdays only, €70/4 courses at dinner, Tue-Sat 19:00-21:00, also open for lunch Thu-Fri 12:00-14:00, Sint-Katelijnevest 23, tel. 03-231-8994, www.degodevaart.be).

Near Hendrik Conscienceplein: The streets branching off from Hendrik Conscienceplein (about a block northeast of the cathedral), with its very Italian-feeling Baroque Jesuit church, are a charming cobbles-and-red-brick maze of alleys with intriguing little eateries. **Neuze Neuze** is a dressy and romantic place serving classic Belgian cuisine under old beams (€20-30 starters and main dishes, Mon-Sat 12:00-14:00 & 19:00-21:30, closed for lunch Wed and Sat and all day Sun, Wijngaardstraat 19, tel. 03-232-2797).

Treats near the Grote Markt: Of the many guilty-pleasure options near the Grote Markt, locals favor **Frituur No. 1** for a cone of *frieten*, or fries (open long hours daily, Hoogstraat 1; for tips on Flemish fast food, see page 336). **Queen of Waffles** sells mostly fresh-made waffles with a variety of toppings (Tue-Sun 10:00-18:00, closed Mon, Grote Markt 60—at far end of square from City Hall).

JUST SOUTH AND EAST OF THE OLD TOWN

In Sint-Andries: The area called Sint-Andries, the center of the fashion district, has its share of enjoyable bars and restaurants. For a quick lunch, try **Fresh 'n Fruity,** selling good €2-5 baguette sandwiches and fresh-squeezed fruit juice (closed Sun, Kammenstraat 19, tel. 03-231-1308).

Lombardenvest and Nearby: Charming pedestrian streets spin off from a leafy little no-name square just a few blocks south of Groenplaats and the Farmers Tower. In addition to a variety of enticing sidewalk cafés and lunch restaurants, this area has some unique shops. **Hungry Henrietta,** tucked away on a businesslike street at the edge of this zone, has mod black decor and good Belgian food (€23-25 main dishes, €17 daily specials, Mon-Fri 12:00-14:00 & 18:00-21:00, closed Sat-Sun, Lombardenvest 19, tel. 03-232-2928).

IN 'T ZUID

Literally "The South," this zone is Antwerp's top restaurant and nightlife zone. Frequented mostly by urbanites, this is where you'll find many of the city's hot new restaurants. Options are scattered around a several-block area, with one or two tempting eateries on each block. It is about a 15-minute walk south of the Grote Markt (along entertaining Kloosterstraat, lined with antique and home-decor shops). Or, from Groenplaats, take bus #180, #181, #182, #183, #291, or #295, or tram #30 or #34. These three areas—all within about a 10-minute walk of each other—have the highest concentration of appealing eateries.

Marnixplaats: The confluence of eight streets facing a dramatic column dedicated to Neptune creates a circle of corner buildings made-to-order for al fresco drinking and dining. While many of these places are drinks-only (sometimes with light snacks), a few are suitable for a full meal. **Fiskebar** is one of the top picks in this area—and in all of Antwerp—and is worth reserving ahead. Focusing on seafood, it's done up like a fish market (as its name implies), and lists a wide range of specialties on its chalkboard menu high on the wall (€19-24 main dishes, €20-30 specials, Mon 18:00-22:00, Tue-Sat 12:00-14:00 & 18:00-22:00, #12, tel. 03-257-1357, www.fiskebar.be). **Lucy Chang,** part of a small and upscale Belgian chain, serves up Asian noodle dishes (€12-16 meals, daily 12:00-23:00, #17, tel. 03-248-9560). **Pasta Plezir** is the less sophisticated option: Order a €10-15 pasta dish at the counter, then eat at the upstairs tables or on a rustic picnic bench out on the square (daily 16:00-23:00, #7, tel. 03-295-9404).

Leopold de Waelplaats: Just a block away from Marnixplaats is another cluster of bars and eateries, which gather around the long, rectangular square in front of the art museum. At the northern end of the square, you'll find several watering holes, as well as **Yam Thai** and **Bar Italia.** The far end feels a bit trendier—with some upscale bars (such as the recommended **Hopper** jazz bar, described later, under "Nightlife in Antwerp") and a wide variety of restaurants, including a pizzeria, sushi, Italian, Egyptian, Middle Eastern, and so on. (**Charleroi** has a very cool interior.)

Vlaamsekaai/Waalsekaai Parking Lot: The long parking lot that runs parallel to the river a block inland (between Waalsekaai and Vlaamsekaai) is lined with several more bars and restaurants, as well as some interesting home-furnishing stores.

Shopping in Antwerp

As a capital of both fashion and avant-garde culture, Antwerp is a shopper's delight, with a seemingly endless array of creative little corner boutiques selling unique items, as well as outlets for big-name international designers. Serious fashionistas and window shoppers alike find Antwerp's quirky browsing culture one of the most delightful in Europe. Note that most shops open between 9:00 and 10:00, and close by the relatively early hour of 18:30.

Shopping Streets

As you explore, you'll discover that each street has its own personality and specialties. For example, **Schuttershofstraat** and **Hopland** are where you'll find famous-label international couture, while **Kammenstraat** is better for young, trendy, retro-hipster fashions.

I enjoy strolling the starburst of traffic-free streets that spin off from the leafy square along **Lombardenvest** (just south of the Farmers' Tower). Each street has a different focus, such as shoe stores on Groendalstraat and clothing on Lombardenvest.

Kloosterstraat, which sticks closer to the river as it heads south from the Grote Markt area all the way to 't Zuid, focuses on home furnishings—from antiques to minimalist furniture to home decor and gadgets. You'll wish you had an unlimited budget to furnish an avant-garde Belgian flat.

Fashion District

Antwerp's status as a fashion mecca is a relatively recent development. In 1988, six students from the Royal Academy of Fine

Arts' fashion department traveled to a London show, where they got a lot of attention. Because their Flemish names were too challenging to pronounce, the English press simply dubbed them the "Antwerp Six." Each one opened a shop in **Sint-Andries,** which at the time was a very poor neighborhood. They put this area on the map, other designers began to move in, and now it's one of Europe's top fashion zones. The academy is still up and running; it has a small enrollment and a strong focus on creativity (www.antwerp-fashion.be).

Sint-Andries is a few minutes' walk south of the Old Town along Nationalestraat. While it's a three-star destination for couture lovers, anybody would have fun window shopping here. In the shops along the streets of Sint-Andries, you'll find top-name international designers, funky hole-in-the-wall boutiques, vintage shops, jewelers, and more. The TI offers thoughtfully designed resources for people interested in delving into Antwerp's high fashion scene, including detailed map/guides and an app that leads you on a self-guided tour through this zone.

Department Stores

The large department stores are on the boulevard called **the Meir,** between the train station and the Old Town. South of the Rubens House, streets like Leopoldstraat, Sint-Jorispoort, and Mechelsesteenweg are noted for antiques and home decor.

Nightlife in Antwerp

In the Old Town

After hours, Antwerp's touristy core (around the Grote Markt and cathedral) hums with activity. Find a café or bar with outdoor tables, order a drink, and people-watch. Below are some favorites; note that most of these serve little or no food—go for the ambience and entertainment, not for dinner.

Den Engel, an old-fashioned pub at the corner of the Grote

Mark (near the City Hall), is an obvious choice but also a local fixture. The cozy interior oozes authentic charm, and feels like it's been the family living room of Antwerpenaars for generations. Outside, it boasts my favorite view in Antwerp, of the dramatic cathedral tower rising up behind a row of fine facades (long hours daily, Grote Markt 3, tel. 03-233-1252). **Den Bengel,** next door, has equally fine views but a lesser interior.

De Muze Jazzcafé is outrageously atmospheric, with happy drinkers filling antique wooden booths on three levels overlooking the bar. Most come for the live jazz (six nights a week plus Sunday afternoons, only 4/week during summer, check schedule at www.jazzcafedemuze.be; open long hours daily, Melkmarkt 10, tel. 03-226-0126).

De Vagant, located at the end of Pelgrimstraat, specializes in *jenever* (gin)—with 200 different kinds on the menu. It has pleasant outdoor seating and a simple, high-ceilinged, traditional interior (daily 12:00-24:00, Reyndersstraat 25, tel. 03-233-1538).

De Groote Witte Arend—which also serves good food (see "Eating in Antwerp," earlier)—is a fine and central spot to sample a Belgian beer.

South of the Old Town

Tucked in a nondescript zone about halfway between the Old Town and 't Zuid—and worth a detour only for beer pilgrims—**Bierhuis Kulminator** is dark and cluttered (almost hoarder-esque), with a narrow little garden in the back. But the beer list literally comes in a binder. It's a rush for beer aficionados searching for a hard-to-find brew (Mon 20:00-24:00, Tue-Sat 16:00-24:00, closed Sun, Vleminckveld 32, tel. 03-232-4538). If you want a meal—or another drink—in the area, check out **Berlin** (trendy brasserie with pub grub, Kleine Markt 1) or **Kapitan Zeppos** (big and inviting beer hall with good food and tables out on an open square, Vleminckveld 78).

In 't Zuid

A 15-minute walk or five-minute bus or tram ride south of the Grote Markt, this area is the more local, somewhat younger alternative to the old core. Bars with outdoor tables cluster around two areas: Marnixplaats and in front of the art museum, at Leopold de Waelplaats (for details, see "Eating in Antwerp," earlier). Along this square, **Hopper** feels urbane and untouristy—like you're in on an insider's tip. The interior is stark but dignified, and they have live jazz a few times a week (usually Sun at 16:00 and Mon at 21:00, also Tue at 21:00 in winter; open long hours daily, Leopold de Waelstraat 2, tel. 03-248-4933).

Antwerp Connections

From Antwerp by Train to: Brussels (3/hour, 40-50 minutes), **Ghent** (3/hour, 50 minutes), **Bruges** (2/hour, 1.5 hours, half change in Ghent), **Ypres/Ieper** (hourly, 2.5 hours, change in Kortrijk), **Amsterdam** (hourly by pricey Thalys, 1.5 hours; also hourly by slower IC train, 2.5 hours), Amsterdam's **Schiphol Airport** (hourly, 1 hour by Thalys, 2 hours by IC train), **Delft** (hourly, 1 hour, change in Rotterdam), **Paris** (about hourly direct on Thalys, 2 hours; more possible with a transfer at Brussels Midi/Zuid/South to Thalys, 2.5 hours). For train information, see www.belgiumrail. be; see also page 352.

ANTWERP SLEEPING, EATING & MORE

GHENT

ORIENTATION TO GHENT

Gent • Gand

Made terrifically wealthy by the textile trade, medieval Ghent was a powerhouse, and for a time, it was one of the biggest cities in Europe. It erected grand churches and ornate guild houses to celebrate its resident industry. But, like its rival Bruges, eventually Ghent's fortunes fell, leaving it with a well-preserved historic nucleus surrounded by a fairly drab modern shell.

Ghent doesn't ooze with cobbles and charm, as Bruges does; this is a living place—home to Belgium's biggest university. Ghent enjoys just the right amount of urban grittiness, with a welcome splash of creative hipster funkiness. It's also a browser's delight, with a wide range of characteristic little shops that aren't aimed squarely at the tourist crowds. Ghent is the kind of town that you visit for a few hours, and find yourself wishing you had a few days.

Visitors enjoy exploring the historic quarter, ogling the breathtaking Van Eyck altarpiece in the massive cathedral, touring impressive art and design museums, strolling picturesque embankments, basking in finely decorated historic gables, and prowling the revitalized Patershol restaurant quarter.

PLANNING YOUR TIME

Ghent, about halfway between Brussels and Bruges and a half-hour from either, is ideally located for day-tripping. It's easy to get the gist of the town in a few hours. Either toss your bag in a locker at Ghent's train station on your way between those two cities, or side-trip here from either one. With limited time, focus on the historical center: Follow my self-guided walk, tour the cathedral, and dip into a museum or two. With more time or a strong interest in art, also visit the art museums in Citadelpark, closer to the train station. Nearly all museums in Ghent are closed on Mondays (though the cathedral and other churches remain open).

Blitz Tour of Ghent

Day-trippers to Ghent can use my Ghent City Walk (see page 284) to weave together the main sights in as little as three hours.

From the train station, take tram #1 to Korenmarkt, where the walk begins. Stop along the way to visit whichever sights interest you: climb the Belfry, tour St. Bavo's with the Ghent Altarpiece, browse the House of Alijn, and scramble up the ramparts of the Castle of the Counts.

From the Castle of the Counts, catch tram #1 back to the station.

Ghent also makes a handy home base for side-tripping to other Belgian destinations. Besides being close to Brussels and Bruges, it's just 50 minutes from Antwerp (though be aware that my recommended Ghent hotels are a tram ride away from the train station).

Ghent Overview

Although it's a mid-sized city (pop. 250,000), Ghent's historic core is appealingly compact—you can walk from one end to the other in about 15 minutes. The train station (with several museums nearby) is a 15-minute tram ride south of the center. Its Flemish residents call the town Gent (gutturally: *h*ent), while its French name is Gand (sounds like "gone").

TOURIST INFORMATION

Ghent's TI is in the Old Fish Market (Oude Vismijn) building next to the Castle of the Counts (daily mid-March-mid-Oct 9:30-18:30, off-season until 16:30, tel. 09-266-5660, www.visitgent.be). Pick up a free town map and a pile of brochures (including a good self-guided walk).

Sightseeing Pass: Busy sightseers might save a few euros with the **CityCard Gent,** but on a day-trip blitz with this book, it's probably not worth it (€30/48 hours, €35/72 hours, includes public transit and entrance to all the major museums and monuments in town). Purchase the card at the TI, any of the included sights, or at the Lijnwinkel transportation office (Mon-Fri 7:00-12:15 & 12:45-19:00) in the train station.

ARRIVAL IN GHENT

By Train: Ghent's main train station, Gent-Sint-Pieters, is about a mile and a half south of the city center. As the station is undergoing an extensive renovation (through 2020), it might differ from what's described here. In the main hall, be sure to look up at the meticulously restored frescoes celebrating great Flemish cities and regions.

The left-luggage desk (daily 6:15-21:00) is across the hall from the Travel Center ticket office, and lockers are just down the same hall.

It's a dull 30-minute **walk** to the city center. Instead, take the **tram:** Buy a ticket from the train station's Relay shop, at the ticket machines outside, or on board (€1.30 if you buy ticket in advance, €2 from the driver; you can also get a shareable 10-ride ticket for €10). Find the stop for tram #1: It's out the front door and 100 yards to the left, under the big, blocky, modern building on stilts. Board tram #1 in the direction of Wondelgem/Evergem (departs about every 10 minutes, 15-minute ride). Get off at the Korenmarkt stop, and continue one block straight ahead to Korenmarkt, where you can see most of the city's landmark towers (and where my Ghent City Walk begins). Figure €10 for a **taxi** into town (€8.50 drop good for about 2 miles, after 22:00 the drop jumps to €11).

To reach the art museums in Citadelpark or the Ghent City Museum, see pages 279-283.

By Car: Exit the E-40 expressway at the Gent Centrum exit, then follow the *P-route* (parking route) to various pay garages in town; the most central include P1 (Vrijdagmarkt) and P5 (Kouter). There's also ample parking at the Gent-Sint-Pieters train station, with its easy tram connection into town (see "By Train," above).

HELPFUL HINTS

Festivals: Ghent is proud of its Gentse Feesten (Ghent Festivities), which last for 10 days and begin around the city holiday of July 21 (www.gentsefeesten.be). This open-air music festival features everything from jazz to techno in venues around town and lots of boozing. Book hotels during this period well in advance. Other events include a jazz festival (the week before the big festival) and a film festival in mid-October.

Market Day: Sunday is the main market day in Ghent, with small markets filling squares around town: a flower market at Kouter, secondhand books along Ajuinlei, clothes and pets on Vrijdagmarkt, and more. There are also smaller markets on Fridays and Saturdays.

Laundry: A handy, unstaffed coin-op **launderette** is in the heart of the Patershol restaurant neighborhood...handy for multitask-ers (daily 7:00-22:00, corner of Oudburg and Zwaanstraat, mobile 048-460-0185). Another option is **Wascenter Netezon,** a few steps west of Vrijdagmarkt square (Mon-Sat 6:00-22:00, closed Sun, Sint-Jacobsnieuwstraat 3).

Tours in Ghent

Walking Tours
Guided two-hour tours of Ghent (in English and usually another language, too) depart from the TI (€8, May-Oct daily at 14:30, Sun only off-season).

Local Guide
Toon Van den Abeele enthusiastically shares Ghent's charms (€70/2-hour tour, book through the local guide agency, tel. 09-233-0772, www.ghentguides.be, info@gidsenbond-gent.be).

Boat Tours
Lazy little tour boats, jammed with tourists listening to the spiel in several languages, cruise the waterways. Several companies offer essentially the same tour for the same price; boats line up along the Korenlei or Graslei embankments (€7, 40-50 minutes, live guides).

SIGHTS IN GHENT

Most of Ghent's sights cluster in one of two areas: in the historic city center or south of the core, near the train station.

IN THE HISTORIC CENTER
▲▲Cathedral of St. Bavo (Sint-Baafskathedraal) and Ghent Altarpiece

This cathedral, the main church of Ghent, houses three of the city's art treasures: the exquisite Van Eyck *Adoration of the Mystic Lamb* altarpiece—famously known as the Ghent Altarpiece; an elaborately carved pulpit; and an altar painting by Rubens depicting the town's patron saint (and the church's namesake).

Cost and Hours: Church free to enter but €4 to see original altarpiece and its facsimile, includes audioguide; April-Oct Mon-Sat 9:30-17:00, Sun 13:00-17:00; Nov-March Mon-Sat 10:30-16:00, Sun 13:00-16:00; Sint-Baafsplein, tel. 09-225-1626, www.sintbaafskathedraal.be.

○ See the Cathedral of St. Bavo & Ghent Altarpiece Tour chapter.

Church of St. Nicholas (Sint-Niklaaskerk)

This beautiful church, built of Tournai limestone, is a classic of the Scheldt Gothic style. There's been a church here since the early 12th century; Ghent's merchants started building this one in the 1300s. Among its art treasures is a massive Baroque altar of painted wood.

Cost and Hours: Free, Mon 14:00-17:00, Tue-Sun 10:00-17:00, on Cataloniëstraat at the corner of Korenmarkt, tel. 09-234-2869.

○ For details, see page 286 of the Ghent City Walk.

Belfry (Belfort)

This combination watchtower and carillon has been keeping an eye on Ghent since the 1300s. For centuries, this landmark building safeguarded civic documents. Nowadays, the mostly empty interior displays an exhibit of bells, and an elevator whisks visitors up the 300-foot tower to views over the city.

Cost and Hours: €6, daily 10:00-18:00, last entry 30 minutes before closing, Sint-Baafsplein, tel. 09-233-3954, www.belfortgent.be.

○ For details, see page 288 of the Ghent City Walk.

House of Alijn (Huis van Alijn)

This museum shows how everyday Belgian lifestyles evolved over the course of time. You walk through an intriguing collection of

bric-a-brac dating from about 1850 to 1980—dishes, toys, cribs, kitchen appliances, and a statue of a woman wiping a baby's bum. You'll see an old-timey candy store, a barbershop, a pharmacy, and a 1980s suburban living room with its TV and Springsteen albums. There are few labels or descriptions, so—for better or worse—you're left to experience the place on your own. It's easy to just browse, and the objects (and their time period) are pretty self-explanatory.

The exhibits are displayed in several buildings around a tranquil courtyard, of what used to be an almshouse—a refuge for poor elderly people. The courtyard hosts an authentic Ghent pub where you can sample *jenever*, or gin.

Cost and Hours: €6, Tue-Sun 11:00-17:00, closed Mon, Kraanlei 65, tel. 09-269-2350, www.huisvanalijn.be.

▲Castle of the Counts (Gravensteen)

Though it dates from 1180, this fortress has morphed over the centuries, and much of it is rebuilt and restored. It's impressive from

the outside, but mostly bare inside and information is skimpy. Still, it's a fun opportunity to get a feel for the medieval world as you twist through towers and ramble over ramparts. It has all the different parts of a typical castle: courtyard and keep, throne room, chapel, 18-foot-deep dungeon, and ramparts. There are displays of swords and suits of armor, along with

GHENT SIGHTS

Ghent at a Glance

▲▲**Cathedral of St. Bavo and Ghent Altarpiece** Main church housing treasures by Peter Paul Rubens and Jan van Eyck. **Hours:** April-Oct Mon-Sat 9:30-17:00, Sun 13:00-17:00, Nov-March Mon-Sat 10:30-16:00, Sun 13:00-16:00. See page 274.

▲**Castle of the Counts** Restored fortress with typical castle ramparts, a dungeon, and good tower views. **Hours:** Daily April-Oct 10:00-18:00, Nov-March 9:00-17:00. See page 275.

▲**Ghent Design Museum** Enjoyable display of Belgian design from the 17th to 20th century. **Hours:** Tue-Sun 10:00-18:00, closed Mon. See page 277.

▲**Fine Arts Museum** Accessible collection of Northern European art. **Hours:** Tue-Sun 10:00-18:00, closed Mon. See page 277.

▲**Ghent City Museum** High-tech museum tracing the city's history through multimedia exhibits and historic artifacts. **Hours:** Tue-Sun 10:00-18:00, closed Mon. See page 282.

Church of St. Nicholas Medieval merchants' church dedicated to their patron saint. **Hours:** Mon 14:00-17:00, Tue-Sun 10:00-17:00. See page 274.

Belfry Landmark 14th-century tower topped by a copper dragon. **Hours:** Daily 10:00-18:00. See page 275.

House of Alijn Knickknacks and re-created scenes of domestic Belgium life. **Hours:** Tue-Sun 11:00-17:00, closed Mon. See page 275.

Stedelijk Contemporary Art Museum Rotating exhibits of cutting-edge European art. **Hours:** Tue-Sun 10:00-18:00, closed Mon. See page 282.

GHENT SIGHTS

a reconstructed guillotine that was last used in 1861. For fans of torture museums, this one has real instruments of "persuasion" (see sidebar), including how waterboarding was practiced by the Inquisition centuries before Dick Cheney endorsed its use as "a no-brainer." If you climb to the top of one of the towers (lots of claustrophobic stairs), you'll get good views—and the feeling that you're the ruler of your own castle.

Cost and Hours: €10, daily April-Oct 10:00-18:00, Nov-March 9:00-17:00, last entry one hour before closing, includes unhelpful audioguide with corny dramatizations, dry €1.50 guidebook tells the history of the place, tel. 09-225-9306, Sint-Veerleplein, www.gravensteengent.be.

▲Ghent Design Museum (Design Museum Gent)

This collection celebrating the Belgian knack for design is enjoyable for everyone, but worth ▲▲▲ for those interested in deco-

rative arts of the 17th to 20th century. It combines a classic old building with a creaky wood interior, with a bright-white, spacious, and glassy new hall in the center. You'll cross back and forth between these sections, seeing both old-timey rooms and exquisite pieces of Art Nouveau, Art Deco, and contempo-

rary design. Just explore: Everything is clearly explained in English and easy to appreciate. The temporary exhibits are well-presented and interesting. Don't miss the 18th-century dining room, with a remarkable wood-carved chandelier.

Cost and Hours: €8, Tue-Sun 10:00-18:00, closed Mon, Jan Breydelstraat 5, tel. 09-267-9999, www.designmuseumgent.be.

MUSEUMS NEAR THE TRAIN STATION

Several museums are closer to the train station than to the historical center, which makes them ideal to visit on your way in or out of Ghent. The Fine Arts Museum and the Stedelijk Contemporary Art Museum are located at Citadelpark, while the Ghent City Museum is a bit farther north of the station.

▲Fine Arts Museum (Museum voor Schone Kunsten)

This museum offers a good, representative look at Northern European art. It's one of the most user-friendly collections of Low Countries art you'll find in Belgium, with lesser-known yet fun works by artists such as Bosch, Rubens, Van Dyck, and Magritte. Information sheets in English are in almost all of the rooms, but you'll get more from renting the excellent audioguide.

Cost and Hours: €8, Tue-Sun 10:00-18:00, closed Mon, €2.50 for great and essential audioguide, in Citadelpark along Fernand Scribedreef street, tel. 09-240-0700, www.mskgent.be.

Getting to the Citadelpark Museums: To reach Citadelpark and its museums from the train station (about a 10-minute walk), exit straight ahead to the modern sculpture in the middle of the plaza. Turn right and walk up the tree- and bike-lined Koningin Astridlaan about five minutes, then cross the road and enter Citadelpark. Walk straight ahead, then curl around the left side of the big, modern building at the center of the park; as you round the far

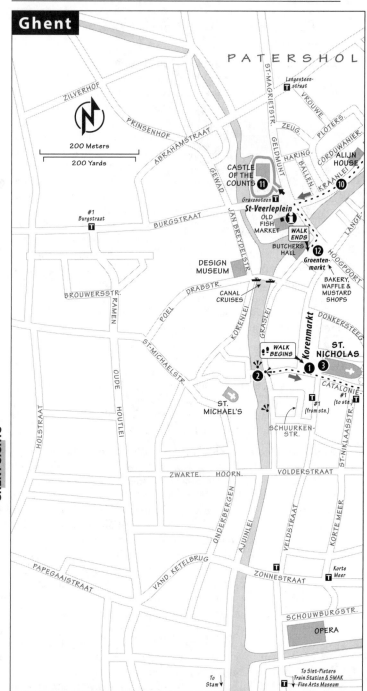

Ghent

PATERSHOL

ZILVERHOF

PRINSENHOF

ABRAHAMSTRAAT

200 Meters

200 Yards

#1 Burgstraat

BURGSTRAAT

ST-MAGRIETSTR.

Langesteen-straat

VROUWE

ZEUG

HARING

GELDMUNT

GEWAD

JAN BREYDELSTR.

CASTLE OF THE COUNTS 11

Gravensteen

St-Veerleplein

OLD FISH MARKET

WALK ENDS

BUTCHERS HALL 12

Groentenmarkt

PLOTERS.

CORDUWANIER

ALIJN HOUSE

KRAANLEI 10

LANGE

HOOGPOORT

DESIGN MUSEUM

DRABSTR.

CANAL CRUISES

BROUWERSSTR.

RAMEN

POEL

KORENLEI

GRASLEI

ST-MICHAELSTR.

OUDE

HOLSTRAAT

HOUTLEI

ST. MICHAEL'S

WALK BEGINS

Korenmarkt

2   1   3

DONKERSTEEG

BAKERY, WAFFLE & MUSTARD SHOPS

ST. NICHOLAS

CATALONIE

#1 (to stn.)

ST-NIKLAASSTR.

#1 (from stn.)

SCHUURKEN-STR.

ZWARTE. HOORN.

VOLDERSTRAAT

VELDSTRAAT

KORTE MEER

ONDERBERGEN

AJUINLEI

VAND. KETELBRUG

ZONNESTRAAT

Korte Meer

PAPEGAAISTRAAT

SCHOUWBURGSTR.

OPERA

To Stam

To Sint-Pieters Train Station & SMAK Fine Arts Museum

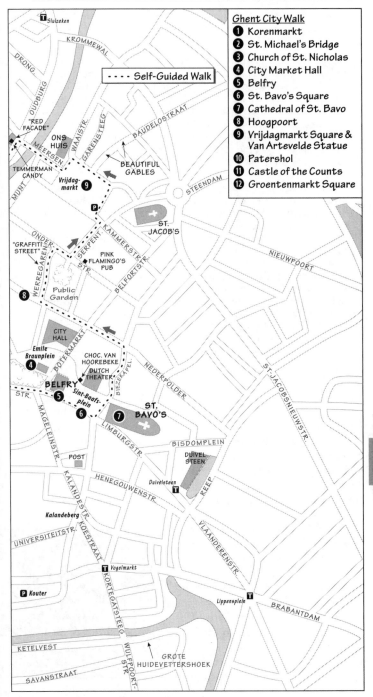

<u>Ghent City Walk</u>
1. Korenmarkt
2. St. Michael's Bridge
3. Church of St. Nicholas
4. City Market Hall
5. Belfry
6. St. Bavo's Square
7. Cathedral of St. Bavo
8. Hoogpoort
9. Vrijdagmarkt Square & Van Artevelde Statue
10. Patershol
11. Castle of the Counts
12. Groentenmarkt Square

- - - - Self-Guided Walk

GHENT SIGHTS

A Torturer's Toolbox

Travelers may think that endless security lines at airports are torturous—but that's child's play compared with what heretics and criminals faced in the Middle Ages. Medieval torture was used to extract confessions and to punish the convicted prior to execution. Torturers had a huge toolkit with which to practice their art.

One device was the rack, designed to pull the victim's limbs apart. A prisoner's arms and legs were tied to opposite ends of the machine. Then the torturer turned the crank, expanding the rack and leaving the victim with dislocated joints or even limbless.

Another nasty tool was a finger screw—a set of bars and screws that tightened to crush fingers and toes. Since finger screws were small and portable, they were a favorite of traveling medieval interrogators.

The iron maiden was a spike-filled cabinet, just tall enough to fit a standing human. It had small holes through which torturers inserted sharp objects to stab prisoners, sometimes killing them. A variant was the torture chair, entirely covered in spikes. Victims' wrists were tied to the arms of the chair, and weights were attached to their legs and feet. Sitting in the chair usually resulted in death from blood loss.

For public executions, a prisoner would be stretched over a wheel, and the executioner would break his or her bones with an iron hammer. The victim was left to die from shock and dehydra-

side, the Neoclassical entrance to the Fine Arts Museum is across the small street, and the Stedelijk Contemporary Art Museum (with a large *S.M.A.K.* sign over the entrance) is on your right.

Visiting the Museum: As you enter, to the right (in numbered rooms) are older works, and to the left (in lettered rooms) are 19th- and 20th-century works and temporary exhibits. To take a counterclockwise, chronological spin though the collection, turn right from the entrance, and keep an eye out for these fine pieces.

In Room 2, **Hieronymus Bosch**'s jarring *Christ Carrying the Cross* (1515-1516) features a severe-looking Jesus surrounded by grotesque faces. Typical of the Middle Ages, Bosch believed that evil was ugly—and all but three faces on this canvas (forming a diagonal, from lower left to upper right) are hideous. The serene woman to the left of Christ is Veronica, who has just wiped his face. In the upper right, with an ashen complexion, is the

tion. For less serious crimes, the prisoner received the gift of one swift and deadly blow to the neck.

Then there was waterboarding. In medieval times jailers  poured water—and often bodily fluids—down the throat of the prisoner. To avoid drowning, "suspects" might drink the liquid, which resulted in a sort of intoxication and often death. The modern variation—practiced by the Japanese during World War II, the French in Algeria, and the CIA at Guantanamo Bay—could be described as "slow-motion drowning." Interrogators covered the victim's face with cloth or another thin material. Then they poured water over the prisoner's nose and mouth, triggering the gag reflex and a sensation of drowning.

Today, although 146 members of the United Nations have ratified an international convention outlawing torture, it remains rampant worldwide. Medieval or modern, it's a practice that won't go away. Carl Jung's observation is still relevant: "The healthy man does not torture others—generally it is the tortured who turn into torturers."

stoic good thief, flanked by a doctor and a taunting monk. Meanwhile, in the lower right, the orange-tinged unrepentant thief sneers back at his hecklers. Nearby, Bosch's portrait of St. Jerome (c. 1505)—who was his personal patron saint—shows the holy hermit having discarded his clothes. Just above his legs, notice the owl (representing evil) sinisterly eyeing a titmouse (good). Also in this room, in **Rogier Van der Weyden**'s *The Virgin with a Carnation* (1480), the Baby Jesus makes a benediction gesture with his little hand. This small painting was designed as a focal point for personal meditation.

Room 5 displays **Peter Paul Rubens**' altarpiece depicting St. Francis of Assisi receiving the stigmata—the wounds of the crucified Christ—from a six-winged angel, whose own hands and feet are fastened to a cross. Francis' brother Leo stares in amazement from below.

Room 4 is devoted to the restoration of **Jan and Hubert van Eyck**'s *Adoration of the Mystic Lamb* altarpiece housed in the Cathedral of St. Bavo. You can watch as conservators work on one panel at a time, removing old varnish and retouching damaged sections. The €1.3 million project won't be completed until 2017.

GHENT SIGHTS

In Room 7, Rubens' student **Anthony van Dyck** depicts the mythological story of *Jupiter and Antiope*—a horned-and-horny god about to inseminate a sleeping woman.

Room 8 features **Pieter Brueghel the Younger**'s copy of his more famous father, Pieter Bruegel the Elder's, much-loved *Peasant Wedding in a Barn*. The elder painter trained his kids to carry on the family business. But Brueghel the Younger was a talented painter in his own right: In his *Village Lawyer*, we see the attorney behind a desk piled with papers, as peasants bring items to barter for his services.

Circle into the modern (lettered) wing. Near the front of this section, in Room B's *Portrait of Physician Ludwig Adler*, Viennese Secessionist painter **Oskar Kokoschka** uses dynamic, expressionistic brushstrokes to capture the personality, rather than a precise reproduction, of his subject.

In Room F you'll find works by homegrown Belgian modernist **René Magritte**. His clever *Perspective II*—part of a larger series—wryly replaces the four subjects on Edouard Manet's famous *Balcony* with coffins. Next to him you'll find similar surrealist works by **Max Ernst** and **Paul Delvaux**. A Belgian artist who studied, worked, and taught in Brussels, Delvaux became famous for his surrealistic paintings of nude women, often wandering through weirdly lit landscapes. They cast long shadows, wandering bare-breasted among classical ruins. Beyond this room, the sculpture gallery underneath the rotunda is also worth a peek.

Stedelijk Contemporary Art Museum (Stedelijk Museum voor Actuele Kunst, a.k.a. SMAK)

This art gallery is constantly changing, both the "permanent" collection and many temporary exhibits. It's worth a visit only for art lovers, and is conveniently located just across the street from the Fine Arts Museum.

Cost and Hours: €6, more for special exhibits, Tue-Sun 10:00-18:00, closed Mon, tel. 09-240-7601, www.smak.be. For directions on how to reach the museum, see "Getting to the Citadelpark Museums," earlier.

▲Ghent City Museum (Stadsmuseum Gent, a.k.a. STAM)

This cutting-edge museum, housed in a beautiful 14th-century Gothic abbey complex called Bijloke, explains the history of Ghent with all the bells and whistles you'd expect in this fashion-forward city. The permanent exhibit traces the city's history in high-tech treatments mixed with historic artifacts. Everything is explained in English, but it's worth paying extra for the excellent audioguide.

Cost and Hours: €8, Tue-Sun 10:00-18:00, closed Mon, last entry one hour before closing, audioguide-€3, Godshuizenlaan 2, tel. 09-267-1400, www.stamgent.be.

Getting There: From the train station, it's a 15- to 20-minute walk: Exit straight ahead, then angle left up the busy, tram-tracks-lined Koning Albertlaan. After the bridge, turn right on Godshuizenlaan. Or, from the station, you could ride tram #1 to the Veergrep stop, backtrack a long block to the first busy road, and turn right.

Visiting the Museum: Begin in the modern annex, where you'll buy your ticket on the ground floor, then head upstairs to the first floor. In the Ghent Today room, you can walk across a giant aerial photograph of the modern city sprawl and (in the middle) examine an elevated model of the old center. Then cross over to the old abbey complex, where you'll slowly circle the courtyard for a clockwise, chronological loop that traces the story of Ghent.

Besides viewing the excellent exhibits, you can peer down into the abbey church, nuns' dormitory, and refectory. Mixed between the six rooms of the main collection are some fascinating themed detours; for example, you'll learn about the theft of the still-missing *Just Judges* panel of the Ghent Altarpiece, housed in the Cathedral of St. Bavo (see page 294). Your visit ends with a walk through the old church building.

GHENT CITY WALK

The heart of Ghent still looks much like it did circa 1500, when this was one of Europe's greatest cities: bristling with skyscraping towers, rich with art, and thronged with upscale citizens.

This self-guided walk starts at the former harbor, where this city of clothmakers plugged into the global economy. Next we pass by the towers for which the city became known. The grandest is the soaring steeple of St. Bavo's, home to the main art sight in town, Van Eyck's famous altarpiece. Then it's down main street (Hoogpoort) through the heart of town, whose many shops make clear that this city of traders lives on. The last part of the walk winds along small lanes, making its way through the trendy residential district. We'll end with the fun-to-tour Castle of the Counts and several photogenic squares. To track the route of this walk, see the map on page 278.

Orientation

Length of This Walk: Allow 1.5 hours to traverse this mile-long walk, plus more time to go inside sights along the way. With limited time, end the walk at the Castle of the Counts, where you can catch tram #1 back to the station. (To use this walk as a spine for a three-hour blitz tour of the city, see page 271.)

Getting There: Take tram #1 from the train station to Korenmarkt (see page 272 for details).

Church of St. Nicholas: Free, Mon 14:00-17:00, Tue-Sun 10:00-17:00.

Belfry: €6, daily 10:00-18:00, last entry 30 minutes before closing.

Cathedral of St. Bavo: Church-free, altarpiece-€4, includes excellent audioguide; April-Oct Mon-Sat 9:30-17:00, Sun 13:00-17:00; Nov-March Mon-Sat 10:30-16:00, Sun 13:00-16:00.

House of Alijn: €6, Tue-Sun 11:00-17:00, closed Mon.

Castle of the Counts: €10, includes corny audioguide, daily April-Oct 10:00-18:00, Nov-March 9:00-17:00, last entry one hour before closing.

The Walk Begins

• *From the Korenmarkt tram #1 stop, walk straight ahead to bustling Korenmarkt square, where our tour begins.*

❶ Korenmarkt Square

You're at the center of historic Ghent. The city boomed in the Middle Ages, when the wool trade made it wealthy. By the 14th cen-

tury, Ghent's population was around 65,000—positively massive in an age when most of Europe was rural farmland (north of the Alps, only Paris was larger). Two-thirds of the city's population were textile workers, making Ghent arguably Europe's first industrial city. Imagine Ghent at its peak around the year 1500, flush with guilders from weaving high-fashion cloth and shipping it around Europe. With its wealth, Ghent became a proud city of soaring towers.

This "Corn Market" is one of many small squares throughout the city. Whereas many Belgian cities (including Brussels, Bruges, and Antwerp) have a single "Great Market" (Grote Markt), Ghent was too big for just one such square. Instead it had a smattering of smaller squares that specialized in different areas of commerce. They retain these traditional names today.

Look down Cataloniëstraat (with its many tram tracks) to see the **spires** of Ghent's three main buildings: the rectangular tower

of the Church of St. Nicholas, the Belfry (with a dragon rather than a cross on top), and St. Bavo's Cathedral.

As you tour Ghent, you can play amateur archaeologist to quickly deduce the age of various structures. Try it with the various materials used to build St. Nich-

olas: The bluish-gray limestone of its tower tells you it was built before 1400, when Ghent was rolling in wool money and could afford to float the valuable blue-hued stone down the Scheldt River from distant Tournai. The yellow sandstone of one of the church's side portals dates it to between 1400 and 1500, when the economy was slowing, and builders quarried local stone. The red brick of the church's lower wall was locally produced after 1500, when competition from Brussels and England, combined with a conservative guild leadership that was slow to adapt to changing markets, caused Ghent's economy to tank. (Proud Ghent natives gleefully point out that their rival, Bruges, is built mostly of brick—indicating that city's lowlier economic status in medieval times.)

The big building with prickly steeples (opposite St. Nicholas) is the former **post office** (now the Post Plaza mall). While it seems to match the classic medieval style of old Ghent, it's much newer—Neo-Gothic, dating from 1913. As throughout Europe, the late 1800s and early 1900s were a time of powerful nationalism, when smaller minority groups (such as the Flemish) rose up against the more dominant groups (such as the French-speaking Belgians) to assert their legitimacy and worth. There was a flurry of Neo-Gothic construction, harkening back to a time when the Flemish had more power.

• *Walk straight ahead—passing the post office building on your right—and out onto the bridge.*

❷ St. Michael's Bridge (Sint-Michielsbrug)

This viewpoint offers Ghent's best 360-degree panorama. The city was founded at the confluence of two rivers: the Leie (*Lys* in

French) and the Scheldt (*Escaut* in French). The waterway under your feet—now plied by tourist-laden boats—was the city's busy harbor. Lining the embankment are several ornately decorated guild houses—meeting halls for the town's boatmen, corn traders, and grain weighers. At one end of the canal, find a castle tower rising above the Old Fish Market (Oude Vismijn, with the TI), which marks the start of the seedy-chic Patershol zone (a residential district sprinkled with great restaurants); behind that is the imposing Castle of the Counts. (We'll circle through town and end near there.)

• *Return to the Korenmarkt and turn your attention to the big church at the end of the square.*

❸ Church of St. Nicholas (Sint-Niklaaskerk)

This stout church was built mostly during the 13th century, a boom time for Ghent. It's dedicated to St. Nicholas, the patron saint of sailors, so it was only natural that it became the favorite of the river traders who sold their goods on the Korenmarkt. The church is a textbook example of Scheldt Gothic style: bluish-gray stone, turrets, and a single tower in the center (rather than twin towers on the facade).

Go inside, using the door facing the tram tracks. You can tell the church was built from the back to the front, as the stone transitions from the blue-gray limestone used first to the yellow sandstone used later. While the building itself is Gothic, the decorations inside—like most in Ghent—are much newer. As this region was at the forefront of the Protestant Reformation in the 16th century, the interior of Ghent's churches suffered at the hands of the iconoclasts—Protestants (Calvinists) who stripped Catholic churches of all adornments to unclutter their communion with God. The church was later partly redecorated by Catholics, who installed the very Baroque altar (painted wood, not marble) and impressive organ (19th century). Iconoclasts destroyed essentially all the medieval glass in Ghent—the modern stained glass above represents the seven sacraments.

• *Exiting the church, look across the street and notice the statue-topped gable of the* **Masons' Guild House.** *This 15th-century facade was only*

revealed in the 1980s, when workers restored the building. They added the decorations at the tops of the gables (bottom row: humans; middle row: devils; top row: angels) as well as a modern glass-and-steel section.

Turn left and head down Cataloniëstraat (away from the river). Beyond St. Nicholas stands the big, wooden roof of the...

❹ City Market Hall (Stadshal)

Just a few years ago, this space was no more than an ugly parking lot. But city leaders decided to beautify and turn this prime real estate into a 21st-century social hub. Now, beyond a small grassy park with a fountain, there's a new public square, partially sheltered by a modern twin-gabled timber roof. While many residents embrace the market hall, some find its modern style jarring, especially in the midst of old Ghent (it's been called the "Sheep Shed" and the "Hall of Shame"). Take a moment to wander beneath the gables, where light filtering in through hundreds of slits scatters in ever-changing patterns. On the lower level is a café, free WCs, and a bicycle parking garage. The woody canopy shelters an original 17th-century bell from the adjacent belfry. Nearby cafés, wine bars, and (often) food trucks offer temptations to office workers on their lunch breaks.

• *The next tall building is the...*

❺ Belfry (Belfort)

Although most of this tower has stood here since the 14th century, the Neo-Gothic top spire (from the gargoyles up) was added when Ghent proudly hosted a World's Fair in 1913. The tower was originally built to house and protect the parchment record of Ghent's favored privileges, granted to the city by the counts of Flanders in exchange for financial support. The dragon topping the spire symbolizes not the devil (as was typical in the Middle Ages), but a protector who never sleeps as it watches over the city's rights. It was also a fire watchtower, represented by the four sentries positioned at the corners. The carillon in the tower often plays the Ghent town anthem at the top of the hour.

Visitors enjoy ascending the belfry for a decent, if not stunning, view over town. It's just a couple of flights of stairs, then an elevator most of the way. Enter on the side facing the tram tracks, and ogle the gorgeous wall painting of old Ghent in the main hall (borrow the English explanations as you enter). Then walk down through some excavations, and spiral up to level 0, which shows off models of the former spires that topped the tower (including an original dragon, from 1380). From here, you can walk or ride the elevator to different levels with exhibits: on level 1, a bell museum, including a film about how bells are cast; on level 2, the giant bell called "Roland"; and on level 3, a big drum for making carillon music.

The long building at the base of (and behind) the belfry is the **Cloth Hall,** which was important to this textile center.

• *The square beyond the Belfry is...*

❻ St. Bavo's Square (Sint-Baafsplein)

This square became a symbolic battleground during the period of Flemish nationalism in the early 20th century. When Belgium gained its independence from the Netherlands in 1830, it was ruled by its Walloon (French-speaking) aristocracy, even though Dutch speakers were in the majority. The Flemish people felt mistreated by their Francophone overlords. (It took a century after independence for Ghent's prestigious university to finally start offering classes in Dutch; to mark that day in 1930, the Walloon-aristocracy-owned electric company spitefully cut power to mourn the university's end of "enlightened" thinking.) For more on the

Flemish-Walloon conflict, see "The Battle for Belgium: Flanders vs. Wallonia" on page 13.

The ornate building on the square is the **Dutch Theater** (Koninklijke Nederlandse Schouwburg, or NT Gent), built in 1899 to provide the town's Dutch speakers a place to perform plays of their own. By embracing Dutch as a language worthy of theater, the spunky Flemish were asserting their cultural legitimacy. The golden mosaic depicts Apollo returning to Mount Parnassus, much as the Flemish felt they were coming home to their beloved language.

The **statue** in the middle of the square—of a muscular man and comely woman—also celebrates the Flemish cultural revival of the 1800s. The figures represent the resurrection of the Dutch language here—notice the lion, a symbol of Flanders, on their flag. The relief on the base (facing the theater) depicts Jan Frans Willems, one of the founders of the Flemish revival.

To the left of the theater is **Chocolatier Van Hoorebeke,** a producer of fine pralines. Peek in the window, or go in the shop and look through the glass floor, to see the chocolate makers hard at work (€4/100 grams, open daily).

• *At the end of the square is Ghent's top sight.*

❼ Cathedral of St. Bavo (Sint-Baafskathedraal)

Ghent's Gothic cathedral can claim plenty of history (Holy Roman Emperor Charles V was baptized here), and it has a beautifully carved pulpit and a Rubens altar painting. But the showstopper here is the monumental *Adoration of the Mystic Lamb* altarpiece by Jan Van Eyck and his brother, Hubert.

❂ For details, see the Cathedral of St. Bavo & Ghent Altarpiece Tour chapter.

• *Exiting the cathedral, turn right and head down the narrow, twisty Biezekapelstraat. You'll pass the medieval-looking turrets and arcades of the back of the (19th-century) Achtersikkel mansion, the home of a powerful aristocratic family. The music you might hear is provided by students rehearsing at the nearby music college. Exiting this narrow street, turn left on Nederpolder and head up to the main street of medieval Ghent...*

❽ Hoogpoort

This "High Gate" street connects Ghent's two rivers. As you walk, notice you're on a slight hill; Ghent was founded at a high point between the rivers, which people made ample use of for trade.

Crossing Belfortstraat, you'll see the giant, eclectic, slightly run-down **City Hall** (Stadhuis) on your left. As Ghent in its heyday was ruled by citizens, not by kings, the City Hall was a kind of monument to self-rule. Notice how it's been augmented over the years. The ornate Gothic core (along Hoogpoort) dates from the early 16th century. The blocky, black-and-white-columned Neo-Renaissance section (down Botermarkt) was added later. Continue along Hoogpoort, observing the many facets of this one building.

At the end of the City Hall, find (on the right) the narrow passageway called Werregaren Straat. Once used to drain water

away from this high ground, today it has a different purpose and an apt nickname: **Graffitistraat.** Walk down the lane, enjoying the artwork provided by the people of Ghent. This is a typically pragmatic Belgian solution to a social problem: Rather than outlawing graffiti entirely, the police have designated this one street to give would-be artists a legal, controlled outlet for their impulses. Halfway down the lane, notice the beautiful fenced-in garden on your right. This restful, city-owned, picnic-perfect space is open to the public. (The entrance is farther ahead, at Onderstraat #22.)

• *Emerging from Graffitistraat, turn right on Onderstraat and find narrow Serpentstraat, on your left. Before turning, check out the* **Pink Flamingo's Pub***, with its avant-garde, funky-kitsch interior and Barbie chandelier. Now, head down Serpentstraat, which is lined with some fun boutiques and colorful secondhand stores (for details, see "Shopping in Ghent," page 310). When you pop out, turn left and you'll be in...*

❾ Vrijdagmarkt Square

While traditionally the big town market was on Friday (as the square's name—Vrijdag—indicates), these days the primary market day is Sunday, when six different locations around the old center are lively with antiques, secondhand books, and—on this square—chirping birds, among other things. Vrijdagmarkt also hosts a smaller market on Friday mornings and Saturday afternoons. But any day, it's a great place to pause for a beverage at one of the cafés ringing the spacious square.

The statue in the square depicts **Jakob van Artevelde,** a clever businessman who saved the day in the 14th century, when Ghent was

caught between powerful France (which controlled the city) and England (which provided it with wool). When the English king refused to export his wool to Ghent, Van Artevelde—not an aristocrat, but an ordinary citizen—boldly negotiated directly with the king to keep Ghent neutral in the conflict and keep the wool coming in. Largely forgotten by history, Van Artevelde's memory was resurrected during the nationalism of the late 19th and early 20th centuries, as a symbol of the Flemish people of Ghent asserting their independence from the Francophones. Today he's still celebrated by the people of Ghent, who sometimes call their city "Artevelde-Stad."

Directly behind the Van Artevelde statue is **Baudelostraat,** a street worth a peek for some particularly beautiful gables dating to the early 20th century. It's also home to a fun antique mall (see "Shopping in Ghent," page 311).

Towering in a corner of the square is the eclectic **Ons Huis** ("House of the People," with the *Bond Moyson* sign), the headquarters for the region's socialist movement. Not surprisingly for a city with a long industrial heritage, Ghent is a hotbed of left-leaning politics and the birthplace of the Belgian Labor Party. Above the door, notice the rooster—crowing to wake up the workers.

Directly in front of the Ons Huis is the popular Frituur Jozef fry wagon; for more on Belgian-style fries and snacks, see page 336.
• *Exit the square down the narrow street just left of the workers' hall (Meerseniersstraat). In a block you reach a bridge. Notice the giant red cannon on the left. Several different tour-guide stories have circulated about this giant piece of artillery, but it's more fun to make up your own.*

Cross the bridge—noticing the walkways that line the riverbank, allowing you a scenic and uncrowded stroll just above the water—to enter the district called...

⑩ Patershol

Until recently a run-down and dangerous district, today this neighborhood is one of Ghent's trendiest. And though it's predominantly residential, Patershol is also a great place for restaurant-hunting (see page 305).

As you cross the bridge, you'll see two particularly fine

gabled **facades.** The red facade features five panels with figures symbolizing the five senses: monkey = taste; eagle = sight; deer = hearing; dog = smell; and humans = touch (since we have no hair on our hands). The other building has panels demonstrating six virtuous acts (the seventh—burying the dead—was deemed too gruesome to depict, so it's symbolized by the urn on top). The ground floor of this building houses a favorite old-fashioned candy shop, **Temmerman** (closed Sun-Tue), with some unique Ghent treats. Wippers are toffee with a sugar coating, marshmallowy Lieve Vrouwkes are shaped like the Virgin Mary, and cone-shaped Cuberdons—the local favorite—are filled with raspberry syrup.

• *Turn left and walk along Kraanlei, passing the* **House of Alijn** *(with a tourable interior—see page 275). Continue along the embankment, curving right with the road. You arrive at a square called Sint-Veerleplein, dominated by the imposing...*

⓫ Castle of the Counts (Gravensteen)

Built in 1180 by Philip of Alsace, this rough-stone fortress was designed not to protect the people of Ghent, but to intimidate the city's independence-minded citizens.

At the time, it was outside the city walls. Today, you can tour the castle (see page 275).

Find the brasserie in the square called **'t Stropke**—"The Noose." The people of Ghent are called "noose wearers" *(Stropkens).* This dates to 1540, when Holy Roman Emperor Charles V (who was born in Ghent but ruled from Spain) demanded a huge tribute. When the citizens refused, he came here personally to crush the rebellion. The leaders of Ghent had to pay the money, then beg forgiveness, on their knees, with nooses around their necks.

Also on the square is the fancy, sculpture-adorned entrance to the **Old Fish Market** (Oude Vismijn), home of the TI and a sprawling brasserie with waterfront seating. Study the facade: That's Neptune on top; below him are Ghent's two rivers: the Scheldt (male) and the Leie (female). It's said that Ghent is the child of these two rivers.

• *If you'd like to end this walk early, you could catch tram #1 to the train*

GHENT CITY WALK

station from right in front of the Castle of the Counts (direction: Flanders Expo).

Otherwise, to continue to a particularly pleasant square, exit Sint-Veerleplein down Kleine Vismarkt street (near the 't Stropke brasserie). Cross the bridge to one final stop.

⓬ Groentenmarkt Square

As you cross the bridge to the Groentenmarkt ("Vegetable Market"), look for the long, medieval **Butchers Hall** (Groot Vleeshuis)

to the right (closed Mon). The hall looks like it's seen better days, but it's worth a peek inside to see its impressive wooden vault (built entirely without nails, and clearly employing ship-builders' expertise). For hygienic reasons, until the 19th century, this was the only place in town allowed to sell meat. You'll see local cured ham hanging from the rafters. The shop inside sells specialty products from East Flanders.

Back out on the square are more snacking opportunities. Across the square from the Butchers Hall is a good traditional bakery (Himschoot); next to that, a café sells delicious takeaway waffles, and to the right of that is the **Tierenteyn Verlent mustard shop** (at #3, closed Sun). Made in the cellar, then pumped into a barrel in the back of the shop, the mustard is some of the horseradish-hottest you'll ever sample. They use no preservatives, so you'll need to refrigerate it—or use it for today's picnic.

• *Head to the far end of the Butchers Hall, then the building beyond it. The bridge here affords another good view of Ghent's canals. Just across the bridge and to the right is the good **Ghent Design Museum** (described on page 277). Near this bridge, various companies sell **boat tours** along the canals of Ghent (see "Tours in Ghent," page 273). Or you can backtrack (turn right along the river) to the **Castle of the Counts** or the **House of Alijn**. Korenmarkt, where we started our tour, is just a block and a half away. In fact, most of what's worth seeing in Ghent is within a few steps of right here. Enjoy.*

CATHEDRAL OF ST. BAVO & GHENT ALTARPIECE TOUR

Sint-Baafskathedraal • Lam Gods

Ghent's cathedral is a vast Gothic oyster housing the pearl of Flemish painting—the Ghent Altarpiece.

Besides this masterpiece by Jan van Eyck, the church itself has a share of quirky sights: You'll see a heavenly pulpit with down-to-earth angels, a painting in which Rubens and the women in his life appear, and Adam and Eve panels depicting the first couple modeling the first clothes.

But it's Van Eyck's altarpiece—displayed all by itself in a darkened chapel—that invites you to linger. This is where modern oil painting was born. It's where invaders—from kings to conquerors to Nazis—have come to steal this potent symbol of civilization. It's where art pilgrims journey to admire the sensuous detail and provocative symbolism of a work that signals a medieval world awakening to the new age of the Renaissance.

Orientation

Cost: The church is free to enter, but it costs €4 to see the original altarpiece and its facsimile (altarpiece tickets are sold inside the cathedral, left of the entrance).

Hours: April-Oct Mon-Sat 9:30-17:00, Sun 13:00-17:00; Nov-March Mon-Sat 10:30-16:00, Sun 13:00-16:00.

Altarpiece Restoration: Some panels may not be viewable due to ongoing conservation, set to be completed by 2017. (You can watch the restoration process at the Fine Arts Museum—see page 277.)

Crowd-Beating Tips: Though the church is big enough to accommodate even the worst crowds, the small altarpiece room can be packed. Avoid the worst of it by visiting right at opening time or in the late afternoon. An excellent-quality replica of

the altarpiece is displayed in a less-crowded chapel. Technically you need a ticket for the replica chapel, though there is
often no one at the entrance to check.

Getting There: The cathedral dominates the central Sint-Baafsplein square.

Information: Tel. 09-225-1626, www.sintbaafskathedraal.be.

Tours: During busy times, volunteer guides can show you around.
The audioguide included with your altarpiece ticket delivers
50 wonderful minutes of commentary about the painting.

Length of This Tour: The church takes 30 minutes. The altarpiece
can be seen in a glance or studied for a lifetime.

Photography: Photos of the altarpiece are not allowed.

Starring: The altarpiece whose unprecedented realism changed the
course of art history.

The Tour Begins

❶ Exterior

Start by taking in the cathedral's sheer
bulk, with its jowl-stretching view up
the 292-foot tower (expect restoration
scaffolding on the tower until 2018).
The church was erected from about 1350
until 1559 on the site of earlier structures dating back to 942. It's named for
a Ghent-area nobleman who gave up his
materialistic existence to help the poor
and founded a monastery here.

• *Step inside and look down the...*

❷ Nave

Appreciate the sheer volume of this structure, with its spacious
100-foot-high ceiling, Gothic arches, and stained glass. Notice
three telltale materials: red brick (the nave walls), yellow stone
(the pillars, also the exterior tower), and—for the valuable area
around the altar—the gray stone of the choir. As in the Church of
St. Nicholas, all of the interior decorations and stained glass date
from the 19th century (following the iconoclasm of the 16th century, when much of the church's Gothic ornamentation was destroyed).

• *Go for a counterclockwise spin around the cathedral's interior, beginning with the rear pillar (to the right as you enter). You'll see two painted
panels showing...*

❸ Adam and Eve with Clothes

These are replicas of Van Eyck's famous nude Adam and Eve from the Ghent Altarpiece (which we'll see later). The clothes were added to cover Van Eyck's nudes during the puritanical 19th century. It wasn't Adam and Eve's nakedness that was offensive—it was the unflinching realism of Adam's hairy legs, Eve's bulging stomach, and their spindly legs. They were just too different from the idealized nudes of the classical world.

Right Side

Along the right wall (second chapel) stands a statue of ❹ **Pater Damiaan** (Father Damien, 1840-1889), a Flemish missionary who went to Hawaii to care for lepers, but after 16 years died of leprosy himself. Canonized in 2009, he's a rare saint with a connection to the United States, and an important figure both to Belgians and to Hawaiians.

Step into the nave to admire the elaborately carved, remarkable ❺ **Rococo pulpit** (1740s), representing the tree of life and the tree of knowledge. Notice the golden serpent entwined around the top of the pulpit; follow its body to find the pudgy, winged baby (a sure sign of Rococo) prying the apple of sin from the snake's mouth. The Carrara marble statues just beneath the pulpit drive

home a Counter-Reformation message: The woman with the sun on her bosom (representing the power of her faith) wakes up the winged old man on the left (representing time): It's time to wake up to the Catholic faith. The smug frat-boy angels at the bases of the staircases offer a lesson in appropriate worship. The angel on the left watches the pulpit intently, and the one on the right points up to the pulpit while glancing scoldingly to the back of the church: Hey, you in the back row—pay attention! Up above, notice the two hard-working cupids struggling to raise the cross.

In the distance, above the main altar, is a white statue backed by a golden sunburst. This is ❻ **St. Bavo,** the beloved local saint, on his way to heaven. For a better view, circle around the side and step up into the choir area. This seventh-century saint was once a wealthy and rambunctious young soldier, but became a born-again Christian after the death of his wife. Bavo rejected his life of ma-

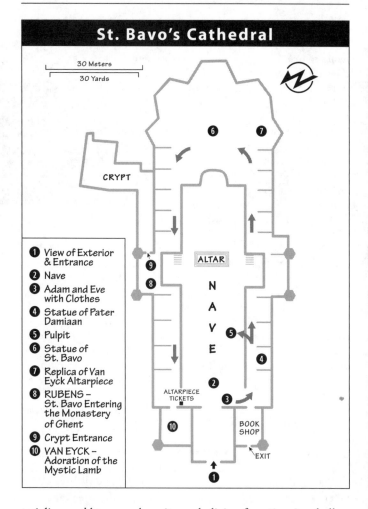

St. Bavo's Cathedral

30 Meters
30 Yards

CRYPT

ALTAR

NAVE

ALTARPIECE
TICKETS

BOOK
SHOP

EXIT

1 View of Exterior & Entrance
2 Nave
3 Adam and Eve with Clothes
4 Statue of Pater Damiaan
5 Pulpit
6 Statue of St. Bavo
7 Replica of Van Eyck Altarpiece
8 RUBENS – St. Bavo Entering the Monastery of Ghent
9 Crypt Entrance
10 VAN EYCK – Adoration of the Mystic Lamb

terialism and became a hermit-monk, living for a time in a hollow tree. He is also the patron saint of Haarlem, in the Netherlands.

To the right of the main altar is the Vijdt Chapel, housing the ❼ **replica of the Van Eyck altarpiece** (it requires a ticket, but discreet individuals can usually slip in for a look). Van Eyck painted his famous altarpiece specifically for this room. In fact, take note of where the replica altarpiece stands in relation to the chapel's windows. Lit from the right, the altarpiece's figures cast shadows to the left.

• *Continue circling the church, rounding the altar to reach the...*

Left Side

In the left transept is Peter Paul Rubens' ❽ *St. Bavo Entering the*

Monastery of Ghent. It depicts the moment this bad-boy-turned-saint started on his righteous course. In the upper half of the canvas, Bavo, in the red cloak, kneels before the abbot to become a monk (Rubens portrayed himself as Bavo). The lower grouping shows Bavo's estate manager distributing his master's belongings to the poor. He's watched by two women on the left, representing Bavo's daughter and her servant. Rubens modeled them after his two wives—his older first wife (in giant hat) and his much younger, more voluptuous second wife, Hélène Fourment, in the red dress.

(The Flemish like to say, with a wink, "An old billy goat loves a young leaf.")

Notice the complex parallel, diagonal composition—Bavo above, women below. Compare this dynamic Baroque canvas, pregnant with motion (1624), with the very static composition of Van Eyck's medieval altarpiece (1432). For more about Rubens, see page 252.

Across from this canvas is the entrance to the ❾ **crypt,** with some of the building's Romanesque foundations and various chapels decorated with ecclesiastical art both old and modern. Along with tombs of bishops, you'll see faint traces of 15th-century paintings that were whitewashed over by Calvinists, then rediscovered in the 1930s.

• *Circling back to the entrance, you reach the grand finale—the chapel with the artistic highlight of Ghent.*

❿ Ghent Altarpiece: *Adoration of the Mystic Lamb*

The highlight of the church (and of all Ghent, for art lovers) is Jan and Hubert van Eyck's *Adoration of the Mystic Lamb* (known as the Ghent Altarpiece, and as *"Lam Gods"* in Dutch). It's been called the most influential painting in art history, as it was the first masterpiece done in the new medium of oil, and the first to portray the unidealized realism of the everyday world.

Hubert van Eyck (c. 1385-1426) began the painting, but after his death, his better-known younger brother Jan (c. 1390-1441) picked up the brush and completed his vision. Finished in 1432, this altarpiece represents a monumental stride in Northern European art from medieval stiffness to Renaissance humanism. The first work signed by Jan van Eyck, it's also considered one of the first works of the Flemish Primitives, characterized by a precise dedication to detail (if imperfect mastery of perspective).

The work is monumental: 15 feet wide and 11 feet tall, composed of a dozen separate panels, depicting hundreds of figures, and weighing more than a ton. It challenges visitors with its complex symbolism, multitude of rich details, and sheer scale, but it rewards those willing to invest the time to take it all in.

Upper Panels: God—in a rich red robe and three-tiered crown—presides over the scene, raising his hand in a solemn blessing. He's flanked by Mary in her traditional blue and John the Baptist in a green robe over his ascetic camel-hair shirt. Though holy, these figures are obviously modeled on flesh-and-blood people with individualized traits, such as God's jug ears, John's scraggly hair, and Mary's parted lips as she reads along from her book. Ogle the incredible richness of the jewels they wear. The hem of God's robe has an inscription written in pearls, one of the numerous quotes woven into the altarpiece (for instance, "King of Kings" and "Behold the Lamb of God").

Serenading God from either side is a heavenly choir. Unlike earlier altarpieces, these musical angels have no wings or halos, and each face is unique. Hymnals of the time indicated which face a singer should make when singing a particular note; today's experts can guess which notes the angels are singing from their expressions.

The outermost panels, depicting Adam and Eve, are probably the first Renaissance-era nudes painted north of the Alps. Though Eve still has the big belly and high waistline typical of medieval Eves, Adam steps boldly forward. His toes break the plane of his niche, a revolutionary example of (still not quite perfect) Italian-inspired perspective. You can actually see each hair on Adam's legs.

Lower Panels and the Adoration: The main scene, playing out across five separate panels, depicts the adoration of the Lamb—that is, Jesus, the sacrificial victim who saved the world from sin. The symbolic ungulate poses proudly atop an altar in the middle of a green field. It's the end of days (Revelation 14:1), and everyone has traveled to the New Jerusalem (the towers in the background)

Coveted, Looted, Stolen, Lost

It's a miracle the Ghent Altarpiece has survived for six centuries. It's been the victim of a half-dozen art thefts—perhaps the most stolen painting in existence—and the focus of several international scandals.

In 1566, Protestant iconoclasts stormed St. Bavo's, hell-bent on burning the altarpiece as a symbol of Catholic idolatry. Fortunately, the priests had hidden it safely away at the top of the cathedral tower. In 1794, Napoleon carried off the altarpiece's four central paintings as war trophies and displayed them in the Louvre (1794-1815). In 1821, the king of Prussia smuggled several panels to Germany. Those works were so prized by the world community that the Treaty of Versailles (which ended World War I) specifically ordered Germany to return the panels.

In 1934, someone broke into St. Bavo's and stole the *Just Judges* panel. The thief left a note justifying the act because the art had been "taken from Germany by the Treaty of Versailles."

In World War II, the Ghent Altarpiece got caught up in the battle between Hitler's gang of art looters and the Allies' Monuments Men, a team of art preservationists. Hitler coveted the work as a symbol of the supremacy of Teutonic art. The altar was on its way to safe storage at the Vatican when it had to be hastily squirreled away in the French Pyrenees. The Nazis discovered it and spirited it away to Neuschwanstein Castle in Bavaria, then stored it in a salt mine. At war's end, the Monuments Men tracked it down and returned it to its rightful home—St. Bavo's.

Today we can enjoy the Ghent Altarpiece in all its restored glory...except for that one pesky piece, the lower left *Just Judges* panel. More than 80 years after it was stolen, the panel has yet to turn up. What you see here is a top-notch copy, and the theft remains Belgium's greatest unsolved art mystery.

to worship the Lamb of God: Angels kneel around the altar, popes wave palm branches (upper left), a legion of virgins gathers (upper right), Old Testament prophets read from their books (lower left), the 12 apostles and Church fathers assemble (lower right), and assorted saints, pagan writers, and Jewish prophets put in an appearance before their savior.

The adoration party spills over into the side panels, as still more worshippers arrive. To the right are groups of pilgrims and hermits, led by the giant St. Christopher. To the left are figures on horseback—knights and judges. Focus in on the bottom-left panel, called the *Just Judges.* It likely has self-portraits of Hubert and Jan van Eyck (the third and fourth figures in), but the painting you see is a copy—the original panel was stolen in 1934 (see sidebar on page 300).

Throughout the lower Adoration panels, notice the diversity of the people assembled, wearing all different styles of clothing and headwear—from Asia, India, and the rest of the known world at the time. In the main panel, a dove (the Holy Spirit) hovers overhead, from which lasers of light stream out over the pristine, shadowless landscape. In the foreground, the Fountain of Life spews water and jewels.

The Lamb of Christ at the center of the work had special meaning here in Ghent, whose wool trade put it on the map. It's too bad that the animal itself—which scholars suspect was later retouched by a lesser artist—isn't particularly well-depicted. He looks more like a fully grown sheep...and is that an extra ear I see?

Exterior Panels: On weekdays, the wings of the hinged altarpiece would be folded shut, showing the paintings on the out-

side panels. You can see them now by circling around the back side. The top panels depict the Annunciation, when an angel (left) came to Mary (right) to tell her she will bear God's child. The angel's announcement—"Hail Mary, full of grace"—is written in Latin across the panel. Mary replies, "I am the servant of the Lord." Notice that Mary's words are upside-down—they're intended for God above. Through the windows of Mary's chamber, we get a glimpse of medieval Ghent. Below, kneeling in the lower panels, are the donors who commissioned the work—the mayor of Ghent and his wife. Between them are depictions of two St. Johns—the Baptist and the Evangelist.

A Final Look: Before leaving, take a moment to review the entire altarpiece and consider what it all means. Scholars mull over the various symbols, the inscriptions, and the cast of saints. The keystone is clearly the venerated lamb at the center of the work. The animal is positioned on a vertical line that descends from God to dove to lamb to the fountain. So—in symbolic terms—God sent the Holy Spirit to Christ on earth who gave his life to bring the faithful the waters of eternal life. John the Baptist is prominently featured on the altarpiece because it was he who proclaimed the arrival of God on earth: *"Ecce Agnus...*Behold the Lamb of God who takes away the sins of the world." At the time the altarpiece was built, the church was dedicated not to St. Bavo but to John the Baptist.

But forget the theology and simply bask in the astonishing

level of detail. The countryside scenes are decorated with dozens of different, identifiable species of plants and flowers. The feathered wings of the angels around the lamb can be matched to a variety of actual birds (peacocks, pigeons, swallows). And in the jeweled amulet around the neck of the singing angel (in the scene next to Adam), you can actually see a faint reflection of the window that decorated the chapel where this altarpiece originally stood. All these lush details—faces, robes, jewels, plants, human flesh—reinforced a theological message that was new to Europe: that the hand of God could be found in the beauty of everyday things.

GHENT SLEEPING, EATING & MORE

Contents

Sleeping in Ghent

A convention town, Ghent is busiest in spring (April-June) and fall (Sept-mid-Dec); things are quieter (and prices lower) in July and August, and even more so in the winter.

$$$ Chambreplus is a three-room B&B run with an impeccable French flair for design. They say the "plus" is for the personal touch they put into their B&B, and this is no exaggeration. With a cozy lounge and an inviting garden, the place oozes class with a contemporary charm (rooms are €95 or €135, "honeymoon" cottage out back with Jacuzzi is €155, 2-night minimum, breakfast-€15, air-con, guest computer, cable Internet in rooms, Hoogpoort 31, tel. 09-225-3775, www.chambreplus.be, chambreplus@telenet.be, Kris and Indira).

$$$ Hotel Harmony is a pricey, classy, four-star, family-run boutique hotel with modern style and 25 rooms ideally located on the embankment in the town center (Sb-€135-210, Db-€154-225, price varies with room size and amenities, air-con, elevator, guest computer, Wi-Fi, very medieval breakfast room and music room/parlor, heated outdoor pool in summer, Kraanlei 37, tel. 09-324-2680, www.hotel-harmony.be, info@hotel-harmony.be).

$$$ Simon Says offers two rooms over a colorful café at the

Sleep Code

Abbreviations   **(€1 = about $1.40, country code: 32)**
S = Single, **D** = Double/Twin, **T** = Triple, **Q** = Quad, **b** = bathroom, **s** = shower only
Price Rankings
  $$$ **Higher Priced**—Most rooms €100 or more
    $$ **Moderately Priced**—Most rooms between €50-100
      $ **Lower Priced**—Most rooms €50 or less
Unless otherwise noted, English is spoken, credit cards are accepted, breakfast is included, and Wi-Fi is generally free. Ghent levies a hotel tax of a few euros per person, per night (typically not included in the prices here). Prices change; verify current rates online or by email. For the best prices, always book directly with the hotel.

far end of Patershol. You're on a small square, so there is some street noise, but you'll feel like a local taking breakfast with the natives in the downstairs café (Db-€110, Wi-Fi, Sluizeken 8, tel. 09-233-0343, www.simon-says.be, info@simon-says.be, Welshman Simon Turner).

$$ Erasmus Hotel, well-run by Peter, has 12 well-maintained rooms around a creaky wooden staircase in a classic 400-year-old building. It's on a boring street, just a short walk from the embankment (Sb-€79-90, Db-€99, large Db-€120-150, prices can flex with demand, no elevator, Wi-Fi, Poel 25, tel. 09-224-2195, www.erasmushotel.be, info@erasmushotel.be).

$$ Ibis Gent Centrum St-Baafs Kathedraal is a good branch of the Europe-wide chain, offering affordable, predictable cookie-cutter comfort in 120 rooms right next to the cathedral (Db-€79-119 depending on season; breakfast-€14, elevator, guest computer, Wi-Fi, Limburgstraat 2, tel. 09-233-0000, www.ibishotel.com, h1455-re@accor.com).

Other B&Bs: Other good accommodations include the **$$ In's Inn,** with one room, in Patershol (Db-€90-98, Wi-Fi, Corduwaniersstraat 11, tel. 09-225-1705, mobile 0494-361-861, www.karienvandekerkhove.com/insinn, insinn@telenet.be) and the **$$ Brooderie,** with three rustic, woody rooms sharing a single bathroom over a café along the embankment in the heart of town (S-€55, D-€75-80, Jan Breydelstraat 8, tel. 09-225-0623, www.brooderie.be, brooderie@pandora.be).

Hostel: **$ De Draecke,** Ghent's very institutional HI hostel, has 106 beds—including some private rooms with bathrooms—in a residential zone a short walk from the castle (€20 for a dorm bed, Db-€50, €3 extra for nonmembers, about €2-3 extra for guests older than 30, includes sheets, towel rental extra, guest computer, Wi-Fi, Sint-Widostraat 11, tel. 09-233-7050, www.jeugdherbergen.be, gent@vjh.be).

Eating in Ghent

RESTAURANTS IN THE CITY CENTER

Pakhuis is a gorgeously restored, late-19th-century warehouse now filled with a classy, lively brasserie and bar. In this light, airy, two-story, glassed-in birdhouse of a restaurant, they serve up good traditional Belgian food with an emphasis on locally sourced and organic ingredients. It's tucked down a nondescript brick alley, but worth taking the few steps out of your way (€15 weekday two-course lunch menu is a great deal, otherwise €9-16 starters, €14-33 main dishes, €27-45 fixed-price meals, Mon-Sat 12:00-14:30 & 18:30-23:00, closed Sun, Schuurkenstraat 4, tel. 09-223-5555).

Belga Queen, an outpost of a similarly popular eatery in Brussels (see page 205), is the most enticing of the restaurants with seating along the embankment in the picturesque core of Ghent. The food is "Belgian-inspired international," and the trendy interior is minimalist/industrialist (three floors of seating, plus a top-floor lounge). While pricey, the place is packed with locals and visitors. Be sure to check out the bathrooms, with windows that turn opaque when you lock the doors (€18 lunches, €15-22 starters, €21-35 main dishes, €33-42 fixed-price dinners, daily 12:00-14:30 & 19:00-22:30, Graslei 10, tel. 09-280-0100).

Belfort Stadscafé occupies the basement of the sleek new market hall in the shadow of its namesake bell tower. Choose between the stylish but casual interior or the covered outdoor tables (€13 lunch special available Mon-Sat, otherwise €18-19 pastas, €19-24 main dishes, daily 8:00-24:00, Emile Braunplein 40, tel. 09-225-6005).

Marco Polo Trattoria is a good choice for Italian-style "slow food" (specializing in fish) at reasonable prices. It fills one long, cozy room with warm, mellow music and tables crowded by locals celebrating special occasions. Reservations are smart (€9-17 antipasti, €15-21 pastas, €8-16 pizzas, Tue-Sat 18:00-22:00, Fri also 12:00-15:00, closed Sun-Mon, Serpentstraat 11, tel. 09-225-0420).

EATERIES IN PATERSHOL

For decades this former sailors' quarter was a derelict and dangerous no-man's land, where only fools and thieves dared to tread. But today it's one of Ghent's most inviting—and priciest—neighborhoods for dining. Stroll the streets and simply drop in on any place that looks good. Peek into courtyards, many of which hide restau-

Ghent Accommodations & Restaurants

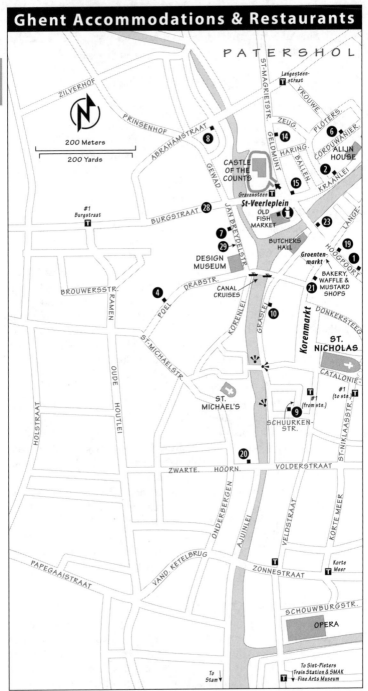

PATERSHOL

ZILVERHOF

PRINSENHOF

N

200 Meters

200 Yards

ABRAHAMSTRAAT

GEWAD

ST-MAGRIETSTR.

VROUWE

Langesteen-
straat

ZEUG

GELDMUNT

HARING

BALLEN

PLOTERS.

CORDUWANIER

ALIJN
HOUSE

KRAANLEI

8

14

6

2

CASTLE
OF THE
COUNTS

#1
Burgstraat

BURGSTRAAT

28

JAN BREYDELSTR.

Gravensteen

St-Veerleplein

OLD
FISH
MARKET

15

BUTCHERS
HALL

LANGE-

HOOGPOORT

23

19

1

Groente-
markt

BAKERY,
WAFFLE &
MUSTARD
SHOPS

DONKERSTEEG

7

29

DESIGN
MUSEUM

BROUWERSSTR.

RAMEN

POEL

DRABSTR.

CANAL
CRUISES

KORENLEI

GRASLEI

4

10

21

Korenmarkt

ST.
NICHOLAS

ST-MICHAELSTR.

OUDE

HOUTLEI

ST.
MICHAEL'S

SCHUURKEN-
STR.

9

#1
(from stn.)

CATALONIE-

#1
(to sta.)

ST-NIKLAASSTR.

HOLSTRAAT

20

ZWARTE.

HOORN.

VOLDERSTRAAT

VELDSTRAAT

KORTE MEER

ONDERBERGEN

AJUINLEI

VAND. KETELBRUG

ZONNESTRAAT

Korte
Meer

PAPEGAAISTRAAT

SCHOUWBURGSTR.

OPERA

To
Stam

To Sint-Pieters
Train Station & SMAK
Fine Arts Museum

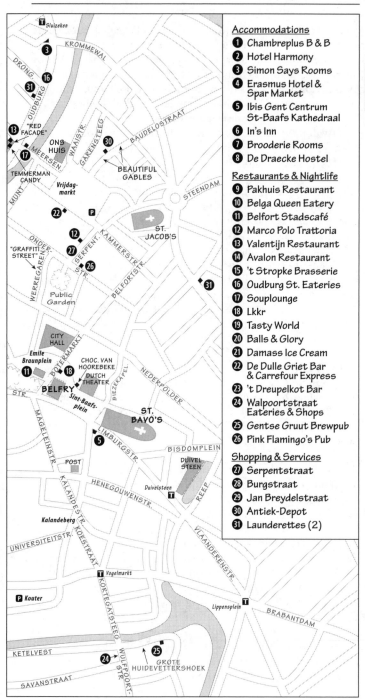

rant and café tables. It's hard to go wrong in Patershol, but here are some particularly well-regarded favorites:

Valentijn, in the heart of the district, has a romantic, dressy interior and a no-fuss menu of classics (€18-30 main dishes, €37 meals, Mon-Wed and Fri-Sat from 18:30, closed Thu, Sun open for lunch only, reservations recommended, Rodekoningstraat 1, tel. 09-225-0429, www.restaurantvalentijn.be).

Avalon, up the street from the Castle of the Counts, offers tasty vegetarian fare (lunch only, €11-13 main dishes, €16-19 specials, daily 11:30-14:30, Geldmuntstraat 32, tel. 09-244-3724).

't Stropke ("The Noose"), down the street from Avalon, is a brasserie with a bright, woody, rustic ambience and a treehouse floor plan. They serve Belgian and French food, with Ghent specialties, such as the creamy *waterzooi* soup (€9-12 sandwiches served until 18:00, €10-14 starters, €16-20 main dishes, Fri-Wed 9:00-22:00, closed Thu, Kraanlei 1, tel. 09-329-8335).

Oudburg street is lined with fun, ethnic, and youthful eateries, including a good Turkish place (Ankara, at #44) and the hip, popular, tight, tasty **Ramen** noodle bar (at #51, closed Sun-Mon). Continue north beyond the end of Oudburg to find **Sleepstraat**, which is lined with cheap Turkish eateries (locals recommend **Gök,** with three branches along here).

QUICK EATS

Souplounge is basic, but cheap and good. They offer four daily soups, along with salads; a bowl of soup, two rolls, and a piece of fruit runs just €4. Eat in the mod interior, or at the outdoor tables overlooking one of Ghent's most scenic stretches of canal (also €5 salads, daily 10:00-19:00, Zuivelbrugstraat 6, tel. 09-223-6203).

Lkkr ("Yum"), tucked behind the Belfry, is a small, modern shop selling sandwiches and salads mostly to businesspeople on lunch breaks. Choose between the cozy interior or outdoor tables (€4-6 sandwiches, big €10 salads, Mon-Sat 10:00-18:00, closed Sun, Botermarkt 6, tel. 09-234-1006).

Tasty World serves up decent €5 veggie burgers with various toppings, plus a wide range of fresh fruit juices and salads (Mon-Sat 11:00-20:00, until 19:00 in winter, closed Sun, Hoogpoort 1, tel. 09-225-7407). They have another branch in the hipster Walpoortstraat neighborhood (see description later).

Balls & Glory, a small Belgian chain that got its start in Ghent, is about a 10-minute walk from Vrijdagmarkt square. They specialize in gigantic meatballs—two flavors per day are noted on the chalkboard menu. Get yours to go (€9.50) or pay a few euros more to eat in their hip dining room at shared stainless-steel tables (Mon-Sat 10:00-21:00, closed Sun, Jakobijnenstraat 6, tel. 0486-678-776).

Dessert: **Damass** is a popular ice cream place where you can hang out and enjoy people-watching or get a cone to stroll with (at the north end of Korenmarkt, #2-C).

Grocery Stores: On Vrijdagmarkt, **Carrefour Express** is handy for picnic supplies and basic toiletries (daily 8:30-19:30 except Sun until 14:30, Mon from 14:30, at #54). Two blocks behind the Design Museum, **Spar** has a more extensive selection (Mon-Sat 8:30-19:30, closed Sun, Poel 22).

GHENT'S BAR AND HIPSTER SCENE
In the Center
Two touristy bars in the center are worth considering if you want to sample a wide range of Belgian favorites: beer or gin.

De Dulle Griet, on Vrijdagmarkt, serves up 249 types of beer in a cozy, sprawling bar with beer glasses hanging from the ceiling (daily 12:00-24:00 except Sun until 19:00, Mon from 16:30, Vrijdagmarkt 50, tel. 09-244-2455).

't Dreupelkot is a cozy little bar along the river, helmed by chain-smoking Pol, who offers a lukewarm welcome and 100 different types of Dutch and Flemish gin, or *jenever* (€2-5 shots, daily from 16:00, or from 18:00 in July-Aug, open until late, Groentenmarkt 12, tel. 09-224-2120).

Walpoortstraat and Nearby
On Walpoortstraat and the surrounding streets, you'll find an enticing bunch of restaurants, cafés, and lively street life. This is Ghent's "Little Portlandia," a 10-minute stroll south from the Belfry (for the most interesting route here, see the walking directions on page 310).

Along Walpoortstraat are Italian eateries, beer halls, a branch of the Tasty World health-food shop (#38), the good OR Espresso Bar (#26), Yogy frozen yogurt (#2), and a gourmet chocolatier (Yuzu, at #11A, described later under "Shopping in Ghent").

One good option for a bite or a drink is **Gentse Gruut,** a brewpub just around the corner from Walpoortstraat. The name comes from the medieval mix of herbs *(gruit)* that flavored beer in the days before hops. You'll sit out on a canal embankment or amid giant copper vats in the industrial-mod interior. Sample one (or more) of the five beers brewed on site: white, blonde, amber, bruin, and inferno—each one well-described by the menu. They also have good pub grub (€4-8 snacks, €12 salads, €14-16 meals, daily 11:00-19:00, Fri-Sat until 23:00, Grote Huidevettershoek 10, tel. 09-269-0269).

Shopping in Ghent

Ghent has an enjoyable real-world feel that makes it a fun place to browse—not for souvenirs, but for interesting, design-oriented items. While not as urbane as Brussels or as cutting-edge as Antwerp, Ghent is creative, yet still accessible. Here are some interesting places to browse:

Serpentstraat

This little pedestrian street, buried deep between the cathedral and Vrijdagmarkt square (described on page 290 of my Ghent City Walk), has a fun, funky collection of creative shops. **Roark**, on the corner with Onderstraat at #1B, shows off cutting-edge/retro home decor; next door is the boutique of local clothing designer **Nathalie Engels** (#1A). Zsa Zsa, with wildly colorful, smartly designed gadgets and toys (for kids and grown-ups alike), has two branches: **Petit Zsa Zsa** for children, at #5, and **Zsa Zsa Rogue** at #22. Between them, at #8, sits the **Zoot** shoe shop.

Streets near the Castle of the Counts

The busy, tram-lined **Burgstraat**, just across the bridge from the castle, isn't particularly charming, but it's an enjoyable place to window-shop several furniture and home-decor shops and art galleries. The side street **Jan Breydelstraat**, which leads to the Design Museum, has an eclectic array of clothing, linens, jewelry, design, and chocolate shops.

Walpoortstraat and Nearby

Walpoortstraat and the adjoining Sint-Pietersnieuwstraat, about a 10-minute stroll southeast of the cathedral, have some of Ghent's most creative and interesting shops.

Shopping Your Way from the Belfry to Walpoortstraat: There are several ways to reach Walpoortstraat from the center, but this route, which strings together mostly pedestrianized shopping streets, is especially pleasant. Beginning at the elongated square at the Belfry, the middle of Ghent's three big towers, head south along the pedestrianized Mageleinstraat, with restaurants, tearooms, upscale shoe stores, and midrange international clothing shops. After two short blocks, you'll pop out at a fine little square ringed by interesting old buildings. Continue straight ahead down Kalandestraat to the handsome Kalandeberg square—with a gurgling fountain, outdoor seating, and a pair of inviting café/bakeries with sidewalk tables. Angle left at the bottom of the square to continue down Koestraat, which takes you to busier Kortedagsteeg. Here the shops and clientele gradually morph from mainstream middle-aged to creative hipster; cross the bridge (you're now on Walpoortstraat), and the transformation is complete.

Shops around Walpoortstraat: The blocks in which Walpoortstraat becomes Sint-Pietersnieuwstraat are fun and picturesque. Wedged between enticing cafés and restaurants are clothing boutiques, vintage and secondhand stores, and some very cool design depots. This area's vibe is exemplified by a couple of stores with bold, creative items for the home: **Piet Moodshop** (at the top of the street, Sint-Pietersnieuwstraat 94) and **Axeswar Design Trendshop** (at #12; both closed Sun).

Closer to the canal, at **Yuzu,** chocolatier Nicolas Vanaise decorates pralines with shiny metallic finishes and infuses them with creative flavors—including Asian elements (closed Sun-Mon, Walpoortstraat 11A). If you want to grab food, coffee, or a beer in this area, see page 309.

Antique Mall

Antiek-Depot is a sprawling antique mall made for browsing. It sits along a postcard-perfect gabled street just north of Vrijdagmarkt square (closed Tue, Baudelostraat 15).

Ghent Connections

From Ghent by Train to: Brussels (3/hour, 35 minutes), **Bruges** (4/hour, 30 minutes), **Antwerp** (3/hour, 50 minutes), **Ypres/Ieper** (hourly, 1.5 hours, transfer in Kortrijk), **Paris** (2/hour, 2-2.5 hours, change at Brussels Midi/Zuid/South to Thalys train), **Amsterdam** (hourly, 2.5 hours, transfer in Antwerp), **Delft** (2/hour, 2-3 hours, transfer in Antwerp and Rotterdam or Roosendaal). For train information, see www.belgianrail.be; see also page 352.

BELGIAN HISTORY

Belgium as a nation is less than 200 years old, but its history stretches back to Europe's roots. Located where France, Germany, and the Netherlands meet, it's a unique mix of all three.

ROMANS AND INVASIONS (A.D. 1-1300)
Julius Caesar invades (57 B.C.), conquering the Belgae people who give the region its name. After Rome's fall (c. 400), the Low Countries shatter into a patchwork of local dukedoms ravaged by invaders, from Franks to Vikings. By A.D. 1000, several self-governing cities begin to emerge, well-located for trade along rivers that flow into the North Sea.

Sights
- Bruges' original fort and Basilica of the Holy Blood
- Brussels' St. Michael's Cathedral, model in the City Museum, and Tour d'Angle (tower) from city wall
- Ghent's Castle of the Counts

BOOMING TRADE TOWNS (1300-1500)
Bruges, the midway port between the North Sea and Mediterranean trade routes, becomes Europe's richest and most cosmopolitan city. English-grown wool is woven into cloth in Flanders factories, then shipped abroad by German merchants, all financed by Italian bankers.

As Bruges' harbor silts up, trade shifts to industrious Ghent and to the bustling port city of Antwerp, which then becomes northern Europe's greatest trading city. Meanwhile, the smaller town of Brussels sells waffles and beer to passing travelers along the Germany-Bruges highway.

Politically, the Low Countries are united through marriage with the cultured, French-speaking Dukes of Burgundy. Duke Philip the Good (c.1450) rules an empire stretching from Amsterdam to Switzerland, and his cultured court is a center of art (Van Eyck, Memling, and van der Weyden), literature, ideas, and pageantry.

But Belgium's medieval Golden Age was threatened by events of the wider world.

Sights

- Bruges' bell tower, the Gothic Room in the City Hall, and the Church of Our Lady
- Flemish Primitive art in Bruges' Groeninge and Memling museums; in Brussels' Royal Museums of Fine Arts of Belgium; and Ghent's *Adoration* altarpiece
- Brussels' Grand Place, medieval street Rue des Bouchers (Restaurant Row), and Notre-Dame du Sablon Church
- Ghent's cathedral and bell tower
- Antwerp's riverfront and Old Town

PROTESTANTS VS. CATHOLICS AND SPANISH RULERS (1500s)

Belgium's economy stagnates after Columbus' discoveries shift trade to a global market. A much-celebrated royal marriage be-

tween the houses of Burgundy and Habsburg (1477) brings Burgundian Belgium under the rule of the Habsburgs in distant Austria and Spain.

Meanwhile, Protestantism spreads through the Low Countries. In 1566, angry Protestants rise up, vandalizing Catholic churches ("iconoclasm"). Belgium—ruled by the ultra-Catholic Habsburgs—becomes the main battleground, as Spanish troops arrive to brutally punish the heretic Protestants. The thriving city of Antwerp falls to Spanish troops (1585), causing that city's best and brightest to flee to the Netherlands.

Ultimately, while the Netherlands wins independence from Spain, Belgium remains under the Catholic Habsburgs, ruled from their regional capital—Brussels.

Sights
- Church interiors (such as Antwerp's and Ghent's cathedrals) that were stripped bare by Protestant iconoclasts and had to be redecorated in Baroque style
- Brussels' tapestry designs

ELEGANT DECLINE (1600-1800)
Belgium languishes under foreign rule while the world moves on. The Netherlands enjoys a Golden Age of self-rule and global sea trade, and France and England rise to superpower status. The Belgians survive as bankers, small manufacturers, and lacemakers—but on a small scale fitting their geographical size. Antwerp rebounds to become a flourishing cultural center of publishing houses and the flamboyant art of Peter Paul Rubens.

Whenever wars between Belgium's neighbors break out, tiny Belgium gets caught in the cross fire. Louis XIV of France bombs Brussels (1695) to punish England. Later, Napoleon invades Belgium and topples the monarchy, ending nearly two centuries of Habsburg rule. When the rest of Europe rallies against Napoleon, where do they send their troops? To Belgium, of course, where they finally defeat Napoleon at Waterloo. Belgium—now little more than a pawn in the game of larger powers—hits rock bottom.

Sights
- Brussels' Grand Place guildhalls
- Antwerp's Paleis op de Meir (Napoleon's palace)
- Brussels' *Manneken-Pis*
- Lace (popularity peaks c. 1700)
- Antwerp's Rubens House, Rockox House, and Museum Plantin-Moretus

A TINY NATION BECOMES AN EMPIRE (1800s)
Europe's nobles install a king to rule all of the Low Countries. Belgians resist this Dutch-controlled government, and—in

August 1830—take to the streets of Brussels to battle Dutch soldiers. They win their independence and choose their own constitutional monarch, King Leopold I (the great-great-great-grandfather of today's king).

Under Leopold I, Belgium rapidly becomes Europe's leader in Industrial Revolution technology. Soon coal from Belgian mines is fueling Ghent factories to make cloth, which is shipped on Belgium's state-of-the-art rail system.

Under King Leopold II, tiny Belgium becomes a global empire. Leopold claims Africa's Congo—a region 80 times bigger than Belgium—as his own private colony. The Belgians brutally exploit the Congo's rubber and ivory resources to finance massive building projects. Brussels becomes a world-class capital of broad boulevards and monumental buildings with columns and domes, all frosted with delicate Art Nouveau.

Sights
- Brussels' Upper Town buildings and Parc du Cinquantenaire
- Brussels' Galeries Royales St. Hubert and BELvue Museum
- Antwerp's Central Station
- Chocolate

WORLD WARS, THE EUROPEAN UNION (1900-2000)

In 1914, prosperous Belgium is suddenly transformed into a horrific battle-scape, as Germany dukes it out with England and France in World War I. Some of the worst fighting takes place at Flanders Fields near Ypres (Ieper).

As Belgium recovers in the 1920s, a new phenomenon appears—newspaper comics—and Hergé thrills Europeans with his tales of the adventurous young reporter, Tintin.

When World War II breaks out, Nazi Germany easily occupies Belgium, imposing five long years of brutal occupation. Late in the war, Belgium is the site of Germany's last-gasp offensive, the Battle of the Bulge.

After the war, Brussels becomes the center of the budding movement toward European unity. It pioneers the Common Market (1957), the BeNeLux economic union (1960), and is a stalwart of NATO. In 1992, Belgium—along with 11 other countries—becomes a founding member of the European Union.

BELGIAN HISTORY

Typical Church Architecture

History comes to life when you visit a centuries-old church. Even if you wouldn't know your apse from a hole in the ground, learning a few simple terms will enrich your experience. Note that not every church has every feature, and a "cathedral" isn't a type of church architecture, but rather a designation for a church that's a governing center for a local bishop.

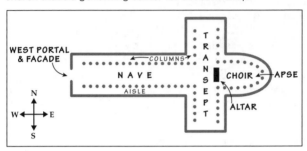

Aisles: The long, generally low-ceilinged arcades that flank the nave.

Altar: The raised area with a ceremonial table (often adorned with candles or a crucifix), where the priest prepares and serves the bread and wine for Communion.

Apse: The space beyond the altar, often bordered with small chapels.

Barrel Vault: A continuous round-arched ceiling that resembles an extended upside-down U.

Choir: A cozy area, often screened off, located within the church nave and near the high altar where services are sung in a more intimate setting.

Cloister: Covered hallways bordering a square or rectangular open-air courtyard, traditionally where monks and nuns got fresh air.

Facade: The front exterior of the church's main (west) entrance, usually highly decorated.

Groin Vault: An arched ceiling formed where two equal barrel vaults meet at right angles. Less common usage: term for a medieval jock strap.

Narthex: The area (portico or foyer) between the main entry and the nave.

Nave: The long, central section of the church (running west to east, from the entrance to the altar) where the congregation sits or stands through the service.

Transept: In a traditional cross-shaped floor plan, the transept is one of the two parts forming the "arms" of the cross. The transepts run north-south, perpendicularly crossing the east-west nave.

West Portal: The main entry to the church (on the west end, opposite the main altar).

Sights

- Belgium's Flanders Fields
- Paintings by René Magritte in Bruges' Groeninge Museum and in Brussels' Magritte Museum
- Brussels' Atomium and European Parliament quarter
- Antwerp's Sint-Andries fashion district, ModeMuseum, "Little Island" area, and 't Zuid district
- Ghent's Design Museum

BELGIUM TODAY: DIVISION, DIVERSITY, AND HOPE

Brussels is the de facto capital of the European Union—a kind of "Washington, D.C." for this "United States of Europe."

But ironically, Belgium itself struggles to unite its own diverse population. Since 1970, it's been a nation officially divided into three semi-autonomous regions: Dutch-speaking Flanders, French-speaking Wallonia, and bilingual Brussels (for more on this divide, see the sidebar on page 13). It also strives to bring the immigrants from its former African colony into the diverse mix.

The Belgian political landscape is splintered into several different parties, divided largely along language lines. Fortunately, Belgium has a popular (if symbolic) ruler—King Philippe and his charming young family. After so many centuries of turbulence, Belgium has grown into a peaceful and forward-thinking nation with a long and rich cultural heritage. It welcomes you to come and make your own history.

PRACTICALITIES

Contents

This chapter covers the practical skills of European travel: how to get tourist information, pay for purchases, sightsee efficiently, find good-value accommodations, eat affordably but well, use technology wisely, and get between destinations smoothly. To study ahead and round out your knowledge, check out "Resources" for a summary of recommended books and films.

Tourist Information

National tourist offices **in the US** can be a wealth of information. Before your trip, request or download any specific information you may want, such as city maps and schedules of upcoming festivals.

For French-speaking Wallonia, go to www.visitbelgium.com; for Flemish-speaking Flanders, check out www.visitflanders.us. At either website, you can request hotel and city guides, brochures for ABC lovers (antiques, beer, and chocolates), maps, and information on WWI and WWII battlefields.

In **Belgium,** the tourist information office (abbreviated **TI** in this book) is generally your best first stop in any new town. TIs are good places to get a city map and information on public transit (including bus and train schedules), walking tours, special events, and nightlife. Many TIs have information on the entire country or at least the region, so try to pick up maps for destinations you'll be visiting later in your trip.

Note that Belgian TIs are state-run, so they're not tainted by a drive for profits. Steer clear of the room-finding services (bloated prices, booking fees, and they take a sizeable cut from your host). Even if there's no "fee," you'll save yourself and your host money by booking directly with the listings in this book.

Travel Tips

Emergency and Medical Help: Dial 112 for police or medical emergencies in Belgium. If you get sick, do as the Belgians do and go to a pharmacist for advice. Or ask at your hotel for help—they'll know the nearest medical and emergency services.

Theft or Loss: To replace a passport, you'll need to go in person to the US Consulate and Embassy (see page 365). If your credit and debit cards disappear, cancel and replace them (see "Damage Control for Lost Cards" on page 323). File a police report, either on the spot or within a day or two; you'll need it to submit an insurance claim for lost or stolen rail passes or travel gear, and it can help with replacing your passport or credit and debit cards. For more information, see www.ricksteves.com/help. Precautionary measures can minimize the effects of loss—back up your photos and other files frequently.

Time Zones: Belgium, like most of continental Europe, is generally six/nine hours ahead of the East/West Coasts of the US. The exceptions are the beginning and end of Daylight Saving Time: Europe "springs forward" the last Sunday in March (two weeks after most of North America) and "falls back" the last Sunday in October (one week before North America). For a handy online time converter, try www.timeanddate.com/worldclock.

Business Hours: Most stores throughout Belgium are open from about 9:00 until 18:00-20:00 on weekdays, but close early on Saturday (generally between 12:00 and 17:00, depending on whether you're in a town or a big city). Sundays in Belgium come with the same pros and cons as they do for travelers in the US: Sightseeing attractions are generally open, while shops and banks are closed, public transportation options are fewer, and there's no rush hour. Popular destinations are even more crowded on weekends. Rowdy evenings are rare on Sundays. Many museums and sights are closed on Monday.

Watt's Up? Europe's electrical system is 220 volts, instead of North America's 110 volts. Most newer electronics (such as laptops, battery chargers, and hair dryers) convert automatically, so you won't need a converter, but you will need an adapter plug with two round prongs, sold inexpensively at travel stores in the US. Avoid bringing older appliances that don't automatically convert voltage; instead, buy a cheap replacement in Europe.

Discounts: Discounts aren't listed in this book. However, many sights offer discounts for children under 18, seniors, families, and students or teachers with proper identification cards (www.isic.org). Always ask. Some discounts are available only for citizens of the European Union (EU).

Online Translation Tip: You can use Google's Chrome browser (available free at www.google.com/chrome) to instantly translate websites. With one click, the page appears in (very rough) English translation. You can also paste the URL of the site into the translation window at www.google.com/translate.

Money

This section offers advice on how to pay for purchases on your trip (including getting cash from ATMs and paying with plastic), dealing with lost or stolen cards, VAT (sales tax) refunds, and tipping.

WHAT TO BRING

Bring both a credit card and a debit card. You'll use the debit card at cash machines (ATMs) to withdraw local cash for most purchases, and the credit card to pay for larger items. Some travelers carry a third card as a backup, in case one gets demagnetized or eaten by a temperamental machine.

For an emergency stash, bring several hundred dollars in hard cash in $20 bills. If you need to exchange the bills, go to a bank; avoid using currency-exchange booths because of their lousy rates and/or outrageous fees.

CASH

Cash is just as desirable in Europe as it is at home. Small businesses (B&Bs, mom-and-pop cafés, shops, etc.) prefer that you pay your bills with cash. Some vendors will charge you extra for using a credit card, and some won't take credit cards at all. Cash is the best—and sometimes only—way to pay for cheap food, bus fare, taxis, and local guides.

Throughout Europe, ATMs are the standard for travelers to get cash. To withdraw money from an ATM (known as a *geldautomaat* in Dutch and a *distributeur* in French), you'll need a debit card (ideally with a Visa or MasterCard logo for maximum usabil-

---

Exchange Rate

1 euro (€) = about $1.40

To convert prices in euros to dollars, add about 40 percent: €20 = about $28, €50 = about $70. (Check www.oanda.com for the latest exchange rates.) Just like the dollar, one euro (€) is broken down into 100 cents. Coins range from €0.01 to €2, and bills from €5 to €500.

---

ity), plus a PIN code. Know your PIN code in numbers; there are only numbers—no letters—on European keypads. For increased security, shield the keypad when entering your PIN code, and don't use an ATM if anything on the front of the machine looks loose or damaged (a sign that someone may have attached a "skimming" device to capture account information).

When possible, use ATMs located outside banks—a thief is less likely to target a cash machine near surveillance cameras, and if your card is munched by a machine, you can go inside for help. Stay away from "independent" ATMs such as Travelex, Euronet, Moneybox, Cardpoint, and Cashzone, which charge huge commissions, have terrible exchange rates, and may try to trick users with "dynamic currency conversion" (described at the end of "Credit and Debit Cards," next).

Try to withdraw large sums of money to reduce the number of per-transaction bank fees you'll pay. Although you can use a credit card for an ATM transaction, it only makes sense in an emergency, because it's considered a cash advance (borrowed at a high interest rate) rather than a withdrawal.

While traveling, if you want to monitor your accounts online to detect any unauthorized transactions, be sure to use a secure connection (see page 351).

Pickpockets target tourists. To safeguard your cash, wear a money belt—a pouch with a strap that you buckle around your waist like a belt and tuck under your clothes. Keep your cash, credit cards, and passport secure in your money belt, and carry only a day's spending money in your front pocket.

CREDIT AND DEBIT CARDS

Credit cards may not be as readily accepted in Belgium as they are in other European countries: Be prepared to use cash for many transactions. In Belgium, train station ticket machines only take Belgian credit cards, but clerks will accept US and Canadian cards at the ticket windows. Most machines in Belgium will only take a chip-and-PIN card (described later) or cash. In general, Visa and MasterCard are more commonly accepted than American Express.

When I do use my credit card here, it's only in a few specific situations: to book hotel reservations, to cover major purchases (such as car rentals, plane tickets, and long hotel stays), and to pay for expensive things near the end of my trip (to avoid another visit to the ATM). While you could use a debit card to make most large purchases, using a credit card offers a greater degree of fraud protection (because debit cards draw funds directly from your account).

Ask Your Credit- or Debit-Card Company: Before your trip, contact the company that issued your debit or credit cards.

• Confirm that your **card will work overseas,** and alert them that you'll be using it in Europe; otherwise, they may deny transactions if they perceive unusual spending patterns.

• Ask for the specifics on transaction **fees.** When you use your credit or debit card—either for purchases or ATM withdrawals—you'll often be charged additional "international transaction" fees of up to 3 percent (1 percent is normal) plus $5 per transaction. If your card's fees seem high, consider getting a different card just for your trip: Capital One (www.capitalone.com) and most credit unions have low-to-no international fees.

• If you plan to withdraw cash from ATMs, confirm your **daily withdrawal limit,** and if necessary, ask your bank to adjust it. Some travelers prefer a high limit that allows them to take out more cash at each ATM stop (saving on bank fees), while others prefer to set a lower limit in case their card is stolen. Note that foreign banks also set maximum withdrawal amounts for their ATMs. Also, remember that you're withdrawing euros, not dollars—so if your daily limit is $300, withdraw just €200. Many frustrated travelers walk away from ATMs thinking their cards have been rejected, when actually they were asking for more cash in euros than their daily limit allowed.

• Get your bank's emergency **phone number** in the US (but not its 800 number, which isn't accessible from overseas) to call collect if you have a problem.

NO CASH
ONLY CARDS
WITH CHIP
AND PINCODE

• Ask for your credit card's **PIN** in case you need to make an emergency cash withdrawal or encounter Europe's "chip-and-PIN" system; the bank won't tell you your PIN over the phone, so allow time for it to be mailed to you.

Chip and PIN: Europeans are increasingly using chip-and-PIN cards, which are embedded with an electronic chip (in addition to the magnetic stripe found on American-style cards). To make a purchase with a chip-and-PIN card, the cardholder inserts the card into a slot in the payment machine, then enters a PIN (like using a debit card in the US) while the card stays in the slot. The chip inside the card authorizes the transaction; the cardholder doesn't sign a receipt. Your American-style card might not work at payment machines using this system, such as those at train and subway stations, toll roads, parking garages, luggage lockers, bike-rental kiosks, and self-serve gas pumps.

If you have problems using your American card in a chip-and-PIN machine, here are some suggestions: For either a debit card or a credit card, try entering that card's PIN when prompted. If your cards still don't work, look for a machine that takes cash, seek out a clerk who might be able to process the transaction manually, or ask a local to run the transaction on his or her card in exchange for your cash.

And don't panic. Many travelers who use only magnetic-stripe cards don't run into problems. Still, it pays to carry plenty of euros; remember, you can always use an ATM to withdraw cash with your magnetic-stripe debit card.

If you're still concerned, you can apply for a chip card in the US (though I think it's overkill). One option is the no-annual-fee GlobeTrek Visa, offered by Andrews Federal Credit Union in Maryland (open to all US residents; see www.andrewsfcu.org). In the future, chip cards should become standard issue in the US: Visa and MasterCard have asked US banks and merchants to use chip-based cards by late 2015.

Dynamic Currency Conversion (DCC): If merchants offer to convert your purchase price into dollars (called dynamic currency conversion), refuse this "service." You'll pay even more in fees for the expensive convenience of seeing your charge in dollars. Some ATMs may try to confuse customers by presenting DCC in misleading terms. If an ATM offers to "lock in" or "guarantee" your conversion rate, choose "proceed without conversion." Other prompts might state, "You can be charged in dollars: Press YES for dollars, NO for euros." Always choose the local currency in these situations.

Damage Control for Lost Cards

If you lose your credit or debit card, you can stop people from using it by reporting the loss immediately to the respective global customer-assistance centers. Call these 24-hour US numbers collect: Visa (tel. 303/967-1096), MasterCard (tel. 636/722-7111), and American Express (tel. 336/393-1111). In Belgium, to make a collect call to the US, dial 0800-10010. Press zero or stay on the line for an English-speaking operator. European toll-free numbers (listed by country) can be found at the websites for Visa and MasterCard.

Providing the following information will allow for a quicker cancellation of your missing card: full card number, whether you are the primary or secondary cardholder, the cardholder's name exactly as printed on the card, billing address, home phone number, circumstances of the loss or theft, and identification verification (your birth date, your mother's maiden name, or your Social Security number—memorize this, don't carry a copy). If you are the secondary cardholder, you'll also need to provide the primary cardholder's identification-verification details. You can generally receive a temporary card within two or three business days in Europe (see www.ricksteves.com/help for more).

If you report your loss within two days, you typically won't be responsible for any unauthorized transactions on your account, although many banks charge a liability fee of $50.

TIPPING

Tipping in Belgium isn't as automatic and generous as it is in the US. For special service, tips are appreciated, but not expected. As in the US, the proper amount depends on your resources, tipping philosophy, and the circumstances, but some general guidelines apply.

Restaurants: Tipping is an issue only at restaurants that have table service. If you order your food at a counter, don't tip.

At Belgian restaurants that have waitstaff, service is included, although it's common to round up the bill after a good meal (usually 5-10 percent; so, for an €18.50 meal, pay €20).

Taxis: For a typical ride, round up your fare a bit (for instance, if the fare is €4.50, pay €5). If the cabbie hauls your bags and zips you to the airport to help you catch your flight, you might want to toss in a little more. But if you feel like you're being driven in circles or otherwise ripped off, skip the tip.

Services: In general, if someone in the service industry does a super job for you, a small tip of a euro or two is appropriate...but not required. If you're not sure whether (or how much) to tip for a service, ask your hotelier or the TI.

GETTING A VAT REFUND

Wrapped into the purchase price of your souvenirs is a Value-Added Tax (VAT) of about 21 percent in Belgium. You're entitled to get most of that tax back if you purchase more than €125.01 (about $175) in Belgium worth of goods at a store that participates in the VAT-refund scheme. Typically, you must ring up the minimum at a single retailer—you can't add up your purchases from various shops to reach the required amount.

Getting your refund is usually straightforward and, if you buy a substantial amount of souvenirs, well worth the hassle. If you're lucky, the merchant will subtract the tax when you make your purchase. (This is more likely to occur if the store ships the goods to your home.) Otherwise, you'll need to:

Get the paperwork. Have the merchant completely fill out the necessary refund document. You'll have to present your passport. Get the paperwork done before you leave the store to ensure you'll have everything you need (including your original sales receipt).

Get your stamp at the border or airport. Process your VAT document at your last stop in the European Union (such as at the airport) with the customs agent who deals with VAT refunds. Arrive an additional hour before you need to check in for your flight to allow time to find the customs office—and to stand in line. It's best to keep your purchases in your carry-on. If your items are too large or not allowed in carry-on (knives, for example), pack them in your checked bags and alert the check-in agent. You'll be sent (with your tagged bag) to a customs desk outside security, where an agent will examine your goods, stamp your paperwork, and put your bag on the belt. You're not supposed to use your purchased goods before you leave. If you show up at customs wearing a Belgian lace wedding veil, officials might look the other way—or deny you a refund.

Collect your refund. You'll need to return your stamped document to the retailer or its representative. Many merchants work with services, such as Global Blue or Premier Tax Free, that have offices at major airports, ports, and border crossings (either before or after security, probably strategically located near a duty-free shop). These services, which extract a 4 percent fee, can refund your money immediately in your currency of choice or credit your card (within two billing cycles). If the retailer handles VAT refunds directly, it's up to you to contact the merchant for your refund. You can mail the documents from home, or more quickly, from your point of departure (using an envelope you've prepared in advance or one that's been provided by the merchant). Then you'll have to wait—it can take months.

CUSTOMS FOR AMERICAN SHOPPERS

You are allowed to take home $800 worth of items per person duty-free, once every 30 days. You can take home many processed and packaged foods: vacuum-packed cheeses, dried herbs, jams, baked goods, candy, chocolate, oil, vinegar, mustard, and honey. Fresh fruits and vegetables and most meats are not allowed, with exceptions for some canned items. As for alcohol, you can bring in one liter duty-free (it can be packed securely in your checked luggage, along with any other liquid-containing items).

To bring alcohol (or liquid-packed foods) in your carry-on bag on your flight home, buy it at a duty-free shop at the airport. You'll increase your odds of getting it onto a connecting flight if it's packaged in a "STEB"—a secure, tamper-evident bag. But stay away from liquids in opaque, ceramic, or metallic containers, which usually cannot be successfully screened (STEB or no STEB).

For details on allowable goods, customs rules, and duty rates, visit www.cbp.gov.

Sightseeing

Sightseeing can be hard work. Use these tips to make your visits to Belgium's finest sights meaningful, fun, efficient, and painless.

PLAN AHEAD

Set up an itinerary that allows you to fit in all your must-see sights. For a one-stop look at opening hours in Bruges, Brussels, Antwerp, and Ghent, see the "At a Glance" sidebars for these cities. Most sights keep stable hours, but you can easily confirm the latest by checking with the TI or visiting museum websites.

Don't put off visiting a must-see sight—you never know when a place will close unexpectedly for a holiday, strike, or restoration. Many museums are closed or have reduced hours at least a few days a year, especially on holidays such as Christmas, New Year's, and Labor Day (May 1). A list of holidays is on page 365; check museum websites for possible closures during your trip. In summer, some sights may stay open late. Off-season, many museums have shorter hours.

Going at the right time helps avoid crowds. This book offers tips on the best times to see specific sights. Try visiting popular sights very early or very late. Evening visits are usually peaceful, with fewer crowds.

Study up. To get the most out of the self-guided tours and sight descriptions in this book, reread them the night before your visit. The Groeninge Museum is much more entertaining if you've boned up on your Flemish Primitives the night before.

AT SIGHTS

Here's what you can typically expect:

Entering: Be warned that you may not be allowed to enter if you arrive 30 to 60 minutes before closing time. And guards start ushering people out well before the actual closing time, so don't save the best for last.

Some important sights have a security check, where you must open your bag or send it through a metal detector. Some sights require you to check daypacks and coats. (If you'd rather not check your daypack, try carrying it tucked under your arm like a purse as you enter.)

Photography: If the museum's photo policy isn't clearly posted, ask a guard. Generally, taking photos without a flash or tripod is allowed. Some sights ban photos altogether.

Temporary Exhibits: Museums may show special exhibits in addition to their permanent collection. Some exhibits are included in the entry price, while others come at an extra cost (which you may have to pay even if you don't want to see the exhibit).

Expect Changes: Artwork can be on tour, on loan, out sick, or shifted at the whim of the curator. To adapt, pick up a floor plan as you enter, and ask museum staff if you can't find a particular item.

Audioguides: Some sights rent audioguides, which generally offer excellent recorded descriptions of the art in English. If you bring your own earbuds, you can enjoy better sound and avoid holding the device to your ear. To save money, bring a Y-jack and share one audioguide with your travel partner. Increasingly, museums are offering apps (often free) that you can download to your mobile device.

Services: Important sights may have an on-site café or cafeteria (usually a handy place to rejuvenate during a long visit). The WCs at sights are free and generally clean.

Before Leaving: At the gift shop, scan the postcard rack or thumb through a guidebook to be sure that you haven't overlooked something that you'd like to see.

Every sight or museum offers more than what is covered in this book. Use the information in this book as an introduction—not the final word.

Sleeping

I favor hotels and restaurants that are handy to your sightseeing activities. Rather than list hotels scattered throughout a city, I de-

scribe two or three favorite neighborhoods and recommend the best accommodations values in each, from dorm beds to fancy doubles with all of the comforts.

A major feature of this book is its extensive and opinionated listing of good-value rooms. I like places that are clean, central, relatively quiet at night, reasonably priced, friendly, small enough to have a hands-on owner and stable staff, run with a respect for Belgian traditions, and not listed in other guidebooks. (In Belgium, for me, six out of these eight criteria means it's a keeper.)

I'm more impressed by a convenient location and a fun-loving philosophy than flat-screen TVs and a pricey laundry service.

Book your accommodations well in advance, especially if you'll be traveling during busy times. See page 365 for a list of major holidays and festivals in Belgium; for tips on making reservations, see page 330.

Some people make reservations as they travel, calling hotels a few days to a week before their arrival. If you'd rather travel without any reservations at all, you'll have greater success snaring rooms if you arrive at your destination early in the day. If you anticipate crowds (weekends are worst) on the day you want to check in, call hotels at about 9:00 or 10:00, when the receptionist knows who'll be checking out and which rooms will be available. If you encounter a language barrier, ask the fluent receptionist at your current hotel to call for you.

RATES AND DEALS

I've described my recommended accommodations using a Sleep Code (see sidebar). Prices listed are for one-night stays in peak season, generally include breakfast, and assume you're booking directly with the hotel (not through an online hotel-booking engine or TI). Booking services extract a commission from the hotel, which logically closes the door on special deals. Book direct.

My recommended hotels each have a website (often with a built-in booking form) and an email address; you can expect a response in English within a day (and often sooner).

If you're on a budget, it's smart to email several hotels to ask for their best price. Comparison-shop and make your choice. This is especially helpful when dealing with the larger hotels that use "dynamic pricing," a computer-generated system that predicts the demand for particular days and sets prices accordingly: High-demand days will often be more than double the price of low-demand days. This makes it impossible for a guidebook to list anything more accurate than a wide range of prices. I regret this trend. While you can assume that hotels listed in this book are good, it's very difficult to say which ones are the better value unless you email to confirm the price.

As you look over the listings, you'll notice that some accommodations promise special prices to Rick Steves readers. To get these rates, you must book direct (that is, not through a booking site like TripAdvisor or Booking.com), mention this book when you reserve, and then show the book upon arrival. Rick Steves discounts apply to readers with ebooks as well as printed books. Because I trust hotels to honor this, please let me know if you don't receive a listed discount. Note, though, that discounts understandably may not be applied to promotional rates.

Sleep Code

(€1 = about $1.40 country code: 32)

Price Rankings

To help you easily sort through my listings, I've divided the accommodations into three categories based on the highest price for a standard double room with bath during high season:

$$$	**Higher Priced**
$$	**Moderately Priced**
$	**Lower Priced**

I always rate hostels as $, whether or not they have double rooms, because they have the cheapest beds in town.

Prices can change without notice; verify the hotel's current rates online or by email. For the best prices, always book directly with the hotel.

Abbreviations

To pack maximum information into minimum space, I use the following code to describe accommodations in this book. Prices listed are per room, not per person. When a price range is given for a type of room (such as double rooms listing for "Db-€80-120"), it means the price fluctuates with the season, size of room, or length of stay; expect to pay the upper end for peak-season stays.

- **S** = Single room (or price for one person in a double).
- **D** = Double or twin. "Double beds" can be two twins sheeted together and are usually big enough for nonromantic couples.
- **T** = Triple (generally a double bed with a single).
- **Q** = Quad (usually two double beds; adding an extra child's bed to a T is usually cheaper).
- **b** = Private bathroom with toilet and shower or tub.
- **s** = Private shower or tub only (the toilet is down the hall).

According to this code, a couple staying at a "Db-€85" hotel would pay a total of €85 (about $120) for a double room with a private bathroom. Unless otherwise noted, breakfast is included, English is spoken, and credit cards are accepted. There's almost always Wi-Fi and/or a guest computer available, either free or for a fee.

PRACTICALITIES

Making Hotel Reservations

Reserve your rooms several weeks in advance—or as soon as you've pinned down your travel dates. Note that some national holidays merit your making reservations far in advance (see page 365).

Requesting a Reservation: It's easiest to book your room through the hotel's website. (For the best rates, always use the hotel's official site and not a booking agency's site.) If there's no reservation form, or for complicated requests, send an email (see below for a sample request). Most recommended hotels take reservations in English.

The hotelier wants to know:
- the number and type of rooms you need
- the number of nights you'll stay
- your date of arrival (use the European style for writing dates: day/month/year)
- your date of departure
- any special needs (such as bathroom in the room or down the hall, cheapest room, twin beds vs. double bed, and so on)

Mention any discounts—for Rick Steves readers or otherwise—when you make the reservation.

Confirming a Reservation: Most places will request a credit-card number to hold your room. If they don't have a secure online reservation form—look for the *https*—you can email it (I do), but it's safer to share that confidential info via a phone call or two emails (splitting your number between them).

Canceling a Reservation: If you must cancel, it's courteous—and smart—to do so with as much notice as possible, especially

In general, prices can soften up if you do any of the following: offer to pay cash, stay at least three nights, or mention this book. You can also try asking for a cheaper room or a discount, or offer to skip breakfast.

TYPES OF ACCOMMODATIONS
Hotels

In this book, the price for a double room ranges from $70 (very simple, toilet and shower down the hall) to $300 (maximum plumbing and more), with most clustering at about $140. You'll pay more at Brussels hotels and less at Bruges B&Bs. Cities in Belgium all charge a hotel tax; it's calculated differently everywhere, but assume you'll pay a few extra euros per person, per night (not included in the prices I list in this book).

Most hotels have lots of doubles and a few singles, triples, and quads. Singles (except for the rare closet-type rooms that fit only a

From: rick@ricksteves.com
Sent: Today
To: info@hotelcentral.com
Subject: Reservation request for 19-22 July

Dear Hotel Central,

I would like to reserve a room for 2 people for 3 nights, arriving 19 July and departing 22 July. If possible, I would like a quiet room with a double bed and a bathroom inside the room.

Please let me know if you have a room available and the price.

Thank you!
Rick Steves

for smaller family-run places. Be warned that cancellation policies can be strict; read the fine print or ask about these before you book. Internet deals may require prepayment, with no refunds for cancellations. If canceling via email, request confirmation that your cancellation was received to avoid being accidentally billed.

Reconfirming a Reservation: Always call to reconfirm your room reservation a few days in advance. For smaller hotels and B&Bs, I call again on my day of arrival to tell my host what time I expect to get there (especially important if arriving late—after 17:00).

Phoning: For tips on how to call hotels overseas, see page 342.

twin bed) are simply doubles used by one person, so they often cost nearly the same as a double.

A hearty breakfast with cereal, meats, local cheeses, fresh bread, yogurt, juice, and coffee or tea is standard in hotels.

Hotel elevators, while becoming more common, are often very small—pack light, or you may need to take your bags up one at a time.

If you're arriving early in the morning, your room probably won't be ready. You can drop your bag safely at the hotel and dive right into sightseeing.

Hoteliers can be a great help and source of advice. Most know their city well, and can assist you with everything from public transit and airport connections to finding a good restaurant, the nearest launderette, or a Wi-Fi hotspot.

Even at the best hotels, mechanical breakdowns occur: air-conditioning malfunctions, sinks leak, hot water turns cold, and toilets gurgle and smell. Report your concerns clearly and calmly at the front desk. For more complicated problems, don't expect instant results.

If you suspect night noise will be a problem (if, for instance, your room is over a beer hall), ask for a quiet room in the back or on an upper floor. To guard against theft in your room, keep valuables out of sight. Some rooms come with a safe, and other hotels have safes at the front desk. I've never bothered using one.

Checkout can pose problems if surprise charges pop up on your bill. If you settle up your bill the afternoon before you leave, you'll have time to discuss and address any points of contention (before 19:00, when the night shift usually arrives).

Above all, keep a positive attitude. After all, you're on vacation. If your hotel is a disappointment, spend more time out enjoying the city you came to see.

Bed-and-Breakfasts

B&Bs offer double the cultural intimacy and—often—nicer rooms for a good deal less than most hotel rooms. Hosts usually speak English and are interesting conversationalists.

Belgium has a variety of cozy, funky, affordable B&Bs well-run by gregarious entrepreneurs and typically located up a flight or two of steep, narrow stairs. There are plenty to choose from in Antwerp, Ghent, and especially Bruges. Urban Brussels has only a few recommended B&Bs. Local TIs have lists of B&Bs and can book a room for you, but you'll save money by booking directly with the B&Bs listed in this book.

Hostels

You'll pay about $30 per bed to stay at a hostel. Travelers of any age are welcome if they don't mind dorm-style accommodations and meeting other travelers. Most hostels offer kitchen facilities, guest computers, Wi-Fi, and a self-service laundry. Nowadays, concerned about bedbugs, hostels are likely to provide all bedding, including sheets. Family and private rooms may be available on request.

Independent hostels tend to be easygoing, colorful, and informal (no membership required); www.hostelworld.com is the standard way backpackers search and book hostels, but also try www.hostelz.com and www.hostels.com.

Official hostels are part of Hostelling International (HI) and share an online booking site (www.hihostels.com). HI hostels typically require that you either have a membership card or pay extra per night.

Other Accommodation Options

Whether you're in a city or the countryside, renting an apartment, house, or villa can be a fun and cost-effective way to go local. Websites such as HomeAway and its sister sites VRBO and GreatRentals let you correspond directly with European property owners or managers.

Airbnb and Roomorama make it reasonably easy to find a place to sleep in someone's home. Beds range from air-mattress-in-living-room basic to plush-B&B-suite posh. If you want a place to sleep that's free, Couchsurfing.org is a vagabond's alternative to Airbnb. It lists millions of outgoing members, who host fellow "surfers" in their homes.

Eating

Belgians brag that they eat as much as the Germans and as well as the French. They are among the world's leading carnivores and beer consumers. Belgium is where France meets northern Europe, and you'll find a good mix of both Germanic and French influences here. The Flemish were ruled by the dukes of Burgundy and absorbed some of the fancy French cuisine and etiquette of their overlords. (The neighboring Dutch, on the other hand, were ruled by the Spanish for 80 years and picked up nothing.) And yet, once Belgian, always Belgian: Instead of cooking with wine, Belgians have perfected the art of cooking with their own unique beers, imbuing the cuisine with a hoppy sweetness.

DINING TIPS

When restaurant-hunting, choose a spot filled with locals, not the place with the big neon signs boasting, "We Speak English and Accept Credit Cards." Venturing even a block or two off the main drag leads to higher-quality food for less than half the price of the tourist-oriented places. Locals eat better at lower-rent locales.

Belgians eat lunch when we do, but they eat dinner later (if you dine earlier than 19:30 at a restaurant, you'll eat alone or with other tourists). Tax and service are always included in your bill (though a 5-10 percent tip is appreciated).

No Free Water: Tap water comes with a smile in the Netherlands, France, and Germany, but that's not the case in Belgium, where you'll either pay for water, enjoy the beer, or go thirsty. You simply can't get tap water for free; Belgian restaurateurs are emphatic about that.

Etiquette at Cafés and Bars: Here are a few tips for ordering at a bar, café, or brasserie.

In general, you can seat yourself, but avoid tables with a sign saying *"reservé"* or *"voorbehouden."* Unlike cafés in Italy or France, the cost of a drink or meal in Belgium is the same at the bar, at a table, or outside on the terrace. If all you want is a drink, you can

The Good and Bad of Online Reviews

User-generated travel review websites—such as TripAdvisor, Booking.com, and Yelp—have quickly become a huge player in the travel industry. These sites give you access to actual reports—good and bad—from travelers who have experienced the hotel, restaurant, tour, or attraction.

My hotelier friends in Europe are in awe of these sites' influence. Small hoteliers who want to stay in business have no choice but to work with review sites—which often charge fees for good placement or photos, and tack on commissions if users book through the site instead of directly with the hotel.

While these sites work hard to weed out bogus users, my hunch is that a significant percentage of reviews are posted by friends or enemies of the business being reviewed. I've even seen hotels "bribe" guests (for example, offer a free breakfast) in exchange for a positive review. Also, review sites can become an echo chamber, with one or two flashy businesses camped out atop the ratings, while better, more affordable, and more authentic alternatives sit ignored further down the list. (For example, I find review sites' restaurant recommendations skew to very touristy, obvious options.)

Remember that a user-generated review is based on the experience of one person. That person likely stayed at one hotel and ate at a few restaurants, and doesn't have much of a basis for comparison. A guidebook is the work of a trained researcher who has exhaustively visited many alternatives to assess their relative value. I recently checked out some top-rated TripAdvisor listings in various towns; when stacked up against their competitors, some are gems, while just as many are duds.

Both types of information have their place, and in many ways, they're complementary. If a hotel or restaurant is well-reviewed in a guidebook or two, and also gets good ratings on one of these sites, it's likely a winner.

wait for the server to come around or order directly from the bar. You generally pay for drinks as you go (especially if you're sitting outside), unless you specify you want to open a tab. If you're also ordering food, you pay for everything—drinks and your meal—at the end, as you would at a restaurant.

BELGIAN SPECIALTIES

Although this book's coverage focuses on the Flemish part of the country, people speak French first in Brussels—so both languages are given below (Dutch/French); if I've listed only one word, it's used nationwide. While the French influence is evident everywhere, it's ratcheted up around Brussels.

Traditional Dishes

Stoofvlees/Carbonnade: Rich beef stew flavored with onions, beer, and mustard. It's similar to French beef bourguignon but often sweetened with brown sugar or gingerbread.

(Gentse) Waterzooi: Creamy soup made with chicken, eel, or fish; originated in Ghent.

Konijn met pruimen/lapin à la flamande: Marinated rabbit braised in onions and prunes.

Filet américain: Similar to steak tartare, this raw beef dish is named for the American meat grinder it was widely made with after WWII.

Luikse ballekes/boulettes sauce lapin: Meatballs made in Liège sauce (a dark syrup from apples, pears, and dates).

Luikse salade/salade liègeoise: A warm salad of green beans, potatoes, tomatoes, and bacon.

Biersoep/soupe à la bière: Beer soup.

Vol-au-vent: A rich and creamy chicken stew made with meatballs and lots of butter, typically used as the filling for a puff pastry sandwich.

...à la flamande: Anything cooked "in the Flemish style," which can mean something made with beer or smothered in a sauce of butter, chopped parsley, and crumbled hardboiled egg.

Seafood

Mosselen/moules: Mussels are served either cooked plain *(natuur/ nature)*, with white wine *(witte wijn/vin blanc)*, with shallots or onions *(marinière)*, in a mushroom cream sauce *(à la crème)*, or in a tomato sauce *(provençale)*. You get a big-enough-for-two bucket and a pile of fries. Go local by using one empty shell to tweeze out the rest of the *mosselen.* From about mid-July through April, you'll get the big Dutch mussels (most are from the coastal Zeeland area). Locals take a break from mussels in May and June, when only the puny Danish kind are available.

Noordzee garnalen/crevettes grises: Little gray shrimp caught off the North Sea coast.

Tomaat garnaal/tomattes crevettes: North Sea shrimp served inside a carved-out tomato.

Grnaalkroket/croquettes de crevettes: Minced North Sea shrimp and Béchamel stuffed in a breaded, deep-fried roll.

Paling in het groen/anguilles au vert: Eel in green herb sauce. This classic dish isn't always available, as good-quality eel is in short supply.

Caricoles/escargots (de mer): Sea snails. Very local, seasonal, and hard to find, these are usually sold hot by street vendors.

Fine Flemish Fried Fast Foods

Just like every village in England has its "chippy" (for fish-and-chips), and every German burg has its *Wurst* stand (for sausages), every Belgian town has a favored *frituur* (fry shop) or *frietkot* (fry shack). While the pinnacle is the fried potato, there's a wider variety of deep-fried treats than you might expect.

Fries (Frieten): Belgian-style fries taste so good because they're deep-fried twice—once to cook them and once to brown them. The best fries are cooked to a crisp in flavorful ox fat. We call them "French fries" and the Dutch call them *Vlaamse frieten* ("Flemish fries")—but to the Flemish they are plain *frieten*. Fries are traditionally served generously topped with mayo, tartar sauce, or another flavored sauce. (Ketchup is sometimes available.)

Sauces (Sausen): Sauce options include curry ketchup (or *currysaus*, without the ketchup), *Joppiesaus* (sweet yellow curry and onion sauce); *samuraisaus* or *samoeraisaus* (mayo with spicy chili flavor and a hint of tomato); *américaine* (mayo with herbs and a dash of Tabasco); *provencaalse* (sweet-and-sour tomato flavor); and *pickles* (mayo with pickle relish). *Stoofvlees,* the rich Belgian beef stew made with beer, is often available as a topping; sometimes it's a mayo-based sauce infused with *stoofvlees* flavor.

Vegetables and Side Dishes

Rode kool/chou rouge à la flamande: Red cabbage with onions and prunes.

Asperges: White asparagus, available only in spring, and usually served in cream sauce.

Witloof/chicoree or **chicon:** Bitter, coarse endive, the classic Belgian vegetable, served both raw and cooked.

Spruitjes/choux de Bruxelles: Brussels sprouts (in cream sauce).

Stoemp: Mashed potatoes and vegetables.

Snacks

Frieten: For more on this Belgian staple, see the sidebar.

Cheeses: While the French might use wine or alcohol to rub the rind of their cheese to infuse it with flavor, the Belgians use (surprise, surprise) beer. There are 350 types of Belgian cheeses. From Flanders, look for Vieux Brugge ("Old Bruges") and Chimay (named for the beer they use on it); from Wallonia, Remoudou and Djotte de Nivelles are good.

You'll generally pay extra (typically less than €1) for any sauce—including mayo.

Frikandel (fricandelle) or **Curryworst:** This minced-meat sausage, the basic Belgian wiener, is usually deep-fried. A *Frikandel speciaal* is served with mayo, ketchup, and chopped onions (it's sometimes called a *curryworst*—not to be confused with a German *Currywurst.*) The skinny, deep-fried variation called *viandel* often has a crunchy, herbed crust.

Bitterballen (petites croquettes): These meat croquettes, battered in breadcrumbs and deep-fried, are typically served as bar snacks, along with a drink made with bitters. **Vleeskroketten** are similar, but bigger.

Boulet, Balleke, Frikadel, or **Gehaktbal (boulette):** These are all terms for meatballs, which can be fried, boiled, or grilled. *Ballekes in tomatensaus* is a tasty meatball dish with tomato sauce. Some meatballs are filled with a surprise; for example, a *vogelnestje* ("bird's nest") meatball is stuffed with a hard-boiled egg.

Bicky Burger: Not your hometown burger, this mystery-meat patty (a combination of pork, chicken, and horse meat) is sold at snack stands nationwide. It's typically deep-fried and topped with a sweet ketchup, a brown spicy sauce, and a secret, yellow "Bicky Dressing" (made with mayonnaise, mustard, cabbage, onion, and other vegetables).

Kip- (de poulet): Something made with chicken—for example, *kippenworst* is chicken sausage.

Croque monsieur: Grilled ham-and-cheese sandwich.

Pistolet: A puffy, round bread-roll sandwich.

Tartine de fromage blanc: Open-face cream-cheese sandwich, often enjoyed with a *lambic* beer (described later) and found mostly in traditional Brussels bars.

Desserts and Sweets

Chocolates: The two basic types of Belgian chocolates are **pralines** (what we generally think of as "chocolates"—a hard chocolate shell with a filling) and **truffles** (a softer, crumblier shell with filling). For more on chocolates, see page 39.

Wafels/Gaufres: You'll see little windows, shops, and trucks selling *wafels,* either plain (for Belgians and purists) or topped with fruit, jam,

Good Belgian Chain Restaurants

While excellent restaurants abound in Belgium, several local chains offer affordable, quick, and predictably good meals. Keep an eye out for these convenient choices.

Exki tries hard to be healthy in a country famous for its deep-fried foods and beer-based sauces. Their prepared meals (soups, salads, wraps) emphasize fresh produce, and while the food can be hit-or-miss, it's a handy break from heavy Belgian fare.

Le Pain Quotidien ("The Daily Bread") began as an artisanal bakery in Brussels...before its relentless march toward world domination. Although it now has 200 locations in more than a dozen countries, it's still considered a local shop among Belgians. It's a reliable fallback for fresh breads, pastries, and sandwiches.

Balls & Glory is a small, fun Flemish chain offering tasty, hand-crafted, softball-sized meatballs. Each day their rotating menu highlights two different flavors of meatball.

chocolate sauce, ice cream, or whipped cream (for tourists). Belgians recognize two general types of waffles. The common take-out version, sold around the clock, is the dense, sugar-crusted, and very sweet **Liège-style waffle** (*Luikse/liègois),* usually served warm. **Brussels-style waffles** (*Brusselse)* are lighter and fluffier, dusted with powdered sugar and sometimes topped with marmalade. Though Americans think of "Belgian" waffles as a breakfast food, Belgians generally have them (or pancakes, *pannenkoeken*) as a late-afternoon snack. Brussels-style waffles are less widely available to go, though you may find them at teahouses or cafés in the afternoon (from about 14:00 until 18:00).

Speculoos: Spicy gingerbread biscuits served with coffee. For the Belgian answer to peanut butter or Nutella, look for *speculoos* spread—thick, creamy, and with the flavor of gingerbread cookies. (Trader Joe's sells this in the US with a "Cookie Butter" label.)

Dame blanche: Chocolate sundae.

Chocolade mousse: Just what it sounds like.

BELGIAN BEERS

Belgium has about 120 different varieties of beer and 580 different brands, more than any other country—the locals take their beers as seriously as the French do their wines. Even small café menus include six to eight varieties. Connoisseurs and novices alike can be confused by the many choices, and casual drinkers probably won't like every kind offered, since some varieties don't even taste like beer. Belgian beer is generally yeastier and higher in alcohol content than beers in other countries. You must be 16 years old to legally enjoy a good Belgian beer (18 to drink wine and hard liquor).

To bring out their flavor, different beers are served cold, cool, or at room temperature, and each has its own distinctive glass. Whether wide-mouthed, tall, or fluted, with or without a stem, tulip-shaped or straight, the glass is meant to highlight a particular beer's qualities. The choice of glass is so important that if, for some reason, a pub doesn't have the proper glass for a particular beer, they will ask the customer if a different glass will be acceptable—or if they'd like to change their beer order.

To get a basic draft beer in Flanders (Bruges, Antwerp, or Ghent), ask for *een pintje* (ayn pinch-ya; a pint); in Brussels, where French prevails, request *une bière* (oon bee-yair).

But don't insist on beer from the tap. The only way to offer so many excellent beers and keep them fresh is to serve them bottled. In fact, because many specialty beers ferment in the bottle, some of the most famous brews come *only* in bottles. Increasingly, though, bars are adding a few high-end brands to their draft menus.

Belgians pair beer with food, much as the French pair wine. In general, lighter-colored beers (blonde or *Tripel*) go well with chicken or pork; darker beers pair nicely with beef; and wheat beers complement seafood.

Specialty Beers

Specialty beers can be much more alcoholic than what you're used to back home, and tourists often find themselves overwhelmed by a single pint of Belgian brew. Bottles (and often menus) list the alcohol percentage of each type of beer. For comparison, most mass-market American beers are between 4 and 6 percent alcohol by volume (ABV), while a heavy Belgian ale can run 7 to 9 percent—and a few powerful beers can reach, or even exceed, 10 to 12 percent.

Monk-run Trappist breweries have given the beer world the terms *Enkel*, *Dubbel*, and *Tripel* (single, double, triple). While originally these indicated the amount of malt used to gain a higher alcohol content, these days they have more to do with the style of beer: *Enkel* is a very light (nearly "lite") blonde ale; *Dubbel* is a dark, sweet beer; and *Tripel* is a very strong, golden-colored pale ale. The less commonly used term *Quadrupel* is a gimmick to emphasize a beer's alcohol content—usually more than 10 percent.

Some beer producers have returned to their medieval roots, flavoring their beer with a secret mix of spices called *gruit*. This can result in some surprising bouquets that charm and puzzle beer aficionados.

PRACTICALITIES

Beers by Type

Here's a breakdown of types of beer, with some common brand names. This list is just a start, and you'll find many beers that don't fall into these neat categories.

Ales (Blonde/Red/Amber/Brown): Easily recognized by their color. Try a blonde or golden ale (Leffe Blonde, Duvel), a rare and bitter sour red (Rodenbach), an amber (Palm, De Koninck), or a brown (Leffe Bruin). *Saison* beers are "seasonal" (summer-brewed), lightly alcoholic pale ales.

Lagers (*Pils*): Light, sparkling, Budweiser-type beers. Popular brands include Jupiler, Stella Artois, and Maes.

Lambics: Wild-yeast beers. *Lambics*—popular in Brussels—get their start in open vats, where they're exposed to naturally occurring wild yeasts in the air. Some brand names include Cantillon, Lindemans, and Mort-Subite ("Sudden Death").

Lambics are often blended with fruits to counter their sour flavor. Fruit *lambics* include cherry *(kriek),* raspberry *(frambozen),* peach *(pêche),* or blackcurrant *(cassis).* People who don't usually enjoy beer tend to like these tart but sweet varieties, similar to a dry pink champagne. *Gueuze*—a dry, sour, double-fermented *lambic* nicknamed "Brussels champagne"—is more of an acquired taste.

White *(Witte* or *Witbier):* Milky-yellow summertime beers made from wheat. White beer, similar to a Hefeweizen, is often flavored with spices such as orange peel or coriander.

Trappist and Abbey Beers: Heavily fermented, malty, monk-brewed beers. For centuries, between their vespers and matins, Trappist monks have been brewing beer. Three typical ones are *Tripel,* with a blonde color, served cold with a frothy head; *Dubbel,* dark, sweet, and served cool; and *Enkel,* made especially by the monks for the monks, and considered a fair trade for a life of celibacy. These styles originated at the Westmalle monastery; other official Belgian Trappist monasteries are Rochefort, Chimay, Orval, Achel, and Westvleteren. "Abbey beers" *(abdijbier)* emulate the Trappist style, but are produced at other monasteries or by commercial brewers; St. Bernardus is one popular abbey beer. Try the Trappist Chimay Blauw/Bleu—extremely smooth, milkshake-like, and complex.

Strong Beers: The potent brands include Duvel ("devil," because of its high octane, camouflaged by a pale color), Verboten Vrucht ("forbidden fruit," with Adam and Eve on the label), and the not-for-the-fainthearted brands of Judas, Satan, and Lucifer. Gouden Carolus is good, and Delerium Tremens speaks for itself.

Mass-Produced Beers: Connoisseurs say you should avoid the mass-produced labels (Leffe, Stella, and Hoegaarden—all owned by InBev, which owns Budweiser in America) when you can enjoy a Belgian microbrew (such as Westmalle or Chimay) instead.

OTHER DRINKS

Jenever: The distilled grain alcohol *jenever* (yah-NAY-ver) is spiced with juniper berries and often called "continental gin" or "Dutch gin" in English. (English traders eventually created a similar drink and called it simply gin.) *Jonge jenever* (young) is sharp and served chilled; *oude jenever* (old) is mellow and more commonly poured at room temperature (the terms refer to whether they use the older or newer distilling technique). I prefer *oude jenever,* which is smooth and soft, with a more mature flavor—like a good whisky. *Jenever* can be sipped, or it can be chugged with a *pils* chaser (this combination is called a *kopstoot*—headbutt; or you can sink the shot of *jenever* into the beer to create a *duikboot*—submarine).

Wine: Belgians drink a lot of fine wine, but it's almost all imported. In general, Flanders prefers Bordeaux wines (which used to be delivered to the busy Flemish ports of Bruges and Antwerp), while inland Wallonia prefers Burgundy wines (which were delivered overland).

Coffee: Belgians love their coffee, enjoying many of the same drinks (espresso, cappuccino) served in American or Italian coffee shops. Coffee usually comes with a small *speculoos* spice cookie. A *koffie verkeerd* (fer-KEERT, "coffee wrong") is an espresso with a lot of steamed milk—the closest thing to a latte.

Orange Juice: Many cafés/bars have a juicer for making fresh-squeezed orange juice.

Water: Belgian restaurants typically charge for tap water. Since you're paying anyway, you might as well spring a bit more for mineral water, still or sparkling (Spa brand is popular).

Communicating

"How can I stay connected in Europe?"—by phone and online—may be the most common question I hear from travelers. You have three basic options (which are explained in greater detail in the following pages):

1. "Roam" with your US mobile device. This is the easiest solution, but likely the most expensive. It works best for people who won't be making very many calls, and who value the convenience of sticking with what's familiar (and their own phone number). In recent years, as data roaming fees have dropped and free Wi-Fi has

PRACTICALITIES

What Language Barrier?

People speak Dutch in Bruges, Ghent, and Antwerp—but with a Flemish accent. It's mostly French in Brussels. But you'll find almost no language barrier in Belgium, as all well-educated folks, nearly all young people, and almost everyone in the tourist trade also speak English. In tourist-friendly Bruges, you also won't encounter any difficulties with English. You will meet some French-only speakers in Brussels, but it's generally a minor language barrier. Regardless, it's polite to use some Dutch or French pleasantries (see pages 371 and 373).

become easier to find, the majority of travelers are finding this to be the best all-around solution.

2. Use an unlocked mobile phone with European SIM cards. This is a much more affordable choice if you'll be making lots of calls, since it gives you 24/7 access to low European rates. Although remarkably cheap, this option does require a bit of shopping around for the right phone and a prepaid SIM card. Savvy travelers who routinely buy European SIM cards swear by this tactic.

3. Use public phones, and get online with your hotel's guest computer and/or at Internet cafés. These options work particularly well for travelers who simply don't want to hassle with the technology, or want to be (mostly) untethered from their home life while on the road.

Mixing and matching works well. For example, I routinely bring along my smartphone for Internet chores and Skyping on Wi-Fi, but also carry an unlocked phone and buy SIM cards for affordable calls on the go.

For an even more in-depth explanation of this complicated topic, see **www.ricksteves.com/phoning.**

HOW TO DIAL

Many Americans are intimidated by dialing European phone numbers. You needn't be. It's simple, once you break the code.

Dialing Within Belgium

The following instructions apply whether you're dialing from a Belgian mobile phone or a landline (such as a pay phone or your hotel-room phone). If you're roaming with a US phone number, follow the "Dialing Internationally" directions described later.

Belgium uses a direct-dial system (no area codes). To call anywhere within Belgium, you always dial a nine-digit number.

Dialing Internationally to or from Belgium

Always start with the **international access code** 011 if you're calling from the US or Canada, 00 from anywhere in Europe. If you're dialing from a mobile phone, you can skip the access code if you insert a + symbol (by holding the 0 key).

- Dial the **country code** of the country you're calling (32 for Belgium, or 1 for the US or Canada).
- Then dial the local number (without the initial zero) if calling to Belgium. To call from Belgium, consult the European calling chart (page 344).

Calling from the US to Belgium: To call a hotel in Bruges from the US, dial 011 (US access code), 32 (Belgium's country code), and then the hotel's number without its initial zero (e.g., 50-444-444).

Calling from any European country to the US: To call my office in Edmonds, Washington, from anywhere in Europe, I dial 00 (Europe's international access code), 1 (US country code), 425 (Edmonds' area code), and 771-8303.

More Dialing Tips

The chart on the next page shows how to dial per country. For online instructions, see www.countrycallingcodes.com or www.howtocallabroad.com.

Remember, if you're using a mobile phone, dial as if you're in that phone's country of origin. So, when roaming with your US phone number in Belgium, dial as if you're calling from the US. But if you're using a European SIM card, dial as you would from that European country.

Note that calls to a European mobile phone are substantially more expensive than calls to a fixed line. Off-hour calls are generally cheaper.

USING YOUR SMARTPHONE IN EUROPE

Even in this age of email, texting, and near-universal Internet access, smart travelers still use the telephone. I call TIs to smooth out sightseeing plans, hotels to get driving directions, museums to confirm tour schedules, restaurants to check open hours or to book a table, and so on.

Most people enjoy the convenience of bringing their own smartphone. Horror stories about sky-high roaming fees are dated and exaggerated, and major service providers work hard to avoid surprising you with an exorbitant bill. With a little planning, you can use your phone—for voice calls, messaging, and Internet access—without breaking the bank.

Start by figuring out whether your phone works in Europe. Most phones purchased through AT&T and T-Mobile (which

PRACTICALITIES

European Calling Chart

Just smile and dial, using this key:
AC = Area Code, LN = Local Number.

European Country	Calling long distance within ...	Calling from the US or Canada to ...	Calling from a European country to ...
Austria	AC + LN	011 + 43 + AC (without initial zero) + LN	00 + 43 + AC (without initial zero) + LN
Belgium	LN	011 + 32 + LN (without initial zero)	00 + 32 + LN (without initial zero)
Bosnia-Herzegovina	AC + LN	011 + 387 + AC (without initial zero) + LN	00 + 387 + AC (without initial zero) + LN
Croatia	AC + LN	011 + 385 + AC (without initial zero) + LN	00 + 385 + AC (without initial zero) + LN
Czech Republic	LN	011 + 420 + LN	00 + 420 + LN
Denmark	LN	011 + 45 + LN	00 + 45 + LN
Estonia	LN	011 + 372 + LN	00 + 372 + LN
Finland	AC + LN	011 + 358 + AC (without initial zero) + LN	999 (or other 900 number) + 358 + AC (without initial zero) + LN
France	LN	011 + 33 + LN (without initial zero)	00 + 33 + LN (without initial zero)
Germany	AC + LN	011 + 49 + AC (without initial zero) + LN	00 + 49 + AC (without initial zero) + LN
Gibraltar	LN	011 + 350 + LN	00 + 350 + LN
Great Britain & N. Ireland	AC + LN	011 + 44 + AC (without initial zero) + LN	00 + 44 + AC (without initial zero) + LN
Greece	LN	011 + 30 + LN	00 + 30 + LN
Hungary	06 + AC + LN	011 + 36 + AC + LN	00 + 36 + AC + LN
Ireland	AC + LN	011 + 353 + AC (without initial zero) + LN	00 + 353 + AC (without initial zero) + LN
Italy	LN	011 + 39 + LN	00 + 39 + LN

European Country	Calling long distance within ...	Calling from the US or Canada to ...	Calling from a European country to ...
Latvia	LN	011 + 371 + LN	00 + 371 + LN
Montenegro	AC + LN	011 + 382 + AC (without initial zero) + LN	00 + 382 + AC (without initial zero) + LN
Morocco	LN	011 + 212 + LN (without initial zero)	00 + 212 + LN (without initial zero)
Netherlands	AC + LN	011 + 31 + AC (without initial zero) + LN	00 + 31 + AC (without initial zero) + LN
Norway	LN	011 + 47 + LN	00 + 47 + LN
Poland	LN	011 + 48 + LN	00 + 48 + LN
Portugal	LN	011 + 351 + LN	00 + 351 + LN
Russia	8 + AC + LN	011 + 7 + AC + LN	00 + 7 + AC + LN
Slovakia	AC + LN	011 + 421 + AC (without initial zero) + LN	00 + 421 + AC (without initial zero) + LN
Slovenia	AC + LN	011 + 386 + AC (without initial zero) + LN	00 + 386 + AC (without initial zero) + LN
Spain	LN	011 + 34 + LN	00 + 34 + LN
Sweden	AC + LN	011 + 46 + AC (without initial zero) + LN	00 + 46 + AC (without initial zero) + LN
Switzerland	LN	011 + 41 + LN (without initial zero)	00 + 41 + LN (without initial zero)
Turkey	AC (if there's no initial zero, add one) + LN	011 + 90 + AC (without initial zero) + LN	00 + 90 + AC (without initial zero) + LN

- The instructions above apply whether you're calling to or from a European landline or mobile phone.

- If calling from any mobile phone, you can replace the international access code with "+" (press and hold 0 to insert it).

- The international access code is 011 if you're calling from the US or Canada.

- To call the US or Canada from Europe, dial 00, then 1 (country code for US and Canada), then the area code and number. In short, 00 + 1 + AC + LN = Hi, Mom!

use the same technology as Europe) work abroad, while only some phones from Verizon or Sprint do—check your operating manual (look for "tri-band," "quad-band," or "GSM"). If you're not sure, ask your service provider.

Roaming Costs

"Roaming" with your phone—that is, using it outside its home region, such as in Europe—generally comes with extra charges, whether you are making voice calls, sending texts, or reading your email. The fees listed here are for the three major American providers—Verizon, AT&T, and T-Mobile; Sprint's roaming rates tend to be much higher. But policies change fast, so get the latest details before your trip. For example, as of mid-2014, T-Mobile waived voice, texting, and data roaming fees for some plans.

Voice calls are the most expensive. Most US providers charge from $1.29 to $1.99 per minute to make or receive calls in Europe. (As you cross each border, you'll typically get a text message explaining the rates in the new country.) If you plan to make multiple calls, look into a global calling plan to lower the per-minute cost, or buy a package of minutes at a discounted price (such as 30 minutes for $30). Note that you'll be charged for incoming calls whether or not you answer them; to save money ask your friends to stay in contact by texting, and to call you only in case of an emergency.

Text messaging costs 20 to 50 cents per text. To cut that cost, you could sign up for an international messaging plan (for example, $10 for 100 texts). Or consider apps that let you text for free (iMessage for Apple, Google Hangouts for Android, or WhatsApp for any device); however, these require you to use Wi-Fi or data roaming. Be aware that Europeans use the term "SMS" ("short message service") to describe text messaging.

Data roaming means accessing data services via a cellular network other than your home carrier's. Prices have dropped dramatically in recent years, making this an affordable way for travelers to bridge gaps between Wi-Fi hotspots. You'll pay far less if you set up an international data roaming plan. Most providers charge $25-30 for 100-120 megabytes of data. That's plenty for basic Internet tasks—100 megabytes lets you view 100 websites or send/receive 1,000 text-based emails, but you'll burn through that amount quickly by streaming videos or music. If your data use exceeds your plan amount, most providers will automatically kick in an additional 100- or 120-megabyte block for the same price. (For more, see "Using Wi-Fi and Data Roaming," later.)

Setting Up (or Disabling) International Service

With most service providers, international roaming (voice, text, and data) is disabled on your account unless you activate it. Before your trip, call your provider (or navigate their website), and cover the following topics:

- Confirm that your phone will work in Europe.
- Verify global roaming rates for voice calls, text messaging, and data.
- Tell them which of those services you'd like to activate.
- Consider add-on plans to bring down the cost of international calls, texts, or data roaming.

When you get home from Europe, be sure to cancel any add-on plans that you activated for your trip.

Some people would rather use their smartphone exclusively on Wi-Fi, and not worry about either voice or data charges. If that's you, call your provider to be sure that international roaming options are deactivated on your account. To be double-sure, put your phone in "airplane mode," then turn your Wi-Fi back on.

Using Wi-Fi and Data Roaming

A good approach is to use free Wi-Fi wherever possible, and fill in the gaps with data roaming.

Wi-Fi is readily available throughout Europe. At accommodations, access is usually free, but you may have to pay a fee, especially at expensive hotels. At hotels with thick stone walls, the Wi-Fi signal from the lobby may not reach every room. If Wi-Fi is important to you, ask about it when you book—and be specific ("In the rooms?"). Get the password and network name at the front desk when you check in.

When you're out and about, your best bet for finding free Wi-Fi is often at a café. They'll usually tell you the password if you buy something. Or you can stroll down a café-lined street, smartphone in hand, checking for unsecured networks every few steps until you find one that works. Some towns have free public Wi-Fi in highly trafficked parks or piazzas. You may have to register before using it, or get a password at the TI.

Data roaming is handy when you can't find Wi-Fi. Because you'll pay by the megabyte (explained earlier), it's best to limit how much data you use. Save bandwidth-gobbling tasks like Skyping, watching videos, or downloading apps or emails with large attachments until you're on Wi-Fi. Switch your phone's email settings from "push" to "fetch." This means that you can choose to "fetch" (download) your messages when you're on Wi-Fi rather than having them continuously "pushed" to your device. And be aware of apps—such as news, weather, and sports tickers—that automatically update. Check your phone's settings to be sure that none of your apps are set to "use cellular data."

I like the safeguard of manually turning off data roaming on my phone whenever I'm not actively using it. To turn off data and

PRACTICALITIES

Internet Calling

To make totally free voice and video calls over the Internet, all you need are a smartphone, tablet, or laptop; a strong Wi-Fi signal; and an account with one of the major Internet calling providers: Skype (www.skype.com), FaceTime (preloaded on most Apple devices), or Google+ Hangouts (www.google.com/hangouts). If the Wi-Fi signal isn't strong enough for video, try sticking with an audio-only call. Or...wait for your next hotel. Many Internet calling programs also work for making calls from your computer to telephones worldwide for a very reasonable fee—generally just a few cents per minute (you'll have to buy some credit before you make your first call).

voice roaming, look in your phone's settings menu—try checking under "cellular" or "network," or ask your service provider how to do it. If you need to get online but can't find Wi-Fi, simply turn on data roaming long enough for the task at hand, then turn it off again.

Figure out how to keep track of how much data you've used (in your phone's menu, look for "cellular data usage"; you may have to reset the counter at the start of your trip). Some companies automatically send you a text message warning if you approach or exceed your limit.

There's yet another option: If you're traveling with an unlocked smartphone (explained later), you can buy a SIM card that also includes data; this can be far cheaper than data roaming through your home provider.

USING EUROPEAN SIM CARDS

While using your American phone in Europe is easy, it's not always cheap. And unreliable Wi-Fi can make keeping in touch frustrating. If you're reasonably technology-savvy, and would like to have the option of making lots of affordable calls, it's worth getting comfortable with European SIM cards.

Here's the basic idea: With an unlocked phone (which works with different carriers; see below), get a SIM card—the microchip that stores data about your phone—once you get to Europe. Slip in the SIM, turn on the phone, and bingo! You've got a European phone number (and access to cheaper European rates).

Getting an Unlocked Phone

Your basic options are getting your existing phone unlocked or buying a phone (either at home or in Europe).

Some phones are electronically "locked" so that you can't switch SIM cards (keeping you loyal to your carrier). But in some circumstances it's possible to unlock your phone—allowing you to replace the original SIM card with one that will work with a European provider. Note that some US carriers are beginning to offer phones/tablets whose SIM card can't be swapped out in the US but will accept a European SIM without any unlocking process.

You may already have an old, unused mobile phone in a drawer somewhere. Call your service provider and ask if they'll send you the unlock code. Otherwise, you can buy one: Search an online shopping site for an "unlocked quad-band phone," or buy one at a mobile-phone shop in Europe. Either way, a basic model typically costs $40 or less.

Buying and Using SIM Cards

Once you have an unlocked phone, you'll need to buy a SIM card (note that a smaller variation called "micro-SIM" or "nano-SIM"—

used in most iPhones—is less widely available.)

SIM cards are sold at mobile-phone shops, department-store electronics counters, and newsstands for $5-10, and usually include about that much prepaid calling credit (making the card itself virtually free). Because SIM cards are prepaid, there's no contract and no commitment; I routinely buy one even if I'm in a country for only a few days.

In Belgium, buying a SIM card is as easy as buying a pack of gum (though some European countries require you to register the SIM card with your passport as an antiterrorism measure).

When using a SIM card in its home country, it's free to receive calls and texts, and it's cheap to make calls—domestic calls average 20 cents per minute. You can also use SIM cards to call the US—sometimes very affordably (Lycamobile, which operates in multiple European countries, lets you call a US number for less than 10 cents a minute). Rates are higher if you're roaming in another country. But if you bought the SIM card within the European Union, roaming fees are capped no matter where you travel throughout the EU (about 25 cents/minute to make calls, 7 cents/minute to receive calls, and 8 cents for a text message).

While you can buy SIM cards just about anywhere, I like to seek out a mobile-phone shop, where an English-speaking clerk can help explain my options, get my SIM card inserted and set up, and show me how to use it. When you buy your SIM card, ask about rates for domestic and international calls and texting, and about roaming fees. Also find out how to check your credit balance (usually you'll key in a few digits and hit "Send"). You can top up your credit at any newsstand, tobacco shop, mobile-phone shop, or many other businesses (look for the SIM card's logo in the window).

To insert your SIM card into the phone, locate the slot, which is usually on the side of the phone or behind the battery. Turning on the phone, you'll be prompted to enter the "SIM PIN" (a code number that came with your card).

If you have an unlocked smartphone, you can look for a European SIM card that covers both voice and data. This is often much cheaper than paying for data roaming through your home provider.

LANDLINE TELEPHONES AND INTERNET CAFÉS

If you prefer to travel without a smartphone or tablet, you can still stay in touch using landline telephones, hotel guest computers, and Internet cafés.

Landline Telephones

Phones in your **hotel room** can be great for local calls and for calls using cheap international phone cards (described in the sidebar). Many hotels charge a fee for local and "toll-free" as well as long-distance or international calls—always ask for the rates before you dial. Since you'll never be charged for receiving calls, it can be more affordable to have someone from the US call you in your room.

While **public pay phones** are on the endangered species list, you'll still see them in post offices and train stations. Pay phones generally come with multilingual instructions. Most public phones work with insertable phone cards (described in the sidebar).

You'll see many cheap **call shops** that advertise low rates to faraway lands, often in train-station neighborhoods. While these target immigrants who want to call home cheaply, tourists can use them, too. Before making your call, be completely clear on the rates.

Internet Cafés and Public Internet Terminals

Finding public Internet terminals in Europe is no problem. Many hotels have a computer in the lobby for guests to use. Otherwise, head for an Internet café, or ask the TI or your hotelier for the nearest place to access the Internet.

European computers typically use non-American keyboards. A few letters are switched around, and command keys are labeled in the local language. Many European keyboards have an "Alt Gr" key (for "Alternate Graphics") to the right of the space bar; press this to insert the extra symbol that appears on some keys. Europeans have different names for, and different ways to type, the @ symbol. If you can't locate a special character (such as the @ sym-

Types of Telephone Cards

Europe uses two different types of telephone cards. Both types are sold at post offices, newsstands, street kiosks, tobacco shops, and train stations.

Insertable Phone Cards: These cards can only be used at pay phones: Simply take the phone off the hook, insert the card, wait for a dial tone, and dial away. The phone displays your credit ticking down as you talk. Each European country has its own insertable phone card—so your Belgian card won't work in a Dutch phone.

International Phone Cards: These prepaid cards can be used to make inexpensive calls—within Europe, or to the US, for pennies a minute—from nearly any phone, including the one in your hotel room. The cards come with a toll-free number and a scratch-to-reveal PIN code. If the voice prompts aren't in English, experiment: Dial your code, followed by the pound sign (#), then the phone number, then pound again, and so on, until it works. Sometimes the star (*) key is used instead of the pound sign. When using an international calling card, the area code must be dialed even if you're calling across the street.

You can buy the cards at small newsstand kiosks, electronics stores, and hole-in-the-wall Internet shops. Ask the clerk which brands have the best rates for calls to America. Buy a lower denomination in case the card is a dud. Some international phone cards work in multiple countries—if traveling to both the Netherlands and Belgium, try to buy a card that will work in both places. Some shops also sell cardless codes, printed right on the receipt.

bol), simply copy it from a Web page and paste it into your email message.

Internet Security

Whether you're accessing the Internet with your own device or at a public terminal, using a shared network or computer comes with the potential for increased security risks. Ask the hotel or café for the specific name of their Wi-Fi network, and make sure you log on to that exact one; hackers sometimes create a bogus hotspot with a similar or vague name (such as "Hotel Europa Free Wi-Fi"). It's better if a network uses a password (especially a hard-to-guess one) rather than being open to the world.

While traveling, you may want to check your online banking or credit-card statements, or to take care of other personal-finance chores, but Internet security experts advise against accessing these sites entirely while traveling. Even if you're using your own computer at a password-protected hotspot, any hacker who's logged on to the same network can see what you're up to. If you need to log on to a banking website, try to do so on a hard-wired connection (i.e., using an Ethernet cable in your hotel room), or if that's not possible, use a secure banking app on a cellular telephone connection.

If using a credit card online, make sure that the site is secure. Most browsers display a little padlock icon, and the URL begins with *https* instead of *http*. Never send a credit-card number over a website that doesn't begin with *https*.

If you're not convinced a connection is secure, avoid accessing any sites (such as your bank's) that could be vulnerable to fraud.

MAIL

You can mail one package per day to yourself worth up to $200 duty-free from Europe to the US (mark it "personal purchases"). If you're sending a gift to someone, mark it "unsolicited gift." For details, visit www.cbp.gov and search for "Know Before You Go."

The Belgian postal service works fine, but for quick transatlantic delivery (in either direction), consider services such as DHL (www.dhl.com).

Transportation

Because of the short distances and excellent public transportation systems in Belgium, and the fact that this book covers four big cities, I recommend connecting Antwerp, Ghent, Bruges, and Brussels by train. Frequent trains connect each of these towns faster and easier than you could by driving. But for other destinations, a car could be a good alternative. In Belgium, cars are best for three or more traveling together (especially families with small kids), those packing heavy, and those scouring the countryside.

TRAINS

The easiest way to reach nearly any Belgian destination is by train. Connections are fast and frequent. Because Belgium is bilingual, the rail system has a complicated identity; it's NMBS in Dutch but SNCB in French (luckily, it has a good English website—www.belgianrail.be). InterCity (IC) trains are speedy for connecting big cities, and the high-speed Thalys is the fastest (the speed comes at a price; see "Reservations for Rail Pass Holders," later). InterRegio (IR) trains connect smaller towns and make more stops along the way. Throughout Belgium, smoking is prohibited in trains and train stations.

Schedules

To get train schedules in advance, consult the Belgian rail site: www.belgianrail.be (tel. 025-282-828). The German Rail (Deutsche

Bahn) website is also useful and has comprehensive schedules for almost anywhere in Europe (www.bahn.com).

To find schedules at train stations, check the yellow schedule posters, or look for TV screens listing upcoming departures. The direction of the train is identified by its final station. If you can't find your train, or are unclear on departure details, visit an information booth or enlist the help of any official-looking employee.

Buying Tickets in Belgium

Belgian train ticket machines only take Belgian debit cards, but you can use US credit and debit cards at ticket windows. It's also possible to purchase tickets online at www.belgianrail.be with a US credit card and print them out at home, or retrieve a hard copy at special ticket-dispensing machines at major train stations.

Ticket Deals

If you're not traveling with a rail pass, consider the region's money-saving deals.

In Belgium, youths under age 26 can get a Go Pass (€51 for 10 rides anywhere in Belgium). A similar deal is available for anyone over 26 for €76. Seniors (age 65+) can get a same-day round-trip ticket to anywhere in Belgium for €6 (valid after 9:00 on weekdays and any time on weekends, but not valid Sat-Sun in July-Aug). There are also weekend discounts for round-trips

(50 percent off, valid Fri after 19:00). For more information, visit www.belgianrail.be.

Bikes on Trains

If you're traveling with a bike, you'll pay extra to bring it on the train. In Belgium, bikes cost €5 extra for a one-way trip, and €8 round-trip.

High-Speed Trains to/from Belgium

Fast **Thalys** trains connect Brussels with Amsterdam, Cologne, and Paris (www.thalys.com). The **Eurostar** train zips between London and Brussels in 2.5 hours—faster and easier than flying (www.eurostar.com). French **TGV** trains link Brussels with Charles de Gaulle Airport, outside Paris, in under two hours (www.tgv-europe.com).

These fast-train services are expensive, but they do offer significant price discounts, with restrictions, on tickets reserved in advance (most available three months ahead, Eurostar available nine months ahead). Each company sells tickets online or through US agents such as www.ricksteves.com/rail. In Europe, you can buy tickets at any major train station in any country or at any travel agency that handles train tickets (expect a booking fee). Note that Thalys tickets between Brussels and Paris and Eurostar tickets between Brussels and London can qualify you for a discounted regional train connection in Belgium. For more on these trains, see page 215.

Rail Passes

Most visits to Belgium don't cover enough miles to justify a rail pass, but if you're traveling beyond its borders, a rail pass could save you money. For instance, good rail pass options exist for those traveling between BeNeLux (Belgium, the Netherlands, and Luxembourg) and either France or Germany; Eurail Select passes (or a Global Pass) make sense if you're touring the Netherlands and Belgium as part of a larger trip (see sidebar). For more detailed advice on figuring out the smartest rail-pass options for your train trip, visit the Trains & Rail Passes section of my website at www.ricksteves.com/rail.

Reservations for Rail Pass Holders: Regional and InterCity trains do not require reservations, allowing you plenty of flexibility. Between Brussels-Amsterdam or Brussels-Cologne, fast Thalys trains require expensive reservations with a rail pass—avoid this extra cost simply by choosing a regular (non-Thalys) train. The only direct service from Brussels to Paris is by Thalys, with reservations costing €30-60. To avoid Thalys fees when heading from Brussels

Rail Passes

Prices listed are for 2014 and are subject to change. For the latest prices, details, and train schedules (and easy online ordering), see www.ricksteves.com/rail.

Benelux = Belgium, Netherlands and Luxembourg. "Saver" prices are per person for two or more people traveling together. "Youth" means under age 26. The fare for children 4–11 is half the adult individual fare or Saver fare. Kids under age 4 travel free.

BENELUX PASS

	Individual 1st Class	Individual 2nd Class	Saver 1st Class	Saver 2nd Class	Youth 2nd Class
3 days in 1 month	$298	$240	$254	$204	$157
5 days in 1 month	$408	$327	$347	$278	$214

Valid on Thalys trains within Benelux (with paid seat reservation), but not to/from Paris.

BENELUX-FRANCE PASS

	Individual 1st Class	Individual 2nd Class	Saver 1st Class	Saver 2nd Class	Youth 2nd Class
5 days in 2 months	$458	$390	$390	$332	$299
6 days in 2 months	$502	$427	$427	$372	$327
8 days in 2 months	$581	$506	$495	$443	$379
10 days in 2 months	$656	$578	$558	$503	$434

BENELUX-GERMANY PASS

	Individual 1st Class	Individual 2nd Class	Saver 1st Class	Saver 2nd Class	Youth 2nd Class
5 days in 2 months	$446	$336	$336	$271	$271
6 days in 2 months	$493	$372	$372	$297	$297
8 days in 2 months	$583	$436	$436	$351	$351
10 days in 2 months	$678	$508	$508	$406	$406

SELECTPASS

This pass covers travel in three adjacent countries, such as Benelux-Germany-Switzerland, but not including France. Please visit **www.ricksteves.com/rail** for four- and five-country options.

	Individual 1st Class	Saver 1st Class	Youth 2nd Class
5 days in 2 months	$524	$446	$342
6 days in 2 months	$572	$487	$373
8 days in 2 months	$666	$567	$434
10 days in 2 months	$762	$468	$497

PRACTICALITIES

or Bruges to Paris, connect in Lille to a TGV with cheaper (but limited) €5-15 reservations.

Eurostar: Any pass that covers Belgium allows you a discounted ticket price on the Eurostar to/from London. (For information on the Eurostar train, see page 215.)

BUSES

While you'll mostly use trains to travel in this region, you can also consider buses. There's no unified national bus company for Belgium—various destinations are served by different companies. Flanders is served largely by De Lijn (www.delijn.be), while French-speaking areas have TEC (www.infotec.be). Eurolines buses connect Belgium to other European cities (www.eurolines.be).

RENTING A CAR

Rental companies require you to be at least 23 years old and to have held your license for one year. Drivers from 21 to 23 years old may incur a young-driver surcharge, and some rental companies do not rent to anyone 75 and over. If you're considered too young or old, look into leasing (covered later), which has less-stringent age restrictions.

Research car rentals before you go. It's cheaper to arrange most car rentals from the US. Call several companies or look online to compare rates.

Most of the major US rental agencies (including Avis, Budget, Hertz, and Thrifty) have offices throughout Europe. Also consider the two major Europe-based agencies, Europcar and Sixt. It can be cheaper to use a consolidator, such as Auto Europe/Kemwel (www.autoeurope.com) or Europe by Car (www.europebycar.com), which compares rates at several companies to get you the best deal—but because you're working with a middleman, it's especially important to ask in advance about add-on fees and restrictions.

Regardless of the car-rental company you choose, always read the fine print carefully for add-on charges—such as one-way drop-off fees, airport surcharges, or mandatory insurance policies—that aren't included in the "total price." You may need to query rental agents pointedly to find out your actual cost.

For the best deal, rent by the week with unlimited mileage. To save money on fuel, ask for a diesel car. I normally rent the smallest, least-expensive model with a stick shift (generally much cheaper than an automatic). Almost all rentals are manual by default, so if you need an automatic, request one in advance; be aware that these cars are usually larger models (not as maneuverable on narrow, winding roads).

Figure on paying roughly $200 for a one-week rental. Allow extra for supplemental insurance, fuel, tolls, and parking. For trips of three weeks or more, look into leasing; you'll save money on insurance and taxes. Be warned that international trips—say, picking up in Brussels and dropping off in Paris—can be expensive (it depends partly on distance).

As a rule, always tell your car-rental company up front exactly which countries you'll be entering. Some companies levy extra insurance fees for trips taken in certain countries with certain types of cars (such as BMWs, Mercedes, and convertibles). Double-check with your rental agent that you have all the documentation you need before you drive off (especially if you're crossing borders into non-Schengen countries, such as Croatia, where you might need to present proof of insurance).

Big companies have offices in most cities; ask whether they can pick you up at your hotel. Small local rental companies can be cheaper but aren't as flexible.

Compare pickup costs (downtown can be less expensive than the airport) and explore drop-off options. Always check the hours of the location you choose: Many rental offices close from midday Saturday until Monday morning and, in smaller towns, at lunchtime.

When selecting a location, don't trust the agency's description of "downtown" or "city center." In some cases, a "downtown" branch can be on the outskirts of the city—a long, costly taxi ride from the center. Before choosing, plug the addresses into a mapping website. You may find that the "train station" location is handier. But returning a car at a big-city train station or downtown agency can be tricky; get precise details on the car drop-off location and hours, and allow ample time to find it.

When you pick up the rental car, check it thoroughly and make sure any damage is noted on your rental agreement. Find out how your car's lights, turn signals, wipers, radio, and fuel cap function, and know what kind of fuel the car takes (diesel vs. unleaded). When you return the car, make sure the agent verifies its condition with you. Some drivers take pictures of the returned vehicle as proof of its condition.

Navigation Options

When renting a car in Europe, you have several alternatives for your digital navigator: Use your smartphone's online mapping app, download an offline map app, or rent a GPS device with your rental car (or bring your own GPS device from home).

Online mapping apps used to be prohibitively expensive for overseas travelers—but that was before most carriers started offering affordable international data plans. If you're already getting a data plan for your trip, this is probably the way to go (see "Using Your Smartphone in Europe," earlier).

A number of well-designed apps allow you much of the convenience of online maps without any costly demands on your data plan. City Maps 2Go is one of the most popular of these; OffMaps, Google Maps, and Navfree also offer good, zoomable offline maps for much of Europe (some are better for driving, while others are better for navigating cities).

Some drivers prefer using a dedicated GPS unit—not only to avoid the data-roaming fees, but because a stand-alone GPS can be easier to operate (important if you're driving solo). The major downside: It's expensive—around $10-30 per day. Your car's GPS unit may only come loaded with maps for its home country—if you need additional maps, ask. Make sure your device's language is set to English before you drive off. If you have a portable GPS device at home, you can take that instead. Many American GPS devices come loaded with US maps only—you'll need to buy and download European maps before your trip. This option is far less expensive than renting.

Car Insurance Options

When you rent a car, you are liable for a very high deductible, sometimes equal to the entire value of the car. Limit your financial risk by choosing one of these three options: Buy Collision Damage Waiver (CDW) coverage from the car-rental company, get coverage through your credit card (free, if your card automatically includes zero-deductible coverage), or get collision insurance as part of a larger travel-insurance policy.

CDW includes a very high deductible (typically $1,000-1,500). Though each rental company has its own variation, basic CDW costs $10-30 a day (figure roughly 30 percent extra) and reduces your liability, but does not eliminate it. When you pick up the car, you'll be offered the chance to "buy down" the basic deductible to zero (for an additional $10-30/day; this is sometimes called "super CDW" or "zero-deductible coverage").

If you opt for **credit-card coverage**, there's a catch. You'll technically have to decline all coverage offered by the car-rental company, which means they can place a hold on your card (which can be up to the full value of the car). In case of damage, it can be time-consuming to resolve the charges with your credit-card company. Before you decide on this option, quiz your credit-card company about how it works.

If you're already purchasing a **travel-insurance policy** for your trip, adding collision coverage is an option. For example, Travel Guard (www.travelguard.com) sells affordable renter's collision insurance as an add-on to its other policies; it's valid everywhere in Europe except the Republic of Ireland, and some Italian car-rental companies refuse to honor it, as it doesn't cover you in case of theft.

For more on car-rental insurance, see www.ricksteves.com/cdw.

Leasing

For trips of three weeks or more, consider leasing (which automatically includes zero-deductible collision and theft insurance). By technically buying and then selling back the car, you save lots of money on tax and insurance. Leasing provides you a brand-new car with unlimited mileage and a 24-hour emergency assistance program. You can lease for as little as 21 days to as long as five and a half months. Car leases must be arranged from the US. One of many companies offering affordable lease packages is Europe by Car (US tel. 800-223-1516, www.europebycar.com).

DRIVING

Road Rules: Traffic cameras are everywhere in Belgium; speeding tickets for even a few kilometers over the limit are common. Kids under age 12 (or less than about 5 feet tall) must ride in an appropriate child-safety seat. Seat belts are mandatory for all, and two beers under those belts are enough to land you in jail. Be aware of other typical European road rules; for example, many countries require headlights to be turned on at all times, and it's generally illegal to drive while using your mobile phone without a hands-free headset. In Europe, you're not allowed to turn right on a red light, unless there is a sign or signal specifically authorizing it, and on expressways it's illegal to pass drivers on the right. Ask your car-rental company about these rules, or check the US State Department website (www.travel.state.gov, search for your country in the "Learn about your destination" box, then click on "Travel and Transportation").

Fuel: Gas (*benzine* in Dutch, *essence* in French) is expensive—about $8-9 per gallon. Diesel (*diesel or dieselolie* in Dutch, *gazole* in French) is less—about $7 per gallon—and diesel cars get better mileage, so try to rent a diesel to save money. Be sure you know what type of fuel your car takes before you fill up. Gas is most expensive on freeways and cheapest at big supermarkets. Some of the filling stations in Belgium are unmanned, and your US credit and debit cards may not work at self-service gas pumps. Look for stations with an attendant or be sure to carry sufficient cash in euros.

Parking: Finding a parking place can be a headache in larger cities. Ask your hotelier for ideas, and pay to park at well-patrolled lots (blue *P* signs direct you to parking lots). Parking structures usually require that you take a ticket with you and pay at a machine on your way back to the car. US credit cards may not work in these automated machines but euro coins (and sometimes bills) will.

FLIGHTS

The best comparison search engine for both international and intra-European flights is www.kayak.com. For inexpensive flights within Europe, try www.skyscanner.com or www.hipmunk.com; for inexpensive international flights, try www.vayama.com.

Flying to Europe: Start looking for international flights four to five months before your trip, especially for peak-season travel. Off-season tickets can be purchased a month or so in advance. Depending on your itinerary, it can be efficient to fly into one city and out of another. If your flight requires a connection in Europe, see our hints on navigating Europe's top hub airports at www.ricksteves.com/hub-airports.

Flying Within Europe: If you're considering a train ride that's more than five hours long, a flight may save you both time and money. When comparing your options, factor in the time it takes to get to the airport and how early you'll need to arrive to check in.

Well-known cheapo airlines include easyJet (www.easyjet.com) and Ryanair (www.ryanair.com), along with Brussels Airlines (www.brusselsairlines.com).

Be aware of the potential drawbacks of flying on the cheap: nonrefundable and nonchangeable tickets, minimal or nonexistent customer service, treks to airports far outside town, and stingy baggage allowances with steep overage fees. If you're traveling with lots of luggage, a cheap flight can quickly become a bad deal. To avoid unpleasant surprises, read the small print before you book.

Resources

RESOURCES FROM RICK STEVES

Rick Steves Belgium is one of many books in my series on European travel, which includes country guidebooks, city guidebooks, Snapshot guides (excerpted chapters from my country guides), Pocket Guides (full-color little books on big cities), and my budget-travel skills handbook, *Rick Steves Europe Through the Back Door.* Most of my titles are available as ebooks. My phrase books—for German, French, Italian, Spanish, and Portuguese—are practical and budget-oriented. My other books include *Europe 101* (a crash course on art and history designed for travelers), *Mediterranean Cruise Ports* and *Northern European Cruise Ports* (how to make the most of your time in port), and *Travel as a Political Act* (a travelogue sprinkled with

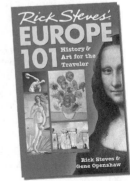

tips for bringing home a global perspective). A more complete list of my titles appears near the end of this book.

Video: My public television series, *Rick Steves' Europe,* covers European destinations in 100 shows, with a show on Belgium. To watch full episodes online for free, see www.ricksteves.com/tv. Or to raise your travel I.Q. with video versions of our popular classes, see www.ricksteves.com/travel-talks.

Audio: My weekly public radio show, *Travel with Rick Steves,* features interviews with travel experts from around the world. All of this audio content is available for free at Rick Steves Audio Europe, an extensive online library organized by destination. Choose whatever interests you, and download it via the Rick Steves Audio Europe app, www. ricksteves.com/audioeurope, iTunes, or Google Play.

MAPS
The black-and-white maps in this book are concise and simple, designed to help you locate recommended places and get to local TIs, where you can pick up more in-depth maps of cities and regions (usually free). For most Belgian cities, look for Use It tourist maps, designed by locals and geared for backpackers, but loaded with insight and informative for anyone.

RECOMMENDED BOOKS AND MOVIES
To learn more about Belgium past and present, check out some of these books and films.

Nonfiction
The Guns of August (Barbara Tuchman, 2004). This Pulitzer-Prize winner details the outbreak of World War I and events along the Western Front, including Belgium.

In Flanders Fields: The 1917 Campaign (Leon Wolff, 1958). This is the classic account of the Flanders battle at Passchendaele, in which Allied forces captured a few thousand yards at the cost of tens of thousands of lives.

King Leopold's Ghost (Adam Hochschild, 1999). A clear-eyed examination of Belgium's exploitation of its Congo colony.

A Tall Man in a Low Land: Some Time Among the Belgians (Harry Pearson, 1999). A wry look at contemporary Belgium through the eyes of an outsider.

Fiction
The Abyss (Marguerite Yourcenar, 1968). The story of an atheist in

PRACTICALITIES

Begin Your Trip at
www.RickSteves.com

My **website** is *the* place to explore Europe. You'll find thousands of fun articles, videos, photos, and radio interviews on European destinations; money-saving tips for planning your dream trip; monthly travel news; my travel talks and travel blog; my latest guidebook updates (www.ricksteves.com/update); and my free Rick Steves Audio Europe app. You can also follow me on Facebook and Twitter.

Our **Travel Forum** is an immense, yet well-groomed collection of message boards, where our travel-savvy community answers questions and shares their personal travel experiences (www.ricksteves.com/forums).

Our **online Travel Store** offers travel bags and accessories that I've designed specifically to help you travel smarter and lighter. These include my popular bags (rolling carry-on and backpack versions), money belts, totes, toiletries kits, adapters, other accessories, and a wide selection of guidebooks, journals, planning maps, and DVDs.

Choosing the right **rail pass** for your trip—amidst hundreds of options—can drive you nutty. Our website will help you find the perfect fit for your itinerary and your budget: We offer easy, one-stop shopping for rail passes, seat reservations, and point-to-point tickets.

Want to travel with greater efficiency and less stress? We organize **tours** with more than three dozen itineraries and 800 departures reaching the best destinations in this book... and beyond. We offer an 11-day Heart of Belgium and Holland tour. You'll enjoy great guides, a fun bunch of travel partners (with small groups of 24 to 28 travelers), and plenty of room to spread out in a big, comfy bus when touring between towns. You'll find European adventures to fit every vacation length. For all the details, and to get our Tour Catalog and a free Rick Steves Tour Experience DVD (filmed on location during an actual tour), visit www.ricksteves.com or call us at 425/608-4217.

Renaissance Bruges, written by one of Belgium's greatest novelists.

The Adventures of Tintin series (Hergé, 1929-1976). Classic comics featuring the irrepressible boy reporter and his dog.

Hercule Poirot series (Agatha Christie, 1920-1975). Appearing in 33 who-dun-its, the Belgian detective Poirot theatrically applies his "little gray cells" to solve all sorts of crimes.

The House of Niccolò series (Dorothy Dunnett, 1999). A three-volume series traces an audacious apprentice who rises to lead a mercantile empire in 15th-century Flanders.

The Lady and the Unicorn (Tracy Chevalier, 2003). The story behind the creation of the famous *Lady and the Unicorn* tapestries, which were woven by a master craftsman in Brussels.

Pallieter (Felix Timmermans, 1916). A Flemish classic about a young man whose life-threatening disease changes his life completely.

Resistance (Anita Shreve, 1995). In a village in Nazi-occupied Belgium, the wife of a resistance fighter shelters a downed American bomber pilot.

The Square of Revenge (Pieter Aspe, 2013). The medieval architecture of Bruges conceals a bizarre mystery for Inspector Van In to solve.

Films

The Adventures of Tintin (2011). Steven Spielberg's adaptation follows the beloved Belgian comic book hero as he sets off on a treasure hunt for a sunken ship.

The Battle of the Bulge (1965). Henry Fonda confronts a surprise Nazi attack.

Get Out Your Handkerchiefs (1978). Shot in the Ardennes, this wacky romantic comedy starring Gérard Depardieu won the Academy Award for Best Foreign Language Film.

If It's Tuesday, This Must Be Belgium (1969). In this comedy, a group of travelers from the US races through seven countries in 18 days on a bus tour.

In Bruges (2008). This dark and violent comedy was filmed just where you'd think.

The Nun's Story (1959). Audrey Hepburn plays a Belgian nun who has a crisis of faith adjusting to cloistered life.

APPENDIX

Contents

Useful Contacts

Emergency Needs
Police: 101 or 112
Ambulance or Fire: 100 or 112

Embassies in Belgium
US Consulate and Embassy in Brussels: Tel. 02-811-4300, after-hours emergency tel. 02-811-4000, Boulevard du Régent 25-27, http://belgium.usembassy.gov.
Canadian Embassy in Brussels: Tel. 02-741-0611, Avenue de Tervueren 2, www.ambassade-canada.be.

Holidays and Festivals

This list includes selected festivals in major cities, plus national holidays observed throughout Belgium. Many sights and banks close on national holidays—keep this in mind when planning your itinerary. Before planning a trip around a festival, verify its dates by checking the festival's website or TI sites: www.visitbelgium.com.

Jan 1	New Year's Day
Feb	Carnival (Mardi Gras)
March/April	Easter Weekend (Good Friday-Easter Monday): April 3-6, 2015; March 25-28, 2016
May 1	Labor Day (some closures)
May	Ascension and Procession of the Holy Blood, Bruges: May 14, 2015; May 5, 2016
May	Pentecost and Whit Monday: May 24-25, 2015; May 15-16, 2016
Late June/ early July	Ommegang Pageant, Brussels (historic costumed parade to Grand Place, www.ommegang.be)
July 21	Belgian Independence Day (parades, fireworks, closures)
Late July	Gentse Feesten music festival, Ghent (www.gentsefeesten.be)
Aug 15	Assumption Day (procession in Bruges, closures)
Mid-Aug	Carpet of Flowers, Brussels (celebrated even years only, www.flowercarpet.be)
Nov 1	All Saints' Day (closures)
Nov 11	Armistice Day (banks closed)
Dec	"Winter Wonders" Christmas Market, Brussels (www.plaisirsdhiver.be)
Dec 6	St. Nicholas Day (Sinterklaas; processions and presents for children)
Dec 25	Christmas

Conversions and Climate

NUMBERS AND STUMBLERS

- Europeans write a few of their numbers differently than we do. 1 = 1, 4 = 4, 7 = 7.
- In Europe, dates appear as day/month/year, so Christmas 2016 is 25/12/16.
- Commas are decimal points and decimals are commas. A dollar and a half is $1,50, one thousand is 1.000, and there are 5.280 feet in a mile.
- When counting with fingers, start with your thumb. If you hold up your first finger to request one item, you'll probably get two.
- What Americans call the second floor of a building is the first floor in Europe.

- On escalators and moving sidewalks, Europeans keep the left "lane" open for passing. Keep to the right.

METRIC CONVERSIONS

A kilogram is 2.2 pounds, and 1 liter is about a quart, or almost four to a gallon. A kilometer is six-tenths of a mile. I figure kilometers to miles by cutting them in half and adding back 10 percent of the original (120 km: 60 + 12 = 72 miles, 300 km: 150 + 30 = 180 miles).

1 foot = 0.3 meter	1 square yard = 0.8 square meter
1 yard = 0.9 meter	1 square mile = 2.6 square kilometers
1 mile = 1.6 kilometers	1 ounce = 28 grams
1 centimeter = 0.4 inch	1 quart = 0.95 liter
1 meter = 39.4 inches	1 kilogram = 2.2 pounds
1 kilometer = 0.62 mile	32°F = 0°C

APPENDIX

CLOTHING SIZES

When shopping for clothing, use these US-to-European comparisons as general guidelines (but note that no conversion is perfect).

- Women's dresses and blouses: Add 30
  (US size 10 = European size 40)
- Men's suits and jackets: Add 10
  (US size 40 regular = European size 50)
- Men's shirts: Multiply by 2 and add about 8
  (US size 15 collar = European size 38)
- Women's shoes: Add about 30
  (US size 8 = European size 38-39)
- Men's shoes: Add 32-34
  (US size 9 = European size 41; US size 11 = European size 45)

APPENDIX

BELGIUM'S CLIMATE

First line, average daily high; second line, average daily low; third line, average days without rain. For more detailed weather statistics for destinations in this book (as well as the rest of the world), check www.wunderground.com.

J	F	M	A	M	J	J	A	S	O	N	D
41°	44°	51°	58°	65°	71°	73°	72°	69°	60°	48°	42°
30°	32°	34°	40°	45°	53°	55°	55°	52°	45°	38°	32°
9	11	14	12	15	15	13	12	15	13	10	11

FAHRENHEIT AND CELSIUS CONVERSION

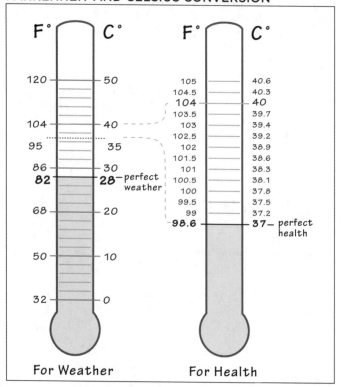

Europe takes its temperature using the Celsius scale, while we opt for Fahrenheit. For a rough conversion from Celsius to Fahrenheit, double the number and add 30. For weather, remember that 28°C is 82°F— perfect. For health, 37°C is just right. At a launderette, 30°C is cold, 40°C is warm (usually the default setting), 60°C is hot, and 95°C is boiling.

Packing Checklist

Whether you're traveling for five days or five weeks, you won't need more than this. Pack light to enjoy the sweet freedom of true mobility.

Clothing

- ❑ 5 shirts: long- & short-sleeve
- ❑ 2 pairs pants or skirt
- ❑ 1 pair shorts or capris
- ❑ 5 pairs underwear & socks
- ❑ 1 pair walking shoes
- ❑ Sweater or fleece top
- ❑ Rainproof jacket with hood
- ❑ Tie or scarf
- ❑ Swimsuit
- ❑ Sleepwear

Money

- ❑ Debit card
- ❑ Credit card(s)
- ❑ Hard cash ($20 bills)
- ❑ Money belt or neck wallet

Documents & Travel Info

- ❑ Passport
- ❑ Airline reservations
- ❑ Rail pass/train reservations
- ❑ Car-rental voucher
- ❑ Driver's license
- ❑ Student ID, hostel card, etc.
- ❑ Photocopies of all the above
- ❑ Hotel confirmations
- ❑ Insurance details
- ❑ Guidebooks & maps
- ❑ Notepad & pen
- ❑ Journal

Toiletries Kit

- ❑ Toiletries
- ❑ Medicines & vitamins
- ❑ First-aid kit
- ❑ Glasses/contacts/sunglasses (with prescriptions)
- ❑ Earplugs
- ❑ Packet of tissues (for WC)

Miscellaneous

- ❑ Daypack
- ❑ Sealable plastic baggies
- ❑ Laundry soap
- ❑ Spot remover
- ❑ Clothesline
- ❑ Sewing kit
- ❑ Travel alarm/watch

Electronics

- ❑ Smartphone or mobile phone
- ❑ Camera & related gear
- ❑ Tablet/ereader/media player
- ❑ Laptop & flash drive
- ❑ Earbuds or headphones
- ❑ Chargers
- ❑ Plug adapters

Optional Extras

- ❑ Flipflops or slippers
- ❑ Mini-umbrella or poncho
- ❑ Travel hairdryer
- ❑ Belt
- ❑ Hat (for sun or cold)
- ❑ Picnic supplies
- ❑ Water bottle
- ❑ Fold-up tote bag
- ❑ Small flashlight
- ❑ Small binoculars
- ❑ Insect repellent
- ❑ Small towel or washcloth
- ❑ Inflatable pillow
- ❑ Some duct tape (for repairs)
- ❑ Tiny lock
- ❑ Address list (to mail postcards)
- ❑ Postcards/photos from home
- ❑ Extra passport photos
- ❑ Good book

Dutch Survival Phrases

Northern Belgium speaks Dutch, but for cultural and historical reasons, the language is often called Flemish. Most people speak English, but if you learn the pleasantries and key phrases, you'll connect better with the locals. To pronounce the guttural Dutch "g" (indicated in phonetics by *h*), make a clear-your-throat sound, similar to the "ch" in the Scottish word "loch."

English	Dutch	Pronunciation
Hello.	*Hallo.*	**hah**-loh
Good day.	*Dag.*	dah
Good morning.	*Goedemorgen.*	**hoo**-deh-mor-hehn
Good afternoon.	*Goedemiddag.*	**hoo**-deh-mid-dah
Good evening.	*Goedenavond.*	**hoo**-dehn-ah-fohnd
Do you speak English?	*Spreekt u Engels?*	shpraykt oo **eng**-ehls
Yes. / No.	*Ja. / Nee.*	yah / nay
I (don't) understand.	*Ik begrijp (het niet).*	ik beh-**hripe** (heht neet)
Please. (can also mean "You're welcome")	*Alstublieft.*	**ahl**-stoo-bleeft
Thank you.	*Dank u wel.*	dahnk oo vehl
I'm sorry.	*Het spijt me.*	heht spite meh
Excuse me.	*Pardon.*	**par**-dohn
(No) problem.	*(Geen) probleem.*	(hayn) **proh**-blaym
Good.	*Goede.*	**hoo**-deh
Goodbye.	*Tot ziens.*	toht zeens
one / two	*een / twee*	ayn / t'vay
three / four	*drie / vier*	dree / feer
five / six	*vijf / zes*	fife / zehs
seven / eight	*zeven / acht*	**zay**-fehn / aht
nine / ten	*negen / tien*	**nay**-hehn / teen
What does it cost?	*Wat kost het?*	vaht kohst heht
Is it free?	*Is het vrij?*	is heht fry
Is it included?	*Is het inclusief?*	is heht in-**kloo**-seev
Can you please help me?	*Kunt u alstublieft helpen?*	koont oo **ahl**-stoo-bleeft **hehl**-pehn
Where can I buy / find...?	*Waar kan ik kopen / vinden...?*	var kahn ik **koh**-pehn / **fin**-dehn
I'd like / We'd like...	*Ik wil graag / Wij willen graag...*	ik vil *h*rah / vy **vil**-lehn *h*rah
...a room.	*...een kamer.*	ayn **kah**-mer
...a train / bus ticket to ____.	*...een trein / bus kaartje naar ____.*	ayn trayn / boos **kart**-yeh nar ____
...to rent a bike.	*...een fiets huren.*	ayn feets **hoo**-rehn
Where is...?	*Waar is...?*	var is
...the train / bus station	*...het trein / bus station*	heht trayn / boos **staht**-see-ohn
...the tourist info office	*...de VVV*	deh fay fay fay
...the toilet	*...het toilet*	heht **twah**-leht
men / women	*mannen / vrouwen*	**mah**-nehn / **frow**-ehn
left / right	*links / rechts*	links / re*h*ts
straight ahead	*rechtdoor*	**re*h*t**-dor
What time does it open / close?	*Hoe laat gaat het open / dicht?*	hoo laht haht heht **oh**-pehn / di*h*t
now / soon / later	*nu / straks / later*	noo / strahks / **lah**-ter
today / tomorrow	*vandaag / morgen*	**fahn**-dah / **mor**-hehn

In a Dutch Restaurant

The all-purpose Dutch word *alstublieft* (**ahl**-stoo-bleeft) means "please," but it can also mean "here you are" (when the server hands you something), "thanks" (when taking payment from you), or "you're welcome" (when handing you change). Here are other words that might come in handy at restaurants:

English	Dutch	Pronunciation
I'd like / We'd like...	Ik will graag / Wij willen graag...	ik vil *hrah* / vy **vil**-lehn *hrah*
...a table for one / two.	...een tafel voor een / twee.	ayn **tah**-fehl for ayn / t'vay
...to reserve a table.	...een tafel reserveren.	ayn **tah**-fehl ray-zehr-feh-rehn
...the menu (in English).	...het menu (in het Engels).	heht meh-**noo** (in heht **eng**-ehls)
Is this table free?	Is deze tafel vrij?	is **day**-zeh **tah**-fehl fry
to go	om mee te nemen	ohm may teh **nay**-mehn
with / without	met / zonder	meht / **zohn**-der
and / or	en / of	ehn / of
special of the day	dagschotel	**dahs**-hoh-tehl
specialty of the house	huisspecialiteit	**hows**-shpeh-shah-lee-tite
breakfast	ontbijt	**ohnt**-bite
lunch	middagmaal	**mid**-dah-mahl
dinner	avondmaal	**ah**-fohnd-mahl
appetizers	hapjes	**hahp**-yehs
main courses	hoofdgerechten	**hohfd**-heh-reh-tehn
side dishes	bijgerechten	**bye**-heh-reh-tehn
bread / cheese	brood / kaas	brohd / kahs
sandwich	sandwich	**sand**-vich
soup / salad	soep / sla	soop / slah
meat / chicken / fish	vlees / kip / vis	flays / kip / fis
fruit / vegetables	vrucht / groenten	fruht / **hroon**-tehn
dessert / pastries	gebak	heh-**bahk**
I am vegetarian.	Ik ben vegetarisch.	ik behn vay-heh-**tah**-rish
mineral water / tap water	mineraalwater / kraanwater	min-eh-rahl-**vah**-ter / **krahn**-vah-ter
milk / (orange) juice	melk / (sinaasappel) sap	mehlk / (**see**-nahs-ah-pehl (sahp)
coffee / tea	koffie / thee	**koh**-fee / tay
wine / beer	wijn / bier	vine / beer
red / white	rode / witte	**roh**-deh / **vit**-teh
glass / bottle	glas / fles	*hlahs* / flehs
Cheers!	Proost!	prohst
More. / Another.	Meer. / Nog een.	mayr / noh ayn
The same.	Het zelfde.	heht **zehlf**-deh
The bill, please.	De rekening, alstublieft.	deh **ray**-keh-neeng **ahl**-stoo-bleeft
Do you accept credit cards?	Accepteert u kredietkaarten?	**ahk**-shehp-tayrt oo kray-deet-**kar**-tehn
Is service included?	Is bediening inbegrepen?	is beh-**dee**-neeng in-beh-**hray**-pehn
tip	fooi	foy
Tasty.	Lekker.	**leh**-ker
Enjoy!	Smakelijk!	**smah**-keh-like

French Survival Phrases

When using the phonetics, try to nasalize the _n_ sound.

English	French	Pronunciation
Good day.	Bonjour.	bohn-zhoor
Mrs. / Mr.	Madame / Monsieur	mah-dahm / muhs-yur
Do you speak English?	Parlez-vous anglais?	par-lay-voo ahn-glay
Yes. / No.	Oui. / Non.	wee / nohn
I understand.	Je comprends.	zhuh kohn-prahn
I don't understand.	Je ne comprends pas.	zhuh nuh kohn-prahn pah
Please.	S'il vous plaît.	see voo play
Thank you.	Merci.	mehr-see
I'm sorry.	Désolé.	day-zoh-lay
Excuse me.	Pardon.	par-dohn
(No) problem.	(Pas de) problème.	(pah duh) proh-blehm
It's good.	C'est bon.	say bohn
Goodbye.	Au revoir.	oh vwahr
one / two	un / deux	uhn / duh
three / four	trois / quatre	twah / kah-truh
five / six	cinq / six	sank / sees
seven / eight	sept / huit	seht / weet
nine / ten	neuf / dix	nuhf / dees
How much is it?	Combien?	kohn-bee-an
Write it?	Ecrivez?	ay-kree-vay
Is it free?	C'est gratuit?	say grah-twee
Included?	Inclus?	an-klew
Where can I buy / find...?	Où puis-je acheter / trouver...?	oo pwee-zhuh ah-shuh-tay / troo-vay
I'd like / We'd like...	Je voudrais / Nous voudrions...	zhuh voo-dray / noo voo-dree-ohn
...a room.	...une chambre.	ewn shahn-bruh
...a ticket to ___.	...un billet pour ___.	uhn bee-yay poor ___
Is it possible?	C'est possible?	say poh-see-bluh
Where is...?	Où est...?	oo ay
...the train station	...la gare	lah gar
...the bus station	...la gare routière	lah gar root-yehr
...tourist information	...l'office du tourisme	loh-fees dew too-reez-muh
Where are the toilets?	Où sont les toilettes?	oo sohn lay twah-leht
men	hommes	ohm
women	dames	dahm
left / right	à gauche / à droite	ah gohsh / ah dwaht
straight	tout droit	too dwah
When does this open / close?	Ça ouvre / ferme à quelle heure?	sah oo-vruh / fehrm ah kehl ur
At what time?	À quelle heure?	ah kehl ur
Just a moment.	Un moment.	uhn moh-mahn
now / soon / later	maintenant / bientôt / plus tard	man-tuh-nahn / bee-an-toh / plew tar
today / tomorrow	aujourd'hui / demain	oh-zhoor-dwee / duh-man

In a French Restaurant

English	French	Pronunciation
I'd like / We'd like...	Je voudrais / Nous voudrions...	zhuh voo-dray / noo voo-dree-ohn
...to reserve...	...réserver...	ray-zehr-vay
...a table for one / two.	...une table pour un / deux.	ewn tah-bluh poor uhn / duh
Is this seat free?	C'est libre?	say lee-bruh
The menu (in English), please.	La carte (en anglais), s'il vous plaît.	lah kart (ahn ahn-glay) see voo play
service (not) included	service (non) compris	sehr-vees (nohn) kohn-pree
to go	à emporter	ah ahn-por-tay
with / without	avec / sans	ah-vehk / sahn
and / or	et / ou	ay / oo
special of the day	plat du jour	plah dew zhoor
specialty of the house	spécialité de la maison	spay-see-ah-lee-tay duh lah may-zohn
appetizers	hors d'oeuvre	or duh-vruh
first course (soup, salad)	entrée	ahn-tray
main course (meat, fish)	plat principal	plah pran-see-pahl
bread	pain	pan
cheese	fromage	froh-mahzh
sandwich	sandwich	sahnd-weech
soup	soupe	soop
salad	salade	sah-lahd
meat	viande	vee-ahnd
chicken	poulet	poo-lay
fish	poisson	pwah-sohn
seafood	fruits de mer	frwee duh mehr
fruit	fruit	frwee
vegetables	légumes	lay-gewm
dessert	dessert	day-sehr
mineral water	eau minérale	oh mee-nay-rahl
tap water	l'eau du robinet	loh dew roh-bee-nay
milk	lait	lay
(orange) juice	jus (d'orange)	zhew (doh-rahnzh)
coffee / tea	café / thé	kah-fay / tay
wine	vin	van
red / white	rouge / blanc	roozh / blahn
glass / bottle	verre / bouteille	vehr / boo-tay
beer	bière	bee-ehr
Cheers!	Santé!	sahn-tay
More. / Another.	Plus. / Un autre.	plew / uhn oh-truh
The same.	La même chose.	lah mehm shohz
The bill, please.	L'addition, s'il vous plaît.	lah-dee-see-ohn see voo play
Do you accept credit cards?	Vous prenez les cartes?	voo pruh-nay lay kart
tip	pourboire	poor-bwahr
Delicious!	Délicieux!	day-lee-see-uh

For more user-friendly French phrases, check out *Rick Steves French Phrase Book and Dictionary* or *Rick Steves French, Italian & German Phrase Book*.

INDEX

INDEX

MAP INDEX

Explore Europe

At ricksteves.com you can browse through thousands of articles, videos, photos and radio interviews, plus find a wealth of money-saving travel tips for planning your dream trip. And with our mobile-friendly website, you can easily access all this great travel information anywhere you go.

TV Shows

Preview the places you'll visit by watching entire half-hour episodes of Rick Steves' Europe (choose from all 100 shows) on-demand, for free.

your travel dreams into affordable reality

Radio Interviews

Enjoy ready access to Rick's vast library of radio interviews covering travel

tips and cultural insights that relate specifically to your Europe travel plans.

Travel Forums

Learn, ask, share! Our online community of savvy travelers is a great resource for first-time travelers to Europe, as well as seasoned pros. You'll find forums on each country, plus travel tips and restaurant/hotel reviews. You can even ask one of our well-traveled staff to chime in with an opinion.

Travel News

Subscribe to our free Travel News e-newsletter, and get monthly updates from Rick on what's happening in Europe.

Rick's Free Travel App

Get your FREE **Rick Steves Audio Europe**™ app to enjoy…

- Dozens of self-guided tours of Europe's top museums, sights and historic walks

- Hundreds of tracks filled with cultural insights and sightseeing tips from Rick's radio interviews

- All organized into handy geographic playlists

- For iPhone, iPad, iPod Touch, Android

With Rick whispering in your ear, Europe gets even better.

Find out more at ricksteves.com

Save time and energy

This guidebook is your independent-travel toolkit. But for all it delivers, it's still up to you to devote the time and energy it takes to manage the preparation and logistics that are essential for a happy trip. If that's a hassle, there's a solution.

Rick Steves Tours

A Rick Steves tour takes you to Europe's most interesting places with great

great tours, too!

with minimum stress

guides and small groups of 28 or less. We follow Rick's favorite itineraries, ride in comfy buses, stay in family-run hotels, and bring you intimately close to the Europe you've traveled so far to see. Most importantly, we take away the logistical headaches so you can focus on the fun.

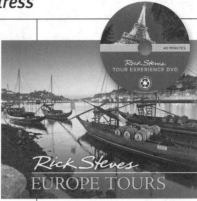

customers—along with us on 40 different itineraries, from Ireland to Italy to Istanbul. Is a Rick Steves tour the right fit for your travel dreams? Find out at ricksteves.com, where you can also get Rick's latest tour catalog and free Tour Experience DVD.

Join the fun

This year we'll take 18,000 free-spirited travelers— nearly half of them repeat

Europe is best experienced with happy travel partners. We hope you can join us.

See our itineraries at ricksteves.com

Rick Steves

EUROPE GUIDES

Best of Europe
Eastern Europe
Europe Through the Back Door
Mediterranean Cruise Ports
Northern European Cruise Ports

COUNTRY GUIDES

Croatia & Slovenia
England
France
Germany
Great Britain
Ireland
Italy
Portugal
Scandinavia
Spain
Switzerland

CITY & REGIONAL GUIDES

Amsterdam, Bruges & Brussels
Barcelona
Budapest
Florence & Tuscany
Greece: Athens & the Peloponnese
Istanbul
London
Paris
Prague & the Czech Republic
Provence & the French Riviera
Rome
Venice
Vienna, Salzburg & Tirol

SNAPSHOT GUIDES

Basque Country: Spain & France
Berlin
Bruges & Brussels
Copenhagen & the Best of
    Denmark
Dublin
Dubrovnik
Hill Towns of Central Italy
Italy's Cinque Terre
Krakow, Warsaw & Gdansk
Lisbon
Madrid & Toledo
Milan & the Italian Lakes District
Munich, Bavaria & Salzburg
Naples & the Amalfi Coast
Northern Ireland
Norway
Scotland
Sevilla, Granada & Southern Spain
Stockholm

POCKET GUIDES

Amsterdam
Athens
Barcelona
Florence
London
Paris
Rome
Venice

Rick Steves guidebooks are published by Avalon Travel,
a member of the Perseus Books Group.

NOW AVAILABLE:
eBOOKS, DVD & BLU-RAY

TRAVEL CULTURE

Europe 101
European Christmas
Postcards from Europe
Travel as a Political Act

eBOOKS

Nearly all Rick Steves guides are available as ebooks. Check with your favorite bookseller.

RICK STEVES' EUROPE DVDs

11 New Shows 2013–2014
Austria & the Alps
Eastern Europe
England & Wales
European Christmas
European Travel Skills & Specials
France
Germany, BeNeLux & More
Greece, Turkey & Portugal
Iran
Ireland & Scotland
Italy's Cities
Italy's Countryside
Scandinavia
Spain
Travel Extras

BLU-RAY

Celtic Charms
Eastern Europe Favorites
European Christmas
Italy Through the Back Door
Mediterranean Mosaic
Surprising Cities of Europe

PHRASE BOOKS & DICTIONARIES

French
French, Italian & German
German
Italian
Portuguese
Spanish

JOURNALS

Rick Steves Pocket Travel Journal
Rick Steves Travel Journal

PLANNING MAPS

Britain, Ireland & London
Europe
France & Paris
Germany, Austria & Switzerland
Ireland
Italy
Spain & Portugal

RickSteves.com **@RickSteves**

Rick Steves books and DVDs are available at bookstores
and through online booksellers.

Photo © Patricia Feaster

Credits

For help with this edition, Rick and Gene relied on...

RESEARCHERS

Cameron Hewitt

Cameron writes and edits guidebooks for Rick Steves, specializing in Eastern Europe. For this book, he taste-tested Belgian pralines in Ghent, explored hipster hangouts in Antwerp, and ogled the glorious Grand Place in Brussels. When he's not traveling, Cameron lives in Seattle with his wife, Shawna.

Amanda Zurita

Amanda Zurita caught the travel bug early—she's been flying since before she could walk. When she's not hovering over a bowl of mussels in Bruges, checking out vintage shops in Antwerp, or dodging cyclists in Amsterdam, she lives in Seattle with her beloved Labrador, Hadrian.

ACKNOWLEDGMENTS

Thanks to Rick Steves tour guide Hilbren Buys for sharing his expertise about Brussels and Belgium.

Avalon Travel
a member of the Perseus Books Group
1700 Fourth Street
Berkeley, CA 94710, USA

Printed in Canada by Friesens.
Second printing July 2015.

ISBN 978-1-63121-064-8
ISSN 2376-5674

For the latest on Rick's lectures, guidebooks, tours, public radio show, and public television series, contact Rick Steves' Europe, 130 Fourth Avenue North, Edmonds, WA
98020, tel. 425/771-8303, www.ricksteves.com, rick@ricksteves.com.

Rick Steves' Europe

Managing Editor: Risa Laib
Editorial & Production Manager: Jennifer Madison Davis
Editors: Glenn Eriksen, Tom Griffin, Cameron Hewitt, Suzanne Kotz, Cathy Lu,
    Carrie Shepherd
Editorial & Production Assistant: Jessica Shaw
Researchers: Cameron Hewitt, Amanda Zurita
Maps & Graphics: David C. Hoerlein, Sandra Hundacker, Lauren Mills, Mary Rostad

Avalon Travel

Senior Editor & Series Manager: Madhu Prasher
Editor: Jamie Andrade
Associate Editor: Maggie Ryan
Copy Editor: Denise Silva
Proofreader: Kelly Lydick
Indexer: Stephen Callahan
Production & Typesetting: Tabitha Lahr
Cover Design: Kimberly Glyder Design
Maps & Graphics: Kat Bennett, Mike Morgenfeld

Photo Credits

Front Cover: Brussels © Getty Images
Title Page: Brussels at Night © Cameron Hewitt
Part-Title Pages: p. 15, Canal in Bruges; p. 113, Brussels Town Hall; p. 219, Cathedral
    of Our Lady, Antwerp; p. 269, Castle of the Counts, Ghent
Additional Photography: Dominic Arizona Bonuccelli, Ben Cameron, Tom Griffin,
    Jennifer Hauseman, Cameron Hewitt, Pat O'Connor, Gene Openshaw, Rick
    Steves, Gretchen Strauch, Bruce VanDeventer, Laura VanDeventer, Wikimedia
    Commons—PD-ART/PD-US (photos are used by permission and are the property
    of the original copyright owners)

More for your trip!
Maximize the experience with Rick Steves as your guide

Guidebooks
Dozens of European city and country guidebooks

Planning Maps
Use the map that's in sync with your guidebook

Rick's TV Shows
Preview Brussels and Bruges with Rick's TV shows

Free! Rick's Audio Europe™ App
Hear Belgium travel tips from Rick's radio shows

Small Group Tours
Including the Heart of Belgium and Holland

For all the details, visit ricksteves.com